INSIGHT GUIDES

The world's largest collection of visual travel guides

Rajasthan

Edited by Samuel Israel and Toby Sinclair
Executive Editor: Bikram Grewal

Editorial Director: Brian Bell

APA PUBLICATIONS

Part of the Langenscheidt Publishing Group

INSIGHT GUIDES

RaJaSTHaN

CONTACTING THE EDITORS: We would appreciate it if readers would alert us to errors or outdated information by writing to:
Apa Publications, P.O. Box 7910,
London SE1 1WE, England.
Fax: (44) 20 7403 0290.
e-mail: insight@apaguide.demon.co.uk.
www.insightguides.com

First Edition 1987
Second Edition 1996 (Updated 2001)
Distributed in the UK & Ireland by
GeoCenter International Ltd
The Viables Centre, Harrow Way
Basingstoke, Hampshire RG22 4BJ
Fax: (44) 1256 817988

Distributed in the United States by
Langenscheidt Publishers Inc.
46–35 54th Road, Maspeth, NY 11378
Fax: (1) 718 784 0640

Distributed in Canada by
Thomas Allen & Son Ltd
390 Steelcase Road East
Markham, Ontario L34 1G2
Fax: (1) 905 475 6747

Distributed in Australia by
Universal Press
1 Waterloo Road
Macquarie Park, NSW 2113
Fax: (61) 2 9888 9074

Distributed in India by
Om Books Services
4379/4b, Prakash House, Ansari Road,
Darya Ganj, New Delhi-110002, India
Tel: (91 11) 326 3363/326 5303. Fax: (91 11) 327 8091
e-mail: obi@del2.vsnl.net.in

Worldwide distribution enquiries:
APA Publications GmbH & Co. Verlag KG (Singapore branch)
38 Joo Koon Road, Singapore 628990
Tel: (65) 8651600. Fax: (65) 8616438

Printed in Singapore by
Insight Print Services (Pte) Ltd
38 Joo Koon Road, Singapore 628990
Fax: (65) 8616438

DISCOVERY CHANNEL

This guidebook combines the interests and enthusiasms of two of the world's best-known information providers: Insight Guides, whose range of titles has set the standard for visual travel guides since 1970, and Discovery Channel, the world's premier source of nonfiction television programming.

The editors of Insight Guides provide both practical advice and general understanding about a destination's history, culture, institutions and people. Discovery Channel and its website, www.discovery.com, help millions of viewers explore their world from the comfort of their own home and also encourage them to explore it first-hand.

Israel

The initial editorial team of **Samuel Israel** and **Bikram Grewal** was joined by **Toby Sinclair**, a travel, wildlife and adventure tourism specialist. In addition to his editorial contribution, Sinclair has written several of the articles and contributed photographs to this volume.

Aditya Patankar, who was commissioned to take a number of photographs for this guide, has been a chronic traveller since his youth. His photographs have appeared in a number of Indian publications and in 1984, he was commissioned to do the photography for *Lives of Indian Princes* by Charles Allen.

Grewal

Writers of varied backgrounds have contributed to this book. Some were chosen for their knowledge and experience, others for their close physical and emotional links with the places they write about.

Dr Kamala Seshan, a geographer on the staff of the National Council of Educational Research and Training, New Delhi, describes the land's often harsh and seemingly unfavourable geography. This forms the background against which the ways of life of its people can be understood – including, in seeming paradox, their colourful art, dance and drama.

Seshan

Professor Harbans Mukhia, as a specialist in medieval Indian history at Delhi's Jawaharlal Nehru University, has drawn together the complex history of a region which

Mukhia

until recently, was split into a score of princely states.

Rajasthan *today*, on the other hand, has, very appropriately, been covered by a senior political journalist based in Jaipur – **Milap Chand Dandia**. Dandia has been a representative of *The Telegraph*, a Calcutta daily, and *Sunday*, a national political weekly.

P.C. Mathur of the Department of Political Science, University of Rajasthan, has provided a survey of the varied groups who, with the minority Rajputs, constitute the population of Rajasthan. This goes beyond bare demography and delves into the area of socio-political roles and interactions.

Jyoti Jafa, a former member of the Indian Foreign Service, is a freelance writer on political, travel and cultural themes. Born a Rathor – a member of the ruling family of the former Bikaner State – her knowledge of Bikaner and its neighbourhood is both personal and intimate.

Nicholson

Jaipur and Jodhpur (and their environs) have been covered by British travel writer **Louise Nicholson**. A student of history and art, Nicholson's first visit to India was on her honeymoon. Her experience as a leader of British and American tourist groups in India makes her contributions to this guide eminently practical ones.

Shail Mayaram, a political scientist, writes for the press on history, women's issues, wildlife and environment, and cultural subjects. She is the convenor of the Alwar Regional Chapter of the Indian National Trust for Art and Cultural Heritage (INTACH), which makes her an authoritative writer on this city and its surroundings.

Mayaram

As co-authors of *Rajasthan, The Painted Walls of Shekhavati*, **Francis Wacziarg** and **Aman Nath** were obvious choices for the article on Shekhavati. They have spent years studying the area, its history and the way of life of its people.

Shalini Saran is a freelance writer and photographer on places of historical interest, peoples, crafts, and lifestyles. Her writings and photographs have been published widely in travel and art magazines.

For Kota, the writer was **M.K. Brijraj Singh** of the former ruling family. For some time he was a member of parliament, and is a wildlife conservationist and photographer.

Indi Rana who contributes on Mewar, is active in a number of fields, from planning, writing, designing and producing books for children, to research on and design of aids in developmental communication.

Uma Anand brings years of experience to her contributions to *Rajasthan* – experience as an editor, broadcaster, actress, commentator, newspaper reporter, journalist and writer of books for children. For 15 years, she was the editor of *Sangeek Natak*, Journal of the Performing Arts of the Indian Sangeet Natak (music and theatre) Akademi, New Delhi.

Dr Geeti Sen who contributes on Rajput painting, is an art historian who has made a special study of the Indian "miniature" tradition. Dr Sen is currently Associated Professor in the School of Art and Aesthetics, Jawaharlal Nehru University, New Delhi.

The famed crafts of Rajasthan are competently covered by **Laila Tyabji**, a designer specialising in textiles and handicrafts, who was also active in graphic and theatre set design and exhibitions. She worked as a consultant on Indian Crafts for the Metropolitan Museum of Art, New York.

There are many others to whom thanks are due for assistance in the course of preparation for the original guide: **Surit Mitra** of Dass Media Pte. Ltd.; **Dr. Sarah Israel**, **Dr. Shobita Punja** and **Jessy Mathew**.

Others who helped in various ways too numerous to mention are **Elizabeth Abraham, Bhim Singh, Divyabhanusing, Kesri Singh** of Mandawa Castle, **Ashish Madan Shgun Mohan** of Special Expeditions, **Tripti Pandey, Naomi Medows, Manju Patankar**, the staff of **Rajasthan Tours, Lakshmi Sinclair, Oliver Sinclair, Maharaj** and **Rani Sultan Singh** and previous updaters **Dagmar von Tschurtschenthaler, Genevieve Stein Sayle** and **Peter Sayle**.

This edition was updated by **Maria Lord** who also prepared the Travel Tips.

CONTENTS

Maps

PALACES, FORTS, PEOPLE

Rajasthan is sometimes presented as an enormous site on which forts, palaces and gardens, the relics of an erstwhile princely order have been frozen for the benefit of posterity and the tourist – as if in a mammoth open-air museum. A museum which offers not only the sights but also, for a price, a living experience of some of the splendour and way of life of royalty – staying in their palaces-turned-hotels and even travelling as they did, till as recently as the 1930s, in special personal trains and coaches, the royal "saloon".

Rajasthan is all this and much, much more – a landscape of singular beauty, whether it is the dunes of the desert, or the craggy, forested hills on which the formidable Ranthambore fortress perches, in the midst of what is today one of India's best wildlife parks, or the lake-studded environs of Udaipur.

The people of Rajasthan are perhaps the most colourful element in a land of colour – their history, religion, music and dance, arts and crafts remain vibrantly alive and active – and are presented here in all their variety and ways.

As one of the contributors to this volume puts it, Rajasthan is very much part of progressive, developing, modernizing India, but nowhere else in the country does the long, continuous past so pervasively press on the present as it does in modern Rajasthan. This, perhaps, is the secret of its charm.

Preceding pages: Maharaja of Pratapgarh's sword; a thoughtful Rajasthani; a day's work; Pushkar Fair; Pushkar Lake; watchful eyes; fairground posing; young girl. **Left**, traffic policeman.

THE LANDSCAPE

Rajasthan is separated from the Ganga basin by the watershed of the Aravalli mountains which run from the northeast to the southwest, displaced by a deep fault which moved the mountains some 1,225 km (765 miles) in its central portion and 300 km (190 miles) in its eastern portion near Delhi.

The topographical regions into which Rajasthan's 342,274 sq. km (132,152 sq. miles) can be divided are the northeastern hill tract, the Vindhyan plateau extensions in the southeast, the basins of the Chappan and Banas, the Aravalli backbone, the Shekhavati uplands in the northwest and the Luni basin of the southwest, merging into the large area on the west – the desert which occupies some 213,000 sq. km (82,000 sq. miles).

Travel across this varied landscape usually begins from the east since most people enter Rajasthan from Delhi, which lies in the Jaipur-Delhi saddle between Rajasthan and the Ganga plain.

Entry point: Entering here, from Delhi, one encounters the northeastern hilly tract. Some 670 metres (2,200 feet) high, the hills near Alwar are a lofty threshold to the plains which stretch out below. Here the Aravallis have elevated plains and high valleys between quartzite ridges.

The northeastern hilly tracts open out into the eastern plains of the Banas and Chappan rivers which lie between the highland plateau of the Hardoti on the east and the Aravalli range and Bhorat plateau on the west.

Known as the Mewar plains to the north and the Chappan plains to the east, this stretch from Jaipur, through Tonk and Bhilwara, up to Udaipur is of hard rock, usually speckled granite. The rocks here have been cut and carried away for ages for carvings, and the silver, lead and zinc deposits from Zawar have been used for making the beautiful jewellery worn here. The Banas and Chappan rivers flow east from the Aravalli watershed and their western tributaries flow from the Vindhyan plateau.

Farther south is the Adivasi belt along the Mahi river's tributaries. A land of hills and deep valleys, it is an area which is deeply eroded and hence very different from the gneissic plain of Mewar. Here separate hillocks stand on a rough uneven land covered with scanty forests.

East of these plains, almost shielding Rajasthan from southern India, stand the sentinels – the Vindhya ranges, known here as the (Haraouti) Hardoti plateau. This area is drained by the river Chambal. Southwards, a steep escarpment overlooks the Bundelkhand area of Madhya Pradesh. Formed by the bending of the Aravallis by a mighty thrust from the southern plateau is this *pathar* or stony upland of the Kota-Bundi area near Banswara and Pratapgarh. It is here that the Deccan lava lands meets the folded Aravalli ranges, connecting the peninsula to the northern plains.

West of the plains of the Chappan and Banas are the Aravalli hills where the massive quartzites mix with metamorphic rocks of an earlier period to produce a stepped arrangement of the landscape, like a hand fan, from the Bhorat plateau near Udaipur, 1,225 metres (4,000 feet) high to the north-eastern highlands.

The southern hilly region of Rajasthan has conical hills, rugged slopes and sheer vertical scarps, and on the plains are hummocky dunes with exposed, now smooth, sides of granite rock.

The areas near Ajmer have extensions of the Aravallis and granites of many colours are found here. Looking back from here to the Banas-Chappan plains through the pass, which is the passage to the east of Rajasthan, rising on each side of the pass, are peaks of reddish granite on blue micaceous slate. Beyond here is a quick ascent through prickly-pear country across to the desert plains.

West of the Aravallis, before entering the Marusthali, or the great desert, is the desert margin. The plains of the river Luni, the Shekhavati region, and, in the north, the saddle between Jaipur and Jodhpur, with the Ghaggar plain, is a desert land with several salt lakes.

The Shekhavati area, because of the low broken hills of the Aravallis in the north, affords a doorway into the desert. The wind gaps here invite the dusts of the desert eastwards, even into the plains of the Banas river. This lake country contains the Sambhar,

Didwani and Degana lakes which collect the rare rain water in the monsoons and in the dry weather become mere muddy pools.

South of here the land has many seasonally dry rivers, the largest being the Luni, which gets its waters from the tiny rivulets that run off the Aravalli hills. This river rises at the Ana Sagar at Pushkar near Ajmer and with its few tributaries flows into a salt marsh in the Rann of Kutch. The Luni, which brings sweet water into the desert, has thick deposits of sand in its channel and the water courses become a mere trickle in summer. The land has steep slopes and large areas of open alluvial plains. Between the river courses are uplands of hard granite and rhyolite.

and coal are seen. These were formed only 60 million years ago. Recently, substantial deposits of oil have been found beneath the desert near Jaisalmer.

The land is neither barren nor uninhabited; it is covered with bushes and shrubs and even small trees. It is a great sandy tract with no streams and just a few rocks that protrude above the lower land now covered with seemingly immobile sand dunes. The grasses on these dunes grow in clumps, indicating the availability of water just beneath the sandy soil. This desert is a rearing ground for camels, buffaloes and cows which are known for their strength and size. They are bred mainly in the Rathi and Tharparkar areas.

Rajasthan's Marusthali desert has many distinctive features. The evidence of plant fossils found in the rocks of Jaisalmer and Barmer and the now stone forests of what were once trees, and of the Barmer sandstone, indicate that during the Jurassic era western Rajasthan was extensively forested.

Fossil remains: The bedrock of Jaisalmer has many fossils which have left their mark on the dark coloured limestones. The jasper rock found here was used extensively in the floral decorations of the Mughals, while further south, in Palana, even seams of lignite

These areas of Rajasthan, a desert in the heart of India, supported a mixture of kingdoms and Adivasi settlements, each with a distinctive personality. The differences in the landscape, the variety of minerals and trees, and the isolation of different desert areas from each other, account for the singularity even in the crafts, from wood carvings to fine embroidery on camel leather, from silver filigree to groundglass *minakari* jewellery.

Rajasthan lies between 22° and 30° north latitude and 69° and 78° east longitude, in the track of the Arabian Sea branch of the southwest monsoon. The Aravallis and, in the

<u>Above</u>, a camel herd.

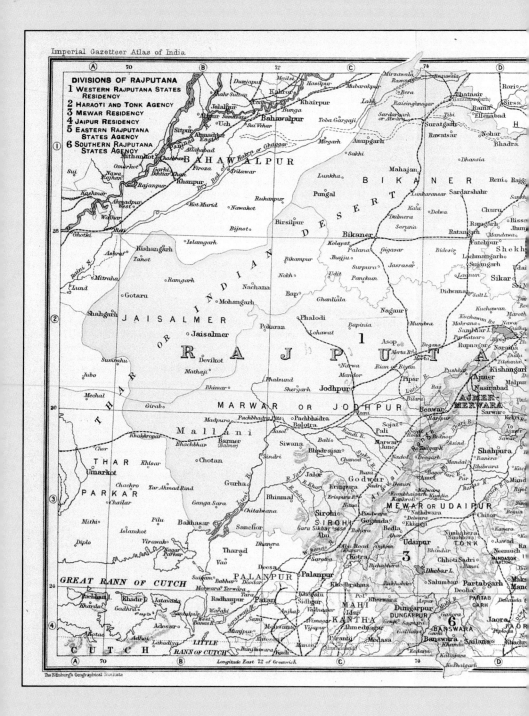

DIVISIONS OF RAJPUTANA
1 WESTERN RAJPUTANA STATES RESIDENCY
2 HARAOTI AND TONK AGENCY
3 MEWAR RESIDENCY
4 JAIPUR RESIDENCY
5 EASTERN RAJPUTANA STATES AGENCY
6 SOUTHERN RAJPUTANA STATES AGENCY

The Edinburgh Geographical Institute

Longitude East 72 of Greenwich

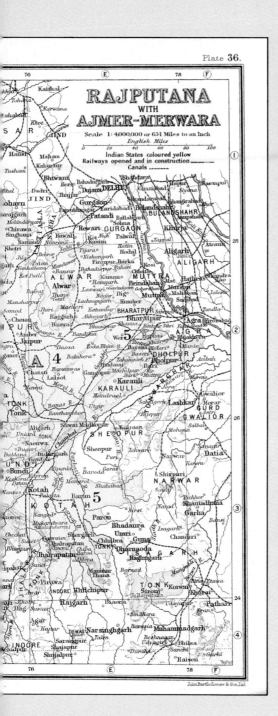

Plate 36.

RAJPUTANA
WITH
AJMER-MERWARA
Scale 1: 4,000,000 or 63½ Miles to an Inch
English Miles

Indian States coloured yellow
Railways opened and in construction
Canals

John Bartholomew & Son, Ltd.

southeast, the plateau of Hardoti being the only highlands, they channel the monsoons coming from Kathiawar and stop the drier eastern flow, creating a desert in the west.

The area of Malwa, a tableland extending up to the Vindhyas, is covered with green forests on black lava soils because of the rain from the monsoons. West of the Aravallis, beyond the desert margin, where the Luni flows over sandy channels, is the land of saline lakes in the north and dunes in the southwest. Here, the summers are hot and with the slightest showers, the white salt encrusted saline marshes become muddy.

The winters that follow the monsoons have an average low of about 12°C (54°F) in the northeastern hills and the Shekhavati and Ghaggar plains. Most of the desert, the Banas basin and across the Vindhyan plateau is warmer, about 14°C (57°F), and southern Rajasthan, which is most of the Bhorat plateau and the lava plains, is above 16°C (61°F).

The wetter parts east and southeast of the Aravallis have taller trees than the drier west. The south and eastern parts between 270 metres (885 feet) and 770 metres (2,530 feet) has the axlewood (Anogeissus Pendula), dhokra and dhak (Butea monosperma) forests.

Flora: The Banas basin and northwards to the northeastern hilly tracts have mesquite or "salai" (Boswellia serrata) forests. The wetter regions support this tall tree which is used for making packing-cases.

Traveling westwards across the Shekhavati and the Godwar tract, the rainfall decreases and so do the khejra (prosopis) forests. Grasses which are tall and yellow fill the patches between the amla trees (Emblica officinalis) with their yellow blossoms. This land with the pipal (Ficus religiosa) marks a boundary with the desert. Deserts, though thought to be treeless, here have a wide variety of trees, the most common being the babul (Acacia nilotica) and the khejra, often found cracking the hard rock surface.

In both the heat of summer and the cold of winter, the desert air is dry. Early morning on the desert plain, one can see phantom towers and arches, groves and domes, reflected on the glowing surface of the plains which vanish with the onset of the afternoon.

Ajmer, previously the seat of a Mughal governor, became the base of a British resident.

Geographically, Rajasthan comprises two distinct regions divided by the Aravalli range running southwest to northeast, its last low ridge spilling into Delhi. Marwar, Jaisalmer and Bikaner are situated in the western and northern parts which are marked by the aridity of shifting sandhills, the major portion of the Thar desert. The other side of the divide features dense forests and fertile irrigated valleys which support the historic cities of Udaipur and Jaipur.

Even western and northern Rajasthan were not always desert. Evidence suggests that elephants once made this part of the land their habitat; indicating it must once have abounded in the dense forest where elephants feel most at home. It is in a relatively recent geological timescale, over the past three to four millennia, that ecological changes have replaced forests with sand dunes and the elephant with the camel.

In the historical timeframe, settled existence may have come to Rajasthan before the rest of India. Harappan culture (2500–1700 BC) is usually considered the first evidence of urban settlement in Indian history, but Rajasthan may take precedence, for some of its pre-Harappan locales, such as Kalibangan, bear evidence of plowed agriculture and therefore of sedentary, organised society. There are, too, several sites of the Harappan period in Rajasthan pointing to the integration of the region with the urban settlements of the Indus valley to the north and east.

The history of early Rajasthan is frequently the history of tribal republics or at best, oligarchical socio-political systems. Often at war with one another and with neighbouring kingdoms, tribal organisations were to give way to the process of internal stratification as well as the impact of external aggression during the centuries immediately preceding and succeeding the birth of Christ. Nor could the region remain immune to the influence of the rise and fall of vast empires in north

India. Thus, even if Rajasthan was not integrated with the Gupta empire of the 4th and 5th century AD, it still bore a subordinate status to the empire.

Warrior clans: The most spectacular development in Rajasthan's history took place between the 6th and 7th centuries, when some new warrior clans were formed. The Rajputs, as they came to be called, were to dominate the history of the region as well as that of many other parts of the country for centuries to come. Their origin, whether indigenous or foreign, has long aroused heated controversy among historians. National pride no doubt played a part in influencing those who insisted that they were wholly Indian. However, the general consensus these days is that the Rajput clans owe their origin to both indigenous and foreign sources. Among the former were some groups – possibly the ancestors of the present-day Bhils – then having low social status but possessed of the skills and determination of warriors. In the given social set-up the two were mutually incompatible: no one too low in the social hierarchy could be allowed to take up the profession of a higher caste, especially the honourable profession of arms. This conflict was resolved through a mythical purification by fire ritual which enabled the warriors to abandon their old low status and assume one that corresponded to their profession. To reinforce their new-found glory even further, they were assigned mythical descent from the sun and the moon.

Also purified were descendants of foreign invaders, such as the Huns, who had become indigenised. They too were given the caste status of a warrior. Thus were the Rajput clans formed, originating in diverse sources but evolving into relatively homogeneous social, if not political, groups. In calling themselves Rajputs (corruption of *rajputras*, sons of princes), they segregated themselves from the rest of society by their social status, profession and code of honour.

The politics that the Rajputs established comprised two levels. At the lower level were the subject people, paying revenue to the rulers and enjoying their protection. At the higher level, political power in all its ramifications was shared by a kind of large kin group. Under this system, the Rajputs of a particular clan were entitled to conventional, if unequal, shares within the territory of that group. The term they used for this collective sharing of power was "brotherhood". However, the clan did not forever remain a homogeneous unit; often there were conflicts within the "brotherhood" leading to splits which in turn established new "brotherhoods" seeking either to wrest territories from their erstwhile allies or conquering new lands. The Rajputs, never exceeding 7 or 8 percent of Rajasthan's population, remained the ruling class *par excellence* for centuries.

come into conflict with Muslim invaders from Central Asia towards the end of the 12th century. In the first battle between them, the Rajput chief inflicted a humiliating defeat on his adversary, Muhammad Ghori. Ghori, described by an eminent Indian historian as "a hero of three stupendous defeats", possessed one cardinal quality: he never allowed himself to be crushed by a reverse on the field of battle. Thus, as the Chauhan warrior imagined that the last had been seen of Ghori on Indian soil, he reappeared to claim the final victory.

Prithviraj Chauhan's defeat in 1191 is the subject of a local epic composed two centuries later. The poet wove a beautiful story around

As the Rajput clans spread, they divided up a great deal of Rajasthan and the neighbouring region among themselves. By about the 12th century, some of the leading houses of Rajput rulers had fairly long traditions of chivalry behind them. The house of the Chauhans, ruling from Ajmer, was the foremost among them, though several others, such as at Ranthambore and Chittaurgarh, were also significant. Needless to say, in situations of constant warfare and intrigue, the relative importance of these houses changed constantly over the centuries.

Muslim invaders: Prithviraj Chauhan of Ajmer was the first great Rajput ruler to

the grand event, a story that has all the elements of medieval drama – chivalry, treachery, war, sex and, of course, nemesis. In this epic, Prithviraj is left alone in the field of battle, his fellow Rajputs keeping aloof. History, however, records that several of the Rajput houses in the Chauhan neighbourhood did come to his aid, though one Rajput ruler, Jai Chand, whose daughter Prithviraj was supposed to have kidnapped (much to her delight) continued to watch from the sidelines. He too was to lose to Ghori a little later. In Rajasthani folklore, Jai Chand has become the archetype of a traitor, much as Judas has in Christianity.

Prithviraj Chauhan's defeat gave the invading peoples from Central Asia a foothold in India that was to expand into a vast empire which lasted well over 500 years. Ghori had ruled over his Indian territories from Ghazni in Afghanistan, capital of his impressive empire that included territories in almost all directions. In 1206, Ghori died and his viceroy in India, one of his thousand slaves, whom he fondly used to refer to as his thousand sons, became an independent ruler. The Delhi Sultanate was thus established, the empire that ruled from Delhi and lasted 320 years. It gave way in 1526 to another invader from Central Asia – Babur, founder of the Mughal empire.

The Delhi Sultanate and the Rajput States: With the establishment of the Delhi Sultanate, the history of the Rajput states of Rajasthan became inseparably intertwined with it. For over 350 years, relations between them were characterised by incessant conflict.

The peoples who had migrated to India from Central Asian regions via Afghanistan and had established their kingdom here had initially adopted a two-pronged strategy. They had incorporated into their state structure the established administrative machinery as well as the existing administrative personnel at the village level. Thus, in the vast countryside, organisation remained in the hands of the Hindus. At the higher echelons of this administrative system, and especially in the towns, the new rulers helped themselves to positions of power. At the same time, in the first flush of victory, they showed extreme reluctance to share political power even with fellow Muslims who happened to be from different regions. However, acute tensions generated by keeping the power base extremely narrow led to a situation in which, a century after the establishment of the Sultanate, the floodgates were thrown open, the old policy given up, and entry into the highest offices was permitted to persons without "respectable" lineage.

However, the Rajputs comprised a rival ruling class with an even longer tradition than that of the new invaders. Their territories,

individually or even collectively, were not very large compared to the Sultanate; their resources were not as great either, but their determination was, for it was based above all on their sense of honour that brooked no surrender to anyone. Tension between the Rajput states and the Sultans of Delhi was therefore inevitable.

Conflict was unavoidable for another reason too. Starting with the region around Delhi as its nucleus, the Delhi Sultanate, right from its inception, was on an expansionist spree made possible by a centrally controlled, highly organised and efficient army, and a nobility that had often to fend for itself. Within half-a-century of the Sultanate's inception, most of north and east India had been brought under its domination. Further expansion was possible only southward and westward.

The west was attractive for another reason: it was the location of the enormously rich region of Gujarat. The very fertile soil of Gujarat was particularly conducive to the cultivation the very valuable crop, cotton. Furthermore, the port of Cambay opened India to sea trade with West Asia. But the route from the northern plains, the heartland of the Delhi Sultanate, to Gujarat lay via Rajasthan. To secure this route permanently, the sultans had to conquer Rajasthan.

Many battles were fought between sultans and rulers of Rajput houses. However, power was so divided between the two sides that, if the Rajputs failed to throw the sultans out of India, the sultans failed to crush individual Rajput houses, even if they defeated them in battles. Thus it was that for over 350 years the two remained locked in conflict without either side obtaining a decisive advantage over the other.

Three and a half centuries was by any standards a long enough stretch of time for realisation to dawn that a lasting solution to the problem had to be found outside the battlefield – through mutual accommodation. The initiative in working out such a political solution was taken by the Mughal emperor Akbar who ruled over most of northern India from 1556 to 1605.

Akbar and the Rajputs: Akbar had inherited from his grandfather, Babur, an admirable cultured bearing and a breadth of vision that treated religious and other diversity with tolerance and understanding. From his book-loving father Humayun, Akbar, at the age of

13, inherited a tiny piece of territory as his "empire"; a half century later he bequeathed on his son Jahangir the Mughal empire that spanned the land from Kabul in Afghanistan in the west to Bengal in the east and Kashmir in the north to the northern parts of South India. Perhaps more important than this vast territory was an administrative structure and a set of strategic policies that gave the Mughal empire an unequalled grandeur and a long term stability that made it the longest lasting empire in Indian history.

Akbar's tolerance of religious diversity was translated from a personal attitude to a state policy. He achieved this by, on the one hand, reducing every single group in the higher echelons of the ruling class, including his own kinsmen, to a small minority; and on the other, by incorporating newer local elements at those levels. As each group was a minority, none could dictate to the rest. Mutual tolerance thus became rooted in the day-to-day functioning of the imperial polity.

Among the new elements invited by Akbar into the high precincts of the imperial nobility were the Rajputs. The emperor realised that nothing could lend the nascent empire a firmer rooting in the soil than the support of the local ruling class; he would not have been unaware of the fact that a clash of arms with that class could only prove futile. Perhaps on an experimental basis, he sought an alliance with what was then a minor Rajput house situated at Amber (or Amer), near Jaipur, by proposing marriage to a princess of the family and offering high positions in the imperial hierarchy to some of the princes.

Akbar was willing to accommodate the many susceptibilities of the Rajputs: although they had to surrender their kingdom to the empire, in return for which they would obtain often disproportionately high positions and incomes, he would refrain from depriving them of the ancestral capital of the kingdom, on which they tended to stake a great deal of prestige. And the princess who became Akbar's queen did not have to give up her religion and convert to Islam. In fact, Hindu temples were constructed within the palace precincts to facilitate worship by the princesses in their own tradition.

Man Singh-Rajput Prince, Mughal noble:

Among the most illustrious sons of the house of Amber was Man Singh, whose father's sister was the first Rajput princess to become Akbar's queen. Man Singh was to become the most trusted of Akbar's nobles, fighting battles on his behalf in almost every corner of the fast expanding empire. Mainly thanks to his loyalty to the empire and his capable generalship, the Amber house acquired a lustre that still lends the family a halo in the region. The descendants of the ruling family at Jaipur trace their lineage to him, though the city of Jaipur was founded by another eminent son of the family, Raja Jai Singh, in the first half of the 18th century.

Encouraged by the early success of a new policy towards the Rajputs, Akbar extended it to several other Rajput houses, entering into matrimonial alliances with them and elevating them to high positions. The Rajputs, who had until then been a provincial ruling class, became integrated with a larger imperial ruling class; in return, they gave the empire their support, in place of earlier hostility. Within this broad framework of alliance, Akbar was willing to accommodate predilections of individual Rajput houses. Thus when the ruler of Ranthambore made it a condition that no princess of the family would be demanded in marriage by the emperor, the latter found the condition perfectly reasonable. However, defiance of imperial authority by a Rajput house was something he was unwilling to brook and he was prepared to go to any lengths to enforce obedience.

Valiant Chittaurgarh:

The most glowing case of such defiance was that of Rana Pratap Singh of Chittaurgarh, where a ruler with relatively small resources stood up to an enormously superior imperial power with an almost superhuman determination. He and his family, including very young children, often had to starve for days and sleep on straw spread out on the ground under the open sky; but the more they suffered, the more their will was steeled. Even in a region where war was the chief preoccupation of the rulers and the code of chivalry the sole guiding spirit, Chittaurgarh's case stands out to inspire awe in the heart of admirer and critic alike. Indeed Chittaurgarh's extremely colourful story goes back long into the past, far beyond Rana Pratap's time, and is therefore worth narrating in some detail.

The rulers of the Mewar region of Rajasthan, with Chittaurgarh as its capital, claimed descent from the Sun. The state of Mewar came under the dominance of the Rajputs early in the 8th century.

At the beginning of the 14th century the reigning Sultan of Delhi, Allauddin Khalji, besieged Chittaurgarh, apparently to seize the beautiful queen, Padmini, the lotus-faced, word of whose beauty had reached his ears. Not succeeding, he professed to retire from Chittaurgarh if only he were allowed a glimpse of the queen. The Rajputs took the sultan at his word but agreed to let him look at her only in a mirror, to guard her chastity from being defiled by his direct carnal glance. Allauddin laid an ambush and was able to get hold of Padmini's husband whom he promised to release in exchange for her.

massive force. The defenders soon realised the hopelessness of their situation. Any other group of warriors would have sued for peace; but in the Rajput code of honour there was nothing more disreputable than shying away from battle, no matter what the situation. Thus they decided on a ritual that has marked the end of many a desperate battle in Rajasthan's history: *johar*. Whenever Rajput warriors realised the inevitability of defeat, they prepared to join battle and perish fighting, to the last man. Since concern for the chastity of their womenfolk was an inseparable part of their code of honour, the women would dress themselves in all their finery and sacrifice themselves in a huge fire

Seeing no way out, the condition was agreed to and Padmini set out in a veiled palanquin accompanied by "maids" in 700 similarly veiled palanquins. In reality the "maids" were some of the bravest Rajput men. At an opportune moment they threw the veils away and pounced on Allauddin's men, putting them to flight and rescuing their master, Padmini's husband.

Allauddin, however, was not one to forget the slight. He attacked the fort again with a

Above, unusual sight of three princesses and a prince playing polo. Mehrangarh Museum, Jodhpur.

so that their men would not have them on their minds while fighting. This was the *johar* which led to the destruction of Padmini and Rattan Singh, her husband, and the defeat of Chittaurgarh, though the kingdom was to become independent again in a short while.

The story, even on the face of it, has clear marks of a legend. It is of course true that Sultan Allauddin Khalji conquered Chittaurgarh early in the 14th century; the performance of *johar* is also a fact in Chittaurgarh's history, as in the history of several other princely states of Rajasthan. It is difficult, however, to vouch for the historical existence of Padmini; at any rate,

Allauddin Khalji, one of the greatest conquerors in the history of medieval India, who gave himself the title of the second Alexander, was not known to be moved by feminine beauty in his desire for the territorial expansion of his empire. Indeed, the story of Padmini and Khalji was the creation of a mid-16th century poet. Ever since this work of poetry was composed in the popular language of the region, the story has become so much a part of folklore that its veracity seems to have become irrelevant.

Three who ruled Chittaurgarh: The subsequent history of Chittaurgarh, although in many ways far more romantic than the story of Padmini and Allauddin, is nonetheless

imperial forces and crushed them in battle. But the imperial forces by this time had retained nothing of their former grandeur or strength and therefore defeating them was not a real feat.

Much more well known throughout north India, and someone whose achievements have been much longer lasting, is one of Rana Kumbha's wives, Mira Bai, herself a Rajput princess of some stature. Mira Bai is one of the most eminent of medieval Indian poets who devoted herself to the love and worship of Krishna, one of the two chief deities of the Hindus. In singing of her love for Krishna, which increasingly filled her entire being, she caused considerable scandal in

more firmly grounded in historical fact.

The 15th and 16th centuries saw Mewar scale high peaks of glory in war under the generalship and determination of three eminent rulers: Rana Kumbha, Rana Sanga and Rana Pratap Singh.

Kumbha, who ruled between 1419 and 1468 was a capable and ambitious warrior who in 1440 defeated the combined forces of the powerful rulers of Gujarat and Malwa (now in Madhya Pradesh). The Victory Tower at Chittaurgarh was built by him in celebration of his feat. At a slightly later stage, Kumbha and his erstwhile adversary, Mahmud Khalji, ruler of Malwa, joined hands against the

contemporary society where upper class women were required to lead a completely secluded life under the protection of their husbands and where the value placed on female chastity was so high that it was unthinkable for a woman to express desire for the company of a man other than her husband, even if this other man were a god.

Rana Kumbha had defeated several of his adversaries, strengthened his kingdom militarily by building as many as 32 new forts to bring the total in the kingdom to 84, and erected some grand temples in his long reign, which was terminated in 1468 with his assassination by none other than his own son, known to history by the epithet "the assassin". Over the next couple of generations, Chittaurgarh's royal chronicle is marked by filial discord.

In terms of material prosperity as well as political stability, Mawar reached its zenith in the first quarter of the 16th century during the reign of Rana Sanga, who ruled from 1508 to 1527. Sanga was frequently at war with his near and distant neighbours, including the Delhi Sultanate. Among the prizes of war he was prone to displaying, with some well-earned pride, were the loss of one eye, an arm and 80 wounds all over his person. However, for all his ceaseless battles, within the boundaries of his kingdom, Sanga proved an able administrator who felt concerned at the need to provide security and prosperity to his subjects.

In 1526 Babur had fought the first major battle with the Sultan of Delhi, Ibrahim Lodi, and defeated him. Thus Mughal rule in India began. However, 1527 was to be the truly decisive year in Babur's Indian enterprise. In that year the Mughal forces came face to face with those of Rana Sanga, who stood at the head of an immense army to which most Rajput princes, tributaries of the Rana, had sent levies. Confronted by such a formidable force, and the awesome reputation of the Rana as a warrior, Babur was utterly unsure of the outcome of the impending battle. However, the vast mass of Rana Sanga's army ultimately proved a handicap in the face of Babur's agile and much better equipped soldiers, and his far superior tactics. In a pithy statement, Babur was to sum up his observation of the Rajput war psychology. "The Rajputs," he remarked, "know how to die in a battle but not how to win it."

In the long chain of outstanding warriors whose exploits fill the chronicles of Mewar state, there were occasional weak links too. Among them was Udai Singh, after whom the city of Udaipur is named. But of course, the same Udai Singh was to father Rana Pratap who, even in his political failure to defend his territory against the imperial onslaught, has filled every little vacant space in the land of Mewar with memories of

almost superhuman achievements of the unbending spirit of defiance.

In 1567, when Akbar laid seige to Chittaurgarh, Udai Singh was its ruler. Defences began to break one after another. It was this desperation that created two of the immortal heroes in Mewar's history, both still in their teens. Their names: Jaimal and Phatta. Phatta's father, ruler of a small state in Rajasthan, had taken on himself the charge of defending one side of the fort and had fallen in the effort. Phatta's mother, witnessing her husband's death, commanded her son to assume charge and, lest his young heart demur, she armed herself and her son's young bride and plunged into the battle.

Phatta followed the two women. On seeing Akbar's cannon balls knocking holes in the fort wall, Phatta placed himself in one of them in a vain attempt to prevent the wall from crumbling. It did not take Akbar's guns long to blow him to smithereens. Jaimal too died a reckless death at Akbar's own hands. The two names became hallowed in folk memory in Rajasthan; Akbar too acknowledged the futile bravery of his foes by erecting statues of them at the gates of the imperial fort at Agra.

Akbar had conquered Chittaurgarh; but he had not defeated Rana Pratap. Pratap succeeded to the titles of his house in 1572.

The thought of recovering Chittaurgarh became obsessive, though he lacked the material resources to do so. He was able to inspire fierce loyalty among his followers, even when they were not Rajputs. The Bhil peoples of Rajasthan, some of the original inhabitants of the region, whose chief had been treacherously murdered by the founder of the Mewar state, nonetheless stuck to Pratap through all his travails. Bhamashah, a great merchant of the region, placed all his enormous wealth at Pratap's disposal in his fight against the Mughals. And of course Rajput leaders, like the sons of Jaimal and Phatta, fought by his side in his quarter-century-long struggle which brought him,

of doing this through a political compromise with Akbar repelled him. He did not succeed in his life's mission, but his last wish, expressed as he lay dying in 1597, was that no mansion ever be built nor any creature comfort be provided to his successors until they had Chittaurgarh back in their hands.

Treachery: If Rana Pratap is an extreme example of the Rajputs' fierce dedication to honour, there were others who were far more down-to-earth in their pursuit of personal ambition and did not allow any scruple to interfere with it. Thus, early in the 14th century Hammira, ruler of Ranthambore, was deserted by the chief commander of his army, who joined forces with his enemy,

his family and his partisans untold privation. The severity of the situation also led some Rajput princes to desert him. Among the several encounters Pratap had with the Mughal army, the most celebrated one at Haldighati (the Yellow Valley) in 1576, had another great Rajput warrior, Man Singh, at the head of the Mughal force. Pratap lost this battle, as he did several others.

The Mughals kept pursuing Pratap through the varied landscape of Rajasthan; and Pratap kept eluding or fighting them. He had taken a vow never to sleep on a proper bed, nor live in a mansion, nor eat off metal utensils until Chittaurgarh had been recovered. The thought

Allauddin Khalji, at a time when Khalji had laid siege to his fort. Some of the other Rajput generals also defected to the opposite side at that critical juncture. On the other hand, some Muslim soldiers, fighting on Hammira's side, stuck with him to the end. One of them, wounded in the battle and captured alive, was asked by Khalji what he would do if his wounds were healed by the sultan's doctors. His reply was unhesitating: he would try to slay Khalji and place the dead Rajput's son on the throne. The sultan had him trampled to death under an elephant's feet, but gave him an honourable burial. Hammira's betrayers were also trampled to death on the sultan's orders, since he never rewarded treachery which he had himself engineered.

Even Rana Pratap failed to command the unreserved loyalty of all his followers; among those who could not stand the enormous strain of his unrelenting struggle against the Mughals was his own brother who went over to Akbar; in return he was given the title of rana and the capital of Mewar.

Barring Rana Pratap, Akbar had been able to come to terms with almost all Rajput rulers who were enlisted as high officials of the empire and many of whom gave their daughters in marriage to the emperor and his princes. Henceforth, alliance with the Rajputs was to become one of the cornerstones of imperial polity. Rajputs became, in the words of a Mughal historian, "at once the props and the ornaments of the (Mughal) throne."

Decline: Henceforth, while an individual Mughal emperor might be more inclined towards one Rajput house rather than another, and might bestow some extra favours on it, the imperial polity always functioned with the support of the Rajputs as a whole. There was an eruption of tension between the empire and one eminent Rajput house in the last quarter of the 17th century. The last of the "great Mughals", Aurangzeb, plagued by one crisis after another, had sought respite from his troubles by accommodating the newly emerging Maratha troublemakers, led by their great leader, Shivaji, at the expense of the Rajputs. This was openly resented by the Jodhpur ruler, but the rest of the Rajputs continued to side with the Mughal empire.

So strong had the interdependence between the Mughal empire and the Rajputs become that Rajput strength, which had stubbornly defied the Delhi Sultans for 3½ long centuries, declined with the loss of authority of the empire in the 18th century. As in the case of the empire's other former as well as existing territories, the subjects and lands of the Rajputs were plundered at will by the rising new power, the Marathas. Several Rajput rulers secured their territories against such plunder by paying large sums in annual ransom to them.

Gone also were the codes of chivalry which had lent so much to the identity of everyday life of Rajput ruling families. Once the overarching Mughal suzerainty was withdrawn, previously buried clan and family tensions rose to the surface within each kingdom and, of course, between them. These were routine, petty tensions, devoid of the grandeur that had marked the relationship between the Rajput states and the great empires of the Sultans of Delhi and the Mughals. Bit by bit, some Rajput states – among them Mewar with its glorious history of defiance of imperial might for over three centuries – were reduced to a situation where they became the protectorates first of the Marathas and later of British power in India. Mewar handed over 6 million rupees to the Marathas for protection and Marwar a similar amount.

Enter the British: The British, along with other European traders, had come to India in the early 17th century, attracted by the fame of Indian cotton and silk textiles and indigo. Their trading interests had expanded over the centuries; with that had grown their attempts to get a foothold in the faction-ridden land. They had brought with them gold and silver to pay for the goods purchased here; but their own value in the local factional policies was enhanced as they brought into the field the most advanced firearms of the time and superior military organisation. They were in great demand in the various states that had emerged following the disintegration of the Mughal empire.

In the ensuing free-for-all, the British and the French were the chief competitors for establishing their hold over the whole of India; in the end, the British emerged the victors, though the French and the Portuguese continued to hold on to bits of Indian territory. The British started on their path of conquest from around the mid-18th century in Bengal; by the end of the century, their presence could also be felt far away in the west and the south.

Out in the west, the British initially let the Marathas plunder the Rajput states by assuming a posture of strict neutrality in the mutual relations of Indian states. This, of necessity, made the Rajputs turn to them for protection. The British did not desire the annihilation of the Rajput states at Maratha's hands, for they were well aware that, along with them, the Marathas were to be the chief contenders for imperial status in India and it would therefore be expedient to preserve a force essentially hostile to the Marathas. This was achieved through a series of treaties between the British Indian Government and various Rajput states. Through them, each side was obliged to treat the friends and enemies of the other as its own friends and enemies, and to render assistance to each other in the event of a threat to either side's security.

Unequal treaties: The conclusion of a treaty did not fully assure assistance in meeting external threats, for often a treaty was violated on one flimsy pretext or another by either

The disingenuous nature of this claim was acknowledged even by Lord Hastings, Governor-General of India, in 1814: "In our treaties with them [the princes] we recognise them as independent sovereigns. Then we send a Resident to their courts…[who] assumes the functions of a director; interferes in all their private concerns; countenances refractory subjects against them; and makes the most ostentatious exhibition of his authority…"

By the second decade of the 19th century, the British had buried any of the Maratha pretensions to imperial status forever, in turn firmly establishing their own claim to it. Thus, although the chief trouble-makers, as far as the Rajput states were concerned, had

side if compliance did not suit it. But, on the whole, the treaties were far more advantageous to the British than to the Indian states. Following these alliances, the British authority in the states came to be represented by Residents – one in each major state. The Resident would emerge as the real centre of power in the state, freely interfering with the internal administration and justifying it with the claim that a properly administered people would secure the prince against any internal disturbance or external threat. "The exclusive aim of our interference," wrote one such Resident, "was the welfare of the Rajput princes and the tranquility of their country".

by and large been silenced, the states were no longer in a position to snap their ties with the mighty new power. Indeed, at an assembly of the princes at Ajmer in 1832, they complained against each other to the British Governor-General and each pleaded for his personal intervention to sort out their petty disputes. They even sought his protection against *dacoits* (robbers) operating in their own territories.

Even as the British Residents interfered with the internal affairs of the states, the Imperial Government wisely refrained from depriving any Rajput ruler or his successor of his throne or his title. The wisdom of this policy was demonstrated in 1857 when almost all the Rajput princes came rushing to the aid of the beleaguered British, and greeted the crushing of the great rebellion of that historic year in India with unconcealed glee.

Not all of Rajasthan was, however, on the side of the British. As in the core of the rebellious territory, intermediate levels of landed aristocracy combined with the civilian population to participate in the uprising in Rajasthan and, for a brief while, met with impressive successes. Often, the common soldiers sent to suppress the rebels expressed their solidarity with them by downing their guns, though their active participation in the uprising remained rather marginal.

administration, justice, education, and so on, gradually came to be introduced in Rajasthan as in the rest of the country. Initially some of these met with resistance, but this was followed by slow acceptance.

Towards the end of the 19th century and the beginning of the 20th, a kind of ferment was agitating the minds of the educated Indian elite, and the ferment was percolating down to the mass of the people. Its main thrust was one of hostility to British rule, initially moderate but growing intense with the passage of time. The Governors-General realised that the princes might prove their chief bastion of support in the face of growing popular agitation. In 1903 Lord Curzon

Immediately following the rebellion of 1857, the princes were engulfed in a sort of euphoria, for Queen Victoria as she declared herself Empress of India, had assured the princes that the earlier reckless policy of depriving them of their thrones was being given up for good. The declaration was reassuring even in Rajasthan where the former policy had hardly ever been implemented. However, various British institutions of

Left, Maharawal Udai Singhji of Dungapur in conversation with General Sir David Ochterlony, first British resident of Rajputana, Jana Mahal Palace, Dungarpur, Above, wall painting.

organised the Delhi Durbar, an assembly of princes at Delhi held to gauge the extent of support for the British Government; the response should have pleased him. Most princes demonstrated an almost excessive eagerness to attend and reiterate their loyalty to their imperial masters.

The Princes and the Nationalist Movement: In 1905 Curzon partitioned Bengal into two provinces, ostensibly for reasons of administrative convenience, but actually to separate the Muslim-dominated east Bengal from Hindu-dominated west Bengal in the hope of creating dissensions between them. This single act electrified the mass of the people in Bengal and galvanised them into a most uncompromising hostility to the Government. The effect of the agitation naturally spilled over into all of South Asia. In Rajasthan, the princes, loyal to Britain, took several steps to prevent the spread of the agitation (termed "sedition" by them) to Rajasthan: severe restrictions were placed on the press in the reporting of agitation. All the restrictions notwithstanding, Rajasthan did not remain untouched by some of the revolutionary activity that had engulfed much of India at this time.

The outbreak of World War I witnessed the princes in Rajasthan similarly eager to demonstrate their loyalty to Britain. The was established with the professed objective of achieving closer cooperation between the two sides. The Chamber was thus visualised as a bulwark against popular agitation.

The rest of the story of Rajasthan conforms closely to the story of the freedom movement in India as a whole. The combined force of the British Government and the Indian princes could not hold back the widespread and popular demands for independence. The movement used diverse methods to achieve its ends: sometimes depending solely on non-violence under the leadership of Gandhi; at other times taking to revolutionary violence and paying for it with life itself. When Independence finally came to India in 1947,

character of India's freedom movement began to change considerably after the peace treaty of 1919. While British imperialism remained the chief target of hostility, especially in the territories directly under British administration, attention also began to be directed towards the problems of the subjects of the princely states. Consequently, agitations were launched to secure redress of their grievances. Clearly the agitations in the princely states were double-edged: they were directed both against the Indian princes and their British masters.

This necessarily threw the two even closer into each other's arms. A Chamber of Princes the different strands of the movement began to fragment into political factions, although the Congress Party remained all-powerful.

Independent India: 15 August 1947 brought to India both Independence and Partition of the country into India and Pakistan. The princes had been given the option of either merging with India or Pakistan or retaining their autonomy. Since the partition had taken place on the basis of the Hindu-Muslim divide, it would have been unthinkable for the Hindu princes of Rajasthan to throw in their lot with Pakistan. Long history and common religious identity with the rest of India made it inevitable that they should merge with India. The new Government of independent India – largely through the efforts of the new Home Minister, Sardar Patel – made it attractive to the princes to opt for India by providing them with a generous Privy Purse and several other privileges; on the other hand, it was made clear to them that the Indian Government did not quite like the idea of several independent states scattered all over its conventionally bounded territory. Rajasthani princes were quick to grasp the message and one by one came over to merge with India. They enjoyed the Privy Purse and other privileges until 1970 when Indira Gandhi abolished them through an Act of Parliament.

Art and commerce: In two other spheres of human activity, the cultural and the economic, Rajasthan has made impressive contributions. During the 18th and early 19th centuries, a Rajasthani school of painting developed from the Mughal style and earned considerable recognition. The chief centre of the Rajasthan school was at Bundi.

In the economy, the term "Marwari" (from Marwar, around Jodhpur) has come to signify a trader *par excellence*. The Marwaris had spread themselves out from west to east as carriers of trade from the 17th century onwards and by the 18th century had established themselves well enough to be the chief bankers and money-lenders to

Although Rajasthan has, with the rest of India, changed a great deal over the past four decades, history and tradition continue to play an important part in Rajasthani identity. Almost every Rajasthani citizen will enthusiastically recite the history, often generously mixed with a great deal of charming fantasy, of almost every fort, palace or former ruling family from its beginning to the present day, to any willing listener.

Left, the infant Maharaja of Jaisalmer surrounded by his courtiers. **Above**, Maharaja Col. Sawai Bhawani Singhji of Jaipur receiving *nazar* on his birthday in the Zenana Deodi.

provincial governments such as the one in Bengal. The tradition continues to this day, though their business now includes industry.

While the Marwaris have taken to modern commercial activity with great zeal, their social and family life remains steeped in tradition. The sense of family solidarity remains extremely strong with them and their children's marriages are mostly arranged by the parents. It is still rare to come across a non-vegetarian Marwari. The Marwaris represent an interesting case of how traditional social practices and structures have been adapted to life in post-Independence India.

Rajasthan is a recent addition to the political map of India. Prior to March 31, 1949, when 22 princely states were merged into one single administrative unit, the area used to be identified as Rajputana – the land of the Rajputs or rajas. Each state was ruled by a prince, one of whose ancestors had entered into a subordinate treaty relationship with the British Crown. The princes governed their subjects through *jaghirdars* (land-holding nobility). With the end of British rule in India on 15 August, 1947, the British government relinquished its rule over the princely Indian states, leaving them technically free of all central control since there had been no formal transfer of paramountcy to the successor governments of India and Pakistan. This posed great danger to India's national integrity, already sorely damaged by partition. Efforts were therefore made to get the princes to accept the control of the Government of independent India as they had that of the British Government of India.

The task was a formidable one, as most of the princes were reluctant to accept any arrangement that curtailed or deprived them of their privileges and denied them absolute power over their territories and subjects, and they strived hard to retain them. However, the wily Home Minister, Sardar Vallabhbhai Patel, accomplished the seemingly impossible task peacefully. His political and religious affiliations as a right-wing Hindu were of great help in gaining the trust of the rulers of the princely states. Rajputana's princes accepted the sovereignty of the Government of India. They even agreed to surrender their rights to rule their individual states, paving the way for their integration into a single administrative unit. In lieu of this, the princes were granted certain privileges and a fixed annual privy purse.

Creation of a State: Rajasthan, as a single, unified administrative unit, was created in stages. The first step in this direction was the formation of the Matsya Union, integrating the princely states of Alwar, Bharatpur,

Preceding pages: desert housing. Left, Rajasthan villages are now electrified. Above, Jaipur at night.

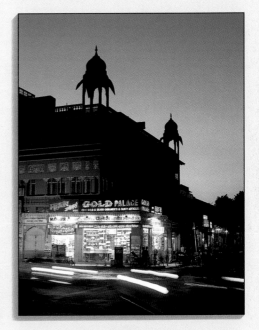

Dholpur and Karauli. Within a week of this, on March 25, 1948, another merger took place forming the Rajasthan Union, unifying the states of Banswara, Bundi, Dungarpur, Jhalawar, Kishangarh, Shahpura and Tonk. Three days later the Maharana of Mewar also agreed to merge Mewar State into the Rajasthan Union, which was renamed the United State of Rajasthan. The process of merger and unification of the princely states of Rajputana was completed on March 30, 1949, with the rulers of all the remaining states of the region, including the princes of Jaipur, Jodhpur, Jaisalmer, Bikaner and Kota, agreeing to integration. With this, a new unified state, the United State of Greater Rajasthan, was formed, comprising the area of these states, the Matsya Union and the United State of Rajasthan. The Maharana of Mewar was appointed Maharajpramukh and the Maharaja of Jaipur Rajpramukh of the United State of Greater Rajasthan.

A single administrative unit for the whole of the geographical area of Rajputana, however, came into existence only on November 1, 1956, when the centrally administered state of Ajmer was also merged with the United State of Greater Rajasthan. After this merger, the state was renamed Rajasthan. Simultaneously, the offices of the Maharajpramukh and Rajpramukh were abolished and, a governor was appointed in Rajasthan also. Just over a decade later, the privileges and privy purses granted to the ex-rulers and their families were withdrawn by amending the constitution.

The days of the Jaghirdars: Under British protection, many princes and their *jaghirdars* had severely oppressed their people. Civil liberties and elementary human rights were denied them. The will of the rulers was law. The farmers were entirely at the mercy of the *jaghirdars* or rajas who enjoyed unlimited

There were, of course, some honourable exceptions both among individual princes and states. For example, in Bikaner and Jaipur in the late 1940s, these princely states and several others made a move towards providing some form of civil rights by inducting public representatives into their governments. However, full democracy in Rajasthan dawned only in 1952, when, for the first time, a Vidhan Sabha (Legislative Assembly) was constituted on the basis of universal adult suffrage.

Princely influence: Many of the ex-rulers and *jaghirdars* found it difficult to reconcile themselves to their changed status. Some, under the leadership of the ruling Maharaja

and unchallenged authority and power. People in authority often treated the majority of the people as slaves.

Before the advent of British rule, the princes and *jaghirdars* had spent most of their time on wars, personal feuds and palace conspiracies, and during British rule, indulging in personal whims, luxuries and extravaganzas. Their relationship with the public was in many cases limited to collection of land revenue with little concern for welfare activities. As a result, Rajasthan, which was once flourishing and prosperous, gradually became the most economically disadvantaged part of the country.

of Jodhpur, made a bid to regain power collectively through the ballot box in the elections to the first Vidhan Sabha. The fact that groups opposed to the Indian National Congress were able to capture 78 of the 160 seats, was a measure of the influence of the princes and *jaghirdars* even after they had ceased to exercise ruling powers. Some of this influence is to be attributed, no doubt, to fear of economic and other powers of reward and reprisal still meted out by the princes and *jaghirdars*. But for the premature death of the Maharaja of Jodhpur in an air crash, before the newly elected Vidhan Sabha could assemble, the formation of a government by the Congress party in Rajasthan would have been extremely difficult. With the untimely removal of the leader around whom the opposition to the Congress party could have rallied, the alliance of ex-princes and their supporters fell apart and Rajasthan's first democratically elected government was formed by the Congress party.

When Maharani (now Rajmata or Queen Mother) Gayatri Devi of Jaipur entered politics and contested the Lok Sabha (Parliamentary) election from the Jaipur constituency in 1962, she smashed all electoral records by winning the largest-ever lead over her nearest rival, the Congress party. She even rose to the position of Vice-President of the right-wing Swatantra Party at the national level.

The ex-princes in Rajasthan thus posed a potential electoral threat to the nationally dominant Congress party, which held power in the desert state until 1977, when the Janata Party won the elections on a near all-India scale. In less than three years their meagre performance culminated in an anti-Janata wave, bringing the Congress back to power in Rajasthan. The first party following India's

Independence, over-confident in its strength and traditional vote, and in a general atmosphere of increasing political tension and economical stagnation, itself fell victim to an anti-Congress move in February 1990. The State was taken over by a coalition government, led by the Janata Party and the Bharat Janata Party, a Hindu chauvanist group with links to several extreme religious organisations. In 1998, after scandals and political infighting in the BJP, Congress won sweeping election victories in both the Lok Sabha and state elections. They were led by the current Chief Minister, Ashok Gehlot.

As the years went by, the ex-princes adjusted themselves to the new situation and

their new circumstances. The services of some of them were utilized by the Government of India on diplomatic assignments; the younger generation competed with other young Indians for higher government services and executive and managerial positions in commerce and industry. Many of Rajasthan's ex-princes turned to business and some even converted their palaces into luxury hotels. The Rambagh Palace Hotel, Jaipur, the Lake Palace Hotel, Udaipur, the Umaid Bhawan Palace Hotel, Jodhpur, and the Lalgarh Palace Hotel, Bikaner, are all former palaces of *maharajas*. These palace hotels now attract tourists from all over the world.

Left and **above**, the conversion of royal residences into hotels has created an infrastructure for tourism and brought employment to many areas.

Though the princely order came to an end in 1949, the *jaghirdari* system persisted for quite some time. After Rajasthan's first elected government came to power in 1952, steps were initiated to free the peasants from the clutches of the *jaghirdars*. A law abolishing *jaghirs* was enacted and far-reaching land reforms were gradually introduced. To further strengthen the democratic system, the administration of the local affairs of the villages was handed over to elected *panchayats* (village councils) in 1959.

Then and now: At the time of the formation of Rajasthan the state had a population of 15.2 million. Only 8.95 percent of the people were literate. Facilities for education were

Only an area of a little more than 740,000 acres (300,000 hectares) was irrigated. Electricity was then a luxury used only to illuminate royal palaces. At the time of the formation of Rajasthan, total power generation in the state was only 8 MW. Only a couple of big industrial units existed and the total number of registered smallscale units was unbelievably low at 16. The low level of industrialisation was discernible in almost every sphere of public life.

The scene has since changed considerably. The state's annual budget of expenditure which was Rs 172.3 million (US$14.33 million) in 1951–52, went up to Rs 25 billion (US$2.08 billion) by 1986–87, and the an-

meagre. The first university of the state was set up in 1947. The only medical college of the state had only just started. Medical facilities were available in only the capital towns of eight erstwhile states. Piped water supply was available in only five towns, and wells or village tanks were the only source of drinking water elsewhere. In the arid region at many places, the water table for tube wells was as low as 100 metres. Even today, in many villages, at least one member of the family spends her/his whole working life in meeting the family's water needs. Major irrigation schemes, except for the Ganga Canal in Bikaner, were conspicuously absent.

nual plan for 2000–1 is set at Rs 44.12 billion (US$980 million). The state's first 5-year plan (1951–56) had an outlay of Rs 675 million ($56.25 million). The outlay for the seventh 5-year plan which stretched into the 1990's rose to Rs 30 billion (US$2.5 billion). A sum of Rs 11.12 billion (US$926.7 million) had been spent on the power sector before the seventh 5-year plan began. As a result, electricity has even reached small hamlets. By 1996–7, the power availability in the state had gone up to over 17.8 million MW. The farmers irrigate fields from electrically pumped wells and drawing water with the help of bullocks for agricultural purposes is becoming a thing of the past. Over 24,000 villages now have piped water supply though "safe water" reaches only around 40 percent of the population.

Many major irrigation projects like those on the Chambal in Kota, the Mahi in Banswara and the Indira Gandhi Nahar (canal) were launched and commissioned after the formation of Rajasthan. Irrigation facilities are now available (figures for 1997–8) for an area of over 6.6 million hectares (16.3 million acres). This has given a big boost to agricultural activity in this once desert state of India.

The waters of the Himalaya, carried to Rajasthan by the Indira Gandhi Nahar Project (IGNP) have helped agricultural production in the desert of northwestern Rajasthan. In 1951, total foodgrain production in the state was 3.9 million tonnes. With the creation of additional irrigation facilities and adoption of modern farming practices by the farmers, foodgrain production has now risen beyond 14 million tonnes per annum. However, despite this, the state is still largely dependent on the rains for a good crop. The monsoon has been very erratic for the last few years, resulting in recurring droughts, the most severe in 1987 and 2000, with a further drought and famine predicted in 2001.

Industrial development: The industrial scene too has witnessed a rapid transformation. Over the years more than 175 industrial areas have been developed and almost every part of the state has at least some industrial activity. Today the number of registered small-scale industries in the state is more than 125,000. Over 200 large and medium-sized industries are in production, with some 10,200 registered factories. According to one rough estimate, about Rs. 20 billion ($1.7 million) stands invested in the industrial sector in the state. The annual industrial growth was estimated at 2 percent during the 1990s.

Education: Educational facilities, earlier limited to major towns, have now reached many villages. The state has five universities, five medical colleges, five engineering colleges, a number of *ayurvedic* (traditional system of medicine) colleges, a National Institute of Ayurvedic Research, a large number of industrial training centres and

Left, the daily passenger train from Nawalgarh to Jaipur serves as a convenient milk run for local farmers.

colleges of general education. However impressive this may sound, the overall literacy rate stands at only 38.5 percent – one of the lowest in the country – with female literacy generously estimated to stand at a paltry 20 percent. Medical facilities have been expanded, although in 1991 there was still only one hospital bed for every 2,027 inhabitants.

What investment in social welfare, and agricultural and industrial development has taken place has been greatly overtaken by the increase in population – somewhere around 50 million, according to recent estimates.

The Indira Gandhi Nahar Project: When the idea of irrigating Thar Desert with water from the Beas and Ravi rivers in the Himalaya was mooted, most people did not take it seriously. However, Himalayan water is now flowing among the sand dunes of Thar through the Indira Gandhi Nahar Project.

Of the various projects initiated after the formation of Rajasthan, the Rajasthan Canal Project (it was renamed after the death of Prime Minister Indira Gandhi) was the most ambitious. The main canal building work was implemented in two stages, beginning in 1958 and finishing by 1986. In the first stage, a network of canals to irrigate sandy lands in the districts of Ganganagar and Bikaner were excavated, providing irrigation facilities to about 70,000 hectares (1.73 million acres) in Ganganagar and Bikaner districts. The second stage takes the main canal another 256 km (159 miles) as far as Mohangarh in Jaisalmer District.

On the plus side, the areas adjacent to the canals now produce wheat, paddy, groundnut, cotton, sugarcane, oil-seeds, pulses and other commercial crops. Ganganagar District, once dependent on others for its food requirements, has acquired a degree of self-sufficiency. The IGNP has also provided some relief in the desert districts from the droughts that regularly plague the state.

However, its overall operating capacity has fallen well short of initial expectations. The canals themselves have become stagnant waterways, clogged up with water hyacinth. Perhaps the main effect of these large standing bodies of water has been to provide a fertile breeding ground for mosquitos, turning Rajasthan into one of the most malarial regions of India.

Despite ecological adversity and a long feudal history which, while it made Rajasthan a fascinating land of palaces and forts, left the state with very low agricultural productivity and a near-total absence of modern industry until a few decades ago, Rajasthan's inhabitants are noted for their ability to shape and decorate their environment. No visitor to Rajasthan will fail to notice the colourful local dress, vibrant traditions of music and dance and the murals painted on many walls.

It is not uncommon for large tracts of Rajasthan to face water, food and fodder scarcity for several consecutive years; even in years of normal rainfall, in many villages, women daily trudge several miles to fetch a head-load of water; yet the people have managed to evolve lifestyles which sustain them in this harsh environment.

Scattered population: The ecological adversities responsible for continuous agricultural scarcities kept Rajasthan's population in check till the early 1920s but, since India became an independent country in 1947, the growth rate of Rajasthan's population has taken demographers as well as policy-makers by surprise. During the decade 1971–81, Jaipur, Rajasthan's capital and premier city, recorded the second-highest growth-rate amongst all urban centres in India, becoming a city of some 1.5 million people. Rajasthan's total population grew by 32.36 percent against the all-India average of 24.75 percent. Some districts of Rajasthan recorded even higher growth rates, setting off alarm bells. However, these growth-rates have to be understood in the context of small absolute population totals in sprawling arid and semi-arid regions, which with appropriate investment in irrigation, agriculture and other infrastructure could sustain a far higher level of population.

According to the 1991 census, Rajasthan had a population of 43.9 million (up from 34.1 million in 1981 and 25.76 million in 1971), estimated ahead of the next census in 2001 to be creeping up to 50 million. This would constitute 5 percent of the country's

total population of 1 billion. However, Rajasthan occupies nearly 10 percent of India's total area, which gives it a very low spatial density of around 146 persons per square kilometre with some districts having startlingly low densities – Jaisalmer 6, Bikaner 31, and Barmer 39, for example, on 1991 figures. The people of Rajasthan thus inhabit a sparsely populated space, a factor which shapes not only political and administrative policies but also the rhythm of social and cultural life, based as it is on long-distance

communication and periodic congregations of people belonging to several villages. The latter gatherings have a ritual as well as great social significance, which extends even into the economic sphere as the people of rural Rajasthan are virtually forced by territorial ecology to make the bulk of their purchases at colourful fairs and *hats* (periodic, usually weekly, markets) organized at frequencies regulated by seasonal necessities.

The people of Rajasthan, then, occupy a large territory with a harsh climate and low level of agriculture, which have resulted in a persistently low per capita annual income, compared to the all-India average. On the

Preceding pages: turbans provide insulation from the desert heat; a Rajput woman. **Left**, village elder. **Right**, shepherd boy.

other hand, as a percentage fewer people in Rajsthan fall below the average all-India "poverty line" as defined by the Planning Commission. This is helped by staple foods such as *jowar* (barley) and *bajra* (millet), which compare favourably with rice and wheat in nutritional value.

However, the people still face a very low per capita availability of social provision like health care and education, as well as economic infrastructure (e.g. railways, roads and electricity). The material base of Rajasthan's economy should be rich enough to sustain a reasonable standard of living for all the state's people – the feudal system in place until Independence has yet to die out

However admirable the Rajasthani's will to overcome the difficulties posed by its environment, one cannot ignore the region's abysmally low level of literacy; 38.5 percent against 52.11 percent for the country as a whole in 1991. In important districts for tourism like Jaisalmer and Barmer, the literacy rate is virtually non-existent (1.64 and 1.68 percent respectively according to 1991 figures). This low level of education is reflected in such social customs as child marriage and *sati* which persistent legislative and executive efforts have failed to eradicate. Many are still "married" in their infancy with some marriages even being arranged, on a mutual-exchange basis, by potential parents

completely, and the raising of the general standard of living is hampered by a massively unequal distribution of wealth. That said, the Rajasthanis have sustained a wealth of cultural creativity and mass participation in leisure festivities, as any visitor to Jaipur can note while witnessing *tij* and *gangaur* processions. The durable nature of urbanisation sustained by the people of Rajasthan is, indeed, remarkable in the context of the internecine and external armed warfare its princes indulged in for nearly 10 centuries. As a bonus, this long history of urbanisation has left cities which contain a wealth of monuments and historical sites.

while the partners are still in their mother's womb. Similarly, cases of *sati* even now occur every year in Rajasthan and newly built memorials devoted to such *satis* are a common sight even though the government is committed to ending the practice.

One of the most infamous cases of recent years was the death of Roop Kanwar in 1987. The *sati* of this 18-year-old on her husband's funeral pyre in the village of Deorala shocked the nation. However, her memorial soon started to attract pilgrims, and the more reactionary members of the nation's religious right defended the practice of *sati* – conveniently ignoring the issue of coercion.

Warrior-caste: The Rajputs constitute the social fulcrum of community life in Rajasthan. Although many families have been stripped of their titles and power as hereditary rulers, a past stretching over nearly a thousand years cannot be expected to just vanish without traceable remnants and residues, short of a violent revolutionary upheaval of a type which India's power-elite have been consciously trying to avoid, let alone advocating or advancing the cause of sudden and total social change. Although the Rajputs never constituted more than a tenth of the total population, they have controlled policy and wider society in Rajasthan for nearly a thousand years. This is now coming to an end

epitomizes the actual political role of the Rajputs in this part of India. This was, to consolidate autonomous princely states amidst the emergence of chaotic conditions in the wake of the decline of empires, like that of Harsha in the 6th century and, later, fiercely resisting invasions and encroachments over their territories, by the Muslim (and Mughal) armies.

The political role of the Rajput rulers of the princely states of Rajasthan is borne out by the fact that, amongst the 22 princely states and chiefdoms which were merged into Rajasthan in a multi-phase consolidation between 1947 and 1950, as many as 19 had Rajput rulers. The more prominent among

with the accession of the territories over which they ruled to the Indian Union and the gradual de-recognition of their special privileges and prerogatives, culminating in the dramatic abolition in 1970 of the privy purses of the ex-rulers.

Who are the Rajputs? Romantic mythology ascribes their origins to the *Agni-kula* ceremony performed by Brahman priests at Mount Abu, which is the highest point along the Aravalli range of mountains in Rajasthan. Be that as it may, this consecration story only

Adivasi and nomadic women are known for their love of silver jewellery.

these were Bikaner, Jaipur, Jodhpur, Kota and Udaipur – the order is alphabetical as any other rank-ordering of these princely states is bound to arouse acrimonious debate. Even though these feudal fiefdoms were abolished over 50 years ago, the ex-rulers continue to exercise a disproportionate influence on the politics of the state, and many voters still maintain their allegience to their local ruling Rajput families through the ballot box.

The Rajasthani Rajput community was accustomed to a military existence. Their personal and family expenditure was met out of tax and non-tax revenues collected from the cultivators and other rural producers from the villages assigned to them as *jaghir*, in lieu of their commitment to perform military service at the command of the *durbar*, the ruler. The Rajput *jaghirdars* were not, however, mere land-grantees of the *durbars*; all of them claimed kinship with the rulers whose ancestors their forefathers had helped in their territorial conquests and political consolidation.

The Rajputs of Rajasthan, thus, constituted a warrior aristocracy divided into a number of prominent clans, each of which regarded a princely state as its traditional patrimony, whose ruler was the social head of the clan besides being the political ruler. The princely

The advent of *Pax Britannica* in the early years of the 19th century signaled the virtual end of the Rajputs' fighting days, while the growing sophistication and technological modernisation of warfare made their traditional attitudes redundant. True, most Rajputs had acquired some *jaghirdari* rights but, in actual practice, very few had learnt the tricks of either estate administration or assets management which modern tax laws and commercial prudence demand. For nearly 150 years after the princely states signed "Treaties of Friendship" with the British, the Rajput *durbars* and *jaghirdars* were able to maintain a life of sumptuous luxury and ostentatious consumption – at the expense of

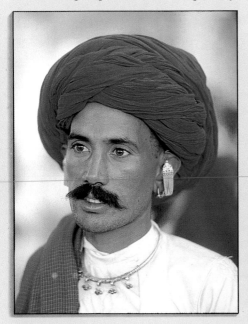 

state of Jaipur was thus ruled by the *Kachchwaha* Rajputs, the *Rathors* ruled in Jodhpur and Bikaner, the *Hadas* in Kota, and the *Sisodias* in Mewar (Udaipur).

For nearly a thousand years, these Rajput clans ruled, and virtually every generation of each Rajput family lost one or more members in armed warfare. Sometimes entire families perished at one stroke: the men rushing out to meet attacking armies which enjoyed overwhelming superiority, and the women performing *johar* by entering mass funeral pyres, in what now seems a twisted code of honour that held that death was preferable to being ruled over.

the vast majority of their subjects who lived in a state of serfdom. But their growing family budgets gradually became imbalanced as their subjects became increasingly conscious of their rights and refused to pay excessive taxes and non-tax levies. The spread of modern concepts of statutory taxation and the separation of a ruler's personal income from public treasury receipts climaxed in the statutory abolition of *jaghirdari* (1954) and princely privy purses (1970). True, some of the more canny Rajput *jaghirdars* and *durbars* did manage to play their cards well and were able to retain substantial land and other properties under their personal possession, but India's legislators continued to gnaw away at such assets, although little seems to have been distributed where the wealth is most needed. These developments have placed the Rajput nobility facing the economic realities of existence for the first time in many generations, which several have tried to overcome independently by converting their palaces into hotels and adding many modern amenities. This is perhaps the only way out of the crisis while still retaining some control over their family property, and some Rajputs have acquired the necessary skills – sound management over money and materials – whereas others continue to bewail their fates.

"Brahmanical Hinduism" prevalent in other parts of India. This makes the people of Rajasthan much more heterodox as far as the Sanskritic norms and forms of Hinduism are concerned. While this heterodoxy allowed the rural people to sustain many of their traditions woven round local deities and heroes such as *Pabuji*, *Ramdeoji*, *Tejaji*, *Gogaji* and *Jambhoji*, it also enabled the princes to maintain a cordiality towards Islam and its followers within their territories, even while indulging in virtually non-stop warfare against Muslim rulers over several centuries.

The Brahmans' failure to dominate the courts of Rajput princes thus imparted a secular flavour to the social life of the people.

Priests and scholars: Like the Rajputs, the Brahmans also constitute less than a tenth of the total population of Rajasthan but, unlike in most of the rest of India, they do not occupy the top rungs of the socio-political and socio-economic ladder although they do enjoy the ritual esteem which the Hindus traditionally accord to Brahmans as priests and scholars. In fact, if we are allowed to coin a phrase, Hinduism in Rajasthan has a distinctive profile which can be described as "Rajput Hinduism" in contrast to the

Different styles of turban indicate the class, caste and region of the wearer.

At the time of India's partition in 1947, Muslims remained unmolested in Rajasthan. In November 1984, following Mrs Gandhi's assassination, not a single Sikh was killed in Rajasthan, even as anti-Sikh passions were raging in adjacent areas.

At the apex of Rajasthan's social pyramid, unlike the situation in most other parts of India, not only do two castes, the Rajputs and the Brahmans, vie for top honours, but these two groups have also to reckon with people belonging to several other social strata who also enjoy elite status. In the economic sphere, the Marwaris of Rajasthan are well-known for their trading skills, but what strikes a newcomer to Rajasthan even more forcefully is the fact that people belonging to such lowly castes as *Kayasthas* and *Charans* (traditionally a caste of epic singers) occupy prominent places in the public and private sectors while Jains (especially the Oswals amongst them) who constitute less than 2 percent of the total population, are conspicuous by their substantial presence in public service and education and also vie with the Marwaris in trade and other economic activities.

Muslims: Islam is the religion of about 10 percent of Rajasthan's population, and Muslims occupy a distinct place in its sociopolitical topography. Outside the Muslim-

which are very nearly indistinguishable from the Hindus living in the same area, sharing with them as they do many life-cycle rituals and social customs. Many such communities (e.g. *Meos*, *Kayamkhanis* and *Chitahs*) have been thus living in peaceful coexistence with their Hindu neighbours in several parts of Rajasthan for centuries. Of late, they have become the unwilling objects of a tug-of-war between Hindu chauvanists and Islamic radicals, as seen by the long period of BJP (Bharatiya Janata Party, right-wing Hindu nationalists) rule during the 1990s.

In southeast Rajasthan there is a sub-community of Shi'ite Muslims, the Bohras, really an extension from the main homeland

majority state of Jammu and Kashmir, Rajasthan was the first in the Indian Union to have a Muslim Chief Minister, while the Rajasthan unit of the erstwhile Jan Sangh, an all-India political party usually considered to be Hindu-oriented, had the distinction of being the first party in the state to field a Muslim for the state legislative elections.

As in other parts of India, Rajasthan's Muslims are mainly concentrated in the cities and bigger towns where their skills as artisans in dyeing, bangle-making, paper-making, etc. are in great demand. Nevertheless, a large number of Muslims also live in the countryside, many forming communities

of the community in Gujarat. Like other Gujarati communities, the Bohras are a highly mercantile group doing extensive business in Bombay, Ahmadabad and Karachi (Pakistan) and numerous other centres in Western India. Though small in numbers, it is said that it was the electoral support of the Rajasthan Bohras that turned the balance in favour of former Chief Minister Mohan Lal Sukhadia and kept him in office for 17 years without a break.

Adivasis: According to the 1981 census, some 12.2 percent of Rajasthan's population belongs to the constitutional category of Scheduled Tribes – government-speak for

Adivasis ("indigenous peoples"). To be included in a "Schedule" means essentially, to identify groups requiring special assistance for their economic and educational development. This is possibly not true of the Minas, who constitute the largest Adivasi group in Rajasthan. Today's Minas are descendants of the peoples who controlled most of the later princely state of Jaipur before the Kachchwahas established their rule there nearly a thousand years ago. A Mina leader was always associated with the coronation ceremonies of Kachchwaha rulers and a sizable percentage of Minas were employed as watch-and-ward staff by the Jaipur *durbar* and his *jaghirdars*. Another

nated against – like many of India's Adivasis – living in small rural communities and occasionally taking casual work in the towns to eke out their meagre incomes. Every February, the Bhil's Baneshwar festival is held at the confluence of the Som and Mahi near Dungarpur. Thousands gather here to sing, dance and pray.

The Bhils and Minas account for roughly 50 and 40 percent of the total Adivasi population of Rajasthan. Of the rest, Garasias and Sahariyas constitute roughly 3 and 1 percent respectively. The tiny community of Dangis are famous for their musical skills. The small group of Gaduliya Lohars have also become well known as India's first prime

significant chunk of Minas became skilled agriculturists, cultivating substantial landholdings, making the Mina community comparatively well-off.

In contrast to the Minas are the Bhils, the next largest Adivasi group, most of whom live in the hilly forests of southwestern Rajasthan. Despite their high socio-political status on account of their military support to the Sisodia rulers of Mewar in general and Maharana Pratap in particular, today the Bhils remain impoverished and discrimi-

Left, winowing *bajra*. **Above**, women at the carpenter god *puja*, Pushkar.

minister, Jawaharlal Nehru, took a personal interest in ensuring their settlement in fixed homes and the abandoning of their nomadic life, whose beginnings their oral traditions ascribe to the days of the sack of the fort of Chittaurgarh at the hands of Akbar nearly 500 years ago. Whether such well-meaning changes to the Adivasis' traditional patterns of existence are beneficial to the recipients are open to question.

While members of all these Adivasi groups, with the partial exception of the Bhils, are highly "visible" in Rajasthan, systematic documentation of their customs, kinship-patterns and cultural beliefs has yet to be undertaken. The social and economic discrimination they face in part dates back to the way in which the British administrators applied the designation "criminal" or "notified" to certain groups. Although such appellations have now been done away with in India, the Adivasis are perceived as outsiders by many caste Hindus and they continue to be exploited as a source of cheap labour.

Scheduled Castes: The "Scheduled Caste" population of Rajasthan (17 percent of the total) is larger than that of the "Scheduled Tribes" (12 percent). This government category again is on the basis of economic discrimination and the need for special assistance and consideration. Rajasthan's

Dalit ("the oppressed") – who continue to suffer from economic and social discrimination in rural Rajasthan. However, the degree of social discrimination suffered by these groups has traditionally been less severe than those suffered by corresponding castes in, say, the neighbouring territories of Uttar Pradesh, Bihar and Madhya Pradesh. The same observation applies to the Bhangis, the traditionally hereditary community of scavengers, who are, primarily, residents of towns and cities where the purity-pollution norms tend to be more relaxed. Besides these majority Scheduled Castes, other imprtant groups include the Madaris, Naths, Bazigars and Bhands whose dance, dramatic and

Scheduled Caste population is scattered throughout the state, Chamars constituting 45 percent of the total.

Chamars are the traditional leather-workers of India and suffer because of orthodox Hindu notions concerning purity and pollution. Nevertheless, they occupy a higher social rank than Meghwals and Balais (who constitute 9 percent each of the total) whose traditional occupation involves the handling of animal carcasses and hides and skins.

All Scheduled Castes are ex-"Untouchables" or "Harijans" ("children of God") – many of whom have now adopted the more radical, and less patronising label

acrobatic performances still entertain the people.

A pastoral people: Despite ecological limitations, agriculture and animal husbandry constitute the primary occupation of the bulk of the people of Rajasthan, with pastoralism adapted to suit the arid and semi-arid lands. Rajasthan's minimal vegetation has been skillfully exploited to sustain large herds of sheep, goats and camels. In addition the people of Rajasthan have evolved varieties of cattle, amongst the best in the country, well adapted to these conditions. In recent years, these well-adapted techniques of agriculture and animal husbandry have been threatened by new policies of agricultural development which have little relevance to the ecology of Rajasthan. The farmers are taking full advangage of the new methods – irrigation, improved seeds, agro-machinery and credit – but their traditional life-styles are being abandoned without taking due account of the possible long-term impact of these new techniques. While the increased use of electrically-pumped bore wells and the planting of high-yield crop varieties dependent on large amounts of water initially brought increased profits, recent droughts have exposed the weaknesses in these technologically dependent methods of agricultural production.

of agricultural production, including irrigation and the use of tractors, coupled with the absence of wool processing facilities in Rajasthan, is endangering their future in regions where large communities of animal farmers have adapted themselves over many years to cope with a waterless regime.

Hardy farmers: Despite all appearances to the contrary, the soil of Rajasthan does support a substantial agricultural population who harvest protein-rich crops like *jowar* and *bajra*. With the arrival of high-input extensive agriculture, castes like the Jats have been able to make considerable profits by turning to the production of cash-crops such as sugarcane and cotton.

These developments have led to great changes in Rajasthani rural life. Whereas previously most dairy produce was consumed locally, the non-nomadic livestock farmers now produce a great quantity of milk which is collected by public sector dairies for pasteurisation and consumption as far away as Delhi.

Rajasthan produces nearly 40 percent of India's wool and a large number of people in rural Rajasthan are engaged in sheep husbandry. The introduction of new methods

Left, a traditional royal wedding. **Above**, village labour being transported to work.

The origins of the Jats, who excel at agriculture, not only in the water-rich regions of Punjab and Haryana, but even the arid Thar desert in Rajasthan, remains obscure. There is some ground to believe that the Jats were the anterior rulers of modern Churu and its adjacent areas before the Rajput state of Bikaner subdued them.

The princely states of Bharatpur and Dholpur also had Jat rulers, but their history dates back only to the late-17th century, when the Jat rulers of Bharatpur defeated even Mughal armies and carried away valuable booty from Delhi and Agra which is on display in the famous palaces of Deeg. In more recent times, however, the Jats have been known mainly for their farming skills which have been enhanced in the wake of the land reforms enacted in post-1947 Rajasthan – the abolition of the *jaghirdari* system and the granting of inheritable property rights on the lands previously farmed by them as tenants. The Jats are now one of the most conspicuous upwardly-mobile communities in Rajasthan. They constitute a only a tenth of the total population, but they are limited to some 10 districts, and this, coupled with their growing consciousness as a political group, has made the Jats one of the most "visible" communities in Rajasthan, despite their long history of poverty and exploitation at the

hands of *jaghirdars* and their revenue-collectors. In this respect they have much in common with members of the Jat community in neighbouring Punjab and Haryana.

Conservationists: Another rural community of Rajasthan which deserves a special mention is that of Bishnois, who have shot to international prominence on account of their conservationist religious beliefs which forbid the wanton taking of animal and vegetable life – which has a contemporary resonance with environmental movements in both India and the West.

As far back as in the 16th century, the Bishnois were known to have resisted a number of royal edicts ordering the felling of trees by literally wrapping their bodies around them, and even today it is extremely difficult for poachers or others to kill any animal for pleasure in any village where a substantial number of Bishnois live. The environment protectionist beliefs of the Bishnois are rooted in the religious teachings of their spiritual mentor, Jambhoji, and are currently the focus of attention of policy-makers concerned with development, as they constitute an indigenous model which might minimize the hazards to the environment of technology.

The heavy shadow of history: The people of Rajasthan are people with a long, continuous past which, possibly more than in any other part of India, dominates the present. The long period of Rajput rule, which was characterised by constant warfare ended nearly 200 years ago, but the people of Rajasthan are still steeped in its customs and ideologies, even though much has changed in material and political terms since Independence in 1947.

Although, like all the other previously distinct regions of India, Rajasthan is being enveloped by all-India patterns of economic liberalisation and increasing access for all members of society to the mass media, the life of its people still retains a distinctive identity. Even in the face of the pan-Indian hegemony of the cinema, traditional entertainments still continue to be performed – even if the audience is sometimes largely made up of tourists. Indeed, the tourist industry has given a new lease of life to many traditional dwellings, crafts and occupations. Visitors to Rajasthan will encounter a largely rural population, that still retains many traditional forms of agriculture, and many may readily ascribe it to the long "feudal" history. Such catch-all labels do not do full justice to the complex nature of Indian society and Rajasthan is no exception. The curious traveller will be tempted to look beyond the forts, palaces and tales of bloodshed, and will discover the equally fascinating histories and cultures of the non-Rajput Rajasthanis who have done just as much to shape the state, though often in more subtle and gentle ways than their warring overlords.

Left, a Bhil Adivasi takes aim, Banswara. **Right**, the late G.D. Birla, the foremost Marwari industrialist, in London.

MARWARIS – MERCANTILE COMMUNITY

The Marwaris are Rajasthanis both by origin and orientation. Although their business operations are spread all over India, they maintain a social base at their "home" villages. They are well known throughout India as traders *par excellence*, and since Independence they have established substantial industrial empires.

For reasons not yet adequately fathomed, either by historians of Mughal India or by historians of British India, Rajasthani businessmen began to migrate and establish trading outposts outside Rajasthan. Some of these operations commenced as early as the 16th century, when Marwari businessmen accompanied the princes of Jaipur, Jodhpur and Bikaner, all of whom were appointed governors of far-flung provinces in eastern and northwestern India by successive Mughal emperors.

Marwari emigration from Rajasthan, however, expanded only in the late 18th century with the business "presence" of Marwaris in such metropolises as Calcutta being felt only as recently as the late 19th century.

From small beginnings, the Marwaris began to build a strong tradition of trading and business management. Their management style involved sophisticated techniques of accountancy, cash and credit conveyancing, and economic intelligence. At the same time, their cultural and community linkages provided a social fence for protecting this stock of economic skills.

During the decades of the 18th and 19th centuries before British rule was firmly established all over India, the Marwaris were able to sustain an all-India economic network mainly because of their social cohesion. Social bonding within the Marwaris community was periodically renewed at family reunions at their original villages where they continued to maintain residences.

As their home-bases were situated in the princely states of Rajasthan, most Marwari businessmen were hardly in a position to participate actively in India's freedom struggle (which, at that time, was aimed primarily at freedom from *British* rule). However, many Marwari businessmen maintained close personal links with the leaders of the Indian National Congress and even provided liberal financial support to its campaigners. It has been argued that Marwari industrialists such as G.D. Birla were indispensible to the creation of the Indian state. The British had been careful to keep industrial production in their own hands and, for the most part, in Britain. In 1947, the newly independent India was left with a tiny industrial base, and its rapid expansion owed a great deal both to the determination of Jawarhalal Nehru, and the commercial expertise of the Marwaris and Parsis.

Over the centuries, the Marwaris had acquired considerable skills in judging the political moods of rulers and in building up a network of contacts, skills which, even when India was committed to its public sector, allowed them to expand their

businesses and spheres of economic influence.

Back in 1964 a Monopolies Inquiry Commission Report found that 17 Marwari Industrial Houses had assets worth Rs 7.5 billion out of a total of Rs 19.6 billion owned by 37 large Industrial Houses.

The commanding position that the Marwaris occupy in the Indian economy as a whole is derived from their control of of trade, finance, commerce and marketing – irrespective of whether the goods are manufactured in the public or private sector, or whether they originate from India's organised corporate sector or the vast unorganised sector. ∎

RELIGION, MYTH AND FOLKLORE

Religion in Rajasthan ranges from the worship of local deities to austere Sanskritic ritual. Most Rajasthanis are either Hindus, Jains or worship Adivasi deities, but there is also a substantial Muslim population as well as Christians.

Hinduism: The wealthy Indo-Gangetic region attracted foreign invaders, who brought their religions to India. Around 1500 BC, invading peoples from Central Asia arrived who worshiped deities like Surya (sun), Indra (rain), Varun (water), and Marut (wind), personifying nature's forces. In the course of time they absorbed the Indus Valley gods. Hinduism thus developed from this mixture of Harappan and the new invaders' beliefs. One interpretation of the central Hindu belief is that every living thing is a manifestation of the One, Unchangeable, Absolute and Impersonal Being, Brahman.

In the Hindu pantheon, the Supreme Being has three manifestations: *Brahma* the Creator, *Vishnu* the Preserver, and *Shiva* the Destroyer. Brahma has four heads, each of which rules a quarter of the universe.

Vishnu, preserver of the world, is a popular aspect of the Hindu trinity who often incarnates on earth when humanity is in danger. He is depicted as a divinely handsome warrior wearing a crown and holding the Sudarshan Chakra (a deadly, divine discus), a conch shell, a long mace, and a lotus flower. It is Vishnu's duty to protect the weak, remove suffering, and punish evildoers. So far, Vishnu is believed to have incarnated 10 times in a rather Darwinian sequence – as a fish, a tortoise, a boar, a lion, a horse, and a dwarf. The Buddha is believed to be his latest incarnation. The most popular of his incarnations are Rama and Krishna, divine heroes of the epics, the *Ramayana* and *Mahabharata*, respectively.

The Hindu epics are based on a mixture of historical legend, myth and folklore. The *Ramayana* tells the story of King Dashrath's eldest son Rama, his exile due to his stepmother Kaikeyi who wanted the throne of Ayodhya for her own son, Bharat; the abduction of Rama's beautiful wife Sita by Lanka's king, Ravana; and Sita's rescue after a long war. Rama is the embodiment of all the qualities of the perfect son, husband, brother, and king. His faithful wife, Sita, is the traditional role model for Indian women. His brother Lakshmana is the perfect, self-sacrificing younger brother. The fearless monkey god, Hanuman, who helped Rama recover Sita from Ravana, is the perfect devotee, venerated throughout Rajasthan. Hanuman's statue guards the entrance to forts and villages, and people ask him to protect them from evil spirits, black magic, and powerful enemies.

The dark-skinned Krishna of the *Mahabharata* is a very different incarnation from his Braj persona as the handsome, playful pastoral god who charmed all creation with his magic flute. As a cowherd he danced with his beloved Radha, and all the milkmaids round Brindavan. As lord of Dwarka, Krishna helped the Pandavas, his friends, in their just war against their wicked cousins, the Kauravas, who had usurped their kingdom and dishonored their shared wife, Draupadi. The *Bhagvadgita* (often referred to as just the Gita) consists of Krishna's eve of battle counsel to Arjuna, the Pandava prince, torn by doubts about the morality of fighting and killing his own kith and kin, however evil they might be.

This scripture, just a small part of the *Mahabharata*, is one of the most basic to Hinduism. The core of its teachings is that each individual must perform his or her duty, *dharma*, without concern for the outcome because God himself is the doer, the deed and outcome. Everything flows from God, and lapses back to God. The path to *moksha*, *nirvana* or merger with the infinite, lies for different people through *karma* (action), *bhakti* (devotion), or *gnyan* (knowledge), according to his or her nature and abilities.

Shiva, the Destroyer, often symbolized by the Shivalinga (phallus), is depicted in sculpture and painting as Mahadeo, the Great God, with a third eye, through whose matted hair the sacred Ganga flows gently to earth,

Preceding pages: a young dancer strikes a pose in Phul Mahal, Mehrangarh Fort, Jodhpur. **Left,** Tejaji, an Adivasi deity; painted terracotta plate, Molela, near Nathdwara.

having spent its destructive momentum in Shiva's locks; as Pashupati Nath, protector of animals, he is depicted garlanded with snakes, wearing a tigerskin, holding a *trishul* (trident), a *damaru* (pellet drum), and ritual fire in three of his hands, with the fourth raised in blessing. Shiva is also depicted as the detached yogi *par excellence*, meditating in the Himalaya; the cosmic Dancer, Nataraj, from whom the universal life force flows, and into whom it lapses. In his destructive aspect, Shiva is Maha Kal, garlanded with human skulls. Shiva's mount, the bull Nandi, is also worshiped and a statue of Nandi is often seen in the courtyard of Shiva temples, facing the main image of the deity.

shrines of Ganesh are installed over many Hindu thresholds in Rajasthan.

The second major source of Hindu belief and observance is the *Vedas*, the oldest written religious texts in the world. They consist of four huge collections of religious, historical, mythological, and philosophical Sanskrit material written by sages, priests and poets and called the *Rig*, *Sama*, *Yajur*, and *Atharva Veda*. Additions called *Brahmanas* contain instruction, incantations, and sacrificial formulas or *mantras* for invoking the help of specific gods and goddesses for specific purposes. The *Upanishads*, which are complementary to the *Vedas*, provide the philosophical foundations of Hinduism.

Shiva's consort, Pravati, takes many forms: the Mother Goddess who manifests whenever the gods need her; the eternally faithful and happy wife, Gauri; the mighty 10-armed Durga, wielding awesome weapons; or Kali, the dark goddess of death. She is symbolized as the female *yoni* round the Shivalinga, which is worshiped as symbolic of creation's fountainhead.

The elephant-headed Ganesh, son of Shiva and Parvati, is the lord of wisdom and good fortune. A popular deity, he is invoked before starting a religious ceremony, wedding, or other functions. He clears away obstacles, ensuring success and good luck. Images and

Among the ancient Hindu texts are also the *Puranas*, a miscellany of legend, myth and history.

Jainism: Mahavira, revered as the founder of Jainism, was born in 599 BC. Like Gautama Buddha, renounced a throne and and left his family to preach the message of non-violence. He joined the Parasnath monastic order, which followed the teachings of a succession of *tirthankaras* ("perfect souls"). Mahavira who went about naked all the time – a sign of his detachment from worldly things, the triumph of mind over matter – became the 24th and last *tirthankara* of the Jains. To gain salvation or *nirvana* from the cycle of birth and death, the Jains practice the Triple Jewel: Right Belief, Right Conduct and Right Knowledge. Jain monks and nuns take five vows: to be non-violent, to be truthful, not to steal, not to become attached to possessions, and to be celibate (*brahmacharya*).

Mahavira starved himself to death at the age of 72. His teachings were spread by itinerant monks and nuns who preached that all living things had a soul, and deserved equal respect with humans. His teachings were codified in the 3rd century BC. A schism divided Jain monks into *Digambaras*, or "sky-clad," naked ascetics like Mahavira, and *Swetambaras*, who wore white robes. There is no fundamental difference between

they believe that the universe functions according to an eternal law of progress and decline.

Jains today are a prosperous commercial community, noted for their endowments for charitable institutions, hospitals, schools, colleges, animal shelters and veterinary hospitals. Jains are tolerant of all religions, and the magnificent Jain temples built by wealthy merchants between the 7th and 14th centuries AD at Abu, Ranakpur, Ossian, Jaisalmer, Bikarner and Chittaurgarh include images of many Hindu deities.

Islam: Rajasthan has had a Muslim population from the time of the Ghori invasion in 1193. Islamic mystics, known as *Sufis*,

their respective doctrines, but the Digambaras are wandering ascetics, practicing severe penances, while the Swetambaras are great scholars and teachers. Thanks to the Jain love of learning and their belief that it is a meritorious act to make a copy of a worthwhile manuscript, many ancient texts and literary works have been preserved in copies prepared by them.

The Jains do not worship a deity, because

Left, shrine of popular Hindu God Shiva. **Above left**, the Maharaja of Bikaner at Karni Mata Temple, Deshnok. **Above right**, a *pandit* (priest) at the shrine of Baba Ram Dev, Pokhran.

became very popular in medieval India at the same time as its Hindu counterpart, the *Bhakti* (devotional) movement. To a certain extent, they both drew on the interaction between Hinduism and Islam during the 14th and 15th centuries. One of the world's greatest Sufi shrines lies in Rajasthan. It is that of the Sufi saint, Khwaja Muin-ud-din Chishti (1142–1256 AD), a direct descendant of the Prophet Muhammad's son-in-law, Ali. He came to Ajmer during the reign of Prithviraj Chauhan, who gifted the saint with the land on which his shrine now stands. At the age of 114, the saint locked himself in his cell to pray. Six days later his disciples broke open the door and found the Khwaja Sahib dead. That is why his *urs* (feast) is celebrated for six days. His *dargah* (mausoleum) is the most popular Muslim pilgrimage centre in South Asia. Hindus, Muslims, Sikhs, and Jains alike believe that this benevolent Sufi saint intercedes with God on behalf of his devotees.

Haminuddin Nagori was a disciple of Moinuddin Chishti. His tomb at Nagor, the Atarki Dargah, is also a pilgrimage centre where many miracle cures are said to have occurred. Sayed Fakhruddin, a saint of the Ismaili Shias, has a shrine at Galiakot. As with Sufi shrines elsewhere in India, several other Muslim *pirs* (saints) are venerated by people of all faiths seeking healing, freedom

been considered sacred since the protohistoric Harappan and Kalibangan period. The bo or banyan tree (*Ficus indica*), under which the Buddha attained enlightenment, is also considered sacred.

Rajasthan has five major local gods: Pabuji, Gogaji, Mehaji, Harbhuji, and Ramdeo Baba. Belief in the supernatural power of these departed folk heroes to mediate in their devotees' lives has made them deities, and shrines dedicated to them are to be seen in many towns and villages.

Pabuji's mother was reputed to be divine. She asked her husband, a 13th-century Rathor chieftain, never to hide and watch her. But he broke his promise, and found her assuming

from the evil eye and evil spirits, or the birth of a child.

Local cults and deities: There are hundreds of local shrines in Rajasthan, some of which may date back thousands of years. The Adivasis and most villagers revere a variety of deities connected to the natural world. Snakes, cows, monkeys and peacocks are considered sacred. There are sacred trees in every village and town, and sacred groves which cannot be cut down. Tree worship is extremely old, and Hindus and Jains revere the *Kalpa Vriksha*, or Tree of Life, portrayed in mythological paintings and temple carvings. The pipul (*Ficus religiosa*) has

the form of a tigress whenever she suckled their son. She returned to heaven, and Pabuji became a great warrior, who protected the oppressed, and broke caste barriers. He is invoked during times of misfortune and sickness by people who hold *jagrans* (night vigils), with Pabuji's *bhopas* (priests) singing his epic in their homes.

Gogaji was an 11th-century warrior who was so true to his word that the Snake God gave him the power to heal snakebite victims. Revered by Hindus and Muslims (the latter call him Gogaji Jahir Pir), snakebite victims are carried to his shrine and kept awake by the beating of drums and gongs so that the poison cannot take effect. Stone carvings of Gogaji on horseback always include snakes. Gogaji's chief *than* (shrine) is at Gogameda near Ganganagar, where a huge cattle fair is held every year.

Mehaji and his son Harbhu are deified as *bhomiyas* (braves) who died heroic deaths while protecting the village community, specially its cattle. Because the village economy in medieval Rajasthan was based on milk and milk products, Rajput feudal chiefs were expected to emulate Meha and Harbhu, and save cattle from raiders and predatory animals at all cost.

Ramdeo Baba, the legend goes, appeared miraculously in a cradle beside the newborn son of a hitherto childless Rajput couple. He became an invincible hero, devoting his life to the poor. His white horse, on which he covered vast distances to help needy people, is believed still to carry grain to drought-stricken areas if he is properly invoked.

The Bishnois are followers of Jambhoji, who made environment and wildlife protection a devotional act in the early 15th century. The Bishnoi cult spread from Bikaner to Jodhpur, and even today the most well-connected *shikaris* (hunters) dare not shoot game in Bishnoi territory, for Bishnois are ready to die for their beliefs. A great *shaka* (sacrifice) took place at Dhawa in the 19th century when the Maharaja of Jodhpur ordered the chopping down of a forest which was a *dacoit* (bandit) hideout. Hundreds of Bishnois gave their lives trying to save the trees by tying themselves to the trunks.

Today, the Bishnois are a wealthy farming community of pure vegetarians, who are very orthodox about observing the 29 (*bish nao* in Hindi) principles laid down by their enlightened guru.

For many Hindus in Rajasthan, the Mother Goddess (Mataji or Devi), the embodiment of *Shakti*, the Cosmic Life Force, is the most important deity – giver of wisdom, wealth, victory and peace. The most famous Rajasthani incarnation of Devi is Karni Mata of Deshnok, who lived for 151 years. A *Charan* (bard) by birth, this 15th-century miracle-worker could not revive the only son of a distraught Charan couple who came to

her for help. Yama, the Lord of Death, told Karniji that the boy had already been reborn. So Karniji decreed that henceforth all dead Charans would be reborn only as sacred *kabas* (rats) in her temple, to escape Yama's clutches and reincarnate as humans at her command. She made a blind carpenter carve her image, which is enshrined at Deshnok near Bikaner. Her body is said to have disappeared into a dazzling orb of light in 1538 AD, and, ever since, Karni Mata's temple has attracted worshipers.

In Rajasthan, certain *Sati Matas* are also worshiped. But all *satis* (women who immolate themselves on their husband's funeral pyre) are not deified. Rajput women who committed *sati* for political reasons (like Queen Padmini of Chittaurgarh), or as a result of a husband's death on the battlefield, are not local goddesses. Only those *satis* who were supposedly under no social compulsion to do so, but chose to burn alive with their dead husbands, are deified and continue to manifest and perform miracles after their self-sacrifice.

Folklore: Each area of Rajasthan has its enduring myths and folklore, but some folklore motifs are widespread. The epic of Heer-Ranjha is sung when there is a cattle epidemic, and several prohibitions are imposed on the entire village for 36 days. Cures in such cases have been recorded, but how they came about, no one can say. Customs that have proved beneficial have become adopted as rituals or taboos.

There is widespread belief in astrology, and the power of the nine planets, the gems and metals worn, celestial beings, demons, and departed souls of ancestors, and on the life of every human being. A person's present status, looks, and luck are believed to be the outcome of his or her past *karma* (actions). But the intervention of supernatural forces can help anyone to overcome trouble and evolve spiritually. Knowledgeable persons can forecast the weather and coming events by studying animal, bird and insect behaviour.

Folklore, myth and Rajasthan's religious institutions communicate something of the region's value system, and concept of a well-lived life. Religious tolerance has been a striking feature of Rajasthan. The harsh climate and terrain make people tolerant of each other's beliefs, and at the same time impose discipline on public life.

Rajasthan is home to a fascinating range of music and dance which varies from region to region and is often associated with local festivals. Particularly important is the long and complex history of patronage that sustained many different groups of performers.

Professional musicians: The desert region of western Rajasthan is home to three castes of settled, hereditary musicians: the Muslim Manganiyars (also known as Mirasis) and Langas, and the Hindu Dholis (sometimes called Kathaks). Although Muslims, the Chamund Devi and Bhaironji (Shiva) who perform for high-caste Hindu patrons. Dholans (female Dholis) sing at life-cycle ceremonies, while male Dholis play the *dhol* (large cylindrical drums which give the caste its name) for processions and celebrations.

Other professional groups of performers include the Bhands (actors), Jogis or Saperas (snake charmers who play the *murli* double clarinet), and Nats (acrobats who play the *dhol* and *thali*, a metal dish used as an idiophone). Another group were the

Manganiyars perform Hindu devotional music in temples for Hindu patrons. The male members of the caste traditionally play the *kamaycha* (a bowed lute), now often replaced by the harmonium, the *dholak* (barrel drum) and *kartal* (wooden clappers). The Langas sing ballads for Muslim patrons, accompanied by either the *gujaratan* or *sindhi sarangi* (bowed lutes). They also play the *satara* (double flute) and *murli* (double clarinet). The music of the Langas and Manganiyars bears similarity to Hindustani concert music with its use of *raga* and *tan* (fast improvised passages).

The Dholis are devotees of the goddess professional female courtesan dancers and singers, known as *kalavant* or *tawaif*, who use to perform at the courts or for landowning patrons.

Epic performance: *Kathputli* or puppet shows are performed at night by couples of the itinerant Bhat community, who are also genealogists. The woman plays the *dholak*, and sings the ballad to which the man makes the puppets act and dance. A discussion goes on between the two, serving as a running commentary on the show. The puppet plays are based on popular legends.

Pabuji ki par is very popular with those who worship Pabuji, a 14th-century hero.

Believers in Pabuji invite his *bhopas* (epic singers and priests) to their homes in times of sickness and misfortune to sing this ballad at all-night vigils. Pabuji's *pad* (ballad) is sung before an open scroll, about 10 metres (30 feet) long and 2.5 metres (8 feet) high, depicting his life. The *bhopa* sings and plays the *ravanhatta* (a bowed lute), while his wife sings and dances, holding an oil lamp to illuminate Pabuji's images on the scroll at appropriate points in the narrative.

Devotional music: As elsewhere in India, the Hindus of Rajasthan gather in temples to sing collective devotional songs known as *bhajan*. Attached to the Krishna temple in Nathdwara is a group of professional

musicians who perform devotional songs known as *pad* and *kirtan* at all rituals. They are accompanied by *pakhavaj* (barrel drum), *sarangi* and *jhanj* (cymbals).

Dance: Of all traditional Rajasthani dances, the best known is the *ghumar*, a circle dance performed by women at the Gangaur festival and also by Rajput women at festivals and family celebrations. Each region and community has its own variation; usually women wearing wide skirts and veils, in

Left, *kalavant* dancers, Jaisalmer. <u>Above</u>, Langa musicians playing the *satara* (a traditional flute) in Badnawa village, Barmer district.

groups, pairs or individually, spin around in alternating directions. The dancers wear pellet bells *(ghunghru)* around their ankles. The dances are performed to songs which articulate women's concerns, accompanied by a *dholak*. *Ghumar* in Udaipur is danced with small sticks in the dancers' hands which are struck together to the rhythm.

In contrast, the *ger* dance (of which there are also many versions) is performed only during the Holi festival by men alone. The singers play huge *daphs* (frame drums) to accompany the dance, which is circular. The *ger* is sometimes performed as a stick dance.

The composite *ger-ghumar* dance of the Bhils is also performed at Holi and during spring. To start, the men dance in the outer circle, and the women dance in an inner one. All the dancers sing and strike sticks with attached pellet bells together, to the rhythm of a drum beat. The men and women change circles with every change of rhythm.

Kacchi ghori is a spectacular dance performed during wedding processions by three or four pairs of elaborately costumed men riding hobby-horses and waving swords. The dancers, usually of the Bavaria, Kumhar and Sargara castes, are accompanied by *dhol* and *bankia* (trumpets). Occasionally a female singer will narrate the exploits of the Bavaria *dacoits* (bandits) of Shekhavati.

The *jasnathi agni* (fire dance) is performed by the Sidh Naths of Bikaner, and is an act of devotion to the saint Jasnath. An ensemble of trumpets and drums begins to play as the devotees dance on the embers of a wood and charcoal fire. The music and dance gradually increase in tempo to a frenetic pace.

The Kalbelias (snake charmers) are a nomadic Adivasi group famous for their skillful *bin* (a double clarinet with a gourd air chamber) playing, and hypnotic, rhythmic dances. They play the *bin* and *bhapang* (a plucked variable tension chordophone) to lure snakes. Kalbelia women and men perform the *indoni*, *panihari*, and *shankaria* dances. The women wear striking bead- and cowrie-decorated veils, skirts and blouses.

The *tera tali* ("13 cymbals") dance of the Kamar women of western Rajasthan is performed in honour of their deity, Ramdeoji. A pair of dancers play the 13 cymbals *(manjira)* tied to each other's bodies, accompanied by Kamar men who play the harmonium and *dholak*.

RAJASTHANI CRAFTS

Jaipur is a city built on a formalised, square grid but the bustle, colour and vibrant rhythm of its streets prevent one from perceiving it. Extensive areas of Rajasthan are monotone, beige-brown desert, but the dramatic spectacle and visual variety that pervade it make it one of the most vibrantly colourful of Indian states. These paradoxes are seen again and again – a recurring motif reflected in its decorative arts and crafts.

It is one of the poorest and and least industrially developed parts of India, yet it houses the most opulent and rich treasures. Its history is a long saga of blood feuds and violent battles, but the forbidding stone battlements of its forts shield mirrored rooms and marble carvings of delicacy and grace.

The same high-balconied prisons that prevented women from venturing out into the outside world were marvels of exquisite ornamentation. The jewelled belts and anklets that proclaimed their status as ornamental chattels were at the same time rich symbols of love and pride.

Mughal influence: Rajas who sacrificed wealth, power, territory, life itself, to withstand the Mughals, generation after generation, at the same time borrowed freely from Mughal art and aesthetics, taking styles, symbols and techniques, often stealing artisans, and incorporating them into their own eclectic, rich tradition.

Some contrasts, however extreme, seem almost inevitable. It seems natural that a landscape so parched and brown should produce paintings bursting with vibrant flowers and foliage and running water; that people starved of natural colour and beauty should almost obsessively decorate everything – be it a camel or a king's crown; that warriors going into battle should arm themselves with delicately decorated, jewelled shields and swords.

Other contradictions are more inexplicable, even reprehensible. Why were women forced to spend their lives embroidering garments to embellish themselves, and sat, bejewelled and bedecked, locked away in mirrored rooms, merely so their husbands could view them and boast of their virtue and beauty?

Rajasthan and its crafts are a source of endless fascination – whether one approaches them for purely visual, aesthetic pleasure or pauses to savour the underlying history, culture and symbolism.

Behind the main squares and streets of its cities, Jaipur, Ajmer Udaipur, Jodhpur, and in every village, artisans still live, practicing crafts handed down orally generation to generation. It is worth bypassing the big tourist souvenir emporia and going to watch the craft-workers themselves in action.

Just as one's eye, dazzled by the colour and pageantry of Jaipur streets, forgets the geometric symmetry of their right-angled layout, the richness and colour of Rajasthani craft can lead one to forget the religious or cultural symbolism from which they derive their inspiration, but colour, shape and motif also have meanings. To ignore them is to miss much.

The Indian stone-mason carves "frozen lace" filigree on the sandstone trellised balconies of Jaisalmer with four basic tools: a pointed punch or *tanki*, a cold chisel or *pahuri*, a *hatora* (hammer) and a *barma* (borer). But the principals underlying the carving were laid down in the *Manasara* and *Shilpshastras*, Sanskrit texts on art and aesthetics dating back 2000 years. For example, the height, width and diameter of every shaft, arch and building detail is strictly defined. Within these formal principles individual creativity can run riot. One generation finding inspiration in flowing arabesques of peacocks and poppy flowers, another in Mughal-inspired geometric squares and stars.

Colour – a vital element of much Indian design – is supplied by the dyer and the printer. Each town and village has some distinctive skill. On both sides of the road from Jodhpur to Udaipur via Pali, lengths of material gleam in the sun as they dry on tall sticks, and the printing process continues by the river.

Preceding pages: traditional dance during the Holi festival, Kanasar, Barmer district. **Left**, a modern miniature painter from Udaipur still uses traditional methods.

Expert dyers: In Alwar a few families still exist who are able to perform the apparently miraculous feat of dyeing one side of a sari red and the reverse side of it green, without any overlapping of colour. In Kota they dye the warp one colour and the weft another to create a shot effect. All over Rajasthan the *bandhani*, tie-dyed sari, veil and turban can be found.

Different designs have different names. *Laharia* is the diagonal-striped version, done mostly in Udaipur; *chira*, when the stripes are of variegated colours; *chunari* is the dotted one; *ekdali* has small circles and squares; *tikhunti, chaubandi* and *satbandi*, have groups of three, four, and seven dots

remain uncoloured. The more intricate *bandhanis* are tied and dyed several times, separately for each colour, starting with the lightest one.

Weaving of all kinds is practiced as a cottage industry. Men and women, and sadly often their children as well, steal a few hours from the fields to sit down at the pit loom in their courtyard and weave a few inches of a *durry* (cotton carpet), a goat-hair blanket or intricately patterned camel-hair bag. Camels, peacocks, eight-pointed stars or the triangles of a tented settlement are familiar stylized motifs. The fine self-checked cotton saris of Kota are famous, and the people of Jaipur make beautiful woollen knotted carpets in

respectively; in *dhannak* the designs form flowering circles; in *jaldar* and *beldar*, the dots form diagonal or flowering patterns; *shikari* is a design with human, tiger, horse and elephant figures. Patterns may be simple or complex, the technique is the same: the cloth is bleached and washed repeatedly to remove all starch and chemicals, and the design block-printed on with washable *geru* (earth colour). The village women then take over, their left hand thumb and little finger nail specially kept long for this purpose. They push and pinch the fabric up into small points which they tie with two or three twists of thread. When dyed, the knotted parts

the Mughal tradition.

Block printing, too, is a traditional art of Rajasthan, and towns like Sanganer and Bagru have been devoted exclusively to this occupation since medieval times; their products exported as far afield as China, Europe and the Middle East. The towns of Sanganer, Barmer and Bagru between them produce about 250,000 metres (275,000 yards) of printed fabric a day, all printed by hand with carved wooden blocks also made locally. Sanganer specializes in delicate floral

Left, the intricate and laborious craft of block printing continues to thrive in Sanganer.

patterns, Barmer in red and indigo geometric *ajraks*, Bagru in brick and black, linear and zigzag stripes. The motifs and layouts are delicate and subtle; the colours are spectacular. Fabrics with stunning combinations of scarlet and shocking pink, purple and orange, turquoise and parrot green, saffron and crimson, often shot with gold and silver, and set with shining mirrors, are worn by women as flared skirts, veils or saris, and sometimes by men as colourful turbans.

Until recently the dyes were vegetable and earth colours extracted from flowers, bark, roots and minerals: jasmine, saffron and myrobalan producing oranges and yellows; mulberry bark and the kirmiz insect, reds and purples; indigo and pistachio galls, blues and greens; sulfate of iron, black. The ingenuity of the Indian dyer knew no bounds, with over 250 different shades in common use in the mid-19th century, with a very successful green being extracted from the soaked green baize exported from England for billiard tables.

Woven, dyed and block-printed, the fabric is then further embellished by embroidery. Though Rajasthani women, curiously enough, seldom stitch their own clothes, depending on the local tailor to do this, they do embroider them. Skirts, bodices and veils, as well as coverlets and decorative pieces for their homes, are covered with beautiful, often ad-lib designs of dancing figures and flowers, peacocks, the tree of life and the *mandala* (a circular religious motif). The Barmer region is known for its flat, geometric, surface satin-stitch motifs, other areas use chain and herringbone stitch, and worn fabric is excitingly recycled into stunning patchwork quilts, cushions and shoulder bags.

Wealth of silver: Clothes – their colour, design and cut – may tell people which village and caste someone comes from, but it is jewellery in which people's wealth is invested. In the Rajasthani villages it is silver. Huge, heavy chunks of it are worn around ankles, waist, neck and wrists, dangling in rings from ears, nose and hair, in chains of buttons down *kurta* or *choli* fronts. The beautiful, ornate designs of Adivasi jewellery have now become fashionable among the urban élite, and can be bought everywhere. Silver is too soft to be durable on its own and is generally mixed with copper before being worked. The silver in the shops ranges from 65 to 90 percent pure silver, and prices vary accordingly. Jewellers will assure you that their silver is 95 percent pure. Pure silver has a coarse, dull sound when struck, unlike the shrill, vibrating sound of other metals. Apart from jewellery, Rajasthani silversmiths make beautiful boxes, trays, small statues of Krishna and Ganesh, and ornamental *objets d'art* – birds, horses and elephants, enamelled as well as plain.

The aristocracy and the well-to-do did not wear silver. *Kundan* and enamel jewellery inlaid with precious stones was a speciality of Rajasthan, particularly of Jaipur. Rajasthan is rich in precious and semi-precious stones. Emerald, garnet, agate, amethyst, topaz and lapiz lazuli are all found locally. Other stones came from further afield as the fame of the Jaipur jewellers and gem-cutters spread. Men as well as women wore elaborate jewellery, and the hilts and scabbards of swords and daggers, goblets and condiment boxes were all equally heavily ornamented.

Unlike European jewellery, though stones were sometimes etched or embossed into decorative shapes and patterns, they were not cut or faceted to remove flaws or accentuate colour. The size of the stone and the elaboration of its setting rather than its depth of colour or brilliance were of greater importance. The back of each piece, set in heavy gold *kundan* or *jarao*, was embellished with delicate enamel ornamentation using the champlevé (raised field) technique. The design, usually entwined flowers and birds, sometimes human and animal figures, was hollowed out, each colour segment separated by a fine raised gold line and the enamel painted in and fired. Each colour was fired separately, in a furnace sunk deep into the ground, starting with those requiring greatest heat. The enamel colours and techniques have poetic names: *ab-e-leher*, waves of water; *tote-ka-par*, parrot's wing; and *khun-e-kabutar*, pigeon's blood (a most highly prized deep translucent red).

Each piece of jewellery is formed by a specialised chain of crafts: the *nyarriya* refines the gold, the *sangsaz* polishes and cuts the stones; the *manihar* prepares the enamel; the *sonar* makes the bezels for setting the stones and fashions the jewel, using patterned moulds; the *chattera* engraves the ground; the *minakar* enamels and fires it; the *kundansaz* sets the stone in a mixture of lacquer and antimony and, when it has solidified, cold-sets it with hammered gold wire. The *sonar* polishes and cleans the piece and the *patwari* puts the finishing touch of twisted gold and silk cord, with its tasseled pendant and beaded knot, twisting the threads in an intricate cat's-cradle between a big toe, knee and index finger.

Stones and metals are also symbolic of the deities of the Hindu pantheon, the nine planets of the Indian astrological system, and sacred sites or rivers. For example, diamond denotes both Agni and Venus, sapphire the god Vishnu as well as Saturn, ruby Indra and the sun, etc. Gold and silver symbolise the sacred rivers Ganga and Yamuna.

The skilled gem-cutters of Jaipur also carve enchanting little animals and birds from rock, crystal, jade, smoky topaz and amethyst, and you can buy intaglio beads and buttons, and crystal scent bottles as well. The wearing of highly coloured decoration is not restricted to women. Rajasthani men traditionally wore vibrant and embellished clothes, from the stiff starched furl of a saffron or shocking-pink turban (8 metres/9 yards of it twirled into convoluted folds weighing more than 2 kilos/4 pounds) to the tips of the turned-up toes of the traditional *juthis*.

The *juthis* or slippers are made of locally tanned and flayed leather. Each village has its own community of a few families who

To complicate matters further, each gem is supposed to have both positive attributes and flaws. For example, the pearl protects the wearer from evil, and a house where pearls are kept "is chosen by the ever-fickle Goddess of Wealth, Lakshmi, as her permanent abode", but a pearl of the wrong shape or colour can cause leprosy, loss of sons, poverty or death. Emeralds, which cleanse you of sin, according to Sanskrit texts, can bring wealth and success in war, and protection from poisoning, but here again, the wrong colour or shade or flaw can cause disease, fatal wounds in battle, or even, apparently, death by snakebite.

practice this trade, collecting dead animals from the local farmers and making *juthis* for them. For centuries they were considered outcastes, but this did not mean they were not consummate craft-workers. The leather was tanned and dyed by vegetable and mineral formulae handed down from generation to generation, and made into shoes and sandals, water bags, fans, pouches and saddles, and musical instruments. It was embroidered, punched, gouged, studded, sequined and stitched in a variety of intricate designs, varying from region to region – sequins and

Left, young carpet weavers at work.

tassels in one village, brass studs and machine-stitched motifs in another. Men did the tanning, cutting and stitching, women the embroidery and ornamentation. Most of the slippers and sandals are available in the big cities – Jaipur, Jodhpur and Ajmer. They are incredibly sturdy, being made to withstand water-logged fields, wind and weather, and they pinch and squeak excruciatingly for the first few days. Persevere and they become the most yielding, comfortable footwear you have ever worn, and certainly the longest lasting.

In Bikaner the inner hide of the camel is put to another use. It is scraped till it is translucent and tissue-fine and then molded into perfume bottles, water jugs, vases and lamp shades, painted with delicately gilded gesso-work floral designs.

Interior decor: In the same way as Rajasthanis decorate themselves, they also decorate their homes. The walls of their dwellings, be they palaces or huts, are painted and decorated. The palaces with inlaid mirror mosaics or marble engraved in floral bas-reliefs set with precious stones; the village homes and city walls with murals of elephants and tigers, illustrations of legends of gods and goddesses, or scenes of everyday life. Doors, windows, pillars and balconies are carved and fretted, inlaid with brass, ivory or mother-of-pearl, or painted. Domestic furniture is also often carved and decorated – chests, chairs, cradles and low tables, inlaid with brass sheet-work or – in the past – ivory, or painted with dancing Radhas and Krishnas. Shekhavati and Jodhpur are famous centres for wood-carving. Jaipur specializes in brass-wire inlay on ebony and sheshum wood. Fine brass wires are set in intricately intertwined geometric or floral patterns and made into ornamental boxes, trays and mirror-frames. The minutely carved wooden blocks used for textile printing are so exquisite that nowadays they are bought by tourists for their own sake. Udaipur is noted for its mirror and mother-of-pearl inlay, Bikaner for its plaster and gold gesso murals, Jaipur for its marble carving, and Jaisalmer for the incredibly intricate stone *jalis* (lattices).

Most of the motifs found in the painted wood and wall murals derive from the miniature and *pichwai* paintings of the 16th and 17th centuries, when every small Rajput ruler had at least one painter in their entourage. They were commissioned to paint court portraits, scenes from the epics, incidents from history, and make records of local flora and fauna which were then incorporated by court artisans into their textiles, carpets and carvings. Each court had a distinctive style of painting – the attenuated, elegant figures of Kishangarh with their soaring eyebrows and sidelong smile; the elaborately detailed court and battle scenes of Mewar; the Bikaner horses and Kota hunting scenes; the harsh simplicity of Bundi.

Done on paper made from cotton, jute or bamboo fibre polished to smoothness with an agate stone, the artist first did a line sketch in *geru* terracotta, covering it with a coat of white. This was then painted on with mineral and vegetable colours ground and extracted from indigo, lapiz, cochineal, cinnebar, mercury sulphite and orpiment, as well as pure gold dust, using squirrel-hair brushes often as fine as one hair. The paintings had no perspective, but intricate details of clothes, jewellery and head-dresses were meticulously rendered, and natural scenes were vividly portrayed, uninhibited by considerations of seasons or climatic conditions. Both in the paintings made for the royal courts and the *pichwai* cloth hangings used in the temples, the Radha-Krishna legend was a favourite theme, depicted in a Ragamala series, each painting linked to a musical mode in turn associated with seasons, months, days and hours and personifications of different phases of love and emotion, both temporal and spiritual.

Phad paintings, with their brilliant flaming orange, red and black stylized cartoon strip illustrated scrolls, are a more popular art form. They are used by the Bhopas, itinerant epic singers who play at fairs and festivals to the accompaniment of the *jantar*, a bamboo stick zither with two gourd resonators. Their songs, and the *phads*, recount the legend of Papuji Ramdeo of the Rabari tribe and his famous black mare, whose neigh warned him of danger; or of Dev Narainji, another Robin Hood-type hero.

Miniatures, *pichwais* and *phads* are all still being painted today, but are fast becoming slick, assembly-line copies. Simultaneously, copies of Audubon birds, Redoute roses, Japanese geisha prints and Persian manuscripts are all being turned out to meet the demand of the market. The skills are still there, although the patrons and inspiration have changed.

Miniature paintings were also done on ivory in Udaipur and Nathdwara. The smooth, matte surface was a perfect foil for the delicate, stylized pictures highlighted with gold.

Ivory is traditionally a popular medium in Rajasthan, from the heavy bracelets worn by Bhil women, to delicate carvings and inlay work. Ivory dust is used medicinally in both the *unani* and *ayurvedic* schools of Indian medicine for abdominal disorders. Ivory is subject to a world-wide ban on exports – do not attempt to take it out of the country – and bone is often used in its place.

Another metal inlay technique is damascening, done by the swordsmiths and armourers of Udaipur and Alwar, whose wonderful shields, swords and armour were chased with floral arabesques, hunting scenes or calligraphic Koranic verses, depending on the tastes of Rajput or Mughal patrons. They now make cutlery, areca-nut crackers, buttons and paper knives to suit the needs of a less belligerent age. Pratapgarh gold filigree and enamel is another beautiful, unusual, but dying craft. Court, religious or hunting scenes are cut out of a fine gold sheet and the resulting silhouette relief mounted onto a backing of deep red or blue enamel and set in box tops or as decorative plaques.

Muslim artisans specialize in metal-work of all kinds, especially brass enamel. There are two types, *sadha* and *siya kalam*. In *sadha*, the brass is coated with a thin layer of tin which is then cut to reveal the pattern in the underlying brass, gleaming in contrast to the tin. In *siya kalam*, the design is left in relief, and the rest of the surface cut away. The depressions are filled with black lac or coloured enamel – red, white, pink or green. When finished, the relief pattern in plain brass stands out against the coloured enamel. There are three different styles – *chikan*, *marori* and *bidri*, each with its repertoire of traditional motifs and designs.

Distinctive to Jaipur today, though originally Iranian and Turkish in origin, is the famous Blue Pottery. It is unique in that no clay is used. It is made from a mixture of fuller's earth, quartz and sodium sulphite that needs firing only once. It is made in moulds with only the neck and lip turned on the wheel. Its characteristic turquoise blue is made from copper sulphate extracted from old scrap metal and the deep blue is cobalt oxide. Most of the pottery made today is formulaic, but a visit to the studio of Kripal Singh Shekhavat, a local painter, shows a different side of the craft. Borrowing inspiration from Persian miniatures and the

Ajanta frescoes, and reintroducing long-forgotten colours such as pinks, greens and yellows into the glaze, he has taken traditional shapes and forms and revitalised them.

All over Rajasthan, village potters turn less elaborate but equally beautiful jars, water-pots, urns, and utensils for the local market. Made of unglazed red terracotta, their simple, perfectly proportioned shapes are a blend of utility and elegance that industrial designers often strive for. Their creation is deceptively simple, but it requires great skill. They appear from a lump of mud on a roughly shaped wheel, all it seems to take is a spin and a flick of dextrous thumb and forefinger, and the pot is ready.

and more of their products are deteriorating into mass-produced knick-knacks for the unwary tourist. Exploitive middlemen urge craft workers to produce in the quickest possible time at the lowest possible price. What then emerges can be a rather unworthy object with just a faint flicker of its former glorious self. The tourist can help by being selective about what they buy. Some shops, such as the chain Anokhi, pay a fair price for their products and support schemes that empower women and do not use child workers. Children are often exploited as a source of cheap labour, and travellers should not buy goods produced in this way – shopping in government stores and buying

Come festival time, the potter will turn to creating tiny toys and images – elephants and chariots, many-armed Devi, mounted warriors, caparisoned camels, and tiny lamps. These beautiful lamps, normally lit by oil wicks, are traditionally made for the festival of *Divali*, when they are used to light up Rama's path back to Ayodhya from his battle against Ravanna in Lanka.

The pressures on Rajasthani artisans, as on all Indian traditional skills, are great. More

Left, a potter using a simple wheel creates vases for the Jaipur blue glazes. **Above**, a master-craftsman repairs a stone statue, Osiyan.

directly from the producers are two ways to ensure that either the money goes straight to the workers, or that they have at least a degree of protection.

The strength of Rajasthani crafts is that they have always been embedded deeply in the everyday lives of the people and were not merely produced for the court or urban market. They are part of the social structure and an abiding cultural tradition. It is this that has helped Rajasthani crafts to survive the stresses of technology, the tourist trade and ever-changing life-styles. They have suffered and changed, but are still recognisably the product of a vibrant society.

THE ALLEGORY OF LOVE: RAJPUT PAINTING

In the 16th and 17th centuries, there was an extraordinary flowering of artistic expression at the courts of Rajasthan. An intense revival of Hindu devotionalism brought about a vital link between poetry and drama, and painting, creating vivid pictorial narratives which were inspired by the literature and the dramas of the time.

Rajasthan, or "Rajputana", included 20 feudal states in the heart of northern India. In a small tract that was 800 km (500 miles) long and 700 km (450 miles) wide, seven states contributed significantly to the impassioned fervour of court painting: Mewar, Bundi, Kota, Marwar, Bikaner, Jaipur and Kishangarh. Each of these courts produced a distinctive idiom, influenced of course by the royal patrons who commissioned these paintings, but also by the environment: by the undulating countryside, by the hills and shrubs, the deserts and forts and gardens in which this art form was nurtured.

Forest paper: Paper was introduced into India in the 14th century. It was used initially only in business transactions and trade. Prior to this, the manuscripts of the 12th and 13th centuries, preserved to the present day in the Jain *bhandars* (libraries) of Gujarat and Rajasthan, were on horizontal strips of palm leaf. They were inscribed with a stylus pen and adorned with tiny miniatures. The value of these early manuscripts is that they have inscriptions giving dates and the provenance; but their style remains unchanged through the centuries – seen in the *Kalpa Sutra* and the *Balagopala Stuti* texts. Even when paper had replaced palm leaf, the horizontal format continued to be used in Rajput paintings of the *Bhagavata Purana* and the *Gita Govinda* in the 16th century.

The illustration of Hindu religious narrative received fresh impetus with the revival of Vaishnava literature. The *Ramayana* was translated into the local languages, becoming a popular source for oral recitations and stage performances. In the Malwa set of

paintings dating from the 17th century, the geographical location for the invasion of Lanka is mapped out with reference to the stage. The heroes Rama and Lakshmana are profiled on one side of the Indian Ocean, with the army of monkeys leaping across the great blue chasm. On the other side, Ravana, the ten-headed king of Lanka and the abducted Sita are depicted in two separate pavilions. The use of gestures and animated movement, and vivid colours to distinguish the characters, are essential to the dramatic narrative.

Dance dramas (*natakas*) provided a vital source of entertainment in medieval India. It was Krishna who captivated the minds and hearts of the people. Krishna, the butter thief and the miracle child, the darling of the milkmaids *(gopis)* and the irresistible lover, became the embodiment of romantic love. Earlier texts such as the *Hari Vamsa* and the *Vishnu Purana* had explored his childhood adventures. Later texts, such as the *Bhagavata Purana* and the *Gita Govinda*, dramatise his romance with the *gopis* and with Radha. These texts are still revered today, read out aloud in gatherings and enacted during annual festivals, such as on the extremely popular *Krishna Lila* and *Janmashtami*.

The vibrant set of paintings of the *Bhagavata Purana*, for instance, are each "staged" in domed pavilions, with the starched contours of costumes, the use of intense dark eyes and rehearsed gestures for communication. Whether seated or standing, each figure is isolated against a red, blue or, sometimes, yellow background that acts as a brilliant back-drop or stage "curtain". The movement of figures is invariably in single file, laterally in one direction, as though on stage moving both through space and time.

Such paintings provide evidence for a miniature style that flourished in the first half of the 16th century, before the Mughal studio of painters was formed. It has been suggested that the Mughal emperor Akbar recruited much of the talent for his new and dynamic school of painting from other court centres that existed in central India: in Gwalior, Jaunpur, Mandu, Gujarat, and in Chittaurgarh in Rajasthan. This is upheld not only by the overwhelming majority of Hindu

Preceding pages: Krishna meeting Nanda, Mewar school C. 1575. Left, a medieval painting of a Rajput royal.

artists at the Mughal court, but also by the eclectic vigour and different idioms in early Mughal paintings of the *Tuti Nama* and *Hamza Nama*.

Yet, by what seems a curious paradox, some of the earliest surviving manuscripts of Rajasthan have been worked upon by Muslim artists. The first definitive proof of painting in Mewar, is in a *Ragamala* set of paintings that are dated to the year 1605, by a painter called Nasir-ud-din. Again, the spectacular and recent discovery of another *Ragamala* set in the Bundi style, but painted at Chunar in Uttar Pradesh, states clearly that it was painted by three artists who had learnt their trade with the Persian masters of the Mughal

and flowers. During the interim 30 years of warfare and stubborn defiance of Mughal authority, it is interesting to note that the Mewar Rajputs employed Muslim painters in their service, who in all probability came from the Mughal court. This subtle interaction brings a new pitch to the miniatures.

Pure passion: From the start, Rajput painting is unmistakably different from the refined court art and book illustrations of the Mughals. It developed its own set of priorities, its own sensibility. In the early paintings from Mewar and Bundi, the colours are inflamed with pure passion, and used undiluted. In *Ragini Bhairavi*, a 16th-century Bundi miniature illustrated here, a brutal,

atelier. Yet this set, which is dated to 1591, belongs to the formative style of Bundi, and is already imbued with the vibrant colours and lyricism of Rajput painting.

In the 17th century, all of North India lay under the rule of the Mughal emperors. It was natural that the exuberant burst of Mughal art would affect and influence the art of the Rajput courts. It seems that a seminal school of painting had already developed at Chittaurgarh in the 16th century. A set of the *Gita Govinda* may belong here, depicting the idealized lovers in intense communication, set against flat expanses of colour with a schematic treatment of trees

brilliant red serves as the background to a captivated woman seated before the Shiva *linga*, performing a *puja*. White flower garlands draped on the *linga*, a triangular corner of the blue sky, the peacock on the roof, and the intensely black eyes and hair of the woman are the only accents here. The use of bold colours brings a savage intensity to these early paintings. A remarkable affinity is shared between the woman profiled and the dark peacock above, as though they indulge in the same ecstatic response to life. These early paintings are infused with an emotion that demands a response, and which shocks almost as much as it elevates the viewer to a sense of religiosity. The atmosphere is one that is "not so much mystic as almost violently vital".

Ragamala paintings seem to have been the preserve and privilege of the Rajputs in North India. In the second half of the 16th century, the songs of Mirabai were sung at the Rajput courts in a surge of religious awakening. At Orcha, the *Rasikapriya* of Keshava Das had just been composed in 1594, and soon after was set to pictorial illustrations in Mewar. In the early 17th century, the hundred verses of the poet Amaru, the *Amaru Sataka*, was also set to pictures and poems of the Malwa school, in a heightened exaltation of the heroine. The depiction of the *nayika* (lover),

in her different moods and situations, becomes the obsession in both poems and visual imagery. As a concept, *raga* lends credibility to the translation of sound into image. Derived from the Sanskrit root *ranja*, to colour, *raga* literally means "colouring." With reference to music, it implies some means being used to "colour" or influence the mind with a definitive emotive response, to inflame it with a certain passion. Since music then is coloured and tinged with specific overtones,

Far left, detail from the Gita Govinda. **Left**, Bhairavi from the Bundi school C. 1600. **Above**, Nata Raga C. 1650.

how appropriate to introduce colour, form and visual aids to enhance the expression of a mood, or a time of day, or a season. It is wise not to take the correspondence between the *ragas* and paintings too literally, they are meant more as an evocation than a scientific description of the music.

Every detail, from the mention of sandal paste or musk or camphor, or ashes smeared on the body, to the leaves quivering with excitement and dewdrops glistening on the lotus, to the sound of parrots in the forest, is used to arouse our sensations. It is the *physical* summoning that awakens us to the sound, smell and colour, and which contributes to the essential vitality of these paintings. Some of them, at least those that are exquisitely finished, remain as images in the mind when the music has died away.

A young lissom woman, her body smeared with a paste of saffron and camphor, is shown wandering through the forest with her *vina*, followed by deer who seem infatuated with her, as might be described in a verse placed above the picture. This is *Ragini Todi*, which is said to embody the anguish of *vipralabdha*, of being separated from her lover.

Quite a remarkable number of *raginis* portray the *nayika* as practicing *tapas*, leading a remote and austere life. Among them is *Ragini Bangali*, where the subject has retreated from the world to assuage her ardour by focusing her mind and heart on Lord Shiva. An unusual origin is found for *Asavari Ragini*, also known as *Ragini Ahiri*, which suggests a connection with the Ahirs, the cowherd nomads living in the hills. Invariably the *nayika* is seated upon a rock, in a skirt of leaves, her skin gleaming in dark blue to suggest her Adivasi origins. Summoned by the music of the *shehnai*, the inscription says, snakes desert their sandal trees and swarm up to the rocks to coil at her feet; white cranes by the water listen, enchanted, and the forest is vibrant with the sound and colour of birds. In some depictions, she herself plays the *shehnai* (oboe).

In literature and painting, there is a sensuous delight in the charms of nature: in the colours of the sky, of the rivers in space, of animals responding to the change of seasons. An entire body of literature developed on the seasons, beginning with the classic poem by Kalidasa of the *Ritusamhara*. The depiction of each month in poems and paintings is known as the *Baramasa*. In the month of *Magha* (January–February), the poet Keshava says, forests and gardens echo with the cries of the peacock, pigeon and koel. Bees hum around. The air is scented with musk, camphor and sandal. The sounds of the *pakhavaj* (barrel drum) and other musical instruments are heard. All are celebrating the advent of spring. "If you love me," the beloved entreats her lover, "do not leave me in this month of Magha".

The theme of romantic love is celebrated in a 12th-century poem by the poet Jayadeva, who singles out Radha for the first time as the heroine. In his *Gita Govinda*, the *dramatis personae* are Krishna, Radha and the *dutika* or messenger, who serves as their confidante. The meetings of these lovers in a secret grove, the anguish of their estrangements and reunion, the different phases of Radha pining for Krishna are described in successive cantos. In these verses Krishna grows to become more than a lover or a mere hero; he becomes the personification of love itself.

In the devotional literature that followed, romantic love was conceived as an exalted experience. Jayadeva's poem received instant recognition, and inspired a wide body of love poems. In the west, Bilvamangala composed a genealogy on the child Krishna, known as the *Balagopala Stuti*. In Bengal in the 15th century, the poets Vidyapati and Chandidasa wrote poems in which the poet indentified himself wholly with the disorders of the mind, the sensations and the passions experienced by the lovers. In Mewar state, the princess Mirabai composed ecstatic songs for her patron deity, Krishna, in the form of *Giri Govardhana*. The Bhakti movement, initiated in Rajasthan by Shri Vallabhacharya, established a cult centre, and inspired his disciples such as Sur Das and Krishna Das.

Krishna, the cowherd boy or Gokula, emerges from the forests of Vrindavan to lead home the cows during a golden dusk. The haunting melodies of his flute fill the village girls with longing, for they recognize it to be the call to love. On the autumn nights they steal into the forest where Krishna stands before them, wearing a crown of peacock feathers and a yellow *dhoti*, his blue-black skin shimmering in the moonlight. Using his powers of delusion, he provides each girl with a semblance of himself, and they dance as the moon rises, saturating the forest.

The love play of Krishna and the *gopis*, known as the *Krishna Lila*, becomes one of the enduring elements of village life. In Vaishnava experience, the flute is the call of God, causing the souls of men and women to give up their worldly attachments and to gather to adore him. In one such incident, he steals up and carries away the clothes of the *gopis* as they bathe in the river Yamuna, and then he sits on the Kadamaba tree, enticing them to come out of the water naked. The next intimate moment of passion between the lover and his beloved is ecstatic.

In pictures illustrating texts such as the *Gita Govinda*, the artist employed poetic symbols – lotuses swaying in a stream, trees

bursting into bloom – to suggest the intimate passion of the lovers. The movement of clouds, of rain, of lightning, of rivers, were each charged with implicit meaning. In literature, they sometimes served as a catalyst, bringing lovers together.

There seems to have been a continuous exodus of artists from the Mughal court, and also from the Deccan, to feed the demands of North India. When Emperor Aurangzeb determined upon a return to Islamic orthodoxy in the 1660s, the artists of the Mughal court were set free to join and influence other centres of court painting. The impact of Mughal artists is keenly felt in

Bikaner painting, which seems to assemble the best of both idioms. Delicate pages of a *Devi Mahatmya* are suffused with subtle tones of muted greens and greys rarely found in other Rajput painting, with a pink demon who defies the usual iconography and brandishes instead a double-barrelled musket. In the royal portrait of Shri Karan Singh of Bikaner, the drawing is tinted with pink and green wash, and illuminated with pearl strands – achieving the formal elegance typical of portraits from the reign of Shah Jahan.

A new genre of painting developed in the 18th century to depict the pastimes, amusements and romantic ideals of Rajput court life. This includes a large number of

portraits in durbar, equestrian studies of rulers, and hunting scenes, especially from the smaller states and *thikanas*. For instance, a magnificent page depicting Raja Umed Singh of Udaipur enjoying a dance performance, inscribed with the names of two courtiers and of the dancer, in a dynamic rhythm that is quite different from the frozen assemblies in depictions of later durbars.

The Rajput rulers are now depicted in different ceremonies of state, and religious festivals. Women out on a hunting expedi-

Left, Nayalha-Nayika theme *circa* 1650. **Above**, Kishangarh school *circa* 1750.

tion shoot at tigers, while the sky is stained the hot orange of monsoon sunsets, and birds raise a clamour at sundown. Even when the women are shown idling away their time on a terrace, beside a game of *chaupad*, the subtle curve of the horizon and the silver moon cupped into the sky betray their secret yearnings.

Courtly love: The most eloquent expression of Rajput chivalry is to be found in paintings from the state of Kishangarh. In this small state that was founded in 1609, the subjects include hunting scenes and portraits, but they also explore most explicitly the scope of courtly love. The delicate refinements and technique derive from an appreciation of the Mughal style at Delhi and at Avadh; yet the heightened sense of lyricism owes much to the sensibilities and influence of the ruler, Savant Singh. He was not only an accomplished poet, but also a religious devotee, writing poems under the name of Nagari Das, to revive once again the romance of Krishna, with a personal identification. His own romance with the singer and poet, Bani Thani, served to strengthen and to generate a new genre of courtly love. From 1740 to 1756 he withdrew to live in Vrindavan, in adoration of Krishna; after which he abdicated the throne in favour of his son, Sardar Singh.

During the 14 years that followed, a small group of paintings were conceived that were large in size, but exquisite in their detailing and finish. With just a few exceptions, they celebrate the romantic encounter between Radha and Krishna. The setting here may be deep in the woods, but the lovers possess the elegance of a prince and princess. Figures are reduced to miniature scale, set against the vast expanse of a lake or against a carpet of towering trees – to suggest perhaps the sense of eternity that encompasses them.

The final gesture of courtly love is conveyed in a painting where, amidst their many attendants, Radha and Krishna are enthroned, against the far distant mirage of marble palaces. Male followers play upon the flute, while a female attendant offers *pan*. In Rajput etiquette, the offering of the betel leaf is a matter of social form; but the offering of *pan* by Radha to Krishna becomes a token of her deep adoration. So Krishna becomes immortalized in poetry and in painting, as the prince and the ideal lover.

Rajasthan

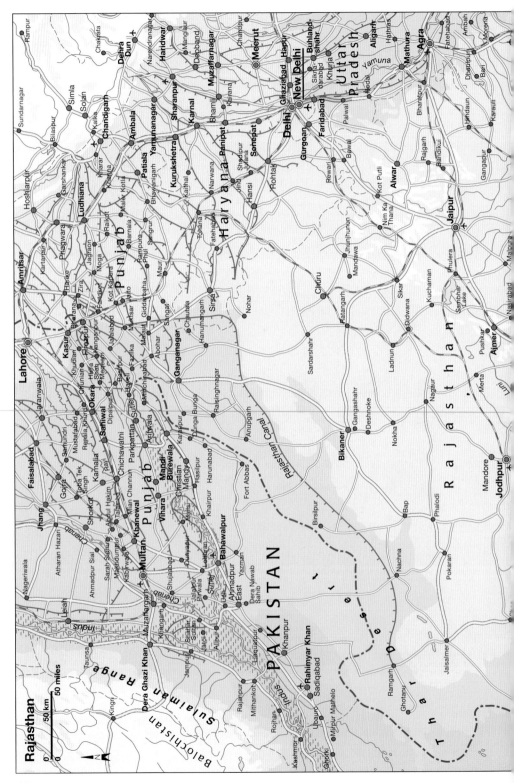

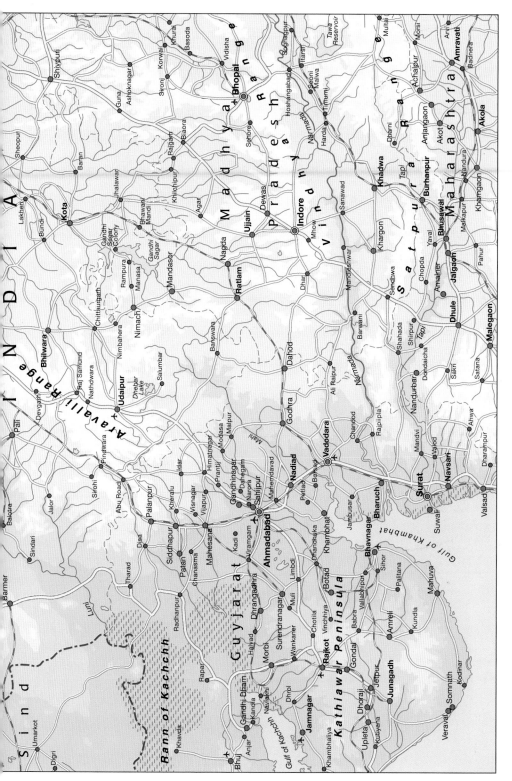

PLACES

Rajasthan, or Rajputana as the area used to be called when it consisted of 20-odd "native states" under British paramountcy, is, literally translated, the land of the Rajputs, who were, for well-nigh a thousand years, the traditional ruling and landed aristocracy of most of the states in the area. Though a minority in term of population, their political and military dominance have left their mark, giving the whole of Rajputana an overall unity of outlook and attitudes. This persists in Rajasthan today. Historically, however, despite Rajput dominance, Rajasthan seldom presented a united face to external aggression, whether of the Muslim invaders down to the Mughals or, ultimately, of the British.

So, in a sense, in Rajasthan we have 20-odd sub-histories to contend with, with all their implications in cultural and material terms. Therefore, while the contributions that follow essentially cover places, the presentation of specific historical backgrounds, to supplement the overall historical essay in Part I of this volume, cannot be avoided.

The emphasis is on leading visitors from the familiar to the less familiar, but equally exciting, byways of the destinations covered, always keeping in mind the practical aspects. The pattern adopted is coverage from a series of central, nodal points, radiating outwards, often across the old princely state boundaries and even those of Rajasthan's modern districts. This should help visitors to plan their trip on a modular basis, adding or subtracting modules according to individual interests and the time available.

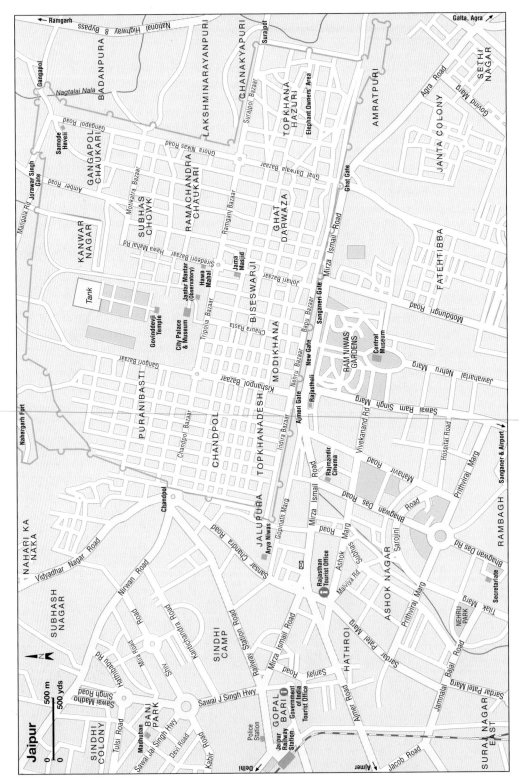

Jaipur

JAIPUR

Soon after he came to the Amber throne in 1699, the 11-year-old Jai Singh II went to pay his respects to Emperor Aurangzeb in Delhi. The aged Mughal, the story goes, grasped the young man's hands, and asked just how he expected to be powerful if his hands were tied. Jai Singh's reply was quick and clever. When a bridegroom takes his bride's hand, he is vowing to protect her for life. Thus, after the royal gesture, he would need no arms because the mighty Mughal would protect him.

Such bare-faced cheek impressed Aurangzeb. And to show how Jai Singh outshone both his ancestors and his fellow Rajputs, he later rewarded his crafty impertinence with the hereditary title *Sawai*, meaning one-and-a-quarter. Jai Singh lived up to the compliment. First he excelled at the Rajput soldiering game. Later, confident of peace and stability, he encouraged his Kachchwaha clan to change from war-loving Rajputs to peace-loving citizens. On a dried-up lake beneath his crammed hill-fort, he built a new capital, naming it Jaipur after himself – although *jai* conveniently means victory, too. It was a beautiful example of humanist town-planning. Merchants and craftsmen flocked to it. Affluence – and the famous pink colour of its buildings – followed. And it continues to thrive today.

Jai Singh envisaged this first planned Rajput city as the capital of a united Rajputana, a centre of government, trade and worship. Some 250 years later, his foresight brought ambition to reality. In 1948, after Independence, Maharaja Man Singh II became Rajpramukh, head of the newly formed Rajasthan Union, consolidated as the state of Rajasthan the following year. Jaipur became the administrative and commerical capital of a democratized collection of former princely states.

It is a busy, bustling city with over 1.5 million people. Gossip and debate in the corridors of its Assembly affect the lives of around 50 million people sprawled over the whole state – Jai Singh's state was only the fourth-largest Rajput state, a mere 40,150 sq. km (15,500 sq. miles).

Commercially, old and new constantly clash. Traditional Jaipur crafts of jewellery, enamelling, metalwork, printed cloths, handloom weaving and carving thrive alongside engineering, distilling, shoe-making, drugs, glass and sports equipment industries. Successful *durri* makers, carpet weavers and jewellers have their world headquarters here.

The founder: Jaipur is a living testament to one of the most remarkable men of his age. Jai Singh II was supremely talented – politically, intellectually and on the battlefield. Indeed, the more prosaic historians claim he won his title of *Sawai* aged 14 at the siege of Khalna in 1702, skillfully defending Mughal interests against the Marathas.

This triumph set the tone. And by 1723, aged just 35, Jai Singh had performed an impressive feat of political juggling. Having backed both contenders for the imperial throne after Aurangzeb's death in 1707, he was

understandably thrown off his own throne by the suspicious winner, Bahadur Shah. Undaunted, he reunited the big Rajput states against the Mughal. As usual, marriage cemented the alliance. First, the Rajputs threw the Mughals out of Jodhpur. Next, they threw Bijai, Jai Singh's brother and the Mughal puppet, out of Amber and Jai Singh reclaimed his throne.

Warring over, Jai Singh left the battlefield to indulge himself and his intellectual passions: science and the arts. The result was Jaipur. And, despite its importance and activity today, Jai Singh's city stands as it was originally planned.

A good place to start is at the statue of the founder, Maharaja Sawai Jai Singh II (ruled 1699–1743). It stands just outside the southern wall. Behind him lies the city he designed with a young Bengali, an engineer and scholar named Vidyadhar Bhattacharaya.

The foundation stone was laid on 25 November 1727. Their plan was a simple grid system: seven blocks of buildings divided by very wide, tree-lined avenues. At its heart lies the palace, covering the space of another two blocks. The whole is surrounded by a crenellated wall with seven gates. Orientation is to the northeast, on two temples standing on the surrounding hills. Essentially, it follows the principles of the ancient Hindu architectural treatise, the *Shilpa Shastra*.

Pink welcome: To these Jai Singh added revolutionary ideas: hygiene, beauty and commerce. But Jaipur's all over pinkness is probably not his. A few of the grander public buildings were indeed built of expensive pink sandstone. But it seems to have been Maharaja Man Singh who dressed up the rest of the city in the symbolically welcoming colour when the Prince of Wales, later Edward VII, visited Jaipur in 1876. During this vast spring clean, he repaired the walls and gates and gave sloping roof verandas to the old shops. Today, every home-owner within the city is obliged by law to maintain their facade – and if they fail, the city does it and charges them.

Peacock doorway, City Palace.

Moving along Mirza Ismail (M.I.) Road, **Singpol** (Lion Gate) is the gate farthest west on the south wall. Like all the gateways, it has two kiosks above and projecting parapet over the entrance. And like all the gateways, it was until the 20th century locked at night, leaving passengers arriving on night trains stranded until daybreak. The wall it pierces averages 7 metres (20 feet) high and a stout 3 metres (9 feet) thick, with plenty of bastions and towers, a parapet loopholed for musketry and holes for cannon to fire through. This was not all of the city's defenses. The vulnerability of the plains was further protected by forts crowning all the important summits of the surrounding rugged hills.

Inside the gate is **Khajana Walon ka Rasta**, the market where the marble carvers work. This is the first of many *mohallas*, rectangular blocks each designed for a particular trade or craft. Each was planned with a precise number of shops and houses built in a distinctive style. At the top of the street, a right turn into another market, **Chandpol Bazaar**, leads to the first of three big crossroads where the widest avenues meet. **Choti Chaupar** is the first, where local villagers come to sell their produce.

The spaciousness and formal elegance of the city is seen on Chandpol and the other main streets, which are an impressive 36 meters (111 feet) broad. Secondary streets maintain their airiness at 18 metres (55 feet) and alleys are half as wide again.

Such detailed planning did not hamper speed. Lakes to supply water, the sturdy walls and the principal buildings were up in 6 or 7 years. Jai Singh's religious tolerance encouraged the Digamber Jains to come, who have since produced a regular flow of scholars and administrators. Also, his Vaishnavism brought temples of the major sects here.

To entice more wealth, Jai Singh invited merchants to come and build houses of their own designs, so long as they conformed to the architect Vidhyadhar's general plan and high standards. They flocked here, together with bankers to serve them.

Feeding pigeons as an act of piety.

Thakurs (landowners) built smart townhouses, although they later moved outside the walls for more space. They were the maharaja's courtiers, whose lands were hereditary royal gifts or rent-free presents to a royal favorite. All courtiers danced attendance on their ruler on important festivals, birthdays and whenever they might be summoned.

In the palace corridors, they peppered the ceaseless hum with gossip and intrigue. In the ceremonial processions, they provided colour, sparkle and fine clothes. Even into the 20th century, the Thakur of Isarda would appear decked out in jewellery worth 25,000 rupees and proudly wearing his gold anklet, a privilege of the Tazimi Sardars. And at each ceremony, he and his fellow nobles knelt to offer their maharaja a gold coin in the *nazar* ritual, symbolizing a reaffirmation of loyalty.

Crossing Choti Chaupar, the avenue continues as **Tripolia Bazaar**, where cooking utensils and costume jewellery are sold. But down **Maniharon ke Rasta**, a lane on the right, craftsmen make multicoloured, striped lacquer bangles.

Back on Tripolia Bazaar, the tall tower on the left is **Iswari Minar Swarga Sal** (Minaret Piercing Heaven). It is a proud monument built by a weak ruler, Iswari Singh (ruled 1743–51). Only five of Jai Singh's multitude of children lived to maturity and Iswari, who succeeded him, did not take after his father. Unable to face the advancing Maratha army, he committed suicide by taking poison and making a cobra bite him. But the moment was given a degree of Rajput honor by his women: three *ranis* and a concubine also took poison and 21 wives joined Iswari's funeral pyre as *satis*.

Jaipur's days of glory thereafter became clouded. As the Marathas pushed up through northern India, they kept close control over their puppet Jaipur rulers. Suddenly, the tables were turned when the Marathas quarrelled amongst themselves. The British then swapped sides to defend the Rajputs, closing their pincer-hold on the princes. An alliance with Jaipur in 1803 helped counter further Maratha onslaughts but Jaipur had

Jantar Mantar, the observatory of Maharaja Jai Singh II.

sacrificed independence for British domination and protection. However, life for the rulers was not bad. Massive amounts of wealth poured in. And, after 1835, Jaipur had no wars to pay for, so rulers indulged themselves and their fancies in their luxurious City Palace.

City Palace complex: **Tripolia** (triple-arched) Gate, just beyond the minaret, is the grand entrance to the City Palace complex, cutting through the centre of the southern wall. Maharajas, dazzling in a sun-burst of gold and jewels, would emerge here, seated atop their painted and silk-bedecked elephants. Lesser mortals now enter through **Atish Pol** (Stable Gate) to the left. After another tunnel gate and a right turn, this city in miniature begins with its **Chandni Chowk** (Moonlight Square), the courtyards of the palace stables.

Further on, huge geometric shapes dot the area on the right like forgotten surrealist stage props. This is the **Jantar Mantar** (*j(y)antra*, instrument/device; *mantra*, (magic) formula), Jai Singh's open-air observatory of outsize astronomical instruments. In mathematics and astronomy, as in war and town-planning, Jai Singh did nothing by halves – his scientific inventiveness was supposed to have emerged when, aged 13, he devised an irrigation system to water the hanging gardens of Amber Fort.

Jai Singh first built a Jantar Mantar in Delhi in 1724–27, the first observatory in India, believing size would improve accuracy. Later, while governor of Agra, he built three more, at Ujjain, Varanasi and Mathura, ancient centres of religion and learning. But for daily observations and constant consultations with his guru, Pandit Jaganath, he needed an observatory at home. The Jaipur set, built 1728–34, is the largest and best preserved. Not only was it built of stone, but in the 19th century Lieutenant A. Garret and Pandit Chandradhar Guleri carefully restored it. It was in use until the 1940s keeping track of Jaipur's solar time. This was read off the quadrants on either side of the vast gnomon (right angle) that acts as a huge sundial called the *Samrat Yantra* (Supreme Instrument). Size made

Jai Singh II also built observatories in Delhi, Mathura, Ujjain and Varanasi.

the readings accurate down to 3 seconds. It was then announced to the people: less important times by a drummer at the top of the steps; more important times by a gun fired from Nahargarh fort above the city. The purposes of the other instruments are less obviously practical. The large, circular *Ram Yantras* are for reading altitudes and azimuths – distances in the sky. The dozen *Rashivilayas* are for calculating celestial latitudes and longitudes.

Gainda ki Deorhi (Rhinoceros Gate), round the corner, leads to the main buildings of the City Palace. They are a showpiece of palace architecture, mingling Hindu and Mughal styles. Following the Rajput fortress pattern, a series of increasingly private rooms leads to the centre of the palace. Following the Mughal tradition of Delhi and Agra, the buildings for various uses stand separate from one another. They are well ventilated to catch the breeze and are often quite small. Thus, the stables and administrative offices lead ultimately to the royal residence, the **Chandra Mahal**.

Royal wardrobe: First comes the dazzling white **Mubarak Mahal** (Palace of Welcome), built in 1900 by Maharaja Madho Singh II (ruled 1880–1922) as a guest house. Later it served as the *Mahakma Khas* (Royal Secretariat). Now it houses the textile part of the **City Palace Museum** and is called the *Tosha Khana* (Royal Wardrobe).

The suite of rooms on the first floor, encircled by an elaborately carved balcony, contain the black and gold Diwali festival dress, whose *odhni* (shawl) alone has some 8 kg (18 pounds) of gold woven into it. Then there are Maharaja Ram Singh's riding clothes, Pratap Singh's wedding outfit, fine muslins, striped silk pajamas and locally printed cottons.

The wardrobe also houses the royal accouterments of hookah bases, Jaipur pottery, Mughal glass and an exceptional collection of musical instruments. But the most extraordinary piece is the *atamsukh* of Madho Singh I (ruled 1750–68). This raspberry-pink garment of Banaras silk, glowing with gold *butti*

The present Maharaja of Jaipur with courtiers.

(dotted) designs, is vast. Legend tells that its owner was 2 metres (6 feet) tall and weighed 225 kg (500 pounds).

Madho Singh II has left his mark throughout the palace, although as a ruler he was not a great innovator and merely continued to support the revolutionary improvements of Ram Singh who, heirless, had adopted him on his deathbed. In fact, the problem of heirs haunted the Kachchwaha house. When, in 1931, the first male heir for two generations was born to a ruling maharaja, such quantities of champagne celebrated the event that the baby's English nanny nicknamed him Bubbles. And on the right wall of the courtyard, beside **Singh Pol** (Lion Gate), stand two white marble elephants to mark the great event.

But first there is the **Sileh Khana** (Armory) which lies behind the Mubarak Mahal. Here, one of the finest collections of Indian weaponry testifies to Kachwaha valour. Among every kind of bejewelled dagger, sword, shield and gun, Jai Singh I of Amber's turban-shaped helmet and shield are especially

Family retainers at the City Palace.

opulent. Far less genteel is a steel mace in the shape of a lotus bud. Once lodged firmly in the victim's stomach, it would spring open into a fan of sharp spikes.

The photographs on display are by Ram Singh, who ruled in quieter times. Aided by an Englishman, T. Murray, he put studios and dark-rooms in the palace, snapped away, and later even founded a photography school.

Back to Singh Pol, a typically Hindu square gatehouse with delicate balconies supported by ornate brackets. Its large bronze double doors lead into a pretty courtyard whose frilly white arches on the salmon-pink walls are 18th-century Rajput decoration. But the **Diwan-i-Khas** (Private Audience Hall) in the center is firmly Mughal, a descendant of Fatehpur Sikri. Within its scalloped arches stand two huge water flasks. Currently the largest single pieces of silver known in the world, they measure 160 cm (5 feet 3 inches) high, with a capacity of 8,812 litres (1,800 gallons). The craftsman, Govind Narain, made them for Madho Singh, using 242.7 kg (10,408 troy oz) of silver. Loyalty to the British crown had persuaded Madho to witness the coronation of Edward VII. So he chartered a liner, built a temple on board, flung bags of gold, silver and silk into Bombay harbour to invoke the oceans to give him safe passage, and stowed away his urns filled with Ganga water to help him avoid the pollution incurred by crossing the ocean.

To the right is the **Diwan-i-Am** (Public Audience Hall), an enclosed room built for the splendour and pageantry of sumptuous court durbars and ceremonies, watched by the ladies from behind the carved screens of the gallery. Now it forms the focus of the **Sawai Man Singh II Museum**. Founded in 1959 by the former ruling family, the museum was set up by the distinguished art historian, Dr Asok Das. After the royal wardrobe and armoury, there are carpets from Lahore, Herat and Agra cover the walls and one of India's largest chandeliers hangs from the ceiling. Royal palanquins and a chosen few of the magnificent collection of miniature paintings and manuscripts fill the room.

Jai Singh established the Jaipur library and gave the painting school its distinctive character. Akbar's magnificently illustrated *Ramayana* and *Razmnama* are here but rarely on view. However, you may well see a painting from the *Sarasrasagrantha* series, such as Krishna playing *holi* with the *gopis*, painted in 1737 for Jai Singh and marking the ultimate refinement of the Jaipur style.

Back across the pink courtyard, under the delicate *jali* (lattice) work of the ladies, the corridor to the Hawa Mahal, **Ridhi Sidhi Pol** leads to **Pritam Niwas Chowk**, known from its decoration as the Peacock Courtyard. It is a magical, enclosed courtyard with ochre walls, whose four gateways were elaborately decorated by Pratap Singh (ruled 1778–1803) to represent the four seasons. Above the parrot gate, girls would sing from the balcony.

Next, through a Wedgewood-blue hall, **Pritam Niwas** houses more Mughal glass and leads to **Chandra Mahal** (Moon Palace), the seven-tiered, pyramid-like inner sanctum of the palace. These were the royal apartments, complete with an internal garden. Crowning them, the **Mukut Mandir** has superb views.

The **Chandra Mandir**, the ground floor, has air-cooling water channels and delicate floral designs on the ceiling. From its terrace the ruler could look across the Jai Niwas garden to the **Sri Govinda Temple** where the deity was placed so he could see it. Here at the centre of his creation, Jai Singh II spent his last years, seemingly alternating between pious studies of Vaishnavism and more carnal play.

Later Madho Singh II followed his illustrious predecessor in his two passions: orthodox Hinduism and sex. To satisfy his sexual appetite, Madho's three secondary *ranis* and 18 concubines were supplemented with city women. Perhaps he entertained them in his newly decorated **Shish Mahal** at the top of Chandra Mahal. When the floral inlaid doors are closed and the lights lit, the whole room is like an inverted medieval reliquary. Walls, ceiling, and scalloped arches are inlaid with red and green glass and mirrors, the floral designs,

diamond-shapes and cartouches outlined with thick bands of gold.

Leaving the palace museum complex, the road straight ahead leads to **Jalebi Chowk** (Sweetmeat Square), where drums and the *shehnai* (a reed instrument) used to help announce Jaipur time from the **Nakkar Khana** (Drum House).

Patron deity: In this square is Sri Govinda Deva Temple. The Jaipur rulers were devotees of Krishna, and Govinda is Krishna's name when he is a cowherd, enjoying fiery romances with Radha and other *gopis* (female cowherds) at Vrindavan, near Mathura. From there Jai Singh brought the image of Govinda and put it in his brand-new temple in 1735, establishing it as the guardian deity of Jaipur rulers. From this time, the maharaja would begin addressing his people with the words "subjects of Govinda Devji," implying they ruled merely as an instrument of the all-powerful deity.

Crowds of devout locals come daily to the temple to perform *puja* (worship), offering songs, music, flowers,

Left, Jal Mahal or Water Palace. **Right**, Hawa Mahal or Palace of Winds.

sweetmeats, coloured powders and spices. Each of the seven *pujas* lasts about half an hour and marks a part of the daily ritual of the deity. Thus, Krishna's awakening is around 5am, his dressing around 10.30am. and his evening prayers around 8pm.

Back through Jalebi Chowk and **Siri Deorhi Gate**, up **Hawa Mahal Bazaar** to the right, the **Hawa Mahal** (Palace of the Winds) adjoins the outside of the palace wall. It was built by Maharaja Pratap Singh (ruled 1778–1803) in 1799. A poet and devotee of Krishna, one of his couplets suggests it was dedicated to Krishna and Radha. Its five-storey, gently tapering facade of pink sandstone is encrusted with lace-fine screens and carved balconies around its 953 niches and windows. The top three stories are just a single room thick. It served as a giant, well-ventilated grandstand from which royal ladies confined to *purdah* could watch the activity of the street below. Now it is another museum concentrating on the arts of Jaipur, with good views from the top.

Lively bazaars: South of the Hawa Mahal, **Johari Bazaar** is the other side of the **Badi Chaupar** crossroads. Attracted by the city and court patronage, many jewellers, goldsmiths and silversmiths settled in this area and made Jaipur a major centre for gem stone-cutting. And it still is, with about 40,000 stone-cutters working here in the narrow lanes of **Gopalji ka Rasta** and **Haldiyon ka Rasta**.

The most fascinating work to watch is *minakari*, or enamelling. Like *champlevé* work, the delicate patterns of birds and flowers are fired in glowing red, deep green, peacock blue and white; the gold jewel is then given further sparkle with precious stones and dangling pearls. This painstaking, high-precision art was probably introduced into India by the Mughals and into the Amber court by Man Singh I. Today, descendants of those court craftsmen work quietly in the Jaipur lanes, taking up to a fortnight to enamel both sides of a pendant.

There are plenty of cotton shops in Johari Bazaar too, their owners shaking

One of the several uses of *Elephas maximus*.

out for potential buyers yard upon yard of cloth, each priced according to weight. Further down, past the famous LMB shop selling snacks and sweets, a delightful vegetable market nestles behind grand merchants' houses on the left.

Above some of the delicate facades, men work on the flat roofs block-printing cotton or hanging out tie-dyed fabric to dry. **Rangwalon-ki-Gali** and **Kishanpol Bazaar** are the real areas to see the two main tie-dying methods being practised: *bandhani* work is dyed, knotted and bleached to make dark dots on a pale background; *laharia* work is sold as a twisted rope which, unfolded, reveals a blaze of diagonal, rippled stripes.

For the best choice of prints, turn right at the bottom of Johari Bazaar into **Bapu Bazaar** which leads into **Nehru Bazaar**. Here shop after shop is stacked high with the traditional floral prints in soft blood-reds or blues. Between the fabrics, other shops stock heady Indian perfumes, banks of bangles and fun costume jewellery versions of the fine *minakari* work.

Through **New Gate**, between Bapu and Nehru Bazaars, the road leads out of Jai Singh's city into its sprawling overspill. **Ram Niwas Public Gardens**, straight ahead down Jawaharlal Nehru Marg, was laid out by Maharaja Ram Singh (ruled 1835–80), its original 31 hectares (76 acres) – now 14.5 hectares (36 acres) – landscaped by Dr de Fabeck.

After 16 years of impotent rule as a minor, Ram Singh reached majority in 1851. Under him the Public Works Department was set up in 1860. Results were speedy. The state postal system began in 1861, carried by camels and runners. Seven years later, the municipality was established. In 1874, the city's piped water was pumped along iron pipes from Aman-i-Shah river west of Chandpol Gate. Street lighting came later.

The Ram Niwas Gardens are a microcosm of Ram Singh's achievements. On the left, a former theatre now houses the **Ravindra Rangmanch**, the gallery of modern art. On the right, past the zoo and a crocodile breeding farm, is the **Maharaja College**. When founded in

City policeman attempts to control Jaipur traffic.

1845, it taught Urdu, Persian and basic English. Later, Ram Singh established Oriental and Sanskrit Colleges and, in 1868, a School of Art which, with notable foresight, laid particular emphasis on the local Jaipur crafts. However, literacy in the state had only reached 2.52 percent by the 1901 census.

The focus of the gardens is **Albert Hall**, housing the **Central Museum**. As its name suggests, it was modelled on the educational Victoria and Albert Museum in London. Prince Albert's son, the then Prince of Wales and the future Edward VII, laid the foundation stone in 1876, although the collection had been forming since 1833. The building was designed by Colonel Sir Samuel Swinton Jacob (1841–1917), a British engineer who from 1867 spent most of his career here. While building the museum, the water-works and other civic buildings – with more in Lucknow, Jodhpur, Bikaner, Simla, Chennai and Delhi – he published a portfolio of Indian architectural details which became the colonial architect's handy source-book for fashionable hybrid styles. A virtuoso of Indo-Saracenic style, he was later consulted for the Viceroy's Palace at New Delhi.

Inside the sandstone and white marble treasure-house, there are amusing models of Rajasthan festivals, occupations and trades, and collections of puppets, costumes, ivory, pottery and jewellery. There are also sections on geology, armour and a corner for the rest of the world. The brasswork is well worth a look, with plaques, salvers, toys and vases embossed with repoussé work or engraved and lacquered. The brass shields illustrating scenes from the *Ramayana* and the *Mahabharata* with eye-straining precision are especially elaborate.

It is also well worth asking to see the magnificent Persian Garden Carpet kept under lock and key in the detached **Durbar Hall** in front of the museum building. Made in 1632 in Kerman, Iran, its fresh silks show a ravishing garden divided by fish-filled water channels and full of blossoming trees, chirping

Central Museum, Albert Hall.

birds and frolicking animals. It is one of the earliest and best of its kind.

Further down Jawaharlal Nehru Road is a later temple to education, the **Museum of Indology**. In Narain Singh Marg, off to the right, stands the grand town house, **Narain Niwas**, which Madho Singh's emissary, Narain Singh, built in 1881. Rich in *fin de siècle* finery – Afghan carpets, chandeliers, four-poster beds and East India Company furniture – it typifies the Raj taste that Madho Singh and his courtiers lapped up. With grandeur gone, it is run as a hotel and therefore possible to visit. In fact, several enterprising ex-nobles have followed their ex-ruler's example at Rambagh Palace and gone into the hotel trade, including the Achrols down on Civil Lines Road and the Bissaus and Khetris up at Chandpol Gate.

Palace, prison, treasure trove: Back on Jawaharlal Nehru Road, at the far end on the left lies an incongruous flight of fancy, the **Moti Dungri**. It is a fort shaped like a Scottish Castle. One of its inmates in the 1930s was Lallji Moti Singh, an illegitimate son of Madho Singh, imprisoned for chopping off a boy's testicles. Although at court *Tazimi Sardars* (senior landowners) were above the law, the British police chief locked him up. However, his food was delivered daily from the royal kitchens.

Later, during the 1970s, Gayatri Devi, third wife of Man Singh II, lived in the Moti Dungri. Although reportedly plagued by nighttime mosquitoes and daytime monkeys, the views over the city from the refurbished interior compensated for any discomfort. The personal royal treasure was stored here, too. And when in 1975 the taxmen swooped, they found gold worth US$4–6 million in one room, and piles of sparkling jewellery in another. All this was documented and legitimate. However, the £19 sterling found in her dressing table was not!

But the place Maharaja Man Singh II and his glamorous wife had made famous was their home along Bhawani Singh Marg, the luxurious **Rambagh Palace**.

Left, a street photographer plies his trade. **Right**, a vendor offers a variety of roasted grams and pulses.

The Rambagh began life as a few pleasure pavilions outside the walled city. Ram Singh later organized them into a hunting lodge, *Ram Bagh* (Garden of Ram). It was Madho Singh II who transformed it into a princely playground. On his return from England, he built deep English herbaceous borders in the garden, still beautifully maintained. In the palace, he followed the growing royal Rajput passion for the latest international leisure activities. Helped by Sir Swinton Jacob, he added a squash court, tennis courts and an indoor swimming pool, complete with trapeze swing suspended across the water. And, since Madho was a polo fanatic, he built a private polo field adjoining the gardens. Later, when a broken arm forced him to relinquish the saddle, in true maharaja style he turned to flying and, like his fellow Jodhpur ruler, built himself an aerodrome.

This fun playground was just one of many palaces Ram Singh's adopted son and successor Man Singh II inherited when he came to the throne in 1922, aged just 11 years. Later, he chose it as his principal home, enlarging and modernising it in 1931 to be his official residence. And when in 1940 he finally married Princess Gayatri Devi, the emancipated and well-travelled socialite from Cooch Behar in northeastern India, Man Singh yet again revamped the royal suites and enlarged the public rooms. Much of his palace survives today: the black marble bathrooms, the boldly geometric furnishings, the Lalique fountain and the London-designed dining rooms.

From the cocoon of this luxurious lifestyle, Maharaja Man Singh II ruled Jaipur State until India's independence in 1947. He was then made Rajpramukh of the new Rajasthan Union and later served for seven years as India's first ambassador to Spain. His wife went on to play a prominent role in politics of the new state. He remained immensely popular with his former subjects, right up to his death in 1970 which resulted from a fall while playing polo at Cirencester in England.

Chilums (smoking pipes) and surais (water pots) are the fastest selling items in a potter's shop.

Like Ram Singh before him, Man Singh mixed tradition with modernity. But the extremes were fiercer. The see-saw life of feudal kingly responsibility at home and modern fun abroad set the pattern for his life. For Jaipur in the 1920s and 1930s still had an undisturbed, medieval flavour, given piquancy by the outdated Rajput reverence for valour and honour.

When Man Singh went driving, his route was closed an hour beforehand so the air would be clear of dust. Literacy, even among the *thakurs*, was around 12 percent in the city. And court life was a continual mire of intrigue, bickering, jealousies over betrothals, wrangles over adoptions and jockeying for royal favour and position. For the king's word and wish were law.

On 14 March 1931, the Viceroy, Lord Irwin, invested Man Singh with his full powers as His Highness Sarada-i-Rajaha-i-Hindustan Raj Rajendra Maharaja Dhiraj, Lieutenant-General Sir Sawai Man Singhji Bahadur the Second, Maharaja of Jaipur, the 39th and last ruler of the Kachchwaha Clan.

Man Singh now indulged his two loves: the army and polo. He created a new regiment, the Sawai Man Guards, modelled on the British Foot Guards. As for polo, his playing brought him and his team worldwide fame. Today, the 61st Cavalry, one of India's few mounted regiments, is headquartered in Jaipur and renowned for its polo skills, best seen at the **Polo Grounds** during the annual March season.

By 1958, Man Singh and Ayesha's lives were considerably less grand. Rambagh became the first palace hotel of Rajasthan, providing Jaipur with a good hotel, the palace with maintenance and Man Singh with income. The couple moved down the road to **Raj Mahal Palace**, the former British Residency – yet again easy to visit as it is now a hotel stuffed with royal knicknacks, trophies and photographs.

Trips out of town: To see Jaipur is to see only the second part of the story. For Jai Singh II had conceived it from his fortress-palace at **Amber**, where the

A typical Jaipur street.

Kachchwahas had risen to power and wealth. Amber is just north of Jaipur, with the royal *chatris* (cenotaphs) and some of Jaipur's protective forts in the same direction, and **Samode** and **Bairat** beyond it. To the east lie the **gardens of Sisodia**, the **gorge of Galta** and beyond them **Dausa** and **Lalsot**. To the south lie first **Sanganer** with its crafts, then **Chatsu** and **Tonk**. And both eastern and southern routes lead to **Ranthambore fort** in Sawai Madhopur.

Out of Jaipur through **Zorawar Singh Gate** in the north wall, a road off to the left leads to **Gaitor** (6 km/4 miles), the Kachchwaha royal cremation ground. Here, the white marble *chatris* of Jaipur's rulers stand majestically silhouetted against Nahargarh hill and fort. Naturally, Jai Singh II's is the finest, the white marble dome supported by 20 pillars richly carved with Hindu mythological scenes.

Back on the Amber road, *chatris* of the maharanis, the queens, stand on raised ground on the right. Just beyond them is **Man Sagar**, a lake with what looks like a pleasure palace but is in fact **Jalmahal**, a giant blind for aristocratic duck-shooting parties.

The road opposite twists up steeply, then follows the ridge (with spectacular views) to reach **Nahargarh** (Tiger) **Fort**. Alternatively, it is a 1.5 km (1 mile) hike up a paved pathway northwest of the City Palace. The effort is worth it: the sunset views over the city are stunning. First built in 1734 to defend his new city, this was also a retreat for Jai Singh's maharanis, later enlarged with an elaborate upper story by Ram Singh in 1868. Jaipur time was boomed out across the city from here. And this is where the maharaja's personal treasure was kept until Man Singh II moved it to Moti Dungri.

Amber: Back on the main road, Amber is reached through high cliffs of two ranges of Aravalli hills. It is an arresting first sight, the honey-coloured palace and its snaking walls sprawled over the hill, softly reflected in **Maota Lake**, the whole protected by hills on every side with **Jaigarh fort** overseeing it all.

Pilgrims rest in the shade near the Govindji temple.

The Kachchwahas had eyed this site from nearby Daosa. They belonged to the Kshatriya, or warrior caste of Hindus. But, as usual in Rajput history, their story blends fact with fiction. Origins are celestial, traced to the sun via Kusa who was the twin son of the god Rama, king of Ayodhya and hero of the Hindu epic, the *Ramayana*. The clan migrated in the 3rd century from Rohtas on the Son river to Gwalior and Narwar in what is now Madhya Pradesh. Here they ruled for 800 years. The mists of legend begin to lift. Taj Karan, known as Dulha Rai (The Bridegroom Prince), left Gwalior in 1128 – possibly thrown out by his uncle – and married the beautiful Maroni, daughter of the Bargujar Rajput chief of Daosa. Soon afterwards, Dulha Rai's generous father-in-law is said to have given him Daosa. The Kachchwaha dynasty was established. And around 1150 Dulha Rai's descendant wrested Amber from the Susawat Minas. Stories vary. One says he got them drunk and then butchered them; another that the Minas gave refuge to a Kachchwaha who took the hospitality, then usurped the throne. Anyway, Amber remained the Kachchwaha capital for six centuries and the Minas became hereditary guards of their treasure.

The town's original name was possibly Ambikishwara – a name for the god Shiva, a member of the all-powerful Hindu Trinity – later contracted to Ambiner, then Amber. Other theories take it back to Ambarisha, a king of Ayodhya, or to Amba Mata, goddess of earth and fertility.

Relations with Delhi began early. Before the end of the 12th century, the chief Pajun married the sister of Prithviraj Chauhan, the last Hindu king of Delhi who was killed by Muhammad Ghori in 1192. But it was the special relationship between the Kachchwahas and the Mughals that brought them real power, influence and wealth.

The moment Muslim power looked like a force to be taken seriously, Bihar Mal (ruled 1548–74) ensured he was first to pay homage to Humayun. They set the typical Mughal-Rajput exchange

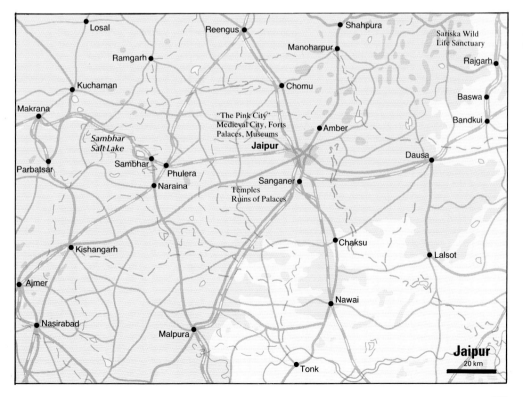

of gifts: Humayun gave Bihar Mal command of a 5,000-strong army, and Bihar Mal gave his daughter to Humayun's son, Akbar, and placed his adopted grandson, Man Singh, in Mughal service.

The next chief, Bhagwan Das, intensified relations. He became a good friend of Akbar, apparently saving his life at the battle of Sarnal, and in 1585/6 gave his daughter to Akbar's son, Prince Salim, who later became Emperor Jahangir. Akbar's gift was the command of 5,000 horse soldiers and governorship of Punjab. For it was under Akbar (ruled 1556–1605) that the Mughal empire expanded and Kachchwaha power grew. The initial reason was that the pilgrimage route to the Muslim shrine at Ajmer crossed Kachchwaha territory and needed to be kept free from bandits. The Kachchwaha-Mughal alliance began.

It was two 16th-century rulers, Man Singh I and Jai Singh I, who benefited most. And with booty from the battlefield, they built and embellished their magnificent fortress complex. In the hierarchy of forts, it has been ranked second only to that of Gwalior in Madhya Pradesh. It may lack Gwalior's raw stamp of Hindu originality but the setting is sublime, the stern, rambling exterior belying the well organized, bejewelled interior whose richness increases as the rooms go higher, opening on to striking views of the gorge.

Visitors can mount the long, steep ramparts by elephant, serenaded by a local playing his *ravanhatha*, a bowed lute. As the elephant plods up, the natural advantages of the site become clearer. With these, Man Singh I (ruled 1589–1614) had confidently begun building his fort around 1592. Through **Jai Pol** (Victory Gate), there are shorter elephant rides around the large courtyard. But be careful not to fall victim to the fate of Man Singh's great-grandson, who died after a fall climbing up a ladder to mount his elephant.

Jai Singh I (ruled 1621–67) became the finest of all Kachchwaha generals. He came to the throne aged 11. By 13, he was commanding 3,000 in the Deccan. **Amber town and Palace with Jaigarh Fort above.**

With a clear idea of where his interests lay, he first fought all over India for Jahangir's successor, Shah Jahan. Then he made a shrewd change of allegience. While Shah Jahan's sons squabbled for power, he shifted his support from Dara to his brother, Aurangzeb, promptly captured Dara who was then murdered by Aurangzeb.

For this and other loyal deeds Aurangzeb heaped prizes on Jai Singh, and the title Mirza Raja with command of 7,000 troops, the maximum permitted to non-members of the royal emperor's family. With this, Jai Singh's finest hour was the defeat and capture of the almost god-like Maratha leader, Shivaji.

Family shrine: To the right of the huge arched gateway, the **Singh Pol** (Lion Gate) steps lead up from the courtyard to the **Kali Temple**. This is the Kachchwaha family shrine built by Man Singh in 1604. It is dedicated to Shila Mata, an aspect of Kali, the goddess of war. Man Singh brought the deity's image back from Jessore in Bengal, housing it amid green marble pillars carved into plantain trees. In this century, Man Singh II would drive up here in his Bentley and sacrifice a goat to Shila Devi with his own hands. And in 1939 he built the solid silver entrance doors as thanks for his recovery from a plane crash. Even today, a Bengali leads the *puja* (worship) with noisy bells and drums and the temple is the Jaipur family's island in the otherwise state-owned fort.

Back down, then up again to the **Diwan-i-Am** (Public Meeting Hall), where the ruler would give audience to his people. Set on a dazzling white terrace overlooking the whole gorge, this is Jai Singh's masterpiece. A double row of columns have capitals decorated with elephants supporting a canopy and galleried terrace. Its delicacy was so much to Mughal taste that Jai Singh had to cover it with stucco before the jealous Jahangir's commissioners arrived to see if the Rajput was getting too big for his warring boots. Now, as the stucco wears, the fine decoration begins to be revealed.

Ganesh Pol (Elephant Gate), a magnificent burst of colour, is Jai Singh's ceremonial gate, built around 1640. It is smothered in mosaic, fresco and sculpture, with lattice-work above so the ladies could watch processions. Over the doorway sits Ganesh, the elephant-headed god of learning and good fortune.

Through this gate lies a very Mughal formal garden court. To the right is the **Sukh Nivas** (Hall of Pleasure), with air-cooling water running through. To the left is the **Jai Mandir** (Hall of Victory), Jai Singh's private apartments whose sophistication is the perfect blend of Hindu and Muslim traditions executed with the highest skills. The decoration on the walls and ceilings is perhaps the finest among all Rajasthan fortress-palaces. Murals are of bold cypresses, tiny flowers or pictures of Rajput pleasures: hunting and war. All is made silky smooth by adding powdered marble, egg shells and even pearls to the final coat. Glass and precious stones set into the plaster add royal glamour. *Taks* (niches) were filled with flowers, deities or candles, to make the jewels sparkle.

The **Diwan-i-Khas** (Private Meeting Hall) is on the ground floor, the boldly

Reservoir at Jaigarh Fort.

scalloped arches giving shade to a deep veranda leading to rooms decorated with delicate murals. Above, the gossamer-fine *jali*-work of the alabaster windows in **Jas Mandir** (Hall of Glory) are at ground level so reclining royals could enjoy the superb views. But the jewel is the **Shish Mahal** (Hall of Mirrors), whose interior is encrusted with tiny mirrors. By candle light, with the doors closed, it is like being inside a vast twinkling diamond.

Behind the garden court lie Man Singh's apartments, the oldest parts of the palace. In the *zenana*, Man Singh's dozen wives each had a separate suite. Murals of Krishna and Radha still decorate some of them.

Back in the courtyard, the path through an archway leads down to old **Amber village**. Of the several Hindu and Jain temples, the most interesting was built by Bihar Mal and dedicated to Sri Jagat Saromanji, with stone elephants to guard its marble gateway. The Amber rulers' *chatris* stand nearby. On the banks of Maota Lake the beautifully restored

Dilaram Gardens are almost encircled by water. A small **Archaeological Museum** is housed among their buildings. Indo-Greek coins, fragments of Ashoka pillars and decorated pottery from Bairat are among its exhibits.

Kachchwaha treasury: Hovering above Amber like a watchful eagle is **Jaigarh Fort**, built by Jai Singh II in 1726. Romantic legend fills its palatial rooms, courtyards and reservoirs. For Jaigarh housed the legendary Kachchwaha treasury. The loyal Mina people, former rulers of Amber, guarded it, using their skills as archers and mountain fighters to protect it. The massive **Jaiwaan cannon**, one of the largest in Asia which had a range of around 20 km (13 miles), gave added protection. It was said that the Minas would take each Kachchwaha chief, blindfolded, into the treasury just once, where he could choose one item from all that booty from Mughal warring. The legend lived on, and in 1976 the taxmen spent 6 months and some £75,000 digging for it. They found nothing. Some say Jai Singh II used treasure

Left, gaily painted elephants take visitors to the Amber Palace.
Right, the Ganesh Pol, built circa 1640, Amber Palace.

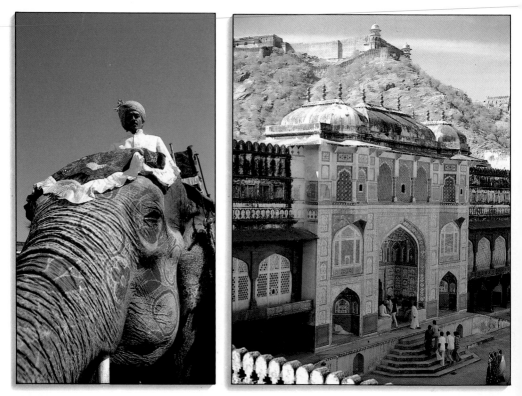

amassed by Man Singh I to build his model city. Others say it is still there.

Beyond Amber, a pretty road leads to the ancient city of **Bairat** (53 miles/85 km from Jaipur), or **Viratnagar**. It is an archaeologist's delight. Two rock edicts of the ruler Ashoka (272 BC–232 BC), hoards of Greek and Indo-Greek coins, remains of a large Buddhist monastery and *chaitya* (temple) – together with the Chinese pilgrim, Hieun Tsang's travelogue – all point to Bairat being a major Buddhist centre in the 3rd century BC. In Hindu legend, Bairat is believed to be Biratpuri, where the Pandavas, heroes of the epic *Mahabharata*, spent their 13th year of exile. So the Minas celebrate these heroes with song and dance here at the annual Benganga Fair. Beyond Bairat is Sariska Wildlife Sanctuary.

Another delightful trip north from Jaipur is to **Samode** (40 km/25 miles). The narrow lanes lead up through massive gateways to a delightful palace built by Jai Singh II's finance minister. The grand staircase leads to rooms elaborately decorated with murals set between panels of fine mirror work. Downstairs, the magnificent durbar hall has delicate paintings and quantities of gilding. Samode is yet another palace-turned-hotel, run by the minister's descendants, and has been beautifully preserved. It is easy to visit and makes a good stop en route to touring Shekhavati.

Heading east from Jaipur, out of Surajpol, a branch to the left reaches **Ramgarh** (25 km/15 miles), a Kachchwaha hilltop stronghold which now overlooks Jaipur's main water supply: a large lake good for boating and picnics. Back on the main road, the temple-filled gorge of **Galta** (10 km/6 miles) plunges down from the Aravalli hills. The **temple of the Sun God** on its summit (yet more stunning views) can also be reached via a short hike from Jaipur. Waters from the Gomukh, believed to have curative properties, flow from the mouth of a stone cow to fill the seven tanks set amid pavilions.

For some more picturesque treats, leave Jaipur by Ghat Gate. First comes **Vidhyadharji ka Bagh** (8 km/5 miles),

Samode Palace with older fort above.

a garden named after Vidyadhar Bhattacharaya, Jai Singh's architect. Next is the **Sisodia Rani ka Bagh** (8 km/ 5 miles) built by Jai Singh II for his Udaipur queen, his second wife, whom he took to cement the revived Rajput alliance. The glorious murals of the domed palace show hunting scenes, strolling lovers, polo playing and moments from the life of Krishna. Peacocks strut in the fine terraced garden with fountains and statues surrounding it. At about 4pm every day, crowds of langurs come to the hillside temple dedicated to *Hanuman*, the monkey god, where the priest feeds them sweetmeats. The crowds are even bigger on the god's special day, Tuesday. Galta's **Sun Temple** is found on the hilltop.

Beyond, en route to Agra, **Daosa** (50 km/30 miles) was the first Kachchwaha capital in the area known as Dhundhu. And to the south lies **Lalsot** (a further 40 km/25 miles), where the Jaipur and Jodhpur forces defeated the Marathas under General de Boigne in 1787 in the Battle of Tonk.

From here, the road leads to the remarkable **Ranthambore fort** (*see page 259*) and game reserve. And one final good trip out of Jaipur, this time southwards, leads here too.

Prints and paper: Leaving by Ajmeri Gate, the road towards Jaipur airport leads to **Sanganer** (16 km/10 miles). Within the majestic **Dausa Gate**, amid the camel-filled alleys, lie an **old palace**, a **Krishna temple**, some statue-packed **Jain temples**, and the homes of several thousand craftsmen whose ancestors made Sanganer the "metropolis of calico printing". The delicate flower, bird, tree and animal prints for the gathered Rajasthani skirts could easily be made fast because the waters of the Aman-i-Shah helped to fix them. Even if chemicals have replaced both the local waters and the vegetable dyes, the work is fascinating to watch. Each craftman practises one particular art. The designer separates the colours, a second man cuts the woodblocks, and a third, a *chippa*, prints each colour down the whole length of his fabric. Finally,

Jian temple, Sanganer.

after fixing, some fabrics are given *kari-printing* – embossed printing with gold or silver. With modern techniques, their turnover is now about 20 times faster.

The spin-off from printing is paper-making, using the offcuts of cotton or silk to make bright pink or yellow sheets, some polished silky smooth and speckled with gold and silver. Whereas little rivulets of colour are the clue to finding some fabric printing activity, sheets of paper pegged out on a washing line leads to a paper-maker. The other main craft of Sanganer is Jaipur blue pottery. Traditional designs are distinctive for their special inky cobalt-blue glaze which serves as a background for rich floral arabesques painted in white and copper oxide green.

Bagru (35 km/20 miles from Jaipur), just west of Sanganer, is also famed for its block-printing, especially large, floral, circular designs printed in deep rich colours using traditional vegetable dyes. South from Sanganer lies **Chaksu** (27 miles/43 km from Jaipur), where Vikramaditya, legendary king and

founder of the Samvat era (57 BC), is said to have lived, surrounded by a wall of copper. The annual March fair honours Sitala Mata, goddess of fever, especially smallpox – traditionally, if a Hindu died of smallpox, they were not cremated for fear of injuring the goddess who possessed them.

Tonk (96 km/60 miles from Jaipur) was once ruled by the Buner tribe of Pathans from Afghanistan. The old walled town, supposedly built in 1643 by a Brahman called Bhola, is picturesquely perched on the slopes of a small range of hills. To the south, the grand new town is enriched with the mansions and painted mosques of the Muslim nawab descendants of the Pathans. **Sunehri Kothi** (Golden Mansion) is an especially fine one, its exterior simplicity contrasting sharply with interior splendour: polished floors, stained glass, mirrors, stucco and gilt. In addition, as a former British headquarters, there are fine colonial buildings. From here roads run down to Bundi and Kota or across to Sawai Madhopur.

Sunehri Kothi or Golden Mansion, Tonk.

ALWAR: A TREASURE OF SURPRISES

A visit to Alwar is a re-entry into historical chapters of great antiquity, a return to a time when warfare was a way of life and peace a brief interlude to gild the state with splendour. A fort, a palace, a lake, a temple, and a garden were the five attributes of great Rajput princes: a dictum Alwar's rulers took seriously, judging by the amount of creative activity they sponsored.

A short journey south from Delhi (160 km/100 miles) or from Jaipur (148 km/90 miles) brings you to Alwar, shielded from the desert by the Aravalli range. What Kipling called the "tumbled fragments" of these hills reach up here into peaks loftier than anywhere else in Rajasthan. Chiseled from crystalline rock, they are covered with tropical dry, deciduous forests which are transformed almost overnight by the monsoon rains. Alwar's landscape of undulating hills and deep valleys, populated by plentiful wildlife and interspersed frequently with lush oases, perennial streams, and hot and cold springs – so unusual in Rajasthan – cradled many civilizations. From Matsya to Machari to Mewat, successive stages of its history moved until it settled finally in Alwar city.

Around 1500 BC most of Alwar was included in the territory of the Matsyas known as Viratnagar. Their form of government known as the Matsya *maha janapada* is Rajasthan's oldest recorded kingdom. The Pandavas, heroes of the great Indian epic, the *Mahabharata*, are said to have spent the last year of their exile in disguise at the court of King Virata. It was here that their Kaurava cousins arrived to steal cattle, initiating, when all efforts at mediation failed, the epic war in which the Matsyas sided with the Pandavas. The fast-expanding Mauryan Empire, however, seems to have eclipsed the Matsya state by the 3rd century BC.

Shortly after the 7th century AD, it was incorporated, along with Dausa, into the large kingdom of Machari, south of Alwar, and ruled by the Bargujar Rajputs. Hiuen Tsang, the Chinese traveller, makes brief mention of this area as being under a powerful king in the 7th century. Inscriptions of Machari kings are found up to the 14th century, when it was swallowed up by Amber.

History's mainstream meanwhile shifted north and the crucial interplay of events to Mewat, bordering Delhi, then including both Tijara and Alwar city. Mewat was governed by the famous Khanzadas, fiercely independent Muslim aristocrats. Hasan Khan Mewati, their most important ruler, preferred an alliance with the Rajputs to siding with his Muslim brethren at Delhi and rejected Babur's many overtures. Amongst his people were the Meos, also known as the "bandit Mewatees" whose raids so terrorized the people of Delhi that sultans and Mughal emperors had to resort to punitive raids against them. In this turbulent situation, with Delhi under constant threat, Alwar city, holding as Major Thorn wrote, the keys to the southern gates of Delhi and the plains of northern and central India beyond, assumed great strategic significance. The Mughals conquered it with great difficulty and were fiercely challenged by the Kachchwahas of Amber and the Jats of Bharatpur, with the British and the Marathas also joining the fray.

From the disorganisation and incessant warfare of the 18th century emerged a leader called **Pratap Singh**. By shrewd realpolitik, this remarkable *thakur* (noble) established an independent state by throwing off Jaipur's suzerainty over the south, ejecting the Jats from Alwar, repudiating the Marathas and having his gains ratified by the Mughal emperor. From three small villages of Machari, he expanded his dominions to include almost all of Alwar state. He founded the Naurka dynasty which gave Alwar esthetes and epicurians for kings for almost two centuries.

Pratap Singh's successors consolidated their rule by lending assistance to the British Empire at the historic Battle of Laswari (1803) against the Marathas, and were rewarded with the title of Maharaja and substantial territory. British feelings of gratitude were soon

Preceding pages: village fair. Left, Kankwari Fort, Sariska.

replaced, however, with increasing interference in Alwar's internal affairs in the 19th century, culminating in the appointment of a British Resident. As the momentum of the Indian freedom struggle grew, its reverberations could be discerned in Alwar's middle class and rural peasant movement of the 20th century spearheaded by the Alwar Rajya Prajamandal. After independence, a short-lived limited monarchy was made in a union of the princely states of Alwar, Bharatpur, Dholpur, and Karauli. But eventually this United State of Matsya, headquartered at Alwar, merged with the new state of Rajasthan in May 1949.

With a population of 211,000, Alwar is now the headquarters of one of the premier industrial districts of Rajasthan and a part of the national capital grid, seeking to divert towards itself overcrowded Delhi's prospective immigrants. It offers wildlife, ancient temples and sculptures, medieval forts, exquisite palaces and cenotaphs, and tanks, dams and gardens galore, set in a mosaic of folklore. Amongst its people are the Meos, a unique instance of Hindu-Muslim cultural synthesis. Notwithstanding their dress – notice their women in colourful *shalwar kamiz*, different from the full skirts Rajasthani women normally wear – and the Muslim religion they profess, they share their Hindu neighbours' rituals, customs, festivals, gods, saints, and superstitions. Alwar also has several rare, but unfortunately disappearing, traditions of music and dance, quite distinct from the more public traditional entertainments of western Rajasthan.

Alwar City: On a steep cliff, presiding over the city of Alwar, stands **Bala Qila** (fort). As a police radio station is located here, prior permission to visit the fort must be obtained from the district authorities. The steep, bumpy drive (negotiable only by 4-wheel-drive vehicles) is compensated by the spectacular view it offers of the city 300 metres (1,000 feet) below. The fort, whose ramparts flank a cliff for 5 km (3 miles), was originally constructed by the city's oldest inhabitants, the Nikumbha Rajputs.

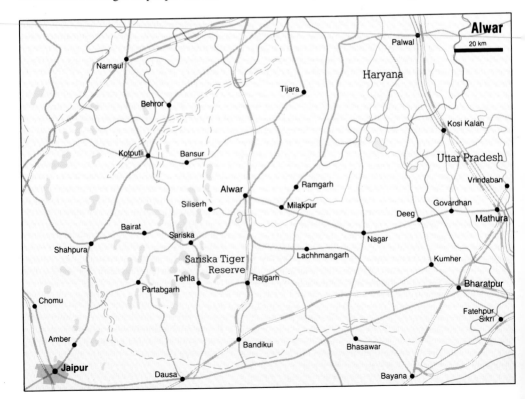

Their old town, known as **Ravana Devra**, lies in ruins at the foot of the hill amidst a bustling village.

Bala Qila was occupied successively by Khanzadas, Mughals, Pathans and Jats. In 1775, Pratap Singh ousted the Jats from the fort. His successor, **Bakhtawar Singh**, extended the existing structure of the palace, and added some fine gold leaf painting on the ceiling. Being quintessentially Hindu in style, the fort is one of the few examples in Rajasthan of pre-Muslim fortification. According to old manuscripts on Alwar, Babur spent a night here after crushing the Khanzada-Rajput alliance at the decisive battle of Fatehpur Sikri, and handed over its treasure to his son Humayun.

Below the fort, in the heart of the old city, is the magnificent **City Palace**. Five massive gates were once closed and caged tigers let loose at night to keep intruders at bay. Today Alwar's district government inhabits the rooms of the former armoury, library and treasury. In the grand courtyards where women once danced to entertain the maharaja and his courtiers, crowds now seek succour in the offices and courts of the district administration. The palace is particularly noted for its darbar room (access to it now requires the permission of the former maharaja, resident at Delhi's Alwar House) decorated with a frieze of miniature paintings and an upper chamber of mirrors set in gilt. Previously used on state occasions, a contemporary British art critic once wrote that "a durbar at Ulwur recalls the dreams of magnificence which the European is accustomed to indulge in with regard to the East".

Wealthy and exploitative, Alwar's rulers owned many legendary objects such as a solid silver dining table, a cup carved from a solitary emerald, a golden limousine, inside and out. Some of these objects are still in the possession of the erstwhile royal family, others are displayed at the **Museum**, located in the upper story of the palace (closed on Fridays). The Alwar court, renowned for its patronage of the arts and scholarship, attracted famous writers, painters

Alwar Palace complex.

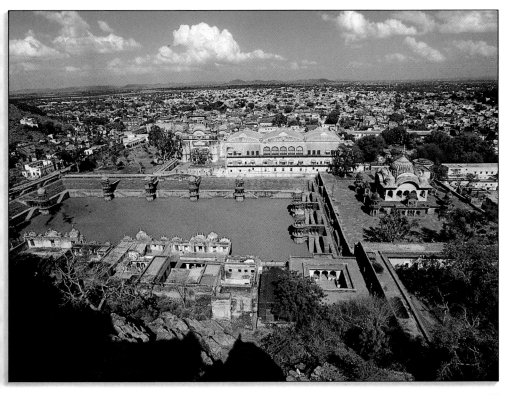

and artists. A copy of the *Mahabharata* minutely written on a single page, 80 metres/87 yards long; an illuminated *Koran,* and an exclusive copy of the Persian *Gulistan*, lovingly created over 10 years, are the gems of a choice collection of manuscripts in Sanskrit, Arabic, Persian and Urdu.

The armoury section has weapons dating back to the days of Hazrat Ali, the Prophet Muhammad's son-in-law and as renowned as the swords and armour of Muhammad Ghori, Akbar and Aurangzeb. The daggers, swords, shields and sabres are often richly ornamented and encrusted with jewels.

Objects in jade, ivory and sandalwood are delicately filigreed, inlaid and enamelled and a silver table with a trick impression of coloured fishes floating in channels of water across it are other highlights of its collection. The museum is most reputed, however, for its miniature paintings, particularly a rare folder of the Bundi school. The juxtaposition of the Mughal and Rajput schools shows their respective treatment of the *ragamala* (garland of music) series – the moods evoked by a particular musical "mode" or *raga.*

While at the museum, remember to look out of the windows, for another "miniature" – the spectacular view of a huge tank below, lined by a chain of temples on one side and dominated by a marvellous cenotaph, all cradled in the lap of high hills crowned by the ramparts of the fort. The impressive **Musi Maharani Chatri** (cenotaph) is popularly identified and named after Bakhtawar Singh's mistress who performed *sati* here. Her footprints, it is said, are embedded in the ground and water washed from them is considered to have medicinal value for children. Like the palace, it is in an Indo-Islamic style. Mythological and court themes in fading gold-leaf painting and sculpture adorn the ceiling. This memorial is regarded as one of the finest of its kind. The tank or *sagar* is a concrete catchment with a symmetrical pattern of stairs and tiny kiosks along the sides.

The environs: On a diversion 10 km (6 miles) away, on the road to Behror, is

Vijay Mandir Palace, the later royal residence, part of which is still inhabited by the royal family. Owned by the former maharaja, entrance is subject to his permission (contact the secretary). But even if it cannot be seen from inside, the drive to the palace and back is highly recommended, particularly if, on return, the circuitous route (previously meant for the exclusive use of the women of the royal family going to and from the *zenana* – women's quarters – of the City Palace) leading behind the fort is taken. It is from the vantage point of this drive that the charming character of the palace, modelled like a ship at anchor, is evident.

Jai Singh (1892–1937), the builder of this palace, was Alwar's most controversial ruler. Talented in many ways and popular, he is nevertheless the subject of many a wild tale. He gave, it is whispered, orders to pickle his dead guru, used babies as tiger bait, sprang a tiger trophy with a hidden mechanism on an unsuspecting viceroy, and was known for his extravagant and eccentric ways. With a penchant for palaces, he also built the Itarana and Sariska Palaces, constructed a club, dams, gardens and roads to the city. Near the exit to the Jaipur road still stands the interesting **Moti Dungri fortress**. Landsdowne, a palace, once graced the flat hill which the fortress still girdles. It was inexplicably dynamited out of existence by Jai Singh, some say in search of hidden treasure, others because he wanted to build a better and bigger palace in its place. A short drive to the top of the Moti Dungri is worthwhile for a circular view of the city.

If *Alpur* or *Arbalpur*, meaning fort on the hills of the Aravalli, is the original derivative of the word Alwar, it should certainly be used in the plural since its rulers built many forts in the region. Of these, the fort of **Rajgarh** 36 km (22 miles) southwards is historically and architecturally the most significant. An hour's drive brings one to this old capital of Alwar, a town of old *havelis* (mansions), citrus fruit gardens and a lake over presided over by the fort known for its secret passages (now unidentifiable) and frescoes. It was built by

Alwar's almost legendary founder-king, Pratap Singh, on the site of an old fort belonging to the Gujar-Pratiharas. The latter ruled around the 3rd century AD from Rajorgarh nearby, which Tod describes as "a city of great antiquity".

More city sights: Back to Alwar city once again, drive briefly past the **old Railway Station**, adjacent to the new one, and the **Fateh Jang Gumbad** (both have examples of local stone tracery) and into the **Vinay Vilas Palace**. This resplendent residence, in a composite style, was once characterised as the Garden Palace because of its long driveways, ornamental shrubs and profusion of flowers, vegetables and fruits including – unheard of in Rajasthan – peaches and strawberries.

This garden and Jai Singh's **Company Bagh** with a rare greenhouse known as **Simla** (named after the summer retreat of the viceroys because of the welcome relief it provided from the terrible heat) were watered by the Silliserh water reservoir 13 km (8 miles) away, via a long aqueduct. This solid stone masonry structure, which transformed the barren soil of the city, is still visible along the road to Silliserh. The disuse of this traditional facility has spelt death to many a garden in the city.

In and around Sariska: On the road to Jaipur (135 km/90 miles to the west of Alwar) is Silliserh's enchanting waterpalace. Built as a retreat by Vinay Singh, Alwar's third ruler, it is one of the most popular and picturesque spots near Alwar. A delightful evening can be spent here, sitting upstairs on the terrace of Rajasthan Tourism's Lake Castle Hotel (the restaurant is open to non-residents) to watch the tranquil waters of the lake, or paddle-boating on it. From the lake, you can also view the palace tucked away amidst the dark, green hills.

The strength of myth and the unwritten word is very powerful in India. Twenty-one centuries after King Bhartrihari wandered about in exile in these parts in penance for his suspicions against Vikramaditya (his younger brother, and the famous king of Malwa), he is still greatly revered. A little away

The sagar or tank – perfect symmetry of steps and kiosks.

from the Alwar-Jaipur road the **Bhartrihari temple** is dedicated to him. Both a fair and an epic music drama lasting 6 hours are massively attended in Alwar in the months of September and October.

Travelling further along the same road, a diversion of 10 km (6 miles), leads to **Talbraksha** past the **fortress of Kushalgarh**. In a clearing above a dense palm grove are several old temples of indefinite history. To the sound of temple bells, numerous pilgrims take a dip in the hot and cold springs. A famous icon of the blue Krishna, appropriately in sapphire, was once stolen from here but has since been recovered and may now be reinstalled. The huge ancient earthenware urn which stands here was discovered in a field and was found to be filled with gold coins. It is believed to be from the Mauryan era.

Around **Sariska** (within 42 km/26 miles of the wildlife sanctuary's gate) there are many delightful spots to visit for both wildlife and those in search of art and archaeology. A couple of days are required to visit them and it is advisable to make Sariska your base.

The **Sariska Palace**, the old watch-towers of Bandipul, small dams and bridges are survivors from the times when Sariska was the private game reserve of the rulers. The palace itself was previously a hunting lodge, now a hotel, originally built in honour of the Duke of Connaught, Queen Victoria's son, at the end of the 19th century.

The typical Sariska tour goes to **Pandupol**, only 24 km (15 miles) away, but involves a long drive punctuated with numerous stops to watch animals in their natural habitat. A tiered stream with a delicate trickle and deep waterholes can be seen on the drive up the hills on either side. The Pandava brothers found the dense forests of this area a good place to hide from their enemies in the 13th year of their exile. At Pandupol, the story goes, Bhima, the strongest of the five brothers, smote the rock face of a cliff with his mace to clear their passage. A little below Pandupol is the old temple called **Budha** (old)

The City Palace now houses an impressive museum.

Hanuman. The newer one further down, however, is more popular and is known for its unusual reclining image. In September devotees crawl, fully stretched out on the ground, all the way from Alwar to attend a crowded fair here.

On the outskirts of the sanctuary (45 km/28 miles), nestling in a green valley towered by hills and facing the plains, are the rarely visited, but breathtaking ruins of **Bhangarh**. Madho Singh, younger brother of Amber's Man Singh (Akbar's famous general), enthralled by its natural beauty, established an extensive city here of some 10,000 identifiable dwellings in 1631. Even in ruin, the attempt at town planning structured in accordance with caste hierarchy is discernible. At the apex, along the hillside, is the former residence of the king. At its base, the mansions (now remnants) and rooms around the verandas of the temple were probably meant for the clergy and aristocracy. Along the main road, for half a kilometre, are symmetrical rooms on either side indicating a remarkable market-place of a prosperous urban

The Sariska Palace is now a hotel.

centre. Gates flanking it at both ends suggest the limits within which the trading and commercial classes were normally restricted. Beyond this, on the periphery, most likely, were the houses of the lower castes.

Specially worth attention are Bhangarh's two **temples**. One of them beside which a perennial spring trickles into a concrete tank, has a particularly beautiful setting. Both temples are ornately carved in stone and marble with floral friezes decorating walls, ceilings and pillars. Images of ancillary gods, of the main deity, Shiva, in a Rajasthani variant astride a camel or peacock, and of typical entrance guardians, river goddesses and musicians grace the shrine. In fact, the contrast between Bhangarh's religious and secular architecture is quite startling. While the latter now consists mainly of crumbling stones, the former is still well-preserved. This and the strong similarity in both architecture and sculpture to the temples excavated at Neelkanth, suggest that Bhangarh's temples are much older than the early

17th century, the period to which they have been previously attributed.

Famine, war, pestilence, a slow decline, or perhaps a queen's curse, led its population to abandon Bhangarh suddenly and it remains hauntingly desolate even today, except for the ubiquitous peacocks and rare visitors. Internecine quarrels had, however, already caused the shifting of the capital of this large kingdom to **Ajabgarh**, founded by Ajab Singh, Madho Singh's grandson. In this picturesque valley 32 km (20 miles) from Bhangarh, once regarded as the richest tract in the state, old temples are still to be seen.

Another immensely rewarding excursion, off the regular tourist track, is to **Kankwari** and **Neelkanth** 35 km (21 miles) in the interior of Sariska. Kankwari (20 km/12 miles) is a very picturesque fortress overlooking a lake, surrounded by forest-covered hills on all sides. Legend has it that Dara Shikoh, heir to the Mughal throne after Shah Jahan, was held captive here by his brother, Aurangzeb.

Imprisonment in this remote spot is credible but it is indeed a wonder how a large fortified temple town like Neelkanth thrived 10 centuries ago, surrounded as it was by a thick forest, populated by dangerous animals, access through which is difficult even today. Neelkanth is home to as many as 80 temples, dating from the 6th to 11th centuries AD. Unfortunately, only some of them have been excavated and in spite of substantial theft, the sculpture lies neglected at the site. They testify to a variety of religious cults and influences, Hindu, Buddhist and Jain. A colossal statute of the 23rd Jain Tirthankara, Parshvanath, an image of the traditionally unmarried god Ganesh with a woman on his knee, and of Vishnu reclining are all important works. The image of Vishnu in his Varaha (boar) incarnation is a theme repeated at Bhangarh and in a black marble statue excavated from Talbraksh which seem strongly to indicate the geographical spread of this Bargujar-Rajput state.

En route to Jaipur (66 km/40 miles) is **Viratnagar (Bairat)**, one of the earliest inhabited sites in Rajasthan. Some 13 km (8 miles) away is **Dhigariya** where caves, rock shelters and stone tools of the paleolithic age have been excavated. Nearer the village, which still reverberates with legends of the Pandavas' stay here, are five huge rocks (representing the five brothers) and atop them are temples dedicated to Bhima and Hanuman – the only instance in India of the monkey god depicted in a human form – thus venerating the heroes of both the epics, the *Mahabharata* and the *Ramayana*. In the third and upper-most layer of history at Bairath are stone inscriptions of the great Mauryan emperor, Ashoka, and a **Buddhist temple** with multiple pillars dating back to the 3rd century BC.

Neemrana: Approximately 10 km (6 miles) south of the state border with Haryana, and some 3 km (2 miles) to the west of the main Delhi to Jaipur road (NH8), the Neemrana fortress occupies a dominant position on a rock overlooking a small village. It has been converted into a stylish hotel.

The Silliserh Palace overlooking a 19th-century reservoir.

SARISKA TIGER RESERVE

On the main highway to Jaipur 34 km (21 miles) south of Alwar, lies the Sariska Tiger Reserve and National Park. Sariska is one of the few remaining pockets of forest in the Aravalli range of hills and the area now consisting of 800 sq. km (308 sq. miles) is the core area. The reserve has been under Project Tiger since 1979 and before that, since 1955, a smaller sanctuary. But earlier still it was a hunting area for the Maharajas of Alwar and was strictly protected.

The forest is mainly hilly with two extensive plateaus, Kankwari and Kiraska, and a wide valley starting at the Baran Tal Gate and running south to Thana Gazi. At the northeastern corner, just off the road between Alwar and Sariska, is the Silliserh Lake. Although there are few large mammals to be seen near the lake, crocodiles are often spotted and, during the winter, there are many migrant water birds.

In spring, the surrounding hillsides are filled with colour as the "flame of the forest"

A male Nilgai or Bluebull.

and other flowering trees bloom. In the summer the park is parched and brown but with the arrival of monsoon becomes lush and green. In the few more moist areas, bamboo is found and, along the banks of streams, jamun and arjan.

Among the undulating hills and wide valleys of Sariska is a rare combination of natural history and archaeology. The ruined temples found in Neelkanth (32 km/20 miles from Sariska) are from the 6th to 10th centuries. The medieval fort of Kankwari was used throughout the Mughal period.

At Sariska, opposite the Baran Tal Gate of the reserve, is a large palace built in 1902 by Maharaj Jai Singh of Alwar as a base for his elaborate shoots. The palace has now been converted into a hotel.

Sariska has a good network of metalled roads. From these main arteries, forest tracks lead into side valleys.

With a low average rainfall of 650 mm (25 inches), water becomes a major limiting factor for the animals. The forest department has provided many artificial water holes along the main roads which attract the animals and make wildlife observation from vehicles in the morning or evening comparatively easy. Because of the scarcity of water, viewing from hides overlooking waterholes at Salopka and Kalighati offers numerous opportunities to watch, photograph and study many of the species, especially during the late afternoon in the summer months of April, May and June.

The dry, open deciduous and thorn forests support increasing populations of ungulates including **sambar**, **nilgai**, **chinkara**, **chausingha** and **chital**. As well as tigers, the predators include **leopard**, **hyena**, **jungle cat** and **jackal**. Also found are **porcupine**, **wild boar** and, occasionally, **ratel**. With the exception of the jungle cat, the carnivores are nocturnal and rarely spotted since there is no nighttime access to the reserve, although daytime tiger sightings are becoming more frequent. Sariska has large populations of **rhesus macaque** and **langur** monkeys.

The range of habitat also supports a rich variety of birds including **shrike**, **parakeet**, **gray partridge**, **golden backed woodpecker**, **peafowl**, **owls** and the **crested serpent eagle**. **Babblers**, **tree pies** and **bulbuls** are often seen from hides and around the forest department buildings. ∎

AJMER AND PUSHKAR

Ajmer is located 130 km (80 miles) west of Jaipur, in a picturesque valley surrounded by the hills of the Aravalli range, and has a population of 401,000. Of strategic importance in erstwhile Rajputana, it is today an important centre of pilgrimage for the Muslims of South Asia, due to its association with the great Sufi saint Muin-ud-din Chishti.

Ajmer was established in the early 7th century by Ajaipal Chauhan. He named the place *Ajaimeru*, the invincible hill, because he built India's first hill fort, **Taragarh**, here. Ajmer was a Chauhan stronghold till 1194. The only remains of their times are the fort and the beautiful **Anasagar Lake**, built in 1150 by Anaji. The legendary Prithviraj, last of the Chauhans, is the inspiration for many heroic ballads sung even today in the villages of Rajasthan.

It was during the reign of Prithviraj, in 1191, that Muhammad of Ghori invaded India. Prithviraj died fighting the sultan's army, and with the establishment of the Sultanate in Delhi, a new era began. Ajmer remained under the Sultanate till 1326. Thereafter, it became a bone of contention between the Sultans of Delhi, the Ranas of Mewar, the Rathors of Marwar and the Sultans of Gujarat. Peace was restored with the accession of Akbar to the Mughal throne in 1556. He made Ajmer a full-fledged province, and the base for his operations in Rajputana. He fortified the city, but only parts of the 3,735-metre (4,045-yd) long wall remain. His palace, the **Daulat Khana**, houses the **Government Museum**.

Mughal Center: Akbar's son, Jahangir, lived in Ajmer from 1613 to 1616. His palace, the Daulat Bagh, is now in ruins. The celebrated English ambassador to the Mughal court, Sir Thomas Roe, was received here by the emperor. During the course of his extended stay, Roe met Jahangir several times and showered him with gifts. But he failed to conclude a commercial treaty between England and the Mughal empire.

In 1659 a battle was fought in Ajmer between the Mughal princes, Aurangzeb and Dara Sukoh, during which Taragarh was greatly damaged. In the first half of the 18th century, Ajmer was affected by the political chaos in Delhi. In 1755, the situation became more complex with the involvement of the Marathas. Finally, in 1818, the Marathas ceded Ajmer to Sir David Ochterlony and, as part of the British empire, it remained under the care of successive superintendents. With the reorganization of the princely states in 1947, Ajmer became a part of Rajasthan.

Commercially, too, the city has been of importance, especially since the 13th century, as it was on the main trade route between Delhi and the ports of Gujarat (it is still on the Delhi–Ahmadabad highway) and taxes were levied on transit goods. The area is also rich in mica, lead and garnet. The 19th century was a very prosperous period, during which several royal families and wealthy *seths* (merchants) came to Ajmer. They built *havelis* to live in, some of which may still be seen off the narrow lanes in the old city.

Ajmer was also considered by the British as an appropriate place to establish a school for Indian princes. In 1874, Mayo College was opened with one pupil – the Maharaja of Alwar. He was attended by a retinue of servants and set out for school each day on an elephant and with considerable fanfare. In 1947 the school was opened to everyone, and is today one of the leading educational institutions in the country.

Islamic shrine: It is, however, as a religious centre that the importance and vitality of the city endures: the **Dargah Sharif**, where Khwaja Muin-ud-din Chishti lies buried, draws pilgrims from all parts of the Islamic world. The saint was born in Sanjar, Persia, in 1142. He became absorbed in spiritual matters at an early age. It is said that while in Mecca (Makkah), he had a prophetic vision directing him to go to Ajmer. He came to India around 1191 and settled in Ajmer, where he established the Chishtiya order, the foremost Sufi order in India. Through his message of love and his devotion to the poor he was able to spread the word of Islam more effectively than Ghori's army. He came to be known as Khwaja Gharib Nawaz, the protector of the poor, and even today beggars plead for alms in his name. Along with fakirs, they seek shelter at his shrine.

Chishti died in 1236 and his devotees now extend beyond Islam. The Dargah Sharif is considered a wish-fulfilling shrine. Akbar is known to have walked on two occasions from Agra to Ajmer in thanksgiving for boons granted. There is a steady flow of pilgrims to the Dargah throughout the year, but during the *Urs* (death anniversary ceremonies) of the saint, celebrated between the 1st and 6th of Rajab, the 7th month of the lunar calendar, lakhs of pilgrims from all parts of South Asia converge upon the shrine.

The **Dargah** and its surroundings have a vitality and character quite apart from colonial and modern Ajmer. The shrine is approached through **Madar Gate** and past the **Dargah Bazaar**. The bazaar is stocked with ritual offerings – dazzling coverlets for the grave, incense, sweet-meats, rose petals and *attar* (perfume). Ajmer is famous for its pink roses and it is here that *attar* of roses was discovered during the time of Jahangir.

The Dargah lies at the foot of the northeast spur of Taragarh hill and is separated from it by a 19th-century water reservoir. The simple brick tomb in which the saint was buried has since been embellished by the lavish gifts of wealthy devotees, and several mosques, pavilions and gateways now surround the mausoleum. To its north lies the **mehfilkhana**, built in 1888 by the Nizam of Hyderabad. It is the scene of all-night *qavvali* (devotional songs) performances during the *urs*. Adjacent to this is the **mosque** built by **Akbar**. **Shah Jahan's** elegant **mosque** in white marble is well preserved and lies west of the mausoleum, while to the east is the ornate **Begami Dalan**, the portico built by Princess Jahanara, the emperor's daughter.

The saint's grave is enclosed by a silver railing and lies in a domed

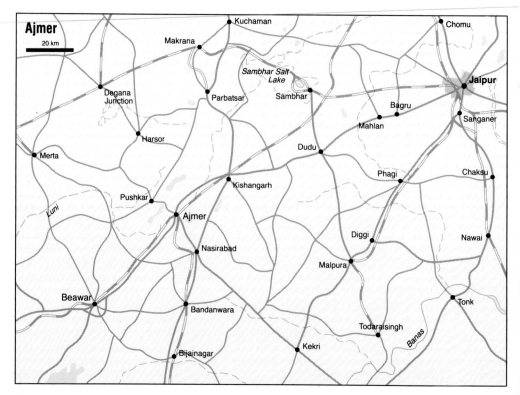

chamber, partially surrounded by a marble lattice screen. *Qavvals* sing in praise of the saint, fakirs plead for alms, while the *khadim* ("servants" of the saint) keep a lookout for pilgrims.

Of particular interest in the Dargah are two huge *deg* (cauldrons) originally presented by Akbar and Jahangir but replaced in the 19th century. The looting of the *deg* is a unique phenomenon which takes place when enough rice has been donated to fill them. (The large *deg* is over 3 metres/9 feet in diameter.) Once the rice is cooked and the names of the donors announced, professional looters empty it with lightning speed, even jumping into the boiling cauldron to scrape the dregs. The event is over in a few minutes and evokes great excitement. The rice is then sold as *tabarrukh* (sanctified food) by the looters.

West of the Dargah Sharif lies the immense **Adhai din ka Jhonpra** (the 2½-day hut). Originally a Sanskrit college built in 1155, it was restructured into a mosque by Sultan Ghori in 1198. It is one of the finest monuments of medieval India, especially noted for the beauty of its decorations and ornate calligraphic inscriptions. The pillars retain Hindu elements but the screen and arches were added in 1266. In the 18th century, fakirs used to assemble here for the *urs* of Panjaba Sahib, which lasted 2½ days, hence the name.

Hill Fort: Taragarh, the star fort, rises 250 metres (800 feet) above the valley. It is accessible by road via Nallah Bazaar and a bridle path from behind the Dargah. Between 1860 and 1920 it was used as a sanatorium by the British. It affords an interesting view of the Dargah and of the valley to the west. The saint's daughter, Bibi Hafiz Jamal, lived in this valley which is named after her. Jahangir built a hunting palace and tanks here, the ruins of which are also visible. Taragarh is important for a mosque and the **shrine of Miran Sayyid Hussain**, governor of the fort. He died in 1202, but sanctity was attached to him around 450 years later, when Akbar visited his grave.

Within the walled city, off Station Road is Akbar's red sandstone palace,

Late-18th century drawing of the *dargah*.

the **Daulat Khana** (Abode of Wealth). Built in 1570, it served the British as the Rajputana arsenal between 1818 and 1862, and was restored in 1905. The central audience hall is now the **Government Museum**. It is especially rich in arms, both Mughal and Rajput, sculptures from the 4th to the 12th centuries, and Bactrian and Kushan coins.

Glimpses of Ajmer's colonial past can be seen at the **Edward Memorial Hall** and **Golden Jubilee Clock Tower**, both on Station Road, as well as the **Ajmer Club** situated near the spacious **Kalka Bagh**.

At the junction of Station Road and Kutcheri Road is the ornate 19th-century **Nasiyan** (Red) **Jain Temple** (also known as the Soni Temple). Although the shrine is closed to non-Jain visitors, the remarkable museum next door has a huge, gold-plated representation of the Jain universe, which can be viewed from a series of different galleries.

A little over 2 km (1 mile) from the Tourist Bungalow, past **Subhash Bagh**, is the tranquil **Anasagar Lake**, situated between hillocks. It is almost 13 km (8 miles) in circumference and its beauty is enhanced by Shah Jahan's white marble embankment and pavilions. This pleasure resort of the emperor was used by the British for official purposes, and Tod and Bishop Herber stayed here. Some of the pavilions are well preserved and it has been restored.

Ajmer forms a convenient base for visits to nearby towns of interest. Foremost among these is **Pushkar** (pop. 11,500), the road to which skirts Anasagar Lake. Just 11 km (8 miles) northeast of Ajmer, Pushkar is a small town sacred to the Hindus and now a tourist attraction for its annual camel fair, the largest in the world. The sanctity of the lake for Hindus is equal to that of Mansarovar in Tibet and according to tradition, a bath in its waters is as purifying as pilgrimages to Badrinath, Dwarka, Ramesvaram and Puri, traditionally the four essential places of pilgrimage for devout Hindus.

The *Padma* (lotus) *Purana* describes Pushkar as the place where Brahma,

Muslim pilgrims at the *dargah*.

148

Lord of Creation, killed a demon with a lotus. The petals fell at three spots where lakes emerged. Pushkar is the most important of them, for Brahma performed a *yagna* (sacrifice) here on the full moon of Kartik (October/November). His consort, Savitri, could not be present on the occasion, so Brahma hastily married a Gurjar girl, Gayatri. When Savitri appeared she was furious. She cursed all those present, and said that Brahma would be worshiped at Pushkar only. Brahma countered this by assigning Gayatri the status of goddess, with powers to undo the curse. However, his temple here remains one of the very few dedicated to this deity in India. Savitri retreated to a hillock north of the lake, where a temple is dedicated to her. On a hillock opposite is another dedicated to Gayatri.

Epics, religious texts, coins and inscriptions bear evidence to the sanctity of Pushkar. Over the centuries it grew into a temple town, and today there are as many as 400 temples in Pushkar. The present town was renovated in the 9th century by a Parihar king of Mandor,

when he was cured of a skin ailment after a dip in the lake.

Pushkar is a maze of temples, *ashrams* (hermitages) and *dharamshalas* (rest houses) and one is never far from the sound of worship, from ascetics and devotees. The most important temples are dedicated to Brahma, Shiva, Badri Narayan, Varaha, Savitri and Gayatri. The *dharamshalas* are for specific castes, Adivasi peoples and sects.

The lake is bounded by 52 ghats, built over the centuries by kings and nobles. (Photography is prohibited on the ghats.) Of these, **Varah**, **Brahma** and **Gau Ghats** are the most revered. Varah Ghat is specially sacred as Lord Vishnu is believed to have appeared here in the form of a boar. A dip in the lake by a woman absolves both her and her husband of their sins. For a complete cleansing of sins, three twilights must be passed at Pushkar with baths at the three important ghats. As a sacred town, the consumption of alcohol and meat is strictly forbidden.

The Pushkar Fair: Throughout the year, life is centred on the lake and temples, and Pushkar has the atmosphere of an ancient religious town, peaceful and secluded. But for 12 days in the month of Kartik it is transformed into a spectacular fairground that spreads over the dunes west of the town. The *mela* is an event of religious and commercial importance. Thousands of men come first, with their camels and cattle, and camp on the dunes to transact business. Three days before the full moon, the women start coming, beautifully attired. The pilgrims bathe and worship, watch the entrtainments and shop at the hundreds of roadside stalls, while on the dunes camels are bought and sold, beautified, raced and paraded. The fair is overwhelming in its magnitude and in its visual impact.

Apart from the tranquil tourist bungalow on the shore of the lake, a miniature tent city is put up during the fair for the convenience of tourists.

Kishangarh, painters' haven: Kishangarh, a charming town well worth a visit, lies 30 km (19 miles) before Ajmer on the Jaipur road. It was founded in

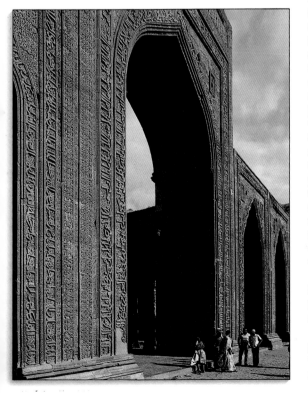

1611 by Kishan Singh, who was the brother of the Raja of Jodhpur. Politically unimportant as a princely state, it has won international renown for having nurtured one of the finest schools of miniature painting in 18th-century India.

Rajput princes had adopted the luxurious lifestyle of the Mughal court, of which miniature painting had become an integral part. By the mid-17th century, artists were already working in the ateliers of Kishangarh. A few decades later, Kishangarh also provided a haven to artists leaving Aurangzeb's court and among those who came were the renowned Bhavanidas, Surat Ram and Nihal Chand.

The greatest patron of Kishangarh art was Raja Satwant Singh. He was himself a painter and poet and wrote verses under the pseudonym of Nagaridas. He fell in love with a court singer, Bani Thani, who subsequently became his mistress. It is said that the famous Kishangarh Radha is made in her likeness, but in fact the lotus-eyed woman had long been an Rajput ideal of feminine beauty. In 1757, Satwant Singh abdicated and left with Bani Thani for Vrindavan. The artists concentrated on the *Krishna lila* theme, but they portrayed Krishna in a courtly instead of a pastoral setting. The paintings belonged to the Rajas of Kishangarh and were first seen by the outside world in the 1940s. Some of these exquisite masterpieces are now on view at the National Museum, New Delhi.

The old city of Kishangarh still has the flavour of the magic world created by the artists. Modern Kishangarh is bustling and crowded, important as a wholesale market for red chillies and a cotton-weaving centre. But Kishan Singh's city is about 4 km (2½ miles) away. A road leads to the fort and buses and *tongas* ply the route regularly.

The **fort** and **palaces** overlook the lake in the centre of which is another palace, accessible by boat. The area is especially beautiful during the monsoon when the lotus blooms. And though the pleasure gardens are overgrown and the palaces unkempt, there are exact

Rose petals being dried, Ajmer.

locations which can be recognized in the miniatures. A walk through the cobbled streets is rewarding. The ambience is decidedly medieval, and in many *havelis* painters of miniatures are still at work. There is also an interesting little bazaar, where goldsmiths and silversmiths can be seen crafting traditional jewellery.

Marble quarries: Due north of Kishangarh and 63 km (40 miles) away via Parvatsar are the marble quarries of **Makrana**, famous for having supplied the white marble for the Taj Mahal and the palaces built by Shah Jahan. More than a century ago Tod wrote: "The quarrries, until of late, yielded a constant revenue but the age of palace building in these regions is no more and posterity will ask with surprise the sources of such luxury." However, marble is being increasingly used in contemporary architecture. Today, Makrana is the biggest centre for marble trade in India and the entire population of the city is associated with it.

The quarries, most of which have

been privately owned over several generations, vary in size and stretch over a distance of 20 km (12½ miles). The finest marble is pure white, followed by white-grained, pink, grey, and grey with blue streaks. Quarrying techniques are mostly traditional. Blocks of marble are often raised by hand-operated pulleys. The stone is dressed for sizing at the site and transported on bullock carts to factories where it is sliced, washed and polished. There are about 500 factories in Makrana which supply marble slabs to all parts of India. Marble is also sent to Agra for inlay work, often pre-shaped on lathes in Makrana itself. There are about 40 carving centers in Makrana as well, and craftsmen can be seen working on statues, containers and pedestals.

Some 32 km (20 miles) west of Makrana, salt is harvested from the **Sambhar Salt Lake**.

Roopangarh, a small, peaceful town about 25 km (15 miles) from Kishangarh, makes a good stopping-off point on the way to Ajmer or Pushkar. A hotel occupies the former fortress complex.

SHEKHAVATI'S PAINTED WALLS

Shekhavati lies in a triangle between Jaipur, Bikaner and Delhi. With the exception of the rocky Aravalli range that divides Shekhavati diagonally, the countryside is flat and almost monochromatic. Today, Shekhavati comprises the administrative districts of Sikar and Jhunjhunu, which are together one-fifth of the Jaipur Division.

Since the 15th century when Rao Shekha opposed the rule of the Amber kings, the region remained a semi-autonomous collection of *thikanas* (feudal states). In the middle of the 19th century, the inhabitants of Shekhavati began to patronize the art of fresco painting, compensating, in a way, for the lack of colour in the landscape of their homeland.

The Rajputs seem to have been the first patrons to have ordered a frescoed room in a fort or on a *chatri* (cenotaph) commemorating a hero. The Marwaris,

Preceding pages: village women escort a bride. Left, Gangaur Festival, Mandawa. Below, painted courtyard as seen through a gate.

the merchant community which prospered on the trade routes between Delhi and the coast and between Central Asia and China, later became even more extravagant patrons.

The roads of Shekhavati, now like any other, were once caravan routes "where the productions of India, Cashmire, and China, were interchanged for those of Europe, Africa, Persia and Arabia". Even though trade rivalry with the British had pushed the Marwaris from Shekhavati to the ports, they never ceased to think of Shekhavati as their own land. And this explains the enormous structures raised in nostalgia.

The merchants built for the community: wells and reservoirs, *dharamshalas* (pilgrims' resthouses), schools, *gaushalas* (shelters for cows), and temples. In memory of their ancestors they constructed cenotaphs, and for their families large *havelis* (mansions).

Framework for a way of life: The word *haveli*, which is of Persian origin, means "surrounded" or an "enclosed place". It has no exact equivalent in the English language. Perhaps "mansion" comes close enough, suggesting the spacious residence that *haveli* connotes, but it fails to capture the essence of a way of life that was more than just a form of architecture. In Mughal times it signified a residential block, usually three to five stories high, around an open courtyard. It accommodated several families who lived together as an economic, civic and social unit, sharing many common amenities. The density of occupation was balanced by the open court that would usually accommodate a common well for drinking water, space for washing and drying clothes, and a play area for children. Just as the joint family system was the smallest macro economic unit in the social structure of medieval India, a *haveli* was the smallest middle-class unit in the urban civic structure.

Havelis are generally town houses, as opposed to *kothis* or garden houses of the suburbs. The original function of a *haveli*, apart from providing a residence, was to wall in the domestic life of a family. Secluded from the outside world, a *haveli* set its own pace of life. All through royal and feudal India the *havelis*, whether inhabited by Hindus or Muslims, represented the rigid lifestyle of a society that segregated its men from its women, and its women from the outside world. The architecture of the *haveli* was conceived around this social norm. Unlike the Mughal *havelis*, the typical *haveli* in Shekhavati consisted of two courtyards, an outer and an inner. The grander ones sometimes had three or four courtyards.

Today, life in the *haveli* continues on much the same pattern, though there are fewer inhabitants. The outer courtyard serves as an extended threshold, since the main gate is seldom shut. The inner one is the domain of the women who are entirely occupied with household chores. In days gone by, their routine began before dawn with the worship of *tulsi* (holy basil), followed by the milking of the cows in the *nora* (pen), the churning of butter, cooking, and collecting and storing water in a special airy room called the *parinda*. When male guests entered the house, the women, who normally remained in *purdah* (literally, "behind the curtain"), retreated briskly into the *zenana*, their private apartments. And from their fretted *zenana* windows they peeped into the men's world.

The *havelis* are guarded at the entrance by large wooden doors reminiscent of medieval forts. Within these, a smaller door is normally used for daily movements. Intricate wooden carvings with fancy brass and iron fittings demonstrate the owner's wealth. The ground floor is normally recessed in such a way that balconies overhang the street. It was from the latticed windows on the balconies and over the courtyards that women were able to get a glimpse of the men's world. The facade, the gateways, the courtyard walls, the parapets and ceilings, were all covered with frescoes.

Wall paintings: The frescoes on the earliest *havelis* date back to the early 1800s (although some on the forts, *chatris* and temples are dated around 1750). The majority were painted **The Char Chowk Haveli, Lachh-mangarh.**

between 1860 and 1900. Starting from purely religious themes, the frescoes move on to ornamental designs, and after 1900 when these became widely available, to imitations of a number of European lithographs and etchings.

The technique of fresco painting in Shekhavati was very close to the Italian fresco (fresh) technique developed around the 14th century. Whether this technique travelled to India through the Mughals, who knew of it from Persia, or whether it was the missionaries to the Mughal court who first introduced this at Fatehpur Sikri, is not known for certain. But the local Shekhavati masons had definitely mastered it by 1800.

Driving through Shekhavati: By road or by train, Shekhavati can be approached with equal ease from Jaipur, Delhi or Bikaner. The region is entered from Jaipur, on the road that armies and caravans once took, on the Jaipur-Sikar road.

The first town passed coming from Jaipur is **Chomu**. A moat and a sturdy medieval wall with machicolations serve as reminders of the town's war-torn past. At the fort, a large iron lock still hangs from its entrance door. The Chomu fort is now a granary, its high walls and large covered spaces providing easy storage and shelter. From Chomu turn right to **Samode**. This detour into the small, sleepy village, is well worthwhile. The road winds through a narrow street, off which paintings, printed cloth and glass bangles are made, under several gates, up to a 19th-century palace, now a lovely hotel, with elaborate decorations and a famous *shish mahal*.

Sikar (42 km/26 miles from Jaipur), the next stop, was the largest *thikana* under the Jaipur State. It is now one of the two districts of Shekhavati, the other being Jhunjhunu. Drive through Sikar's large market to the **Clock Tower** and the older quarter where the painted **Biyani Havelis** will delight your eyes. There is one painted only in blue, reminiscent of Chinese blue-and-white porcelain.

The obsession with blue is understandable, once we know that synthetic blue began to be imported

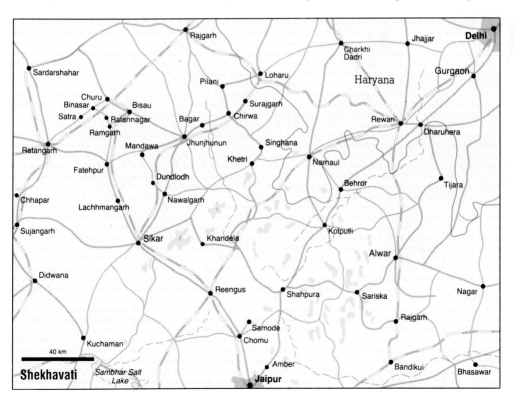

from Germany around 1870. For a wealthy patron, using only blue must have been a step ahead of the others. Then, as now, possession of imported goods was a status symbol.

Sikar has a **Jubilee Hall**, and a palace-turned-temple where women gather and chant prayers all day. The **Sikar fort**, though neglected, is not without charm. Its stone ramps with chevroned patterns lead you to private terraces, painted rooms and fretted windows. The later additions have wrought-iron fences that frame oval portraits of Queen Victoria, Empress of India.

Nawalgarh, a fascinating town founded by Nawal Singh in 1737, is north of Sikar. It has a college with a very British clock tower and hundreds of painted *havelis*, old and new. Many of the better known Rajasthani merchant families come from here. The *Thakurs* (nobles) of Nawalgarh also had a great passion for building. Many structures of the early 20th century still stand. Among them is **Roop Niwas** (with its drive around a fountain) where tourists can stay. Also worth seeing is the **Saat Haveli** complex.

Walking through Nawalgarh's streets, there is much to discover. Try and see the Shiva Temple with a multi-headed *lingam*; the frescoed telephone exchange; the tiled cenotaph near the railway station; the "Company School" paintings (those showing signs of the English influence of the East India Company, 1760–1880). If you can manage to secure the keys, see the painted dome in the fort on which an aerial view of Jaipur has been drawn in great detail. *Trompe l'oeil* frescoes are common in Nawalgarh. A colourful bazaar surrounds the old fort. In Jaipur, the Nawalgarh family has one of the best private art collections.

An excursion from Nawalgarh will take you to **Parasrampura** where some of the earliest frescoes (around 1750) are to be seen in the interior of a temple and inside the dome of the *chatri* of Shardul Singh (the 8th descendant of Rao Shekhaji, founder of Shekhavati) who expanded his territories by ousting

Noblemen chase wild boar.

the Kayamkhani *nawabs* from Jhunjhunu (1730) and Fatehpur (1731), putting an end to three centuries of almost unbroken Muslim supremacy over large areas of Shekhavati.

From Nawalgarh, the more adventurous can tour the Aravalli region where they will be rewarded by visiting towns like **Chirana**, with an elegant fort and grand *havelis* against a rocky backdrop; **Lohargal**, where the mace of Bhima – a hero of the Mahabharata – is said to have been cast, giving the town its name (*lohargal* literally means "iron smelting"); **Raghunathgarh**; and **Udaipurvati** – historically one of the most important towns, as the Confederation of the Shekhavats used to meet here to decide on joint action in times of danger.

Close by is the small and delightful town of **Dundlod**. Here an enlightened *thakur* has modernized his rugged fort (dated around 1765), where tourists can now stay. It now houses a well-stocked library with European-style portraits and chandeliers. The *Diwan-i-Khas* (audience room) is well preserved. Don't miss the **Goenka Haveli**. Very close to Dundlod is **Mukundgarh**, a town built around a temple square, outside the sloping fort walls. This fort is now a hotel too. Here you can shop for local handicrafts in a pleasant white-colonnaded market. Besides textiles, it is also renowned for its brass and iron scissors. The **Kanoria** and **Ganeriwala Havelis** deserve a visit.

A few miles away, **Lachmangarh** offers one of the best forts of the area. It commands an aerial view of the town, the only one to have been planned on the model of Jaipur, with roads at right angles and roundabouts. The **Char Chowk Haveli** with four courtyards is one of the most imposing in Shekhavati.

Next comes **Mandawa**. A medieval fort (dated around 1750) gradually rises on the horizon. A painted, arched gateway adorned with Lord Krishna and his cows leads to the bazaar. Later, three large gates lead you to the cannon-guarded interior of the fort where visitors can stay. The terrace of **Castle**

Demoiselle cranes, Tal Chappar, near Churu.

Mandawa holds a breathtaking view of the town and the semi-arid plains beyond. The stables are now rooms that face the garden, and time is still traditionally marked by a gong sounding on the hour. The Mandawa bazaar has many painted houses, parts of which have now been turned into shops. Hand-painted and tie-dyed fabrics, colourful bangles in lac and shoes embroidered with gold thread can be bought here.

Though the *havelis* of the Chokhanis, the Goenkas and the Sarafs are extravagantly painted, one of the oldest frescoes is within the fort itself. The Mandawa family has a small collection of traditional ceremonial costumes and precious arms with handles of jade and gold. On the outskirts of the town, a temple built by a jeweller has an enormous natural crystal in the shape of a *lingam*. The Mandawa family has built a desert camp for tourists who would prefer to live in village ambience on a dune. Three groups of cottages symbolize the villages of potters, weavers and farmers.

A short road links Mandawa with **Fatehpur**, a town founded and ruled by the Muslim Kayamkhani *nawabs* in the 15th century. The frescoes on the **Devra** and **Singhania Havelis** of Fatehpur are matched by few others. As later, more hybrid examples, the two **Bharitia Havelis** are impressive. These are adorned with mirrorwork on their entrances and Japanese tiles patterned with Mount Fuji. Driving through Fatehpur's confusion of roads can be frustrating as they link with each other when you least expect them to. See the English-style portraits on the crumbling fort and the intricately painted room of a **Goenka Haveli**. Not far off, is **Churu** with its imposing 18th-century fort and large painted *havelis*.

From Churu it is possible to branch off southwest to Bikaner or east to Delhi. As you drive to Delhi you will pass **Bissau** with one of the nicest painted *chatris,* near a massive fort. From here take a detour to **Mahansar** which has a most exquisite room painted in gold (*Soney Chandi ki Haveli*). This was once a showroom for a family of goldsmiths. It also has the fine Raghunath temple. At nearby **Ramgarh**, the entire *Ramayana* is illustrated on the interior dome of the Poddar cenotaph. The frescoes on the **Shani Temple**, dedicated to the Saturday god have been painted with devotion and delicacy.

From Bissau to **Jhunjhunu** the road goes up and down the dunes till it finally straightens out. This too, was under the Muslim Kayamkhani *nawabs* until Shardul Singh recovered it for the Rajput Shekhavats. Besides the painted *havelis* (the **Tibdiwala**, the **Modi** and the **Che** [Six]-**Haveli** complex), the stark pure **Khetri Mahal** is very refreshing and offers a complete view of the town. Just off the road, gaze at the ornate **Rani Sati Temple** where the Marwaris, the mercantile community of Rajasthan, gather once a year for a fair.

En route to Delhi, you can stop at **Baggar** to admire the gigantic *havelis* of the **Rungtas**. Further on, at **Chirawa**, are more stunning *havelis* of the **Dalmias** and the **Kakraniyas**. The Delhi–Jaipur road is regained near **Dharuhera**.

Left, gateway to mosque, Jhunjhunu. **Right**, painted doorway depicting scenes from Indian mythology.

BIKANER: JEWEL IN THE SUN

Bikaner: This desert city, with a population of 415,000, was a major trade centre on the old caravan route linking Central Asia and North India with the Gujarat seaports long before a Rathor prince, Bika, conquered it in 1486 AD, and called it Bikaner. When Muhammad Ghori destroyed their Kanauj kingdom in 1193, the Rathors re-established themselves in the wilds of Marwar. Bikaji was the second son of Rao Jodhaji, the real founder of Jodhpur state, its magnificent fort and city. Bika left Jodhpur with a few kinsmen and followers because his father taunted him in open durbar about concocting expansionist schemes with his uncle, Rao Kandhal.

Fortunately for his descendants, no enemy could withstand the harsh desert that surrounds this rich city nor disrupt its leisurely lifestyle, which still prevails. Bikaner is still off the main tourist route but is starting to attract more visitors as Jaisalmer becomes more popular.

The bazaars round **Kote Gate** bustle with activity. Women in colourful *lehenga-cholis* (flared ankle-length shirts and midriff-baring blouses) and hand printed *odhnis* (veils) seek bargains at the pavement stalls. Inside stores, *baniyas* (merchants) sit cross-legged checking accounts or showing bolts of cloth to customers. TV sets, VCRs, tape recorders, toys, and knick-knacks crowd show-windows. Sari shops, readymade garment stores, *zari* (gold and silver embroidery) shops, tailors, jewellers, booksellers, *pan* (betel leaf) *wallahs*, barbers, boys selling *kulfi* (ice cream) out of vacuum flasks, and hawkers calling out their wares fill the space between the **Vishwa Jyoti** and **Prakash Theatre** cinema halls.

Several local handicrafts and souvenirs are available in the bazaar. Lacquer-work wall panels on camel skin are a Bikaner speciality. Camel skin is used for making all sorts of useful or ornamental items such as embossed water-bottles, slippers, handbags, purses, cushions, and lacquered lampshades. Gold-lacquered pottery, trays, hand-blocked ethnic prints, and tie-dyed fabrics, bedspreads and table linen, exotic silver and gold jewellery, are also good buys. Handwoven cotton *durries* (rugs), camel-hair blankets and silk carpets are local specialities which have long been export items.

Bikaner can be very uncomfortable in summer, which lasts from April to September. There are three distinct seasons in Rajasthan – the long hot summer; a short rainy spell when everything turns miraculously green and the lakes fill up; and the clear, comfortable winter. It is best to visit Bikaner between October and March. The festival of Holi generally falls in March, and for nearly three weeks before that, people start singing Holi songs to the beating of large frame drums call *daffs*. One night, on a date declared auspicious by astrologers and priests according to the lunar calendar, a *daff* player will begin to beat out a rhythm, then others pick it up, and male voices from different parts of the city and the surrounding villages join in. As the singers collect round campfires in various courtyards, this is the sign that winter is ending, and the wheat crop is ready for ritual harvesting on the day of Holi.

Bikaner's villages are very thinly populated, and most of the people live in urban centres. Several lovely *havelis* (mansions) belonging to distinguished merchant families stand in the old quarters of the walled city. Bikaner was a safe haven for rich traders and bankers in Mughal and British India, where they could leave their families while carrying on their commercial ventures in distant places. One of the finest *havelis* in the old town is now a small but exquisite hotel, known as Bhanwar Niwas, or Rampuria Haveli, after its owner. Open to non-residents, it provides an insight into the lifestyle of a wealthy Jain merchant family. It also has an excellent collection of artwork displayed in the guest rooms and lounges overlooking the quiet courtyard, remarkable carved sandalwood doors and windows, airy sandstone balconies, balustrades, and lacy *jharokhas* (latticed stone windows).

Preceding pages: painted roof showing the popular Hindu god, Krishna. **Left,** roadside advertisement for Atlas cycles.

Jain temples: The oldest existing structures in Bikaner are the 14th-century Jain temples built by two merchant brothers, Sandeshwar and Bhandeshwar. Neither had a son to carry on the family name, so each built a temple. The **Bhandeshwar Temple** stands on a high-walled plinth and has a shallow sultanate type of dome over the main entrance. Carved wooden columns with dancing figures surround a dark sanctuary with checkered gold designs, and there is a mass of reflecting mirror-work behind the marble Mahavir. The circular *mandap* (pavilion) features well-preserved frescoes of battles, local historical events, and parades of elephants and camels.

The nearby **Neminath Sandeshwar Temple** is entirely different. Its chief features are stylized enamel and gold-leaf wall paintings, and an interesting vaulted and arched ornamented ceiling. Rows of white marble statues of Jain saints line two marble altars beneath the raised lotus pedestal on which Neminath sits meditating.

Junagarh Fort: Akbar's contemporary, Raja Rai Singh, began building Bikaner's Junagarh Fort in 1587. It is one of the finest of Rajput monuments, even though it lacks the commanding hilltop site of the forts at Jodhpur, Jaisalmer, Amber and Chittaurgarh.

Rai Singh's brother, Prithviraj, a poet, scholar and wit, was one of the distinguished Nine Gems of the Mughal Emperor Akbar's court. And Raja Rai Singh's eccentric youngest son, Kishen Singh, left Junagadh to establish a branch of the Bika dynasty at copper-rich Sankhu.

Junagarh is one of the few forts in India which has never been conquered, though it was often attacked. Women who committed *sati* down the centuries left their handprints on the wall facing the huge spiked gate leading to an eerie enclosure which opens on the main courtyard. The arrival and departure of the ruler was marked by a pair of kettle drums. Thirty-seven palaces, pavilions and temples built by different kings stand protected by massive ramparts

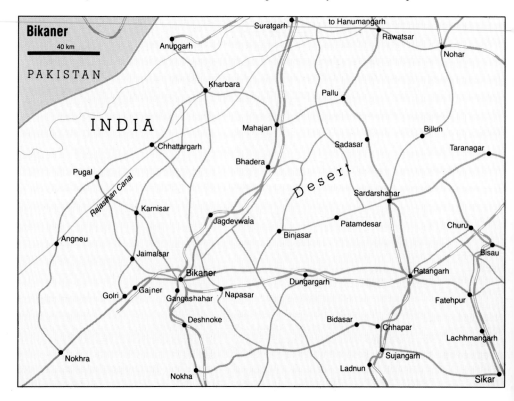

and round towers. They are all connected by paved courtyards, painted galleries and narrow staircases which could be defended by a single warrior. Two marble fretwork windows set in a soaring sandstone wall are particularly impressive. Bikaner's crimson and saffron standard still flies over this Rathor stronghold, cared for by a family trust.

Behind the multi-storied Anup Mahal facade lie well-preserved chambers where the rulers lived, surrounded by relations and retainers. From the latticed windows women watched the outside world without breaking *purdah*. For four centuries Junagarh was the heart of an important autonomous kingdom where the public came daily, as a matter of right, to lay their problems and petitions before their maharaja, or to eat at the communal kitchen from which no one could be turned away hungry. The fort houses a number of historic treasures which are on public display. The rarest of these is the ancient *Pugal* or sandalwood throne of the Kanauj kings,

possibly the oldest piece of furniture existing in India. This was one of the Rathor heirlooms brought from Jodhpur by Bikaji after the deaths of his father and elder brother. Another is Bikaji's small silver-legged bed. Remembering how his grandfather, Rao Riddmall, was tied to his own bed and treacherously killed at Chittaurgarh by enemies who had hidden under the bed, Bika always slept on a low, narrow bed under which no one could hide. Sitting or sleeping on this bed is strictly taboo even for members of Bika's dynasty.

The huge **Ganga Niwas Durbar Hall** with its carved walls and ceiling, used to be a splendid setting for ceremonies in the days of feudal rule. Royal marriages, births, and the yearly Gangaur festival are still celebrated in the **Har Mandir** facing the Anup Mahal courtyard, where the ancient Hiranyagarbh image of Lakshmi-Narayan, the Nav Durgas (nine Durgas) seated on a nine-petalled gold lotus, the holy Dakshina-Vrat Shankh (conch shell), and the sacred Karand casket are housed. Daily worship is

A painter puts the finishing touches to his masterpiece.

performed here by hereditary priests who still serve Bikaji's descendants.

From the fort's roofs and ramparts there is a magnificent view of the crowded city, with the great **Ratan Bihari Temple** in the foreground. In the *zenana*, shady balconies and kiosks surround colourful mosaic courtyards, each different – some studded with pools and fountains to refresh the queens and princesses in the summer months. Each exuberant *chaubara* (four-sided open pavilion), *panchbara* (penthouse), and *sal* (gallery) is ornamented with lacquerwork, mirrored niches, floral panels, portraits and mythological scenes. The vaulted, arched, or panelled ceilings and decorated doors, each different, have to be seen to be believed. The **Gaj Mandir Shish Mahal** (hall of mirrors) with its ivory-inlaid bed, inviting swing-seat, silver chairs, and polished wooden chests and cupboards seems ready and waiting for its master.

The **fort museum** has a valuable collection of illuminated Sanskrit and Persian manuscripts, and miniature paintings. Some art experts rate the extremely elegant and sensitive Bikaner miniatures second only to those of the Mughal school. Outstanding examples of Rajasthani jewellery, enamelware, gold and silver boxes, ceremonial vessels, *hookahs*, costumes, and carpets are displayed here. Historic weapons and armour include jewelled swords inscribed with the names of famous Mughal emperors or great Rajput warriors, jade and enamel hilted daggers, pistols and muskets inlaid with ivory, gold, or silver. The huge double-edged sword of Rajkumar Padam Singh is always pointed out with great pride. With this sword, which few able-bodied men can lift, Padam Singh left a dent on the sandstone pillar of Agra's Diwan-i-Aam (Hall of Public Audience) when he cut down his brother's murderer in front of the Mughal Emperor, Aurangzeb. You can also examine Mughal *farmans* (written orders), British treaties, decorations, medals, and other heirlooms belonging to legendary figures. The gold insignia of rank presented to Bikaner's

Junagarh Fort.

rulers by various Mughal emperors, their gold *howdahs*, palanquins lined with rare brocades, and ceremonial war drums, are also displayed here.

Besides being formidable fighters, the Rathors of Bikaner were sophisticated scholars and art patrons. The walls of the 17th-century **Karan Mahal** are so skilfully painted with gold leaf and jewel tones that it seems like outrageously expensive *pietra dura* inlay. The walls are not even marble, but lime plaster polished to perfection with shells. The 18th-century **Phool Mahal** is decorated with elaborate mirror-work, while the airy **Chandra Mahal** in which the *maharanis* lived has bas-relief friezes of Hindu gods and goddesses over every arched entrance. Hunting and polo scenes cover galleries in the male apartments. The dazzling **Anup Mahal**, where Bikaner's kings received kinsmen and clan chiefs, is ornamented with scarlet and gold Persian motifs repeated in the specially woven carpet. The seldom-visited chamber under the bright blue clock tower has a quaint combination of "wallfellows" – erotic Rajput paintings, Chinese wallpaper, and Dutch tiles. Together they echo the hybrid Eurasian style that swept India during the heyday of the British Raj.

Lallgarh Palace: Aesthetically, few palaces in India match Bikaner's Lallgarh, now one of Rajasthan's most interesting luxury hotels. Set in the open countryside outside the city, this splendid blend of orientalist fantasy and European luxury was designed 100 years ago by Sir Swinton Jacob for Maharaja Ganga Singh, a great moderniser, soldier, and one of the signatories to the Versailles Treaty. Before World War II began, Maharaja Ganga Singh wrote to the Secretary of State for India, the Viceroy, and brother princes, advocating the merger of the princely states with a free, federal India.

Statues of Queen Victoria and King Edward VII greet visitors in Lalgarh's entrance hall. This rambling palace is built round an open garden court overlooked by the *zenana* (ladies' apartments) windows. Local craftsmen

carved the tracery of its cupolas, umbrella domes, balconies, balustrades, pillars, windows and walls with such skill that the solid red sandstone took on the look of delicate lace.

A cloister of peacock arches surrounds the stately marble courtyard of the **Lazmi Bilas**. The main drawing room, library, billiard room, card room, smoking room, and guest suites are located here. All have Belgian or Bohemian crystal chandeliers reflected in huge mirrors over the fireplaces, and carpets repeating the intricate ceiling carvings or moldings. The marble corridors connecting the whole palace are lined with hunting trophies, lithographs, and bronzes. The palace used to house a fabulous collection of oil paintings, Indian miniatures, Chinese jade, porcelain, hand-embroidered silk screens, Japanese eggshell enamel vases, ornamental *ormolu* clocks, antique silver, lamps, bronzes, marbles, and cut-glass ornaments. Maintenance problems created by the abolition of privy purses and lack of staff have led to the dispersal

of this collection gathered over centuries. But the **Shiv Bilas** dining room (seats 400) with its hunting trophies and wild-life paintings remains unchanged. And autographed photographs of European, Asian and India royalty in crested silver frames still stand where they used to, in a reception hall near the ADC Room.

Peacocks roam freely through Lallgarh's grounds, boldly venturing into verandas and posing on domes. Pigeons, parrots, blue jays, doves, bright bee-eaters, and colourful humming birds thrive here. Once goldfish and silver carp filled the lily pools, and fountains played amidst the lawns. Today, even drinking water is a problem in this drought-prone region, so the gardens are difficult to maintain.

The late Maharaja Karni Singhji, former owner of Lallgarh Palace, was a famous clay-pigeon marksman, who took part in the Olympic Games. He had also added India's only private trap and skeet shooting range to the existing sporting facilitites, where he took great pride in training aspiring sporting champi-

ons. The present owners are the Maharani of Bikaner, her two daughters and the Sir Ganga Singh Trust, who continue to run the hotel business.

Manuscript library, archives and museum: The **Anup Sanskrit Library** housed at Lallgarh has one of the world's largest collections of original Sanskrit manuscripts on every conceivable subject. When Maharaja Anup Singh of Bikaner captured Golconda and Bijapur in 1687 at the head of Aurangzeb's army, he saved these priceless manuscripts, parchments, inscribed copper plates, and gold and silver plaques engraved with entire Indian epics like the *Ramayana* and *Mahabharata*, or philosophical treatises like the *Bhagavad Gita*. Research scholars from all over the world come to consult these Sanskrit texts and to study the historical records, documents, letters, Mughal *farmans*, and hand-painted picture albums stored at the **Rajasthan State Archives**. The **Bikaner Museum** has an excellent collection of sculpture, seals, domestic implements and toys

from pre-Vedic archaeological finds. It also has a large collection of coins, marble, stone, and terracotta statues, handicrafts, and metalwork from every period of Indian history. There are colourful Jain, Rajput, and Mughal miniature paintings. A scale model of the former maharaja's Edwardian special train is a popular exhibit. But the real collector's items are the exquisitely carved sandalwood cities, caravans and portraits fitted into almond shells, walnuts, and dry beans, because this is now a lost art.

Modern township: The **Public Park** and **zoo** lie between the medieval city and the modern township dotted with dignified sandstone buildings, offices, colleges, schools, hospitals, and military barracks. Shady trees line wide roads around comfortable bungalows set in large gardens. All this, plus Bikaner's railways, tube wells, powerhouses, excellent club, railway workshop, wool mills, glass manufacturing and carpet weaving centres, sheep and cattle-breeding farms, orphanages and

Throne room, Junagarh Fort.

rehabilitation centres for hearing, speech and sight impaired people, were all built by its dynamic ruler, Maharaja Ganga Singh, whose equestrian statue faces the fort as you enter the Public Park. This large park dotted with fountains, victory towers, shady kiosks, and fish-ponds is a welcome spot in this dusty city. People come here to take a rest, or picnic on the lawns. Many come to see the animals and birds housed in enclosures scattered round the park.

Devi Kund Sagar: Beyond the radio station stand the marble and sandstone *chatris* (cenotaphs) of Bikaner's rulers. Memorials carved with suns symbolise a prince's resting place. Lotus flowers commemorate princesses. Marble footprints beneath warriors on horseback denote spots sanctified by *satis* like Rani Deep Kanwar. To these, local people bring their offerings of coco-nuts, incense, lamps, and flowers. Otherwise, the peace of the place is little disturbed.

These cenotaphs are grouped round a large artifical tank. An 18th-century king built a walled enclosure to protect his father's memorial. It was foretold that all the coming rulers of Bikaner would be cremated in this small enclosure over which the maharaja had set guards. And, strangely enough, with the cenotaph of the last ruling maharaja, Sadul Singhji, built in 1950, the enclosure is full.

Camels are seen everywhere in Bikaner, carrying people, transporting goods, pulling carts, ploughing fields, plodding patiently through trackless sands, or sitting still in camps after a hard day under the blistering sun. Camels are still very important in Rajasthan's daily life for transport, milk, meat and hides. At most festivals, fairs and weddings, people pay tribute to their importance by decking out their camels in colourful *gorbunds* (ornamental harness and camel accoutrements) dripping cowrie shells, coral beads, silver chains, and silk tassels. It's worth spending a little time watching the huge camel herds being watered, fed, and exercised at the **State Camel Breeding Farm** near **Shiv Bari**.

At rest.

Gajner: Just 32 km (20 miles) west from Bikaner, Gajner has a quality of repose quite out of keeping with the bustling imperial sandgrouse shoots to which former maharajas invited viceroys, visiting royalty and brother princes. The lake reflecting a fairytale pink sandstone palace and lush gardens contrasts effectively with the surrounding scrubland, where black buck, chital, sambar, chinkara, nilgai and wild boar and Indian bustard live. From the paved terrace of the palace, main garden and bedroom windows you can see jungle animals coming down to the lake for a drink.

The elegant **Gajner Palace**, with its original furnishings, has been transformed into a hotel. Perched on a hillock overlooking the lake, the small, secluded Shahnam Cottage was built by Maharaja Sadul Singhji and is a favourite with honeymooners. Gajner's lake attracts millions of migratory birds in winter, when its owner, Dr. Karni Singh, held house parties for shooting grouse, duck, and wild boar. Strongly opposed to deer

Drying grain beside Hanumangarh Fort.

hunting, however, he created a deer park and wildlife reserve at Gaijner. Jeep rides through the protected area give visitors the opportunity to see a wide range of wildlife at close quarters.

From Gajner it's an easy drive to **Kolayat**, an ancient pilgrimage centre where Kapil Muni of Vedic fame shed his body under a pipul tree. Kolayat is a collection of delightful marble temples, sandstone pavilions, and 32 *ghats* (bathing places) built round a huge man-made lake which never goes dry even in the worst drought. Here you see *sadhus*, *fakirs*, and pleasure-seekers taking a dip, people picnicking under awnings, and monkeys swinging from old banyan trees. Kolayat has a timeless atmosphere reinforced by the surrounding desert, where you see nothing but its vast emptiness and hear nothing but the wind.

People interested in agriculture and archaeology often undertake the 280-km (175-mile) trip to **Ganganagar** and **Kalibangan**. After witnessing the miseries of the great 1899 famine, the 19-year-old Maharaja Ganga Singh vowed to end starvation by building a canal in his state. The British pussyfooted, refusing water rights from the Satluj river in Punjab and financial aid. But Ganga Singh persevered and raised a loan of nearly £5 million for his irrigation scheme. The Ganga Canal, begun in 1921, was completed in 1927. One of the longest concrete-lined canals in the world, it has changed the desert's face around Ganganagar. Crops of wheat, sugarcane, cotton, mustard and citrus fruit generated industry and a building boom.

Factories and mills today dot the skyline round **Kalibangan**, where extensive remains of the oldest known Indian settlements have been found. More than 3,000 years before Christ, settled societies developed simultaneously in the river valleys of the Nile, Euphrates, Yangtse and Indus. Archaeologists called the Harappa and Mohenjodaro cultures the Indus valley civilization, after the sites of two great cities excavated on the banks of the Ravi and Indus (now usually referred to as the Harappan culture). Kalibangan, the third city, lies along the old Saraswati river, which has since stopped flowing. The Harappan script has not yet been deciphered, so very little is known about the society and culture of its people.

Kalibangan is almost as large as Harappa and Mohenjodaro, and designed on the same plan. Historians have established that Kalibangan formed part of a flourishing urban network protected by a large centralized state stretching from Baluchistan to Sind and modern Rajasthan. The excavations show that Kalibangan too had a well-defined citadel like Harappa and Mohenjodaro, which was used for both religious and government purposes. The streets are regular and well planned. Even the bricks, dating back 5,000 years, are uniform in size, like the weights and measures found in all these cities. The houses, often two stories high, are mostly built round square courtyards. They all have bathrooms provided with drains which flowed into covered sewers under the main streets. This impressive sewage system of the Indus people is as good as the much later Roman system, and must have been maintained by some sort of municipal organization. The special attention paid by the people living at Kalibangan to water supply, social hygiene and public baths shows that, like the later Hindus, they had a strong belief in the purifying qualities of water from a ritual point of view.

Kalibangan had trade links with distant places, as the silver, gold jewellery, turquoise, lapiz lazuli and jade dug up show. Copper and bronze images; domestic vessels; cotton and linen cloth; superb stone and metal seals depicting bulls, rhinoceroses, tigers, lions, elephants and goats; and interesting terracotta figurines of men and women wearing elaborate headdress have been found here. Models of monkeys and squirrels, little toy carts, cattle with moving heads, and terracotta whistles shaped like birds have also been unearthed at Kalibangan. The flat metal swords, knives, spearheads and axes are not strong because they lack the reinforced central rib of such weapons found in Egypt and Mesopotamia, but the saws found have undulating teeth, which suggests that they were good carpenters, though their woodwork has since perished.

Phallic symbols, proto-Shiva and Mother Goddess seals and figures unearthed prove that the Central Asian peoples who overran the Indus valley in around 1500 BC adopted elements of Harappa, Mohenjodaro, and Kalibangan religion, and these earlier cults were fused with Hinduism. But no one knows for certain who these Indus valley peoples were, for the skeletons show evidence of Mediterranean, Proto-Australoid and Mongolian peoples, all inhabiting the same sites.

Karni Mata Temple: Thirty km (19 miles) south of Bikaner stands a unique temple. On his way from Jodhpur to carve out a kingdom for himself, Bika camped at Deshnok village, home of the miracle-working 15th-century mystic Karni Mata, considered an incarnation of Goddess Durga. She blessed Bika, prophesying his victory. Since then she has been worshiped as the titular deity by the Bikaner dynasty, though the Rathor family goddess remains Naganecchya Devi. **Karniji's Temple** at Deshnok derives its fame from the legion of rats which have territorial rights here, rather than from its miraculous shrine. The entrance is through a beautifully carved marble arch which leads to a black and white marble courtyard topped by wire mesh to protect the rats from eagles, crows and hawks. The sanctuary itself has superb silver doors embossed with images of gods and goddesses, given by Ganga Singh. One panel features Karni Mata standing on a footstool holding a *trishul* (trident), surrounded by rats. Visitors are cautioned not to injure these sacred rats, called *kabas*. Whoever does so, however innocently, must present a gold or silver replica to the temple, or suffer a misfortune. These harmless creatures scurry around, or surround the huge metal bowls full of sweetmeats, milk and grain donated by devotees. It is considered highly auspicious to see a white *kaba* near the vermilion-splashed image of Karni Mata.

Protected rats feed from bowls of sweetmeats and grain donated by devotees, Karni Mata Temple, Deshnok.

JAISALMER: DESERT CITADEL

Origin, myth and history: About 850 years ago, a usurping Rajput prince sought the counsel of a hermit who lived in a cave on top of a rocky hill. The prince was Jaisal, of the Bhatti clan; the hermit was Eesul, an oracle; the hill was Tricuta, a triple-peaked rock, and the outcome of that meeting was the foundation of Jaisalmer, the Rock of Jaisal, in 1156.

Prince Jaisal had been appointed regent to his young nephew on the death of his brother at Lodurva, capital of the Bhatti Rajputs. He had betrayed that trust and seized power in his own right, but was uncertain of commanding the loyalty of his vassal princes. Fearing an uprising, he wished to move his capital to a less vulnerable site than Lodurva. Having heard of the prophetic powers of the hermit, he decided to consult him.

The meeting proved fateful, for Eesul related a compelling myth about Tricuta, the place of his hermitage. Centuries ago, Lord Krishna himself had predicted that, in time to come, a distant descendant of his Lunar clan would rule from Tricuta. This fired Jaisal's imagination, for the Bhattis claim descent from the Chandravansh or Lunar clan, and he determined to build his new capital on Tricuta. He was not discouraged by the oracle's warning that the fort he built would be sacked at least twice.

The history of Jaisalmer is as turbulent as the character of its bandit chiefs would lead one to expect. Ferociously independent, inordinately proud of a tenuous "divine" lineage; brave, even foolhardy in battle and often treacherous as allies, the Bhatti Rajputs were the most feared of all desert marauders. When they were on the rampage, the gates of neighbouring fortresses were closed and the cowering citizens barred their doors and windows against these "wolf-packs of the wastes". Their major opponents were the powerful Rathor clans of Jodhpur and Bikaner and endless battles were waged for the possession of a petty fort or meagre waterhole. Cattle-stealing was a major pastime, along with falconry and the hunt. The main source of income was the forced levies on the great caravans that travelled the ancient Spice Route on their way to imperial Delhi.

With the coming of the Muslims in the 13th and 14th centuries, the nature of the conflicts changed. The new enemy was not given to playing war-games according to a chivalric, if bizarre, code of conduct. The outsiders were here to found an empire and to spread Islam. However, since Jaisalmer was situated deep in the desert, it escaped direct Muslim conquest. The Rawals, as the rulers were styled, agreed to pay an annual tribute to the Delhi Sultans in order to preserve a circumscribed independence.

Unfortunately, the Bhatti rulers could not always control their unruly vassal chiefs. The dire prophesy of Eesul, that the fort would be sacked, came about by their own rash actions.

The sieges of Jaisalmer are the subject of traditional ballads about Bhatti heroes. They are still sung at fairs and festivals by hereditary bards, the *bhats* and *charans*, and are the only record of the clan in medieval times. Although elaborately embellished with fabulous deeds of valour, they form the oral history of the period and have inspired the people during difficult times.

According to the ballads, the first siege occurred during the reign of Allauddin Khilji (1295–1315 AD), provoked by a foolhardy raid on the royal baggage caravan. For seven long years, the besieging army tried to starve out the defenders. Finally, they breached the ramparts, and the Bhattis, facing certain defeat, proclaimed the terrible rite of *johar*. Once the women and children had perished by sword or fire, the men, clad in ceremonial saffron and intoxicated with opium, opened the gates and rushed out to meet a heroic death.

The second defeat followed a daring raid on Sultan Ferozeshah's camp at Anasagar Lake, near Ajmer. Jaisalmer was once again overrun and the dreaded *johar* repeated.

The "at least" part of the prophesy came much later, in the 16th century. A friendly Pathan chieftain persuaded the Rawals to permit the *begums* of his harem to pay a courtesy call on the Rajput *ranis* but actually filled the palanquins with armed soldiers who attacked the palace guards. In a moment of panic, Rawal Lunakaran slew several of the princesses of his family, to prevent them being carried off by the intruders, who, as it happens, were beaten off.

Once the Great Mughals established their empire, relations between the imperial court and Jaisalmer stabilised. Several princes served as commanders of the Mughal forces and Bhatti contingents fought in the Mughal army. Royal princesses were married to Mughal rulers and a Bhatti consort of the Emperor Jahangir was the mother of his eldest son. Unfortunately, this prince so distressed his mother by his incessant intrigues and rebellions against his royal father that the Rajput queen, true to the stern code she had been brought up in, killed herself to atone for her son's infidelity.

With the opening of Mumbai's port in the 18th century, the hazardous overland Spice Route lost its importance, and Jaisalmer its main link with the outside world. Gradually the remote desert outpost dwindled in fortune and, in the days of British India Jaisalmer was the least known of the Rajputana principalities. It was the last to sign the Instrument of Agreement with the British, drawn up by Colonel James Tod, the political agent – possibly the first British person to set food in the legendary stronghold of Jaisalmer. Today, the fort is the centre of the largest district in Rajasthan. For anyone who wishes to understand the true spirit of historic Rajasthan, Jaisalmer is a rich source of sights and impressions.

Desert Citadel: Jaisalmer is easily accessible both by rail and road, and a private airline now serves the town. An overnight journey takes you by train from Jodhpur. Two major highways connect Jaisalmer with important centres in Rajasthan. The slightly shorter and usual approach is the excellent one from Jodhpur (288 km/180 miles). The other, longer and less frequented, starts from

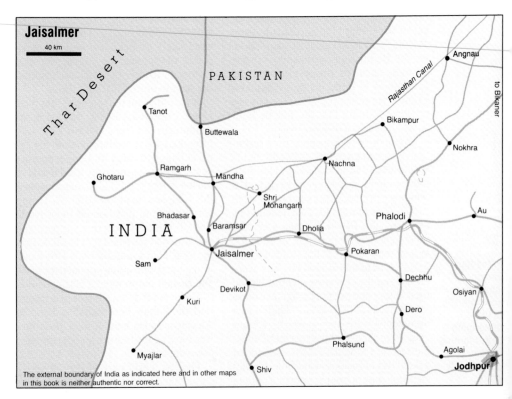

The external boundary of India as indicated here and in other maps in this book is neither authentic nor correct.

Bikaner and is the more dramatic journey, since it goes through stretches of stark desert. It joins the Jodhpur highway at Pokharan – site of India's infamous nuclear test explosions in 1998 – after which a single road runs on to Jaisalmer. Whichever road you take, start early, because there are a few unusual and off-the-beaten-track diversions to make at Pokharan for the more adventurous. Carry plenty of drinking water and snacks.

The Thar is part of the great global desert-belt. The second Mughal, Emperor Humayun, while a fugitive (1540 AD), made his way through it to Persia. It was while he was crossing the Thar that Humayun's son, Akbar, later to become the greatest of the Great Mughals, was born at Amarkot, now in Pakistan.

The desert ambience can be quite overwhelming, with endless oceans of sand broken by dunes, scrub and shattered scarps of the Aravalli range. The gray sand shades into rosy tones and then, beyond Pokharan, takes on an increasingly golden tinge. This is the famous Jurassic sandstone of which Jaisalmer is built – **Sonar Kila**, a Golden Fort, growing out of a rock of brandy-topaz and set in an undulating sea of ochre sand. Glimpsed first at sunset, the triangular rock looks like a huge, crouching beast ready to spring at any intruder.

Jaisalmer, with a population of 39,000, is a true citadel – the entire living area is within the city wall, the main bastion and royal palaces being further protected by huge ramparts, pierced by enormous gates, and protected by guardhouses.

Tricuta is the highest rock-hill in the vast plain. The flat-topped triangle rises in a gradual slope. The **Palace** stands at the highest point of the incline and is contained within double ramparts almost 100 metres (325 feet) above the market-place. Thus, the royal apartments could be shut off in case of need, such as a palace revolt.

Entering through **Ganesh Pol**, the Elephant Gate, from the **Manik Chowk** (main market), leads up a steep incline paved with large flag-stones past **Suraj Pol**, the Sun Gate. The winding path is

Jaisalmer's Fort dominates Gadisar Lake.

wide enough to have permitted four fully armed warriors to ride abreast. The silver **Imperial Umbrella**, symbol of protection, rises on **Megh Durbar**, the Cloud Tower, while nearby, is another tower used as a sentinel's look-out.

Bhointa Pol, the Turn Gate, stands square on a sharp curve. Its name has been corrupted to **Bhoota Pol**, the Haunted Gate, as it has been the scene of many a bloody fight. Nearby is a temple to the Goddess Bhavani, a warlike aspect of the mother deity. As protectress of the warrior Bhattis, it is to her that the Rajputs offered *puja* (worship) before going into battle. Alongside is a smaller shrine to the benign elephant-headed god, Ganesh, remover of obstacles. No doubt he got his share of petitions from the departing soldiers for their safe return.

Finally, **Hava Pol**, the Wind Gate, stands sentinel to the royal palaces and leads to the main enclosure, the Court of Public Audience. It is a spacious square, where the Rawal could hear petitions, review troops or entertain visiting royalty to spectacular shows during festivals or marriages. It was also here that the *johar* took place.

Facing the palace, to the left is a flight of marble steps, at the head of which is an imposing white marble throne for the monarch. By its side is a disused covered well, **Jaisal's Well**, which is said to have been built over a spring visited by Lord Krishna.

Returning down the staircase, to the right is a **Kali Temple**, dedicated to the goddess of destruction. Here, sacrifices were offered during the Dassehra festival and the ancient horse-worship rite, *arsha puja,* was performed. The nearby **Jawahar Mahal**, the Jewelled Palace, has only one wing open to the public.

Manik Chowk: It is a quite a relief to return to the main market-square, with its noise and bustle, after the silent and ominous 12th-century fort. Yet, even here the past still beckons, although the ghosts are more friendly than the blood-thirsty spectres of Bhoota Pol. While looking at the picturesque village, or dodging between boys trundling hand-carts and the rambling sacred bulls, these

<u>Left</u>, ornate Jaisalmer balconies. <u>Right</u>, Patwon ki Haveli.

images blur into the ancient trading centre, where merchants from as far as Africa, West Asia and Iran once brought their swords and scimitars from Damascus, their grapes and nuts from Afghanistan, the famed wines of Shiraz and the high-stepping horses of Balkh, to barter for the spices, birds and animals, the rare gems, rich brocades and fine muslins of India.

The *havelis*: The art of the *silavats* (stone carvers) of Jaisalmer is justly famous. It attained its peak of excellence during the 18th and 19th centuries, rivalling the quality of the carved marble of the Taj Mahal at Agra. The honey tones of the yellow sandstone lend a softer glow to the elaborate facades of the desert *havelis* and are easier on the eye then the dazzle of the reflecting white marble.

Patwon-ki-haveli (House of the Brocade Merchants) is the largest and most elaborate of the famous *havelis* of Jaisalmer. It stands in a cul-de-sac with an imposing gate spanning the entrance to the lane, protecting this prestigious private residence from prying eyes. *Patwas* are merchants trading in rich brocades, gold and silver embroidery, sequins and ribbons. This family expanded their business to include opium, banking and revenue-collecting. In the late 18th-century, Guman Chand Patwa had a chain of 300 trading centres extending from Afghanistan to China. His five sons began building this mansion in 1800, which consists of five separate suites, linked together. It took 50 years to complete. For a while, fearing it would be requisitioned, the family turned it into a Sanskrit school for boys. Fortunately it has been rescued from that fate and is now a protected monument, as is the entire citadel.

Nathmalji-ki-haveli (The Mansion of Nathmalji), the last of the great *havelis* was built in the late 19th century. Nathmalji was the Prime Minister of the state at that time, and his family still lives in the *haveli*. Its facade was carved by two brothers, master-craftsmen of such consummate talent that, in a land of anonymous artists, their names are still remembered: Hathu and Lallu.

Salim Singh's *haveli*: Salim Singh Mohta was a notoriously tyrannical Prime Minister of Jaisalmer in the 18th century. His mansion is distinguished by two main features: the upper story, in cantilever style, supported by carved peacock brackets, and the unique saxe-blue cupolas that adorn its roof.

Badal Mahal and Tazia Tower: Beyond the entrance gate to Tricuta stands the present home of the former rulers of Jaisalmer, **Badal Mahal** (Cloud Palace), from which rises the delicate, pagoda-like **Tazia tower**, its chief claim to architectural fame. *Tazias* are the fragile, split-bamboo and elaborately decorated paper and tinsel models of Taj-like mausoleums made and paraded by Shia Muslims during the period of Muharram, to commemorate the martyrdom of Hassan and Hussain, the Prophet's grandsons. The *silavats* of Jaisalmer, being Shia Muslims, decided to migrate to Pakistan when it was established in 1947. Before leaving their desert home, they expressed their love for their homeland and their ruler by building this tower in the shape of a *tazia* and presenting it to the ruler.

Jain Temples (12th–15th century): An extensive group of Jain temples stands within the fort complex. They were built from donations by the wealthy Marwari merchants. The finest are considered to be the Rishabdevji, the Sambhavnath, and the Ashtapadi Mandir.

Entrance to the **Rishabdevji Temple** is through an intricately carved *toran* (scrolled archway) where shoes, cameras and all leather articles must be left. A porch whose pillars are carved with creepers and flowers, all in yellow stone, leads to the main *mandap* (hall) with columns sporting graceful *apsaras* (heavenly nymphs), *kinaras* and *gandharvas* (celestial dancers and musicians) facing the central image of Rishabdevji. But one's eye is caught by an arresting group of images of Jain *tirthankaras* (saints), sitting in meditation in a circle, to the right of the hall. Made of white marble or red or black stone, all have jewelled third eyes that sparkle. These silent, meditating stylised figures are, in their quiet way, deeply impressive.

Sambhavnath Temple leads off from the left of Rishabdevji. It is a subsidiary shrine, smaller and simpler in design. A basement is reputed to house a library of fabulous sacred manuscripts. It is rumoured that an underground tunnel led from here all the way to Lodurva, the former capital, from where these treasures were secretly conveyed when the migration to Jaisalmer took place.

Ashtapadi Mandi can be entered by a cloistered passage linking it with Sambhavji Temple. It has beautiful images of Hindu deities on the outer pillars and walls of the *mandap*. This margin of religions is an indication of the remarkable religious tolerance of the age, and is a distinguishing feature of Jain sacred architecture. Since they were granted freedom of worship under Hindu rulers, they reciprocated by incorporating Hindu deities on their temple walls. The donors of the *mandir*, seated on elephants, guard its entrance.

A short walk beyond Tazia tower is **Gadi Sagar** (or Gadisar), an artificial lake that was an important source of water in the past. A natural decline was enlarged to catch every drop of rain and, in a season of drought, Gadisar was the mainstay of Jaisalmer.

Many years ago, Telia, a well known courtesan and singer from a neighbouring area, became the lover of a Bhatti prince. In a gesture to him, Telia donated the handsome gateway and *ghats* (steps) that lead down to Gadisar. The princesses of the royal house were outraged by her effrontery and refused to use the gate. They even threatened to pull it down. So the wily Telia installed an image of Lord Satya Narain (Krishna) in the upper chamber and had it consecrated as a temple.

Today, most of the homes of Jaisalmer have the amenity of piped water, but Gadisar remains a useful and pleasurable reminder of the past, and of the generosity of a clever woman.

The City: Ample time should be given to wander through Jaisalmer's narrow lanes and to visit the small silversmiths' shops, the stalls selling leathercraft goods, or the colourful traditional shawls

Pabusa village, West Rajasthan.

and blankets. The homes of the ordinary citizens of the fort – flat-roofed, white houses, with bands of ochre and brown around lintels and folk paintings and geometric patterns on walls and floors – are as picturesque as the splendid mansions of the elite.

Around Jaisalmer: Not far from the town is **Bhattiani Sati-rani** (Shrine of the Martyred Bhatti Queen). The awesome rite of *sati*, according to the ideology of the male rulers, rendered a woman immortal, i.e. by becoming – not committing – *sati* she attained *moksha*, release from the cycle of rebirth. In reality, many women were dragged to their deaths or would have suffered such a miserable existence at the hands of their husband's family if they had not died, that they were, in effect, forced on to the funeral pyre. Jaisalmer has its share of monuments sacred to the memory of such *satis*.

By far the most important and romantic of these is the shrine to a young Bhatti queen known as *Maha-sati* (the great *sati*), since she immolated herself, not on her husband's pyre, but on that of her *dewar*, younger brother-in-law, who was suspected of being her lover. Even now, her shrine is a place of pilgrimage for star-crossed lovers, who come to pray for her favours and blessing.

A curious feature of Sati-rani's shrine is that, while she was a Hindu, the keepers of her shrine are Muslims. They belong to the hereditary caste of Manganiyars, who for eight centuries have been some of the finest music-makers of the Thar. Not only do they look after the shrine, they also sing hymns of praise to the *sati* and the ballads of her epic.

On a rocky eminence on the road to Jaisalmer stands the **Royal Cenotaphs** (*chatris*) of the Rawals in **Barra Bagh** (Big Garden) where the rulers were cremated. A pillared and canopied *chatri*, often of white marble, marks the site of each cremation. Despite the bas-relief tablets depicting the ruler along with his consort-*satis*, a garden of *chatris* does not have the lugubrious atmosphere

Open stairway in a courtyard, Jaisalmer.

of a graveyard. Barra Bagh is no exception and this is the best place from which to watch the spectacular desert sunset, and to photograph the fort.

Lodurva, the former capital of the Bhatti rulers, is still an important place of Jain pilgrimage. It is just 16 km (10 miles) northwest of Jaisalmer. The ancient township lies in ruins about the temples and the seasonal river Kak is usually dry – one explanation for this is provided by a local legend.

One version runs as follows. The beautiful Princess Mumal lived in a palace on the banks of the Kak. The Prince of Amarkot, Mahendru, riding by, heard her singing, fell in love with her, and became her lover. The lovers were parted by Mahendru's jealous wives. Mumal, disguised as an itinerant singer, made her way to Amarkot to seek her beloved, only to die of fatigue and a broken heart at the gates of his fort, where Mahendru found her. And that is why the river Kak refuses to flow.

The desert: Riding to the dunes of Sam on camel-back gives you some idea of the pace and space of desert life. Animals can be hired by the day, or by jeep, the outing would require just a couple of hours. Most hotels offer some sort of longer camel safari, but choose your guide and package carefully, making sure that all the food, blankets (it gets cold in the desert at night) and transport back to Jaisalmer if you fall ill/get too sore, is included. Women should avoid riding with the guide to prevent any sexual harassment. Also, take a hat and lots of sun-block.

The dunes at Sam are treacherous. They look smooth and firm, but the golden sands run like silk through your fingers and you can sink to your knees in a second. A sudden wind has been known to blow a dune up into a moving funnel to deposit it yards away. Cattle sometimes flounder to their death in such shifting sands.

The camel-drovers (*Raikas*) are the best guides. The *Raika* is a handsome, romantic figure, and in local legends and traditional songs, he is referred to as the messenger of love or the bringer of tidings, good or bad. *Raikas* travel with their animals over vast distances and know every pasture and waterhole in their region. They can trace a lost camel by its hoofprints, while the beasts recognize and respond to the call of their drovers.

Another worthwhile diversion from Pokharan, en route to Jaisalmer, is the shrine to the medieval saint, Ramdevra. The **temple** stands on a low hill and is open to all, as Ramdevra is worshiped by persons of all castes and beliefs. At the annual **Ramdevra Fair** (August– September), the dextrous *Tera-Tali* performers are the biggest draw. They are acrobatic dancers who execute feats with cymbals, swords and *divas* (oil-lamps), to the resounding rhythm of drums. The traditional offerings at the shrine are horses of clay, cloth, wood or paper.

The Jaisalmer Desert Festival, is held annually in January and brings together musicians, dancers, puppeteers, fire-walkers and sword-swallowers from all over the desert region. Run by the local tourist office, the festival now attracts many visitors.

If Jaisalmer whets your appetite for desert life, take the National Highway to **Barmer**. On the way, 16 km (10 miles) out of Jaisalmer, is **Akal**, the Fossil Park, proof of the geologic cataclysms that have taken place in the Thar. Here, 180 million years ago, stood a forest of giant deciduous trees whose trunks petrified into fossils, littering a bare hillside with mica and red and yellow stone. The fossil trunks have had to be protected by iron grids as people were apt to hack off bits and pieces for building houses.

Barmer, growing in importance as a border outpost, has the air of a dusty garrision town. But if you are there in January, it is worth enquiring about the great **Tilwara Cattle Fair** on the banks of the salt-water river Luni. Tilwara has a temple which is dedicated to the warrior-saint Mallinath, and the fair is held on the dry river-bed. It is here, according to popular belief, that the saint rides his ghostly steed across the sands every night. Tilwara Fair is the largest cattle-mart held in Rajasthan. Horses, bullocks, camels and other fine cattle are brought here for sale.

DESERT NATIONAL PARK

About 45 km (28 miles) to the southwest of Jaisalmer, the Desert National Park covers 3,162 sq. km (1,220 sq. miles) of scrub, thorn forest, desert and dunes. The range of both flora and fauna is, to many, surprisingly large for a desert area. The unique ecosystem reflects the successful adaptation by a range of mammals, birds, insects and flowers to a harsh climate with temperature ranges from below freezing to over 55°C (130°F).

The rolling landscape of sand-dunes and scrub-covered hills is often breath-takingly beautiful. The active dunes of Sam contrast strikingly with the 180 million-year-old wood fossils at Akal 17 km (10 miles) from Jaisalmer which indicate that this now arid area must have once been hot, humid and luxuriant.

The scant vegetation and the animals dependent on it are in turn dependent on whatever water is available. Waterholes are therefore the ideal spots from which to watch animals and birds.

Chinkara, the smallest Indian antelope.

The small, active desert **fox** is an important predator keeping a natural check on the population of desert **rats** and **gerbils**. The fox, although normally shy, is often seen in the Miazalor area, especially in the winter, basking in the sun. The **wolf** is perhaps the main predator and **jackal** is found on the periphery of the park.

Many of the villages on the edge of the park are Bishnoi and the areas around these settlements are natural sanctuaries where the strong religious beliefs of the Bishnois ensure protection to all living creatures. Groups of **blackbuck**, **chinkara** and **nilgai** are found around the villages and now thrive in the park's areas of sparse, arid grassland. The blackbuck is a true antelope, living in large herds of 50 to 60 animals (mainly fawns and doe) on the open grasslands. The chinkara or Indian gazelle is spread throughout the park, in the sandy areas as well as the scrub grasslands, in small groups or as individuals.

Some smaller mammals have adapted to the desert environment by burrowing like the gerbil, by living in colonies or by being noctural, like the **crested porcupine**.

Desert birdlife is extensive, ranging from a large number of birds of prey to **sandgrouse**, **doves**, **quails**, **partridges**, **shrikes**, **flycatchers**, **bee-eaters**, **warblers** and **desert coursers**. The most remarkable bird of the desert is the **Great Indian Bustard**, weighing up to 14 kg (30 pounds) and standing up to 45 cm (18 inches). A reluctant flyer, the bustard lives on an omnivorous diet of locusts, grasshoppers, seeds, berries, lizards and even snakes. Habitat destruction and hunting threatened this majestic bird but it has thrived here and the population in the Desert National Park alone is now estimated to be over 1,000.

The **Houbara bustard** is also found in the park. Of the three resident species of sand-grouse, the **Indian sandgrouse** is most impressive with its routine of arriving in small groups to join large turbulent flocks in the early morning, all of them gathering to drink at the same place each day. The **pintail sandgrouse** is a winter visitor.

The many insect and reptile species evident throughout the park form important links in the desert food chains. The 43 species of reptiles include lizards, chameleons and snakes. ∎

JODHPUR

It is said that when the defeated Maharaja Jaswant Singh fled the battlefield of the victorious Mughal princes Aurangzeb and Murad in 1658, his proud wife refused to accept this insult to Rajput honour. Slamming the fort gate in his face, she sent him back to redeem the good name of the Jodhpur house. Legend, perhaps, but it captures the pride of the Rajput rulers of this delightful, slow-paced city set on the edge of the Thar Desert.

Jodhpur, former capital of Marwar state, retains some of its medieval character. Beginning in 1549, when the city was called Jodhagarh, the Rathor clan fought and ruled from the virtually impregnable fort until their territory covered 91,000 sq. km (35,000 sq. miles), making it the largest Rajput state.

The clan traces its origins back to the Hindu god, Rama, hero of the epic *Ramayana*, and thence to the sun. So the Rathors belong to the Suryavansha (solar race) branch of the Kshatriyas, the warrior caste of the Hindus. Later, breaking into historical reality, in 470 AD Nayal Pal conquered the kingdom of Kanauj, near modern Kanpur in Uttar Pradesh. The Rathor capital for seven centuries, Kanauj, fell in 1193 to the Afghan invaders led by Muhammad Ghori.

The fleeing ruler, Jai Chand, drowned in the Ganga. But his son or grandson, Sihaji, had better luck. Moving west into the Thar Desert, he achieved glory in battle for the local Solanki prince, whose sister he won as reward. He later set himself up as an independent ruler around the wealthy trading center of Pali, just south of Jodhpur. His descendants flourished, battled often, won often, and in 1381 Rao Chanda ousted the Parihars from Mandore which then became the Rathor seat of government.

Rathor fortunes then turned. Rao Chanda's son and heir, Rainmal, won praise for his capture of Ajmer and was then entrusted with the care of his orphaned nephew, destined to inherit the Mewar throne of Chittaurgarh. Rainmal may have had his eyes on this fine hilltop fort. But court intrigue and treachery stopped him. In 1438 he was doped with opium, and finally shot dead. This triggered bitter feuds, ending with Mewar and Marwar becoming separate states.

Rathor legend continues in various versions. One is that Jodha, one of Rainmal's 24 sons, fled Chittaurgarh and finally, 15 years later, recaptured Mandore in 1453. Five years later he was acknowledged as ruler. A holy man sensibly advised him to move his capital to hilltop safety. It was an obvious and irresistible site and the building of Meherangarh, or Majestic Fort, was begun.

Jodhpur City: Today Jodhpur, with its 770,000 inhabitants, is the second-largest city in Rajasthan. It still fulfils its historical role as the area's main trading centre for wood, cattle, camels, cotton, salt, hides and agricultural crops, as well as handicrafts, marble and granite.

Although the **old city** was founded by Rao Jodha, its walls with seven gates and countless bastions and towers were built by Rao Maldeo in the 16th century when Jodhpur was a booming trading town. Poised on both the international east–west trading route between Central Asia and China and on the strategic Delhi-Gujarat route, the Marwari traders amassed fortunes from the passing camel caravans whose loads included ivory, copper, silks, sandalwood, camphor, spices and opium.

In the maze of old lanes focused on **Sardar Bazaar** and its **Clock Tower** of 1912 are several former palaces, some *havelis* and temples. Many have richly carved facades, such as the **Tulati Mahal**, a palace built by Jaswant Singh which is now a hospital. And many of Jodhpur's traditional craftsmen thrive here, too. With a little help from a taxi driver or the keeper of a large shop, they are easy to find and fascinating to watch at work.

Nearby, in **Mochi** (Cobbler) **Bazaar**, a regular tap-tapping betrays a cobbler. Further west, the nimble-fingered Muslim women and children confined to their houses around Jalori and Siwanchi Gates (or in Bambamola district) create delicate, multi-coloured *bandhani* (tie-dyed) patterns on cotton. Other craftsmen make glass bangles, felt goods and leather water-bottles. Some carve marble and ivory, or make painted wooden horses. Still others emboss silver, weave hand-loom textiles or make carpets.

Then, there are the famous puppet-makers of Jodhpur who re-enact the deeds of such heroes as Amar Singh Rathor of Nagaur. Puppeteering is an ancient entertainment in India. The *kathputliwala* (puppeteer) makes his own two-string, 1 metre (3 foot) high marionettes, gives them carved wooden heads and elaborate costumes. As he makes them perform, he speaks through bamboo or leather to give his voice a distinctive shrillness, while his wife plays a drum and elaborates the story – usually on the Rajputs' favourite themess: love, war and honour. Indeed, such is the place of *kathputli* that there is a special ceremony marking the "death" of a puppet. When, after many generations of use, the puppet is worn out, it is floated down a holy river, accompanied by prayers. The longer it remains afloat, the higher the gods are judging its life.

Modern Jodhpur: Spilling out from the walled city is the more modern side of Jodhpur. To the east lie the **Umaid Gardens**, with zoo, library, and the **Government Museum** founded by Sardar Singh in 1909. Its moth-eaten birds, old weapons and early models of aeroplanes make it a time-capsule in itself. The nearby **Rupayan Sansthan** (Rajasthan Institute of Folklore), run by Komal Kothari, is valiantly trying to record the state's rich but threatened musical heritage. The grand **State High Court** is near here. And, to the south, lie the Air Force, Engineering and Medical Colleges and the University (founded 1965).

As for polo, you can catch some in action at the **Polo Grounds** which are on the airport road. Polo, pigsticking and tennis were the favorite sports of the more recent Rajasthani royals. And Jodhpur has produced some of the most outstanding Indian polo players, including Rao Raja Hanut Singh.

Palace complex: The gentle atmosphere of Jodhpur today belies a stormy, sometime glorious, past. The best way to trace its history is to make a leisurely visit

Moonsoon skies over Mehrangarh Fort.

to the aptly named **Meherangarh** (Majestic) **Fort** (5 km/3 miles), taking a taxi from town up through Nagauri Gate to **Jai Pol** (Victory Gate). Its general inspiration came from Raja Man Singh's stupendous 15th-century fort at Gwalior. But, as the historian Percy Brown observed, "for grandeur of conception and elegance of detail, this palace is unsurpassed" (*Indian Architecture*).

Such was the threat of Rajput warring in 1459 that Rao Jodha and his successors built an almost impregnable fort on already superb natural defenses. The bold bluff soars 121 metres (393 feet) above the flat surrounding plains, commanding views for some 120 km (80 miles) – in post-monsoon clarity, the towers of Khumbhalgarh Fort to the south can be seen. The fort itself is guarded by seven gates piercing walls which are 21 metres (68 feet) wide and 36 metres (117 feet) high in places. When complete, its architect, Bambhi Rajra, was said to have been buried alive with its secrets.

Jai Pol is a late addition to the fort. Maharaja Man Singh built it after he successfully repelled the combined forces of Jaipur and Bikaner in 1808. Above it is the water pump which finally ended the daily slog of carrying drinkable water from **Gulab** (Rose) **Sagar** at the bottom of the steep hill. The water of both lake and well inside the fort is brackish. The story goes that when a hermit's cave was included in the fort buildings, he was so angry that he cursed the water for ever.

Inside the gate, Man Singh also built the wall on the right. Yet another legend says he did this after a trusted Muslim employee was buried outside the fort walls. His spirit returned to complain to his master who solved the problem by building an extra wall.

Passing the Jaipuri's cannon-ball pits on the left side of the original outer wall, **Fateh Pol** is the first of the fort's seven protective gates proper. It is built with a flat lintel supported on corbels between twin bastions. After an acute angle turn, which would slow down any enemy, the road runs up through the elegantly arched **Gopal**, **Bhairon** and (after one lost gateway) **Dodkangra Pols**.

18th-century cannon; Umaid Bhawan Palace in the distance.

The sixth gate, **Amirita Pol**, built by Rao Maldeo, is a sharp turn to the left. Within on the left is **Rao Jodhaji's Falsa**, or Jodha's barrier. Wooden logs were fixed into holes in the stone slabs. Jodha's foes entered here only to be confronted with the strongest gate of all, **Loha** (Iron) **Pol**. Like the other gates, it is built just after a bend so the enemy could not rush it, and reinforced with iron spikes against elephant charges. With such defenses, Rao Jodha subjugated most of Mewar, Nagaur, Sambha and Ajmer before he died in 1489.

Of Rao Jodha's 14 sons, the second, named Suja but known as the "cavalier prince" was to die in true Rajput style, attempting to rescue 140 Rathor women who were being carried off by the Pathans from a fair at Pipli. The sixth son, Bika, founded Bikaner, while others founded Idar, Kishangarh, Ratlam, Jhabua, Sailana, Sitamau and Alirazpur. All eight looked to their Jodhpur ruler as head of the Rathor clan.

Loha Pol was further strengthened by Rao Maldeo (ruled 1532–73), who expanded the Marwar kingdom to reach up to Sind in the north, Hissar in the east and Gujarat in the west. However, in 1544 he met his match at the battle of Khanua, narrowly failing to beat Sher Shah Suri who had ousted the Mughal Emporer Humayun from the imperial throne in Delhi.

For two years, Jodhpur was under Sher Shah's control. But when it was won back, Marwar's territory, power and independence reached their zenith. Maldeo had even out-powered Rana Sanga of Chittaurgarh. And he could refuse to help the ousted Humayun, fleeing Sher Shah. But the tables turned with the Mughal restoration when Akbar came to the throne. Enraged by this snub to his father, he besieged the Rathor ruler who eventually made peace by sending his son, Udai Singh, to the Delhi court.

However, on Udai Singh's succession, the new ruler changed the policy towards the Mughals. He gave his sister Jodhi Bai in marriage to Akbar and his daughter Man Bai to Prince Salim, who later became Emperor Jahangir. Jodhi Bai

Stained glass reflected in table top.

possessed considerable political skills, which she used in persuading Akbar to return all of Jodhpur's territory (with the exception of Ajmer) to her brother, to give him extra land and to bestow upon him the title of *raja* (king), calling him King of the Desert.

Jodhpur flourished under this alliance with the Mughals. When Raja Gaj Singh put down Jahangir's son's rebellion he was made Viceroy of the Deccan. But it was his second son, Jaswant Singh (ruled 1638–78), who was created maharaja (great king), and had the most remarkable career. First, he led Shah Jahan's army against his rebelling sons in 1658. The battle lost, he switched sides and joined Aurangzeb. Then he turned again and plundered Aurangzeb's army. And somehow he later managed to become viceroy of Gujarat, then of the Deccan.

The last gate is the **Loha Pol** (Iron Gate). On its wall 31 hand-prints of the royal *satis*, the sacrificial wives of the maharajas, are still visible. *Sati* was the cruel custom of a widow's death by self-immolation. On the death of her husband, a woman would leave home for the last time, dipping her hand in red pigment and laying it flat on the doorpost or lintel, a moving testimony to the women who suffered such discrimination and violence at the hands of Rajput men.

Nowhere was *sati* more important and nowhere did it persist as long as it did in feudal Rajasthan. Illustrating vividly the position of women at the Rajput courts, a prince's success in life was measured by the number of women who committed *sati* on his death. And for Jaswant Singh's successor, Ajit Singh, 6 queens and 58 concubines joined his funeral pyre in 1731. Later, for many years, the 1829 British law prohibiting *sati* made little impact (one of the few instances when the British outlawed an Indian custom). Indeed, in Jodhpur, the last recorded royal *sati* was in 1953.

Finally, **Suraj** (Sun) **Pol**, the entrance to the fort's palaces. Moving from the fierce battlements into the sumptuous domestic quarters, you are accompanied by hereditary musicians of the Mirasi caste playing traditional music.

Graceful arches, Mehrangarh Fort.

The Fort: The various buildings constructed by Jodha and his successors now serve as the **Meherangarh Museum**. Royal retainers still tend their master's possessions which are arranged in the former public and private rooms and in the *zenana* (women's quarters).

Up the narrow stairs from Suraj Pol is the courtyard of the **Moti Mahal** (Pearl Palace), enclosed by *jali* (lattice) work of gossamer fineness and beauty. It was the Maharaja Sur Singh (ruled 1581–95) who commissioned it. Here the marble **Sringar Chowki** (Coronation Seat), with peacock armrests and gilded elephants, is kept. Apart from Jodha, every ruler of Jodhpur has been crowned on it.

Royal palanquins fill the nearby **Palki Room**, including a massive gold-polished one that was booty from Gujarat and needed a dozen men to carry it. A fine gift from Emperor Shah Jahan to Jaswant Singh sits in the **Elephant Howdah Room** – a silver *howdah* which he presented together with an elephant to put it on and 100 horses. And every royal birth is recorded in the **Jhanki Mahal**, a

room from which ladies could watch events below. Here, the royal cradle of the lastest maharaja is an ingenious mechanical machine. It was given by the electricians' union of Jodhpur, "with profound loyalty", reinforced by a portrait of the young prince's ruling father.

Ministers and nobles would discuss state affairs in the **Chandan Mahal**. A.H. Muller's 1893 mural shows a bearded man clad in white riding a horse and baking some bread at the end of a spear. This illustrates the story of Jodhpur's great hero, Durga Das, celebrated by poets and bards. It recounts how, after Jaswant Singh's death in 1678, the orthodox Muslim Aurangzeb wreaked his revenge. He sacked Jodhpur and plundered the large towns of Marwar, destroyed temples, demanded conversion to Islam and implemented the *jizya* tax on non-Muslims that Akbar had abolished back in 1564. Meanwhile, Durga Das had smuggled Jaswant Singh's posthumously-born son, Ajit, out of the Mughal capital, Delhi. After 30 years of guerilla warfare, hardship and wandering

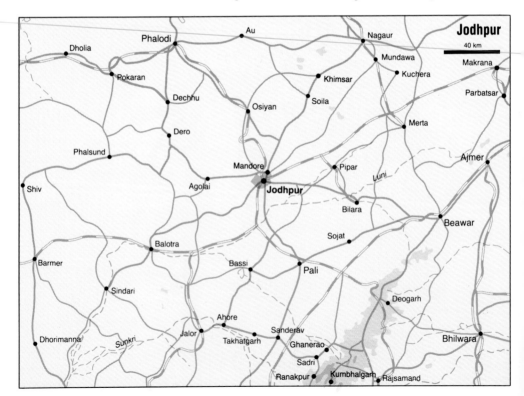

– the subject of the mural – Durga Das courageously re-took Jodhpur and Ajit Singh took up the throne.

Jodhpur, Jaipur and Udaipur finally buried their mutual enmity and formed a triple alliance to throw off the Muslim yoke. Under this fragile security, Jodhpur's internal history entered a stormy period. Meanwhile, external Rajput affairs plunged, too. Despite the alliance, the Rajput inability to unite led to constant inter-clan warfare. From all sides the Marathas, Pathans, Pindaris and British fought over the disintegrating Mughal Empire and its Rajput allies.

Eventually, in 1818, after almost a century of internal and external war, Jodhpur signed a treaty with the East India Company for "defensive alliance, perpetual friendship, protection and subordinate co-operation". Rathor honour was put to shame.

In the **Darbar Takhat**, or Throne Room, one of the last *darbars* (public audience or meeting) was held in 1819. The octagonal *gadi* (throne) was another of Shah Jahan's gifts. Chairs on the right were for nobles, in descending rank. Those on the left were marked for representatives of villages, such as Alniwas, Riyan, Bhadrjun. And lattice windows behind the *gadi* permitted the women to witness the *darbar* and, via messengers, contribute their voice to discussions.

The *zenana* was the sealed area where the women lived in apartments and on roof terraces around the communal **Rang Mahal**. Here, at the spring festival of Holi, the king and his ladies would flirt and play, squirting one another with coloured waters and tossing clouds of crimson and ochre powders.

Miniatures: Umaid Vilas now houses a fine collection of Rajput miniature paintings, well worth a look. In the secular subjects, especially the fine portraits, the prevailing influences of the delicate Mughal and Deccani court styles reflect the Jodhpur alliance with the emperors. In the devotional paintings, the more robust Rajput style asserts itself, with strong lines, bright colours and clear designs. But as Mughal power waned, this bold style took over entirely, as is clear in the large portrait of Maharaja Thakhat Singh (ruled 1843–73) out riding camels with his courtesans.

Other portraits show off the tower-like, voluminous turbans – the biggest in Rajasthan – that were fashionable with Jodhpur rulers during the late 18th and early 19th centuries. But their jodhpurs, those comfortable riding trousers with baggy upper sections that the British adopted from here, are usually hidden beneath a coat.

The adjoining room, built for *puja*, is now called the **Mirror Room**. Thakhat Singh's bedroom is upstairs. Decorated just before his reign, its walls are coated with paintings, its lacquered ceiling is hung with baubles, and its furnishings include a giant, bed-like swing.

Next, a remarkable collection of musical instruments: a stringed *Sindhi sarangi*, a vast *drum*, and a huge conical trumpet called a *karna*, used at court and in the battlefield. Royal costumes of great extravagance fill **Ajit Vilas**. The pearl shoes of Raja Gaj Singh's favourite concubine, Anara Begum, are here.

Upstairs, the airy **Phul Mahal** (Flower

Sati stone marks the spot of self-immolation by women whose husbands died in battle.

Palace) was built by Abhai Singh as his *Darbar-e-Khas* (Private Audience Hall). Former rulers look down from the elaborately painted and gilded ceiling. *Ragamala* paintings decorate the walls between gold cartouches. A pictorial royal family tree helps visitors sort out who's who. And above a couch-like *gadi* hangs the Jodhpur coat of arms.

Downstairs, in the **Tent Room**, is one of Jodhpur's proudest pieces of booty: a portable cloth palace. This is a huge royal Mughal tent made of red silk velvet covered with floral designs embroidered with gold thread. It was made for Shah Jahan as his mobile audience hall, where he would sit on his velvet *gadi* in the inner colonnaded chamber and receive visitors. Aurangzeb inherited the tent. But when Jaswant Singh attacked for the second time, the tent was part of his loot.

Lastly, there is **Maan Vilas** housing the appropriately fine Rathor armory. Here are the tools that upheld their sense of honour and brought wealth to these skilled warriors. Special craftsmen made each weapon and lived inside the fort.

Sikligars (swordsmiths) might cover a hilt with delicate inlay of calligraphy or stud it with precious jewels, giving the blade a leaf-shape or making it double-edged, curved or pointed. Then there were *dhabdars* (armourers) to protect man, horse and elephant. Axes came in all shapes, and shields were made of anything from bamboo or steel to crocodile skin or rhino hide.

A selection of Jodhpur's bigger defense weapons stands on the **ramparts**. Some of the cannons are the spoils of Gaj Singh's warring in Jalore, others of Abhai's triumphs in Gujarat. Nearby, the image of the goddess Chamunda Devi, worshiped by the Rathors since Jodha's time, sits in her temple. The view from the ramparts is stunning.

On the road down from the fort, the splash of blinding white marble on the left is **Jaswant Thada**, Maharaja Jaswant Singh II's *chatri* (cenotaph) built in 1899 – all previous rulers have their *chatris* at Mandore. As with the Taj Mahal, the marble is from Makrana. Inside, the faithful still come to petition

Steam locomotives used to operate on the metre gauge lines.

198

the portrait of Jaswant. Outside, *chatris* of the next four Rathor rulers adjoin it, including that of Umaid whose outsized palace sits heavily on Chittor Hill to the east of the city.

Following two pretty disastrous rulers, Jaswant Singh (ruled 1878–95) ushered in a golden age for Jodhpur. According to rumour, Jodhpur treasure and wealth was sixth in the Indian league – following Hyderabad, Jaipur, Kashmir, Gwalior and Baroda. So Jaswant could not only be photographed in 1890 dripping in egg-sized pearls and precious stones; he could also invest in his state, for he was an energetic and successful ruler. He brought down the level of crime and suppressed the dacoits, began building railways, started much needed irrigation projects, and vastly improved the economy of Marwar with regular revenue and organized customs tariffs. As the *Imperial Gazetteer* noted in 1908: "In every department, wise and progressive policy was pursued" – praise no doubt lavished on him because of his fervent loyalty to the British Raj.

A street in old Jodhpur.

In all this – especially the loyalty – he was helped and encouraged by Pratap Singh (1845–1922), a remarkable man whose strong personality dominated the Jodhpur court from the 1870s to the 1920s, during which time he was three times made regent.

Palace-building as famine relief: It is unlikely the *Gazetteer* would have praised Maharaja Umaid Singh as it had Jaswant and Sir Pratap. For in 1929, aged 27, his solution to long-term famine was to employ 3,000 citizens a day for 16 years to build himself the playtime palace par excellence, completed on the eve of Indian Independence. This latest 347-room royal dwelling is so huge that the former royals now spread themselves airily over a third of it, run the official rooms as a museum, and leave a mere 57 suites plus dining and leisure rooms to serve as a hotel.

From its inception, **Umaid Bhawan Palace** is a catalogue of wild extremes. Astrologers dictated the hilly and arid site, so a railway was built to bring the sandstone up, earth was moved, rock was blasted to make room for tree roots,

and very deep wells were bored.

H.V. Lanchester, a British architect of civic buildings who admired the *Beaux-Arts* Movement and Lutyens' Viceregal Lodge (now Rashtrapati Bhavan) in New Delhi, designed it. It is his *tour de force*. Within a rigidly symmetrical plan full of courtyards, he somehow managed to cater for strict *purdah*, the latest princely European fashions, the Indian royal taste for gilt, his own interest in craftsmanship, and every whim of both Indian and British lifestyles on a small and grand scale. And the sombre, domed building is enlivened by Hindu details. His concession was size: the palace plan measures 195 by 103 metres (212 by 111 yards). It is one of the largest private homes in the world, and one of the more spectacular buildings of the 1930s.

Glorious *Beaux-Arts* doors are the entrance to the part that is now a hotel, still guarded by tall Jodhpuris in orange turbans. In the first hall, sweeping marble staircases lead to suites with art deco mirrors and Belgian crystal. A double dome with a whispering gallery covers the second hall, while an indoor swimming pool lies beneath it. Beyond, the terrace overlooks the restored garden. And in what is now the **museum section** (with fine clocks and more fine miniature paintings and arms), the Polish artist S. Norblin painted scenes from the Hindu epic, the *Mahabharata* on the walls of what has been called the **Oriental Room**.

Raikabagh Palace at the foot of Chittor Hill now houses government offices. Here, Umaid lived in sumptuous splendour on the first floor, while 400 of his beloved horses lived in almost equal comfort beneath him.

Umaid had little time to enjoy his new private paradise. In 1944 he moved in. Early in 1947, pursuing pleasure as usual on a hunting trip to Mount Abu, he died of a burst appendix aged 43.

Further tragedy struck. His son, Hanwant Singh, inherited the title at 28. Like Umaid, Hanwant loved modern toys, and his passion was flying. He developed Jodhpur as a premier aircraft centre in Asia. In 1952, Hanwant stood as an Independent. The vote-count revealed **Mughal tent now in the fort museum.**

he had won a with a majority of 10,000. Just two days later, he flew into some telegraph wires and died instantly.

Trips out of town: After the charm of Jodhpur city and the extravagance of Umaid Bhawan, it is worth making a foray into the desert. It contains some remarkable *chatris*, temples and forts, and a surprisingly rich variety of wildlife. This desert land gets extremely hot: it is best to start early in the day, taking snacks and a supply of drinking water.

Mahamandir (about 2 km/1 mile), or Great Temple, lies on the northeastern outskirts of Jodhpur. This small temple town was founded by Maharaja Man Singh, who was a strong devotee of the Nath sect of Shaivas. His guru was Deva Nath, for whom he built the Mahamandir in 1812 after his escape from Jhalore. Inside, a forest of pillars supports the temple roof. Murals of aspects of yoga cover the walls.

Man Singh combined Rajput warring with serious cultural and religious pursuits. As a scholar, he studied Sanskrit, Urdu and Persian. He was a fine poet and generously patronised other poets, heaping state money, court honours and some 62 villages on his favourites.

The lakeside palace at Balsamand (7 km/4 miles), further north on the same road, has now been converted into a beautiful Art Deco-style hotel with a public park and bird sanctuary. The whole complex was built as a little royal oasis, a pleasure-ground where welcome fresh air wafted off the lake and across the lush green gardens. It is said that Balak Rao Parihar of Mandore cut out the lake in 1159, making it the oldest artificial lake in Rajasthan. Maharaja Sur Singh enlarged the lake and built a summer palace, which seems to have been later enlarged and modified, first by Jaswant Singh II, and then by Umaid Singh.

Just north of here, through a narrow pass between high cliffs, lies the former capital of Jodhpur, **Mandore** (9 km/5 miles). Originally called Mandaya Pura, the city was the capital of the Parihar Rajputs from the 6th century until their defeat by Rao Chanda in 1381. Rao

The maharani *chatris*, Mandore.

Chanda married a Parihar princess, had 14 sons and established Mandore as the Rathor seat of government which held sway until 1459. From the ancient fort set on craggy hills above the fertile gorge, the Rathors fought off the Khaljis and Tuglaqs and other Delhi sultanates.

Mandore's glory are the **six dewals**, the domed royal *chatris* of the Rathors which stand in a line on the right of the lush, shady, landscaped gardens. Each is built on the spot where the ruler was cremated, joined on his pyre by various wives and concubines.

Starting with Rao Maldeo's fairly modest *chatri*, the monuments to Sur Singh, Udhai Singh, Guj Singh, Jaswant Singh and Ajit Singh rise in increasing height and grandeur, neatly mirroring the rise in Marwar's fortunes. Their architecture mixes Buddhist and Shaiva styles. But the rich and fine decoration carved into the hard, brown stone is entirely Jain. Whereas Jaswant's is rather ponderous, Ajit's achieves a rare elegance: a Shaiva-style pyramidal temple with columned interiors.

Across the garden is the **Hall of Heroes**, where 16 life-size figures were carved out of the rock during the reigns of Ajit and Abhai (1707–49) or possibly earlier. The heroes are either Hindu deities or local Rajputs, each one fully armed, mounted on horse-back and gaily painted. There is Chamunda, a form of the goddess of destruction; Kali, another destructive goddess, riding her tiger and crushing a demon; and Nath, the Rathor's spiritual leader, holding a *churri* (rod) to guide his devotees.

Among the warriors is Pabuji on his famous black mare, Kesa Kali (Black Caesar), who so moved the historian Tod that he scratched his name here, and even admitted to the graffiti in his *Annals*. The heroic deeds of Pabuji, an ally of Rao Jodha, are a favourite subject of *bhopas* (itinerant epic singers). Next but one to Pabuji is Hurba Sankla, who helped Jodha win back Mandore from Chittaurgarh's clutches in 1453 and who is celebrated with the **Virpuri Mela** every August.

The larger hall next door is the **Shrine of 30 Crore** (3,000 million) **Gods**. An optimistic title, but the interior is indeed crammed with huge, painted statues of Hindu gods. Nearby are remains of **Abhai Singh's stone palace**, where he would have come to eat the famous Jodhpur pomegranates and to enjoy his garden with its fountains and water-channels.

Ruins of the ancient city litter the rocky plateau above – materials were re-used for the *chatris* and the new **Jodhpur fort**. On the way up, there is a **monument to Nahur Rao**, last of the Parihars. Through what remains today of massive walls and square bastions, there are still traces of the Parihar gateway, arch and fort. There is also a much earlier 8th-century **Gupta temple**.

Beyond the walls lie the *chatris* of four earlier Rathor rulers, of which the carving on Rao Ganga's (died about 1532) is especially fine. Back in the gardens, some 60 elegant *chatris* of royal *maharanis* lie quietly up a steep winding path and across the reservoir.

Luni and Rohet: About 40km (25 miles) south of Jodhpur lie two interesting little estates, both now hotels. Built from red Jodhpur sandstone, Fort Chanwa in Luni

The Hall of Heroes, Mandore.

has some unusual architecture. In the winter Rohetgarh is a sanctuary for the many migratory birds, which nest by the idyllic lake to the rear of the small palace. Many black-buck gazelle can be found in the area around the two properties, as the Bishnoi people revered and protected this particular species.

All Bishnois follow the 21 *(bis-noi)* tenets laid down by the 15th-century Guru Jambeshwar. They fervently believe in the sanctity of animal and plant life, so all animals live near their villages without fear. When Bishnoi die, they are sometimes buried in the sitting position and often placed at the threshold of the house or adjoining cattleshed. But all Bishnoi believe that they will later be reincarnated as a deer – hence the herds often seen near their villages.

Bishnoi villages are immaculate, scrubbed daily by the brightly clad women who are weighed down with jewellery and festooned with bangles the length of their arms. By contrast, the men dress entirely in white, with loosely swathed large turbans.

In the nearby village of Salawa, it is possible to watch a weaver and his family making the traditional *durris*. The outlying region can be explored by jeep or as part of an organised horse-safari.

Peacock Island: A more ambitious trip north, but thoroughly rewarding for its architecture, goes on to **Osiyan** (65 km/40 miles). This small green peacock-inhabited island of greenery in the desert sand, now full of peacocks, was once a great trading centre. Since Jains were the prosperous traders who formed the backbone of the local economy, the Hindu rulers showed them religious tolerance, permitting them to build lavish, often marble, temples which became repositories of historical and cultural manuscripts. The 16 fine **Brahman and Jain** temples of the 8th to 12th centuries testify to the city's former wealth under its Parihar rulers.

The first group, on the town outskirts, are the earlier temples. These 11 represent the first phases of medieval temple architecture in Rajasthan. Standing on high terraces, each has a porch, hall and

Finely detailed carvings, Osiyan.

sanctum. The halls are mostly open, balustrades replacing walls to give more light, and the whole group is richly and elaborately decorated. Vase-and-foliage capitals top the columns, and four or five bands of decoration rise up from river-goddesses to surround doorways and sanctum surroundings.

The largest is **Mahavira**, a Jain temple set up on a terrace and dedicated to their last Tirthankara. The sanctum was built during the rule of the Parihar Rajput, Vatsaraja (783–793). After 10th-century renovations, the graceful *torana* (gateway), with carvings of celestial women and the *sikhara* (beehive-shaped tower) were both added the following century. Behind **Surya** (Sun) **temple**, with two fluted pillars at its entrance, steps by a pool lead down to the ruins of what was possibly a summer palace.

The later **Mahashamardi temple**, known locally as **Pipla Devi**, has a big assembly hall and a row of the nine personified planets adorn the lintel. It is also worth looking at the two temples dedicated to Vishnu and the three 8th-century temples dedicated to Harihara. The 12th-century **Sachiya Mata temple**, well decorated inside and outside, is the focus of the second group which stands on a hill just east of Osiyan, reached through a sandstone arch carved, again, with celestial women.

If the desert has worked its magic, travel another 60 km (37 miles) to **Khimsar**, whose fort is now a hotel. As expected in this area, its history is dominated by the Rathors. Rao Jodha's fifth son, Karam Singh, was the local *thakur* (ruler). He named his fortified *thikana* (ruler's home) Fateh Mahal after a Sufi saint who was buried there.

Karam Singh's descendants now live in an 18th-century annex to the fort. If possible, climb one of the huge sand dunes nearby and watch the sun set over the beautiful surrounding countryside. The radiant and romantic Castle Khimsar is a perfect place to stop and rest and a good starting-point to explore Nagaur and its environs.

Desert city: From Khimsar, **Nagaur** is a 40-km (25-mile) journey (it is 135 km/

A *minar* is all that survives of an old mosque, Nargar.

85 miles from Jodhpur). This ancient, heavily fortified desert city is now the headquarters of Nagaur District, an area famous for its fine bullocks. Indeed, it is well worth timing your visit to take in the huge cattle fairs when there are four days of races and contests for camels, cocks, horses and bullocks, with colourful Rajasthani dancing and singing. The two major festivals are named after local heroes; the **Ramdeoji Fair** is in February and the **Tejaji Fair** in August.

According to legend, Nagaur is named after the Naga Rajputs. But its turbulent history see-sawed between Hindu and Muslim ownership. The old town is surrounded by a tall, thick wall, with sturdy battlements which have been repaired with bits of demolished mosques – hence the occasional Arabic or Persian inscription. The fine decoration on the high gateway is probably by the same artisans who worked on Ajmer mosques in the mid-13th century. A cluster of royal Hindu *chatris* stand outside it.

Inside, the two most interesting buildings are Muslim. One is **Akbar's five-domed mosque**, his shrine for a disciple of Khwaja Muin-ud-din Chishti, the Sufi saint who came to India in 1192 and died at Ajmer. The other is **Shams Masjid**, named after the 13th-century governor Shams Khan.

The remarkable **fort** sits on a hill in the city, further protected by huge double walls: the outer one 8 metres (25 feet) high, the inner one 16 metres (50 feet) high and of a thickness tapering from 9 metres (30 feet) at the base to 4 metres (12 feet) at the top. Inside, Akbar built the 17-jet fountains; Shah Jahan built the mosque; and both Muslims and Hindus claim their saints lived in the cave.

The **palaces**, once set in lush formal gardens, are the delight of Naguar. Delicate murals of cyprus trees and peacock feathers, occasionally framing a dancer or flower, decorate the exterior walls. There are impressive paintings inside.

About 25 km (15 miles) east of Nagaur lies **Manglud**. Its ancient temple has a Sanskrit inscription recording its repair in 604 AD, one of the oldest inscriptions in Rajasthan.

Camels draw water from extremely deep wells.

MOUNT ABU: PILGRIM CENTRE

A tropical hill-resort in the middle of the Rajasthan desert would appear an impossibility. Yet this is exactly what **Mount Abu** is. The broken ridges of the Aravalli hills attain their highest point at **Guru Shikhar**, the Saints Pinnacle, in the southwestern corner of Rajasthan, bordering the State of Gujarat. This range is separated from the main chain of the Aravallis by a valley about 24 km (15 miles) wide. In this vale the fruits and vegetables that feed the surrounding region are grown.

Driving from Udaipur towards Abu, it is incredible how fertile the area appears. From **Sirohi**, once a formidable Deora-Chauhan stronghold, now a neglected stopover, the fields on either side glow with vigorous splendour. During the monsoon, there are piles of scarlet chillies, golden pumpkins, red tomatoes, purple brinjals (aubergines) waiting to be transported by trucks to nearby cities. However, Gujarat is the main destination for the produce, rather than the more distant, less accessible, Rajasthani markets.

Sirohi was once an important centre of Rajput power. The Chauhans, after their defeat by the Afghans in the 12th century, fled southwest. Settling in Kota-Bundi, they were called the Hada Chauhans, while another branch, the Deora Chauhans, made Sirohi their main centre. All branches of the Chauhan clan owed allegiance to the Sisodias of Mewar (the Royal House of Udaipur).

Glimpses of former glory in Sirohi are still evident, such as the beautiful whitewashed temple gleaming on a hill-top about 10 km (6 miles) outside the town. If you have the stamina to go up, the effort will be rewarded by a remarkable view of the surrounding countryside. You will also notice the curious type of local cattle: small, compact, strong and with long, sharp and straight horns. These are often painted in bright colours and little bulls are decorated with necklaces of beads and cowrie shells. These animals are said to be very intelligent and can be trained to do all sorts of tricks. Bulls are often the companions of mendicant fortune-tellers who entertain the crowds at fairs and festivals with their "holy bulls" who can tell the fortune of standers-by, shaking or nodding their heads in answer to questions.

As you climb up the winding road to Mount Abu, the hill become covered by tropical forests with a wide variety of trees. Each curve of the road brings into view silk-cotton and bottle-brush, mango, bamboo, eucalyptus, wild pomegranate, coral, date-palm and lime. There are also the colourful flame of the forest (the famous *pallas* of the ancient poems), gulmohur, jacaranda, amaltash and oleander.

Abu was selected as the site for one of the most sacred rites of the Vedic era, the *yagna* of the *Agnikund*, or the sacrifice of the fire-pit. This ceremony was to have a profound effect on the whole basic structure of Hinduism and its impact on Indian society can still be seen today.

Preceding pages: ceiling detail, Mount Abu. **Left,** devotees at Dilwara. **Right,** Jain nun covers her mouth to avoid harming insects.

The *yagna* was an initiation ceremony, qualifying those who participate to be accepted into the social fold.

After the fall of the great Gupta Empire, northwest India was in a state of chaos. The ancient fighting caste, the Kshatriyas, had been decimated by the endless invaders that entered India via the Hindu Kush: Huns, Gujars, Hellenes, Persians, Scythians, who mixed, married and settled in petty kingdoms. These fighting peoples, after an elaborate, sacrificial ceremony and purification through an ordeal by fire at a Concord of Brahmans, held at Gaumukh in Abu, were now proclaimed Kshatriyas and accepted as the fighting caste, the families of fireborn or *agnikula* Rajputs. They were the Paramars, Chauhans, Pratiharas and Solankis. Even today these castes claim a divine origin and a direct Kshatriya link with the earlier Vedic peoples. This had an important impact on the history of the region. No longer considered as marauding foreigners, these clans went on to set up flourishing kingdoms; the Chauhans in

Delhi-Ajmer; the Paramars in Central India, where the remains of their beautiful temples can still be seen in Madhya Pradesh; the Pratiharas were the direct forerunners of the later Rajput rulers who held power up to the time of the independence of India in 1947.

Abu is also a centre of Jain pilgrimage and here is one of the greatest achievements of the temple-builders' art: the **Dilwara temples**. The carving in marble achieved an impressive degree of subtlety and complexity, delicacy and intricate detail. The stone was manipulated with such skill and dexterity, that many variations on a theme could be encompassed on a single pillar or a frieze. In a way, Dilwara is almost too much. It can overwhelm and satiate, but it cannot be missed.

Gaumukh Temple (literally the "cow's mouth") lies about 4 km (2.5 miles) below Abu on a bridle path. A small shrine to Vishnu has images of his incarnations as Rama and Krishna. A natural spring flows through a cow's head which gives the shrine its name.

Detail, Dilwara Temple roof carvings.

This is the scene of the ancient *agnikund* from which the Rajput clans, *Agnikula*, are said to have sprung. Pilgrims visit this sacred shrine and carry home the holy water of the spring.

Achalgarh: This fort is about 8 km (5 miles) out of Abu along a motorable road up to Uria. From here the ascent is made on foot through steeply rising woods (palanquins are available for those not wishing to walk). There are several temples on the way, many in a ruined state, and only the ramparts and broken walls of the original fort, built by Rana Kumbha of Mewar (14th century) remain. Kumbha was one of the great rulers of the state responsible for making Mewar the leading Rajput kingdom. He was murdered by his son and the fight that followed split the House of Mewar. The first large temple is dedicated to *Achaliswar Mahadev* or Lord Shiva and was built in 1412.

Dilwara Jain Temples: Barely 3 km (2 miles) north of Abu are temples set on a hill in the midst of a grove of old mango trees. These are Jain shrines. The temples are open between noon and 6pm. All cameras, bags, shoes, and leather objects must be left outside. The main temples are not very large and are covered by domes rather than the more usual pyramidal *shikaras*.

Adinath Temple (1031): The older of the two main shrines is dedicated to the first of the Jain *tirthankaras* (pathfinders to the faith). It was built by Vimala, a minister of state. Constructed entirely of pure white marble, this temple is the more pleasing of the two. It is less ornate, allowing the fine carving to be more easily appreciated. The outer porch has a pavilion to the right which shows the donors mounted on elephants, but these have been badly mutilated.

The entrance opposite leads to the main shrine. Elaborate *makaratoranas* or scroll arches decorate the hall, with pillars entirely covered with fine carvings of nymphs and musicians. The inner sanctum contains a figure of Adinath (the first of the *tirthankaras*) in the posture of meditation. The door lintel and jambs are encrusted with carved figures.

The high ground and cool climate have made Abu a popular holiday resort.

The domed ceiling of the hall has a flower-pendant encircled by large female figures in dancing postures. All round the shrine runs a covered cloister, its pillars also carved, and its ceiling divided into innumerable sections, each cut and carved in different patterns. Along the corridor are 52 niches housing statues of the *tirthankaras* and each niche again has delicate carved figures and designs on its facing.

Neminath Temple (1230): This shrine, dedicated to the 22nd *tirthankara*, was built by two brothers, Tejapala and Vastupala, who also built the famous temple at Girnar, Gujarat. There is a profusion of marble work on its convoluted scroll arches, its covered pillars of which no two are alike; the elaborate scenes carved in bas-relief on the corridor ceilings, the stalactite-like pendant from the main central dome, and the magnificent hall of donors at the farther end are especially fine. The carving is exceptional.

The Hall of Donors: Behind the central shrine is perhaps the most interesting and unusual feature of this temple: in a long hall are several figures mounted on elephants, some of black marble. Behind the mounted figures are niches, each containing two or three figures, almost life size, of a donor and his wife, or with two women. The exquisite carvings show the fine texture of the muslin drapery and the delicate designs of the shadow and drawn-thread work.

There is a **museum** at Abu set in a pleasant garden which is worth a visit.

Nakki Lake: A focal point for Indian tourists is a lovely little artificial lake ringed round by hills and overhung by the enormous **Toad's Rock**. Boating and exploring the lake's little islets is a favourite recreation of Indian tourists. The rulers of Rajput states built summer villas round the lake; some of these are now guest houses or hotels. Nakki Lake is said to have been dug by the gods with their nails *(nakki)*, hence its name.

Sunset Point: There are many beautiful walks round the hills. The best mountain view is to be had from Sunset Point southwest of Nakki Lake, where the sun

Nakki lake.

sets between two craggy peaks. Steps lead to a high terrace which offers a magnificent view of the sunset, especially during the monsoon.

Trevor's Tank: A part of the forest around Abu has been turned into a wildlife sanctuary. The road winds through steep hills, thickly wooded and containing peacocks, pheasants, partridges and other birds. In a sudden opening, the hills encircle a deep pool, built by a British engineer named Trevor and now named Trevor's Tank. A small but pretty forest lodge stands on the far bank. The tank is home to crocodiles, which you may see lazing on the banks. In the evening this is a good spot to see local wildlife, as this is the time the animals come down to drink. In the past, shoots were arranged and picnics held by the royal hosts, but now it is an excellent place for the more peaceful pursuit of birdwatching.

While returning from Mount Abu, pause at **Abu Road** at the bottom of the hill. Essentially a stopover for the sacred sites at Mount Abu, Abu Road is where the pilgrims gather. They pause to pick up offerings, or to look for inexpensive lodgings, or just to rest before embarking on the long and arduous pilgrimage to the holy shrines, often made on foot.

The winding lanes in the bazaars are lined with shops heaped with coloured powders. Here you can get the vermilion *sindhoor* or *kumkum* that adorns the forehead and hair parting of Indian women. There are flower stalls selling sweet-smelling jasmine garlands. Incense of many kinds, oil-lamps and beautiful marble images are also favourite offerings.

Since Abu is a sacred city and an important Jain centre, most people there are strict vegetarians. Delicious vegetarian food can be found at the better hotels and guest-houses and it is best to stick to this. As much of the food is highly spiced with chillies, ask for lightly spiced dishes.

Mount Abu is a convenient stop between southwestern Rajasthan and Gujarat to the south. It is also linked with Jodhpur and Udaipur.

UDAIPUR: MEWAR, LAND OF LEGEND

Royal House of Mewar: Legend has it that the Sisodias of Mewar are descended from the Sun God through Lav, the son of Lord Rama whose life story is told in India's great epic, the *Ramayana*. They came from the borders of Kashmir and by the 2nd century BC they had moved south to what is now Gujarat, founding, as they went, several cities along the coast, one of which was called Vallabhi.

The chronicles of the bards tell us that in the 6th century, Vallabhi was sacked by strangers from the west. The Queen of Vallabhi, Pushpavati, who was on a pilgrimage offering prayers for her unborn child, heard of the destruction of Vallabhi and the death of her husband while travelling through the Aravalli hills in the north. Despairing, she took refuge in a cave, and there gave birth to a son whom she called Guhil, or "cave born". Then, entrusting her child to a maidservant, the queen ordered a funeral pyre to be lit, and walked into it to join her dead husband's soul.

Guhil, or Guhadatta, was befriended by the Bhils, Adivasis who had lived in the Aravalli hills since well before 2000 BC. Amongst the Bhils, Guhadatta grew in power, and became a chieftain. His progeny came to be known as *Guhilots*.

In the 7th century the Guhilots moved north, and down to the plains of Mewar, changing their name to Sisodia, after a village they encountered on the way. The descendants of Guhadatta were the great Ranas, Rawals and Maharanas of Mewar, builders of forts and palaces, whose exploits in peace and war are the stuff of legend. By the time of India's independence, the royal line of Mewar had ruled for 75 generations, a total of 1,400 years; the oldest of Rajasthan's feudal dynasties.

The founding of Udaipur: In 1567, the capital of Mewar, Chittaurgarh, was sacked for the third time by the armies of the Mughal Emperor Akbar; Rana Udai Singh II withdrew into the hills and ravines of the Aravalli. One morning, while out hunting by Lake Pichola, the rana saw a sage meditating. The rana dutifully paid his respects to the holy man.

"Where, O Revered One," the rana asked the sage, having recounted the fall of Chittaurgarh, "should I build my next capital city?" And the sage answered, as sages will, "Why, right here of course, where your destiny has brought you to ask such a question." And that's what Udai Singh did.

Udaipur today: The spirit of **Udaipur**, someone once said, gazes toward Chittaurgarh, as at a lost and distant horizon. For it is from the misfortunes of that fort that this city of pleasure was born. Luxurious Udaipur is an interesting counterpoint to stark Chittaurgarh. While the fort stands rugged and battle-scarred, blending with the scrubby country, on a stark plateau, Udaipur nestles like a gem in a valley surrounded by the green Aravalli hills, reflected smooth and white in the clear blue of Lake Pichola.

The old city within the fortifications is built on tiny hills. Narrow medieval roads and lanes wind and bend, with a small temple at each turning, making the city one of the most attractive in all Rajasthan. Interspersed among the old dwellings, temples and palaces which speak of a royal, aristocratic past, is the new and the modern – shops, houses, markets and down-to-earth bus-stands. The population has since grown to 308,000.

The **City Palace**, once entirely the home of Mewar's rulers, is today largely a museum run by the Maharana Mewar Foundation. It actually consists of four major and several minor palaces forming a single breathtaking facade overlooking the Pichola lake. Built by successive kings, every addition was so flawlessly integrated in style and feeling with the existing structures as to make the whole seem one.

From the outside, the palace resembles nothing so much as formidable Rajput fort with sheer impregnable walls rising high out of the water, broken only near the top by an exuberance of domes, arches, cupolas, turrets and crenellations.

The approach to the palace is through the **Hathi Pol** (Elephant Gate) to the

Preceding pages: shy Rajput woman. **Left, city view from across Lake Pichola.**

north on the main street of the city, leading to the **Tripolia** or triple gate of marble arches.

Above the Tripolia is **Hawa Mahal**, built in the 19th century, a facade of windows from behind which the women of the palace could watch the world outside. Beyond the Tripolia is the **Bada Chowk**, the Big Square, in which in the past, a hundred elephants, the rana's infantry, cavalry and artillery were massed for inspection before battle.

The **Toran Pol** on the south side of Bada Chowk leads into the palace buildings, and to its right, high on the wall you will see the sun emblem of the rulers of Mewar. Below this emblem is the **Padgadi-Hathni**, where in the past, visitors to the royal house dismounted from the backs of richly caparisoned elephants.

Entering the palace, there is a profusion of courtyards, rooms, and galleries – so decorated and embellished as to be museum pieces themselves – housing artefacts connected with the history of Mewar and its rulers.

The **Shrine of Dhuni Mata** is the oldest part of the city palace, as well as the oldest building in Udaipur, and said to be built on the spot at which Rana Udai Singh met the meditating sage. It is a simple room containing pictures of the four major Hindu deities of Mewar: Sri Charbhujaji, Sri Eklingji, Sri Nathji (or Krishna) and Amba Mata.

The **Raj Angan** or Royal Courtyard in which the shrine of Dhuni Mata stands has rooms leading off it which house part of the **Museum of Rana Pratap** which was once in the Victoria Hall.

Rana Pratap (ruled 1572–97) was one of the great warrior kings of Mewar. He lived in troubled times: Emperor Akbar, the Great Mughal, was expanding his domains across South Asia. He had already sacked the Mewar stronghold, Chittaurgarh, driving Pratap's father, Rana Udai Singh II, out towards a life in the new capital, Udaipur. Rana Pratap was imbued with stories of the lost greatness of Mewar and obsessed with a desire to recover its territories, and the fort of Chittaurgarh.

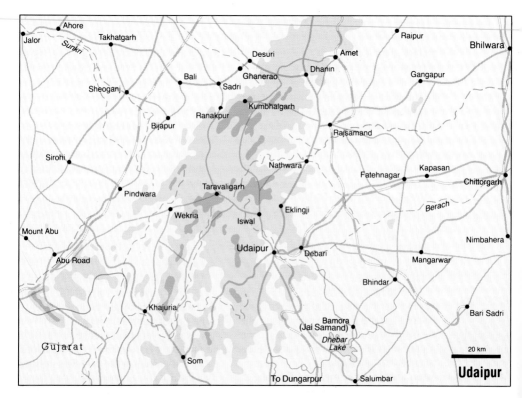

The indomitable Pratap threw himself against the might of the Mughal armies again and again, losing the battle of Haldighati, losing every fort, including Kumbalgarh, retreating to the hills and ravines of the Aravallis where sometimes his family hadn't enough to eat. In these years of adversity, they were aided by the Bhil peoples, whose ancestors had, centuries earlier, supported the rana's ancestor, Guhadatta.

Rana Pratap was one of the two Rajput kings who refused to accept Mughal suzerainty or compromise with Akbar: no daughter of Mewar was ever given to a Mughal emperor or prince in marriage. The other Rajput ruler who similarly held out against the Mughals was the king of Bundi. Akbar allowed both states to survive and the next generation of rulers had to accept reality and sign treaties with the Mughals. Eventually, Pratap freed Udaipur and much of Mewar from the Mughal grip but he failed to win back Chittaurgarh.

In the museum in the City Palace are paintings depicting incidents in the life of Rana Pratap. His armour and weapons and other memorabilia are also on display. **Dil Kushal**, a room created in the 17th century by Rana Karan Singh, has walls lined with mirrors interspersed with miniature paintings.

On the walls surrounding **Mor Chowk**, a courtyard in **Priyatama Vilas** built in the late 19th century by Maharana Sajjan Singh, are intricately crafted peacocks in fine mosaic relief. **Bhim Vilas** has a famous sun window, **Suraj Gokhala**, installed by Maharana Bhim Singh in the late 18th century.

The **Bada** (big) **Mahal** is also called the Garden Palace, for here in the centre, raised 27 metres (90 feet), is a beautiful garden. It stands on a hill in the middle of the palace complex, making the rooms around it appear to be on the top floor of the palace. They are actually ground-floor rooms built around the periphery of the natural rock topped by the garden.

Krishna Vilas: In 1805, the kings of Jodhpur and Jaipur were on the offensive against Mewar where Maharana Bhim Singh was then ruling. Both the rulers

indicated that they would settle for the lovely 16-year-old Sisodia princess, Krishna Kumari. The king of Mewar was in a quandary: he could neither refuse or accept, for appeasing one would set the other against him. When Krishna Kumari heard of her father's dilemma, she resolved it – by poisoning herself. Her heartbroken mother died soon after, and the maharana soothed his grief by building the Krishna Vilas which today holds some of the most beautiful miniature paintings to be seen in Rajasthan.

Manek Mahal (Ruby Palace) houses an exhibition of glass and porcelain, including the **Chini Chitrashala**, a collection of Chinese porcelain. **Khush Mahal** (Palace of Pleasure) was built by Sajjan Singh in 1874.

Zenana Mahal: South of the City Palace Museum and east of the gardens of Chandra Chowk is the Palace of the Queens, begun in the early 17th century, it is now open to the public as a museum.

The Zenana Mahal is entered through the **Zenana Dyodhi**, named the "devious gate", as it guards Mahal's entrance.

Through this gate is the **Rang Bhawan** where heirlooms and state treasures are on display. On the right are shrines to Lord Krishna and Princess Mira Bai, Rana Sanga's daughter-in-law, a renowned *bhakti* (devotional) poet and saint.

Rang Bhawan opens into **Laxmi Chowk** (square) which is flanked by the domed apartments of the queen and her guests. The queen's apartments are decorated with murals of Lord Krishna at play amongst the milkmaids. There is exquisite glass inlay work in the **Osara**, the place of ceremony, in the eastern wing of Zenana Mahal.

In the centre of Laxmi Chowk is a pavilion with a magnificent fretwork peacock spreading its tail. Inside the pavilion are housed musical instruments.

On the first floor of the structure around Laxmi Chowk is a succession of rooms housing miniatures of the Mewar school, showing the minutiae of daily life of the court, a subject peculiar to the Mewar school. And here too you can see some fine old photographs of the British political residents and viceroys. One of

Local tourists add color to the City Palace.

220

the alcoves off these rooms is set up in memory of Colonel James Tod, the devoted historian of Rajasthan, and Resident Representative of the British Crown from 1818 to 1822.

Beyond Zenana Mahal and the garden of Chandra Chowk, or Moon Square, past another square to the east, is the **Durbar Hall**. Lord Minto, the British viceroy, laid the foundation stone of the hall in the reign of Maharana Fateh Singh, a proud and conservative man, constantly at odds with the British in defence of his rights and privileges as a ruling prince. He was virtually dethroned by the British and the *gadi* passed to Maharana Bhupal Singh who led Mewar into the Indian Union in 1947. On the formation of the state of Rajasthan in 1949, the Government of India honoured Maharana Bhupal Singh by making him Maharaj Pramukh (the premier maharaja) of Rajasthan.

Shambu Niwas, adjacent to the Durbar Hall, was built in the mid-19th century. It is not open to the public. Nor are the older apartments of the saint,

Kanwarji Bhaiji, east of the Durbar Hall, where *puja* ceremonies are still performed as they have been through the generations. The Shiv Niwas Hotel is also a part of the city palace complex. Formerly a royal guest-house, its guests today can enjoy the luxurious accommodation – opulent suites, an elegant bar with a huge crystal chandelier and a swimming pool in the inner courtyard – but at a royal price. The Fateh Prakash Hotel is housed in another part of this city palace.

Jagdish Mandir: Close by the main gate of the City Palace, high on a hill is a temple complex dedicated to Jagannath, an aspect of Lord Vishnu. It was built by Maharana Jagat Singh in 1651. Thirty-two steps lead up to it from the main road. The central temple in the group is heavily ornamented with excellent carvings. In its main shrine is an enormous black stone image of Jagannath. At the entrance, in an enclosed shrine of its own, is a fine bronze figure of Garuda (a mythical bird), the *vahana* or vehicle of Lord Vishnu.

In the reign of Maharana Raj Singh, the Mughal Emperor Aurangzeb defeated the combined armies of Mewar and Marwar. While the maharana and his men attempted to defend Udaipur, Naru Bharat, a bard, gathered a small force to defend the Jagdish Temple. He fell to the Mughal sword, and the temple was destroyed. A cenotaph adjacent to the temple commemorates his heroism.

Udaipur today: It is through the streets of today, the markets and the bazaars, that the traveller must wander to get the feel of the city as a whole. The **Bara Bazaar** is close behind the palace, and under the ramparts to the east is **Bapu Bazaar**, a fascinating place.

Here, you will find carpenters in side alleys making wooden toys in the traditional manner, and dressing puppets in traditional styles of dress. Puppet shows re-enact epics of heroism and romance. You can also see artisans at work and jewellers engaged in the craft of *minakari* (enamel inlay on gold or silver). You can buy old coins and images of gods and watch women making *bandhani* (tie-dyed) fabrics and traditional *pichwai* paintings.

Sajjan Niwas lies a little further south, still within the old city walls. In its grounds is **Gulab Bagh** (Rose Garden) laid out by Maharana Sajjan Singh in the late 19th century. The grounds cover 40 hectares (100 acres) with spacious lawns, a zoo, and Victoria Hall (now called Saraswati Bhawan) opened in 1890 by the British viceroy, Lord Landsdowne, to commemorate the 1887 Diamond Jubilee of Queen Victoria. Saraswati Bhawan is now a library.

Farther south, toward Lake Pichola, is **Machchalaya Magra** (Whale Hill), so called because it resembles a whale beached on the sands. It rises about 760 metres (2,500 feet) above sea level and extends right to the lake. The view from this hill, over the city and lake, is magnificent.

From **Eklingji Hill** south of **Dudh Talai** (Pond of Milk), the ramparts of the old city wall ramble down the hills to the east and north, skirting the banks of Lake Pichola.

Lakeside houses in the shadow of the City Palace.

Lake Pichola: This lake takes its name from the small village of Picholi on its west bank. A *banjara* (grain transporter) back in the 15th century, found that the bullocks carrying his load could not ford the stream there, so he built a raised path across it. The path acted as a dam, and a lake began to form behind it. By the time Rana Udai Singh II came to this region, Pichola Lake was quite large. Rana Udai Singh strengthened the dam, **Badi Pal** (Big Dam), and greatly enlarged the lake as a defence measure.

Pichola Lake consists today of a complex of the original Pichola, Amar Sagar, Rang Sagar, Swaroop Sagar north of it, and Dudh Talai toward the south, which is currently dry land covered by a garden. Later maharanas strengthened the dam further. The lake is about 8 sq. km (3 sq. miles) in area, and contains several islands. On two of them the maharanas of Udaipur constructed pleasure palaces, one of which, **Jag Niwas**, is today the Lake Palace Hotel, one of India's most romantic and best known hotels.

Jag Mandir: It is said Maharana Karan Singh built this second island retreat for the family of his friend Prince Khurram, who later became the Emperor Shah Jahan. Huge seamless stone slabs of translucent thinness were used. Cupolas; a lofty dome; spacious courtyards; beautiful rooms embellished with inlaid stones – onyx, jade, cornelian, jasper, agate; and paintings, are a few of the splendours of the palace. As a mark of his gratitude, and a symbol of brotherhood, Prince Khurram exchanged turbans with Maharana Karan. This turban is preserved, still in its original folds, in the City Palace at Udaipur.

The palace was named after Maharana Jagat Singh, the son of Maharana Karan Singh, who made some additions to it and later built Jag Niwas. Today, the western part of the palace is a delightful rest house, with a swimming pool. For bird-watching alone it is worth a visit.

Jag Niwas, the Lake Palace Hotel: Legend has it that, as a youth, Prince Jagat Singh once asked his father's permission to take a group of friends

The Lake Palace by moonlight.

and hangers-on with him to Jag Mandir for a bit of fun. The old maharana refused, saying that for fun Jagat Singh could go build his own palace on the lake. Stung, the prince did just that; he built a most magnificent palace on a rocky island nearby – a sort of posthumous retort to his father.

The Jag Niwas Palace and its grounds, covering an area of 1.6 hectares (4 acres), is an airy stucco complex floored with marble and has graceful granite columns. The gardens, fountains and lavishly decorated rooms are a refreshing retreat.

Arsi Vilas: This small island near Jag Mandir was never built on. It is now a sanctuary for water-fowl and other birds.

Nathani ka Chabutra: A small platform rising out of the water near the Jag Mandir Palace has an interesting history. A professional tightrope walker of the Nat caste was promised half the kingdom of Mewar by a somewhat drunken maharana, if she could walk the tightrope from a village on the west bank of Lake Pichola to the City Palace on the east bank. The confident Nathani gladly accepted the challenge and, toes curled around a tightrope strung for the occasion, gracefully balanced her way over the lake until she had almost reached Jag Mandir – at which point, a canny minister imbued with a strong practical streak, had the rope cut. The girl fell into the lake and drowned. The kingdom of Mewar remained undivided, but a *chabutra*, a small marble platform, was raised in memory of this acrobat.

Lake Fateh Sagar, lying north of Pichola, past Lake Rang Sagar and Lake Swaroop Sagar, was excavated in the late 17th century by Maharana Jai Singh.

Nehru Park: Out in Lake Fateh Sagar is an island. In 1937, intending to create work for his people to alleviate famine conditions, Maharana Bhupal Singh initiated work on the foundations of a water palace. However, the famine passed, and work on the new palace was discontinued. The island was left to birds and animals, reptiles and swamps, for the next 35 years. The state government of Rajasthan has converted it into a park named after India's first

Udaipur has its own style of wall painting.

Prime Minister. Visitors reach it by boat from the **Municipal Rock Garden** on the eastern bank.

Bharatiya Lok Kala Mandal: A little further north is the centre for Rajasthan's traditional culture. Created in 1952, the institution has been recording Rajasthani folklore and music, collecting local arts, staging plays, collecting Adivasi art, and supporting Rajasthani puppetry.

On **Moti Magri** (Hill of Pearls), in a garden named after Bhama Shah, the Prime Minister of Rana Pratap, is a 3-metre (11-foot) tall bronze statue of Rana Pratap astride his horse, Chetak. You enter the garden through a fort-like gate facing Lake Fateh Sagar. The road winds steeply up Moti Magri, past the **Bhama Shah Garden** which is laid out in Japanese style. The view from the top of the hill is well worth the climb.

Sahelion-ki-Bari (Garden of the Maids of Honour) was originally constructed in the early 18th century by Maharana Sangram Singh, using the waters of the Fateh Sagar to feed the pools. It had been the scene of royal parties for centuries and is now a favourite spot with both locals and tourists.

Sajjan Garh Palace was constructed by Maharana Sajjan Singh in the late 18th century. It is 5 km (3 miles) west of Udaipur, high on a hill called Bansdara and visible from miles around. It stands 750 metres (2,468 feet) above sea level. From the palace, there is a breathtaking view for miles around. During the monsoon, clouds shroud the palace, making it seem distant, ghostly and romantic. It is said a nine-storeyed astronomical observatory was planned here, but Maharana Sajjan Singh died when he was 25 years old, when only one storey was completed.

Khas Odi hunting lodge: To the left, off Sajjan Garh road, in the hills on the west side of Lake Pichola, is a hunting lodge called Khas Odi or **Shikarbadi**. This lodge features frequently in Mewar miniatures and is worth a visit. In the centre of the building is a square pit where boars, tigers, and leopards were pitted against each other, spectators cheering from the surrounding wall. You

Wayside dentist.

can stay the night in this peaceful lodge (book through the Lake Palace Hotel).

Haridasji-ki-Magri is a large, walled enclosure on a wooded hill close to the lodge containing wild boar and deer.

No account of the land and people of Mewar is complete without a description of **Chittaurgarh**. (*See Chittaurgarh, page 239.*) However, there are a number of other interesting sites which are easily reached from the two towns.

Nahar Magri (Tiger Hill): On the way to Chittaurgarh from Udaipur, almost opposite the turn off for the airport, pennants fly over a small shrine, the *dhuni* (place of worship) of ascetics. Here, Bappa Rawal, the founder of Mewar, stopped to receive the blessings of the goddess Durga, in the form of a tiger skin presented to him by the solitary old prophetess who kept the holy fire burning there.

Ahar village and museum: Three km (2 miles) east of Udaipur, on a small hillock called **Dhimkot**, archaeologists have discovered a town belonging to a period between the chalcolithic age and Kushan era (*circa* 150 AD). In ancient times, it was called **Tambawati Nagri**. Here, bones of fish, deer and birds, and pieces of pottery have been found, dating back to 4000 BC. Wells and drainage indicate town planning of some maturity. There is a museum near the site.

Before Bappa Rawal wrested Chittaurgarh from his Mori uncle, Ahar was the capital of the ruling house. Every time Chittaurgarh fell to an enemy, and until Udaipur was built, Ahar sheltered the Rana's kinsmen and forces.

Cenotaphs of Kings: The rulers of Mewar were traditionally cremated (along with their wives, who were burnt alive) near a tank called the **Gangabhar Kund** on the banks of the river Ahar which flows out of lake Fateh Sagar. Cenotaphs or *chatris* to the ranas are grouped within an enclosure, each grandson completing the memorial to his grandfather. Every cenotaph contains an image of Shiva, and a single upright stone on which are carved the figures of the rana and his wives. Nineteen ranas have their cenotaphs here. The **Aravalli landscape.**

226

Gangabhar Kund is considered by some to be as holy as the Ganga.

Shri Eklingji Temple: Some 22 km (14 miles) northeast of Udaipur is **Kailashpuri**, which is known for its 108 temples surrounded by a high fortified wall. The whole complex centres around the white marble Shri Eklingji Temple and has been a holy site associated with Lord Shiva for many centuries. The present structures, however, date from the 15th century.

Bappa Rawal spent much of his childhood at Kailashpuri in the hermitage of a sage called Harita Rishi from whom he received religious instruction. The sage invested his favourite pupil with the insignia of royalty and bestowed upon him the title *Dewan* (regent) *of Eklingji*, which succeeding Mewar kings carried with pride.

The main temple is said to be on the spot at which Harita Rishi and Bappa Rawal conversed. It is built of granite and marble and has a large, ornate *mandap* (pillared hall) under a huge pyramidal roof. There is a four-faced black marble image of Shiva in the inner sanctuary. Outside is a statue of the bull Nandi, the mount of Shiva. This is the family temple of the rulers of Mewar and the temple is still visited every Monday by the Maharaja of Udaipur.

The temple was damaged by the Sultan of Gujarat in 1433, restored by Rana Kumbha, and again sacked by Aurangzeb in the late 17th century.

Lakulish Temple stands within the precincts of the Eklingji complex. It was built in 971 AD by a ruler of Nagda. It is the only temple of the Lakulish sect in India and was only discovered relatively recently.

Nagda: Close to Kailashpuri, down a rough country road, is Nagda, once a Solanki stronghold, and now a major railway junction and industrial centre. It is believed to have been established by Nagaditya, the fourth Mewar king, a descendant of the Guhadatta who was born in a cave in the Aravalli mountains after the sack of Vallabhi. There are several temples dating from the 4th century AD, ancient rock edicts, stone

Sas-Bahu temple, Nagda.

inscriptions, and very early shrines at which the Bhils still worship during the Mahashivratri festival in Feburary.

All that is now left of those times at Nagda are the temples of **Sas-Bahu** and **Adbhutji**. The former dates back to the 11th century and is famed for its beautiful carvings. **Sas-Bahu** literally means "mother-in-law and daughter-in-law." Adbhutji is an old Jain temple named after a somewhat odd statue of a Jain saint seated within. *Adbhut* means, quite literally, "peculiar."

Nathdwara: Forty-eight km (30 miles) north of Udaipur, past Kailashpuri and the Eklingji temple is a town once known as Sihar. Now it is called Nathdwara, and is a *dham*, one of the principal places of pilgrimage in Rajasthan.

The Vallabh Sampradhya sect was founded by a Telugu Brahman, Sri Vallabhacharya (1479–1531). Fleeing from Govardhan in the late 16th century to escape the persecution of the Mughal Emperor Aurangzeb, who had proscribed the worship of Krishna throughout the empire, the Vallabhacharis were hoping to reach the sanctuary of Udaipur, capital of the kingdom of Mewar. The Maharaja of Mewar, Raj Singh I, offered sanctuary to the image of Nathji. So it was loaded on to a chariot, but some distance from their destination, the wheels of the chariot got stuck in a rut and could not be dug out. Taking this as divine intervention, the Vallabhacharis built their shrine on the spot. The village of Sirah became known as Nathdwara, home of Srinathji, Lord Krishna. Today, it is an important Vaishnava pilgrimage spot.

Temple rules forbid entry by non-Hindus, but the decision is often left to the official at the temple entrance. Photography and leather belts are not permitted. However, the town is still worth a visit. The streets are narrow, cobbled, and wind up the hill to the temple. Little shops sell all manner of goods: paintings, *minakari* jewellery, and sweets that are sent to relatives abroad after they have been blessed by the deity. Here, you can also see *pichwais* being painted.

Cattle fairs are important local events.

PICHWAIS OF NATHDWARA

Nathdwara, a sleepy, dusty, small town set on a hill some 50 km (30 miles) from Udaipur, is – quite literally by accident – the scene of one of the most lush and vibrant visual art forms found in India, *pichwai* painting.

In the 17th century, when Emperor Aurangzeb prohibited the worship of images, devout Hindus in Mathura, the home of Lord Krishna, became fearful that their sacred statues might be smashed, and decided to remove them to safer locations.

The Maharaja of Mewar, Raj Singh I, offered sanctuary to the image of Nathji and it was loaded reverently on to a chariot and sent on its way to Mewar accompanied by its *goswami* (priest). At Sihar, a wheel of the chariot sank deep into the mud, and it could not be moved despite repeated efforts. This was interpreted as a sign that the image wanted to dwell at that place, and the priests decided that it should stay. A temple was

built for the idol, and the village came to be known as Nathdwara, "Home of Nathji" or Lord Krishna.

Behind the sculpted image of Krishna or Srinathji, elaborately bedecked and bejewelled, hang huge decorative cloth curtains – *pichwais* (meaning "that which hangs behind") – literally backdrops setting the mood and religious significance of each ritualized scene. There are 24 iconographic renderings of the Krishna legend traditionally portrayed in the Nathdwara *pichwais*. Each is linked with a particular festival or holy day; for example, *Gokulashtami* will have Krishna playing the flute to the assembled *gopas*, *gopis* and their cows; *Dana Ekadashi*, the taking of the toll or *dan* from the *gopis* and the breaking of pots. As well as forming a devotional backdrop for the temple, the paintings also serve the purpose of outlining the religious stories to a largely illiterate population.

The *pichwais* were traditionally done in a variety of media: brocaded, blockprinted, embroidered, or worked in gold. In Nathdwara, however, a rich tradition of painted *pichwais* grew.

The *pichwais* are on handspun cloth, sized with starch, and painted in pigments derived from natural vegetable and mineral colours, also mixed with starch (giving the *pichwai* its characteristic strong smell). They have a stylised, rather static format, with frozen figures set in an idyllic landscape of brilliant green trees and midnight-blue skies in which sun, moon, stars, forked lightning, all shine together amid fluffy white clouds; peacocks, parrots and monkeys riot in flowering fields, and swans and storks, fish and turtle swim in lotus-strewn, silver waters. In this Indian conception of paradise – known as Braj – so unlike the bleak, beige Rajasthani landscape, Krishna, the blue boy-god, Radha and the *gopis* play, dance and make love; a pictorial allegory of the soul's yearning for union with the divine.

Today, the *pichwai* tradition is carried on and it is not only devotees of Srinathji who buy the cloth scrolls painted by today's descendants of Raja Raj Singh's original court painters. The *pichwai* has also become a tourist souvenir. They tend to now be painted with chemical fabric paints that have taken the place of indigo, cochineal, lapiz and orpiment. ∎

Kankroli and Rajasamund: Sixty-five km (40 miles) from Udaipur, and a few north of Nathdwara, is Kankroli on the banks of lake Rajasamund. The temple here resembles in many ways that which stands at Nathdwara, and the image, Dwarkadhish, Lord Krishna, was installed by Maharana Raj Singh I in 1676.

An additional attraction in the area is the exquisite **Nauchowki**, pillared buildings by the lake's edge, paved with marble. Emperor Aurangzeb wanted to marry Princess Charumati of Kishangarh. The princess appealed to the Maharana of Mewar, Raj Singh I, to help her, and the maharana gallantly married the princess himself. To commemorate this act, Maharani Charumati built a set of white marble steps on the embankment of Lake Rajasamund. Maharana Sajjan Singh built a palace on the embankment in the late 19th century, and laid out the beautiful gardens around it.

The **mansion of Dayal Shah**, a famous Jain prime minister, is well worth visiting. The sculptures here almost equal those at Mount Abu. There is an inscription of 1,017 verses in Sanskrit in one of the edifices recounting the history of Mewar. Inscribed on 27 slabs in 1675, this is the longest literary work inscribed on stone so far known.

Haldighati: The Battle of Haldighati is celebrated in murals and paintings at Udaipur's City Palace. But you may want to visit the battlefield itself, 27 km (17 miles) north of this city. It falls well within reach on a trip to Eklingji to the northeast or to Kumbhalgarh to the northwest. The battlefield comprises a narrow pass which runs south to northeast and ends in a plain where the main battle took place. The colour of the earth is yellow, like that of *haldi* (turmeric), giving the battlefield its name.

Having learnt the lesson of Chittaurgarh and unwilling to be besieged at Kumbhalgarh, Rana Pratap Singh met the armies of the Mughal Emperor Akbar at the height of summer of June 1576 on this open field. Ranged behind the rana were the Raja of Gwalior, Pathans from the northwest frontier,

Man smoking from a chilum.

and Bhil archers and infantry under their leader, Punj. Three times the intrepid Pratap had to be rescued as the royal umbrella over his head made him the main target. Eventually, one of the Mewar nobles, Jhala Man, took the umbrella, drawing the attacks away from the rana. Wounded and unattended, Rana Pratap was carried off the battlefield by his loyal horse, Chetak. The horse died of its own wounds, but only after he had seen his master out of danger. A cenotaph stands at the spot at which Chetak died. A more contemporary tribute is a daily train from Delhi to Udaipur named after Rana Pratap's war horse – the Chetak Express. Of the 22,000 Rajputs ranged against the Mughals, only 8,000 finally fled the battlefield.

Shri Charbhujaji: Thirty km (20 miles) west of Kankroli, to the northwest of Udaipur, is the temple of Shri Charbhujaji built by Rana Mokal in the early 15th century. A grand fair is held here every year, attracting thousands of pilgrims from all over Rajasthan, Gujarat, and Madhya Pradesh.

Kumbhalgarh: Off a road from Charbhujaji and some 65 km (40 miles) from Udaipur lies Kumbhalgarh, the second most important fortress in the Mewar region. Its very inaccessibility ensured its security as a refuge for Mewar's rulers in times of strife. It was built by the scholarly Rana Kumbha in the mid-15th century.

An aerial view shows a fortified city on top of a rocky peak of the Aravalli hills, 1,100 metres (3,500 feet) above sea level, and 200 metres (700 feet) above the closest pass. Situated on the border between the Rajput kingdom of Udaipur (Mewar) and Jodhpur (Marwar), it was of great strategic importance. Enclosed within its crenellated ramparts spreading over 12 km (8 miles) are palaces, temples, humble dwellings, fields, water sources, farms and kitchen gardens – everything needed to withstand a long siege.

The fort: Kumbhalgarh fell only once in its history – to the armies of Emperor Akbar, combined with those of the Rajas of Amber and Marwar. This siege

A latter-day addition to a traditional dance.

succeeded because the Mughals contaminated the fort's water supply.

A tour of the fort can be linked with a visit to the adjoining wildlife park, a habitat for a number of bird and antelope species. To make the most of the park, aim to visit either between March and June or between September and November. Accommodation is available at the Aodhi Hotel. Once there, you are rewarded by the counterpoint of lovely, domed palaces with beautiful suites, the temples of Nilkanth, Mahadeo and Kumbhaswami, and the inevitable, lovely cenotaphs *(chatris)*.

Ranakpur: The Jain community has a history closely interwined with that of the Hindus of Mewar. Many officials at the Mewar court were Jains. The ranas in turn patronized Jain temples and saints. Rana Kumbha gave a large tract of land to the Jains in the 15th century in a valley deep in the Aravallis where some of the most magnificent Jain temples in India are to be seen. Ranakpur is about 100 km (60 miles) from Udaipur, reached by road through Ghasar and Charbhuja, or from Mount Abu via the Deora-Chauhan stronghold of Sirohi.

The Jains tended to build their temples either on hilltops as at Mount Abu (Dilwara), or in deep secluded valleys as at Ranakpur. The central temple in this complex is called **Chaumukha** (four-faced). It is dedicated to the Jain *tirthankara* (revealer of truth, lit. "ford maker") Adinath. It is the most complex and extensive of Jain temples in India, covering over 3,600 sq. metres (40,000 sq. feet). It has 29 halls containing 1,444 pillars, each one said to be different, and each covered with intricate, delicate carvings. The temple is built on a high plinth which is encircled by lofty boundary walls and graceful turrets.

Seen from the outside and above, there are five spires, each covering a shrine below, the largest covering the central shrine housing the white marble image of Chaumukha. Surrounding the spires are cupolas, each forming the roof of a pillared hall.

The temple has three entrances with double-storeyed portals, each leading

A Jain temple in a forested area.

232

through columned courts into the main halls – a seeming confusion of halls, pillars and courtyards radiating out from the central shrine with a hundred pillars.

Some distance away is a polygonal sun temple, embellished with a running band of solar deities seated in racing chariots. Farther away are two more temples dedicated to the Jain deities, Neminathji and Paraswakathji, built in the 14th century.

Narlai: Some 39 km (24 miles) north of Ranakpur, in the heart of the mainly Jain village and its many temples, lies Narlai. This small 17th-century fort was presented by the ruling maharaja to his brother Ajit Singh. Used for many years as a hunting lodge, it has been lavishly restored and is now a hotel.

Rishabdeo: In this village, also called Dhuler, 40 km (25 miles) south of Udaipur, is the celebrated 15th-century temple of Lord Rishaddeoji, a reincarnation of Mahavira Jain, the founder of the faith. Here, in a lovely temple, an image of this Jain saint, 1-metre (3-feet) high, sits, carved in black marble. On special occasions the image is clothed with the *angia* (a garment studded with precious stones worth several hundred thousand rupees) presented to the temple by Maharana Fateh Singh.

This Jain saint is also considered a reincarnation of Lord Vishnu, so the idol is worshiped by Vaishnava Hindus, Jains and Bhils with equal reverence.

Galiakot: Located 268 km (168 miles) south of Udaipur is an ancient town known for its famous mausoleum of the Saint Fakruddin Shahid of the Bohra Muslims. Saint Fakruddin was the son of minister Bharmal. Fakruddin traveled up from the coast of the Bagar region south of Mewar, preaching the message of Muhammad. He died at the hands of an assassin and a mausoleum marks the site of his burial. Thousands of Bohra Muslims from all over the world come to Galiakot especially at the time of the *urs* on the 27th day of Moharram, to pay their respects to Saint Fakruddin. The Adivasi Bhil people in the area also greatly revere him.

Detail from Jain temple, Ranakpur.

Early in the 13th century, there was serious disruption in the house of Mewar. Samant Singh, the eldest son of Mewar, was cheated of his inheritance by a first cousin. He migrated south to Bagar to make his place amongst the Bhils and other Rajput clans. In time, Samant Singh's heirs came to rule all Bagar. Rana Dungar Singh happening upon a rock 2,100 metres (7,000 feet) high and 8 km (5 miles) in diameter, built upon it the city of Dungarpur.

The Dungarpur Sisodias, unlike split-offs in most Rajput clans, did not long remain hostile to the main line at Chittaurgarh. They fought alongside the ranas against the invaders from the northwest, giving their full assistance to Rana Sangra against Babur during the battle of Kanwa. They did, however, later fall under Mughal control, unlike the main Mewar line which held out. The princely state of Dungarpur ultimately yielded suzerainty to the British East India Company in 1818.

Dungarpur: This small town is easily reached via the main road which links Udaipur with Ahmadabad. It lies about 100 km (60 miles) from Udaipur and 25 km (15 miles) from the main road. Despite its beauty, it is often ignored by tourists, so it has retained much of its old charm. The **Udai Bilas Palace**, now over 150 years old, stands by the banks of a large lake (Udai Sagar), where many migratory birds spend the winter. This delightful palace of grey-green granite is still the seat of the ruling family and part of it has been turned into a hotel. The Ek-Thambia-Mahal (One Column Pavilion) deserves special attention as it is unique in Rajasthan. The pillars at the lower level are covered with friezes and, above these, arches support curved brackets. Twisted pillars and windows around cool marble form a women's room with an encrustation of balustrades and airy balconies.

A 4-km (2½-mile) walk through the well-preserved old town will take you to the former residence of the royal family, the 13th-century **Juna Mahal** which was quite obviously built along the line of the old fortifications. Above the sturdy outer walls there is a jumble of turrets, cupolas, terraces, crenellated watchtowers and ramparts with slits for archers and for pouring boiling oil, all designed to withstand a long siege. The whole interior of the palace bursts with colour and design in contrast to the severity of the fortifications. The lime plaster walls are polished to resemble marble and covered with mirrorwork, frescoes and Chinese tiles. It has some of Rajasthan's finest murals as well as a well-preserved throne. The view from here extends over Dungarpur and the Udai Lake.

Other attractions that can be visited from Dungarpur include February's Baneshwar Festival celebrated by the Bhils at the confluence of rivers Som and Mahi (70 km/43 miles), the excavations at Arthuna (80 km/50 miles) and the Dev Somnath Temple (25 km/15 miles).

Ambika Durga Temple: About 90 km (56 miles) southeast of Udaipur, on a regular bus route, is the temple of Ambika Durga in the village of Jagat. It was built in 960 AD and is dedicated to the various aspects of the goddess Durga, the protector. *Apsaras* (celestial women), and *sur-sundaris* (beautiful women) have also been lovingly sculptured in great detail. Several of the sculptures from the temple dating from the 10th to the 16th century can now be seen in the Udaipur Museum.

Jaisamudra Lake: In 1685, Maharana Jai Singh dammed the river Gomti, creating the Jaisamudra Lake, 51 km (32 miles) southeast of Udaipur. It is a little less than 14 km (9 miles) long and 10 km (6 miles) wide and lies in a beautiful area. Along the lake's embankment stand six cenotaphs with carvings of elephants surrounding a small temple dedicated to Lord Shiva.

Chavand: Some 19 km (12 miles) west of Jaisamudra lake, where the Bhils have always lived, is the village of Chavand, where Rana Pratap lived for the last 10 years of his life. He built a small palace here and a temple to the goddess Chavandji. In 1597, while hunting a tiger, he suffered an internal injury and died. Marking this is a stone *chatri* or cenotaph.

Udai Bilas Palace, Dungarpur.

CHITTAURGARH, HOME OF THE BRAVE

About 115 km (72 miles) east of Udaipur, stands Chittaurgarh (Chittor). With its formidable fortifications and a population of 72,000, the city was one of the most fiercely contested seats of power in India. Bappa Rawal, the legendary founder of the Sisodia dynasty, received Chittaurgarh in the middle of the 8th century, as part of the last Solanki princess's dowry. It crowns a 11-km (7-mile) long hill, covering 280 hectares (700 acres) with its fortifications, temples and palaces.

From the 8th to the 16th century, Bappa Rawal's descendants ruled over an important kingdom called Mewar stretching from Gujarat to Ajmer. But during these eight centuries the seemingly impregnable Chittaurgarh was overrun and sacked three times.

Sacks of Chittaurgarh: In 1303 Ala-ud-Din Khalji, Sultan of Delhi, intrigued by tales of the matchless beauty, wit and charm of Padmini, Rani of Chittaurgarh, decided to verify this himself. His armies surrounded Chittaurgarh, and the sultan sent a message to Rana Ratan Singh, Padmini's husband, to say that he would spare the city if he could meet its famous queen. The compromise finally reached was that the sultan could look upon Padmini's reflection if he came unarmed into the fort. Accordingly, the sultan went up the hill and glimpsed a reflection of the beautiful Padmini standing by a lotus pool. He thanked his host who courteously escorted Allauddin down to the outer gate – where the sultan's men waited in ambush to take the rana hostage.

There was consternation in Chittaurgarh until Padmini devised a plan. A messenger informed the sultan that the rani would come to him. Dozens of curtained palanquins set off down the hill, each carried by six bearers. Once inside the Sultan's camp, four well-armed Rajput warriors leaped out of each palanquin and each palanquin-bearer drew a sword. In the ensuing battle, Rana Ratan Singh was rescued – but 7,000 Rajput warriors died.

The sultan now attacked Chittaurgarh with renewed vigour. Having lost 7,000 of its best warriors, the city could not hold out. Surrender was unthinkable. The rani and her entire entourage of women, the wives of generals and soldiers, sent their children into hiding with loyal retainers. Dressed in their wedding finery, they then said their farewells, and singing hymns, boldly entered the massive communal funeral pyre in the **Mahasati Chowk** and performed *johar*.

The men then donned saffron robes, smeared the holy ashes of their women on their foreheads, flung open the gates of the fort and thundered down the hill into the enemy ranks, to fight to the death.

The second sack or *shaka* (sacrifice) of Chittaurgarh, by which Rajputs still swear when pledging their word, occurred in 1535, when Sultan Bhadur Shan of Gujarat attacked the fort long since retrieved from the khaljis.

The ruler of Chittaurgarh at the time was a 16-year-old prince, Vikramaditya. He was spirited away at dead of night by loyal retainers (the Sisodia line, in any event, had to be continued). His mother, Queen Karnavati herself led the Rajput warriors into battle. But the Mewar troops were hopelessly outnumbered.

The last rana to rule there was no match for Akbar, the Mughal emperor. In 1567, Akbar attacked Chittaurgarh. Forty metres (150 feet) below the ramparts, at the southern end of the fort, is a hillock called **Mohar Magri** (Hill of Gold Coins) which was raised, the story goes, by Akbar. Because the work was so dangerous, the emperor is said to have paid one *mohar* for each basketful of earth placed on the mound. This raised the hillock to a height which was sufficient for the Mughal cannons to fire into the fort.

The road to Chittaurgarh: The road up to the fort zigzags steeply for just over a kilometre (half a mile) and passes through seven huge *pols* or gates, each with watch-towers and great iron-spiked doors. Near **Bhairon Pol** is a cenotaph, a *chatri* (pillared, open-domed structure), a memorial to Jaimal and his cousin Phatta who fell during the third sack of Chittaurgarh. Udai Singh II (who later founded Udaipur) had left Jaimal, a boy of 16, in charge while he went out on guerrilla sorties against Mughal supply lines. Jamil was wounded when inspecting the ramparts. Unwilling to be left to die in bed, he was carried into battle on the shoulders of his cousin Kalia. Linked together, they died fighting by Bhairon Pol.

By **Ram Pol** is a memorial to Phatta of Kailwa, who took charge of the fort after the death of Jaimal. Phatta, too, was 16, and had just been married. His father had already fallen defending Chittaurgarh. Now Phatta's mother urged him to don the saffron robe and die for Chittaurgarh. To free her son from every care, Phatta's mother armed his young bride with a lance and, picking up a sword herself, advanced against the Mughal army. The two women fell within Phatta's sight.

The next day, the women of Chittaurgarh committed *johar*, and the saffron-robed men led by Phatta charged down from the fortress to die fighting. Thereafter, on each anniversary of this third *shaka*, the Maharanas of Mewar gathered at the Mahasati Chowk in the fort to offer prayers for the souls of those who gave their lives in defence of Chittaurgarh.

The great builder: The Palace of Rana Kumbha is the first large palace to be seen inside the fort itself. The original was supposedly built by Rana Hamir on regaining the fort after its first sacking. The city remained the seat of Sisodia power for two centuries, reaching its zenith under Rana Kumbha, the best-loved warrior-king in Mewar. This age also saw a flowering of art and architecture. Rana Kumbha was a great builder, as well as a musician and poet.

To commemorate his victory against the combined might of Sultan Mahmud of neighbouring Malwa and Sultan Ahmad Shah of Gujarat, Rana Kumbha erected the **Vijay Stambh** to the west of the palace. Built of limestone, it is 36 metres (120 feet) high, and has nine storeys and a winding stairway.

Adjacent lies the square *(mahasati)* where the Ranas were burnt when

Chittaurgarh was still the capital of Mewar, as demonstrated by the sobering sight of countless *sati* stones in the vicinity. Further south stands the **Samidhisvhara Temple**, dedicated to Shiva. Behind it, a lonely flight of steps winds down to the **Gaumukh** (Cow's Mouth) **reservoir**. Here, through the mouths of cows carved on the rock face, the waters of an underground spring flow into the reservoir on to a sacred *Shivalinga* placed below. The underground passage leading from Kumbha's palace comes out on the north bank of the reservoir, inside a small Jain temple called the **Paraspath Temple**.

There is another pillar in Chittaurgarh called the **Kirti Stambh** dedicated to Sri Adinath Rishabdeo, the first Jain *tirthankara* (enlighted soul). There are several small Jain temples in Chittaurgarh. Some Buddhist artefacts dating back to the Maurya dynasty are also to be found here.

Rana Hamir also built the **Kalika Mata temple** towards the south end of the fort. It is the oldest there, the original

Tower of Victory.

240

dedicated to the Sun God having been built by Bappa Rawal in the 8th century. It was destroyed during the first sack of Chittaurgarh and, regaining the fort, Rana Hamir put in an image of Kalika, the family's patron goddess, to replace the Sun God. The **House of Chunda** stands near the Kalika Mata temple.

Further south, a road branches off to the southeast, to a compound containing two temples. The **Kumbha Shyam Temple** was built by Rana Kumbha in 1448, and dedicated to the Varaha (boar) incarnation of Lord Vishnu. The smaller temple in the compound is that of the famous devotee of Lord Krishna and the great devotional princess poet, Mira Bai, Rana Sanga's daughter-in-law.

In front of Mira Bai's temple is a *chatri* in memory of Mira Bai's guru, the saint Rai Das of Banaras. In its dome is carved a circle of five human bodies with one head, symbolizing the belief that all castes, Brahman, Kshatriya, Vaishya, Sudra and outcastes, can reach God.

An 18th-century reconstruction of Padmini's palace can be seen at Chittaurgarh by the pool in which her image was reflected for viewing by Sultan Allauddin Khalji.

Panna, the Diamond of Mewar: In 1536, a year after the fort's second sack, Rana Vikramaditya was assassinated by Banbir, a pretender to the throne. Banbir then went after the rana's younger brother, Udai Singh II, left in the care of the nursemaid, Panna, by his mother Karnavati before she performed *sati*.

Bari, the court barber, warned Panna Bai of Banbir's intentions. Panna Bai placed the young prince in a basket and handed him to Bari, telling him to wait for her outside the fort, and put her own son in the prince's bed. Banbir crashed into the room and demanded the prince. Panna Bai pointed to her own child sleeping in the prince's bed. Banbir then disembowelled him with his sword.

Panna Bai wandered from chieftain to chieftain seeking a protector for her charge. Finally, at Kumbhalgarh, the governor, Asa Shah, a Jain, took in Udai Singh and, when Udai was 15, restored him to Chittaurgarh.

Memorial of fallen hero, Rawat Bagh Singh of Deolia, at Padal Pol.

IN AND AROUND KOTA

The city of **Kota** (previously spelt Kotah) is at the centre of the southeastern region of Rajasthan widely known as Hadaoti (Hadavati), the land of the Hadas. The Hadas are a major branch of the Chauhan clan of the Agnikula (fire dynasty) Rajputs. They had settled in the hilly terrain of Mewar near Bijolian at Bambaoda in the 12th century AD and soon extended their rule, conquering Bundi in 1241 and Kota in 1264 (some writers date both these events exactly 100 years later). Originally, all this formed the Hada state of Bundi with Kota as the *jaghir* (land grant) of the eldest prince of Bundi. Kota later became a separate state in 1624. The domain of the Hadas of Bundi and Kota extended from the hills of Bundi in the west to the Malwa plateau in the east, with a similar expanse north to south. The state of Jhalawar was formed in 1838, out of Kota territory.

Hadaoti is an expanse of fertile plain with a rich black-cotton soil irrigated by several rivers. The largest and the only perennial river of Rajasthan, the Chambal (Charmanyavati), rises in the south and flows through this territory to join the Jamuna in the north. It is an ancient river, mentioned in the Upanishads, evident from the great 96-km (60-mile) long gorge it has cut through the rock. It has several tributaries, the chief ones being the Kali Sind, the Parvan and the Parvati.

The Aravalli Hills, the oldest folded mountain range in India, rise near Abu in the south of Rajasthan and one arm crosses Bundi in a south to north direction, while another cuts across Kota from the southwest to the northwest, roughly dividing the plains of Hadaoti from the Malwa Plateau. These hills and the surrounding areas were once thickly forested and teemed with wildlife, including tiger for which Hadaoti was famous. Unfortunately, most of these jungles have been badly depleted in the course of the last 30 years and there is

Preceding pages: Gagron Fort. Below, wall painting, Kota Fort.

hardly any animal wildlife left outside the present game sanctuaries.

The climate of this area is very similar to that of the Indo-Gangetic plain, with hot dry summers and refreshingly cold winters. The monsoon here is, however, quite distinct from the oppressive humid climate of the North Indian plains. Hadaoti receives an average of 88 cm (35 inches) of rainfall, which keeps it cool, and gentle breezes ward off the stifling humidity. Good rainfall has made this area the traditional granary of Rajasthan and it also offers good pasturage in times of drought and famine for the livestock from the arid zones of the state.

Hadaoti had been settled by early peoples, as is clearly evident from several well preserved Upper Paleolithic period cave paintings dating back to 20,000 BC. Legend links it to the epic periods of the *Ramayana* and *Mahabharata*. Being a fertile and prosperous area, it was the ancient battleground between invading peoples such as the Sakas (Scythians) and the entrenched empires of ancient India like that of the Imperial Guptas and of Harsha Vardhana. During the medieval period, Hadaoti attracted the attention of practically every powerful monarch of Delhi, for this region was one of the gateways to the rich kingdoms of Gujarat and Malwa. Numerous battles and sieges have left an imprint on this land. Nevertheless, scores of beautiful temples and countless exquisitely sculpted stone buildings are spread throughout this wilderness; spectacular fortresses and grim strongholds, beautiful palaces and delicate pavilions – all testify to a basic stability and continuity of tradition despite political and military upheavals.

Kota City: The building of medieval Kota began in 1264 (some say 1364), when Rajkumar Jait Singh of Bundi slew the Bhil leader, Koteya, in battle. He raised the first battlements of the *garh* (fort) over the slain chieftain's severed head, treating it as a foundation "stone". Today, the **Sailar Ghazi Gate** stands at this spot. As the fort complex grew, a small settlement outside the

A view of Kota town.

walls also started growing and it was called Kota after the dead ruler. The independent princely state of Kota became a reality in 1624, when Rao Madho Singh, second son of Rao Rattan of Bundi, was made the ruler by the Mughal Emperor Jahangir, an act which was formalised by Emperor Shah Jahan in 1631. Soon Kota outgrew its parent state of Bundi to become bigger in area, richer in revenue and more powerful. It also developed into an artistic, cultural, and religious centre.

In 1947 Kota was a town of 60,000 people, the capital city of the state bearing the same name, with graceful palaces and public buildings, with a modern administration, civic amenities and utilities. The population swelled soon after, first with the refugee influx from the Punjab and Sind and later by the growth of industry. There are now 537,000 inhabitants. Industry moved in because of Kota's excellent geographical location. It is situated on the right bank of the Chambal river which provides an abundant supply of water; electricity is generated at the hydro, atomic and thermal power stations sited on the river. It has a rich agricultural hinterland and has ample vacant land available for industrys' growth and spread. Besides, it is on the main broad-gauge route of the Western railway between Delhi and Bombay and is within easy reach of Jaipur, Ajmer, Udaipur, Indore, Bhopal and Gwalior by road. There is an air service between Delhi and Kota too. All this makes Kota a premier centre of industry, trade and commerce in Rajasthan.

The town's speciality, known throughout India, is the famous *Kota doria sari*, locally known as *masuria* because the original weavers were brought here from the Mysore region in the 17th century by the rulers of Kota.

Palace complex: The foremost tourist attraction in Kota is the *garh*. This large complex, also called the **City Palace**, is built in a predominantly Rajput style of architecture. Each successive ruler has added something to it. The *garh* was the fulcrum of all activities in former times,

Kota Fort from the Chambal river.

being not only the residence of the king but also the seat of power. The presiding deity of the House of Kota, the image of Shri Brijnathji, and other family deities, also reside here. All ceremonials, functions and *pujas* were held here – and some continue to be held here even today.

In keeping with the times, this property is now administered by the Rao Madho Singh Museum Trust which has a rich collection of art and artefacts showing the cultural heritage of the House of Kota and Hadaoti. Some of the finest examples of the famous *Kota Kalam* can be seen among the wall paintings in the palace and the miniature paintings in the *mahals* (apartments) and in the **Art Gallery**. The museum has a rich collection of paintings, old photographs, arms and armour, *objets d'art*, banners and flags, regalia and a wildlife gallery. There is a small **Government Museum** housed in the **Hawa Mahal** of the *garh* which has an excellent collection of stone images and architectural fragments collected from the former Kota State.

The entrance to the *garh* is by the **Naya Darwaza** (New Gate) built around 1900. It is flanked by the **Hawa Mahal** and leads to **Jaleb Chowk** (Big Square) where parades used to be held and processions assembled. To the east of the *chowk* is the **Nakkarakhana Darwaza** (Kettledrum Gate) with the shrine of Koteya outside it, and the **Jantar Burj** (Zodiac Bastion). To the west of the *chowk* stand the **Kunwar-bade-ka-Mahal** (Crown Prince's Palace) and the **Bada Mahal** (Big Palace) and the **Hathia Pol** (Elephant Gate), reminiscent of Hadaoti.

The delicate stonework, the fluted canopies and some fine elephant-shaped brackets give the palace "an air of light elegance". Inside the glittering **Raj Mahal** is the *Raj Gaddi* (throne) on which the kings of Kota were anointed and sat during *durbars* (audiences). The mahal is embellished by medieval gold and glass-work friezes on the walls. It has some fine 18th-century wall paintings in blue-green hues depicting mainly the *Krishna-lila*.

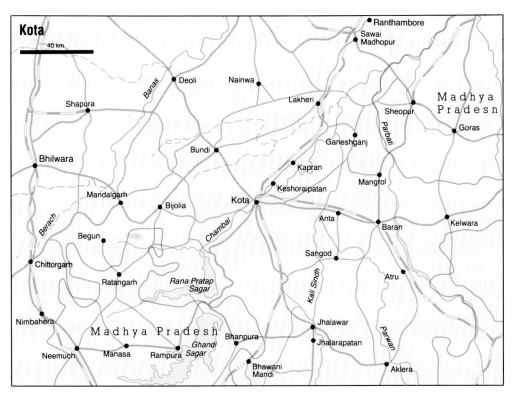

Across the Raj Mahal courtyard is the old **Akhade-ka-Mahal** (Wrestling Palace) in which are displayed the regalia and paraphernalia of state. Next to it are the various galleries housing arms and armour, old photographs, miniature paintings and stuffed birds and animals. On the first floor is the small room of Arjun Mahal. The breezy **Bara Dari**, where private parties were held by the ruler, and the **Bhim Mahal**, which was used as the *Diwan-i-Khas* (private audience chamber), are also on the first floor. Right on top is **Bada Mahal**, the private living quarters of the king. A large open veranda in front has a rich array of paintings of various schools and periods set in the glass on the walls, beautiful white marble friezes and an ornate 17th-century ceiling. Inside the main living chamber there are some very early (1680) Kota Kalam miniatures. A small, beautiful balcony facing the east, called **Suraj Gokh** has rich gold, glass and crystal work. The **Chattra Mahal** has a rare painted ceiling. The imposing pink sandstone latticed **Zenana Mahal** and **Alsi Mahal** were built by Maharao Umed Singh II in the early 1900s. The **Dilkhushal Bagh** (Garden of Heart's Delight) below has a grand white marble *chatri* (cenotaph).

Traditional Kota: The old town was encircled and defended on three sides by a moat and massive fortified crenellated walls, built in two successive rings. They were first erected by Rao Ram Singh in the late 1690s and later enlarged and improved upon by Zalim Singh, the Diwan of Kota around 1780–1800. On the western side, the Chambal river forms a natural barrier.

Kishore Sagar, the picturesque artificial lake in the middle of the town, popularly known as **Bada Talao**, was built in 1346 by Rajkumar Dhir Deh of Bundi. The small island palace, **Jagmandir**, was built around 1740 by the Maharani Brij Kunwar of Kota, a princess of Mewar. Below it are the **Chattar Bilas Gardens,** which are beautiful in spring, with the **Brij Bilas Palace** and the **Sarbagh** (Park of Royal Chatris or Cenotaphs) on either side. Some

Hathia Pol, Kota Fort.

of the *chatris* are magnificent, with beautiful carved friezes and elephant statues.

Of the many **temples** located in the town, the most famous are those of Mathureshji, belonging to the middle 18th century, and of Nilkanth Mahadeo belonging to the 10th century.

Inside the town, near the Sabzi Mandi (vegetable market) are the tombs of two Pathan brothers, Kesar Khan and Dokhar Khan, who seized Kota for a brief interlude between 1531 to 1551. Their yoke was thrown off by the famous Rao Surjan of Bundi after a bloody battle. Adjacent to the public gardens is the British cemetery where some of the officers killed in the uprising ("Mutiny") of 1857 are interred.

Amongst Kota's many beautiful buildings, the pride of place, after the *garh*, goes to the **Umed Bhawan Palace** built in 1905, part of which is the new residence of the Maharaos of Kota, designed by Sir Swinton Jacob. Another part has been converted into a hotel. Next comes **Brijraj Bhawan Palace**, formerly the British Residency, built around 1840 on the bank of the river commanding a beautiful view. It became the State Guest House in 1900 and numerous VIPs have stayed there.

The **Herbert College** (Government College) built in local, white stone, the **Crossthwait Institute**, the **Curzon Wylie Memorial** (Mahatma Gandhi Hall) and the **Bailey Clock Tower** are some of the other buildings noted for their beauty.

A bronze statue of Maharao Umed Singh II (1889–1940) stands in the **Umed Park**. Beside the river are the new **Chambal Gardens** with a pool. The river once used to teem with crocodiles and gharial but, by 1960, they had almost all been exterminated by widespread netting and pollution. Efforts are now being made to revive these dwindling populations.

Next to this garden is **Amar Niwas**, a pleasure-palace built on the bank of the river, with old Hanuman and Surya temples nearby. The **Bitheria Kund** (tank) with its 18th-century Shivalinga (phallic symbol of Shiva) and a rare

Jal Mandir.

image of **Panch-mukhi Ganesha** (five-faced Ganesh), is one of the popular picnic spots around Kota.

Near Kota: Ten km (6 miles) east of Kota lies the **Kansuan Temple** (Karneshwar Mahadeo). It has a stone inscription dating to 740 AD which says that it was built by Raja Shivgana Maurya. Beyond Kansuan, another 6 km (4 miles) away is **Umed Ganj**, a pleasure garden with a pavilion near a lake built by Maharao Umed Singh I (1771–1819). Until the early 1950s, there was a dense forest around it and many types of game were to be seen here, but this has since been severely denuded. Another 3 km (2 miles) further lie the temples of **Dadh Devi**. **Kaithun** village, the weaving centre for the famous Kota *doria* sari is close by. It also has perhaps the only temple in India dedicated to Vibhishan, the brother of the Ravana, the demon king of Sri Lanka who abducts Rama's wife Sita in the epic *Ramayana*.

At **Borkandi**, 11 km (7 miles) east of Kota, on the road to Gwalior, stands a bridge built by the British in 1818, commonly known as **Tod's Bridge**.

To the west, across the river, 6 km (4 miles) away, is the pretty lake and palace of **Abhera**, and just below the bund is the shrine of Karni Mata. Towards the north, 11 km (7 miles) down the river, is the temple village of **Keshorai Patan**. The imposing temple of Keshorai was commissioned by Rao Raja Chattar Sal of Bundi in 1653.

On the road to Jhalawar, on **National Highway 12**, 22 km (14 miles) south of Kota is the small village of **Alnia**. Across the railway line, beyond the cable factory, is an island in the small Alnia stream where there is a group of rock shelters with paintings dating to the Upper Paleolithic age which are still in good condition. This is a delightful spot surrounded by forest.

Towards the south, on the road to Bardoli and Rawat Bhatta Dam, 22 km (14 miles) away is the picturesque **chasm of Gaipar Nath** (Gavyeshwara Mahadeo) with an old Shiva temple set in a deep gorge, with a spectacular view of the rugged forests and the *kerais* of cliffs of the Chambal valley.

Bardoli Temples: (56 km/35 miles southwest of Kota.) The road to these beautiful 8th–9th century temples runs along the Chambal river and enters the southern end of the Darrah Wild Game Sanctuary through a lovely, thickly wooded *ghat* (hill) section. This cluster of temples set in a grove has some of the best temple architecture in Rajasthan. The main temple is that of Ghateshwara Mahadeo. In front is the *mandap* (hall) with exquisite pillars. The entire temple is beautifully adorned with delicately carved figurines of *apsaras* (celestial women), amorous figures and the Ganga and Yamuna deities. On one side is the temple of Ganesh and on the other is that of Kali. There is also a Trimurti temple. Unfortunately, many of the faces of the idols were disfigured by iconoclastic Muslim armies in medieval times.

There is a smaller group of temples set around a small rectangular pool. The famous statue of **Shesh Shayyi Vishnu**, the reclining Vishnu, now on view at the Government Museum, Kota, was originally from here. The entire courtyard is littered with beautiful carved stone pieces from the remains of other buildings, including a *torana* (gate). Some of the good pieces lie in a store near the temples and can be viewed if you get permission from the Archaeological Survey of India Inspector at Kota.

A couple of miles further on is the big **Rawat Bhatta Dam**, with a bronze equestrian statue of Rana Pratap of Mewar dominating the cliff. There is a pretty garden on top which affords a fine panoramic view of the dam and the Pratap Sagar reservoir, somewhat marred by the atomic power station across the lake. However, the rocky bed of the Chambal is most attractive where it flows down through the Chulia Falls below the dam and past the pile of Bhensrodgarh Fort rising above the fields, with the range of hills and forest encircling the whole valley.

Darrah Wildlife Sanctuary: (56 km/35 miles south of Kota.) The forest area was once the hunting preserve of the Maharaos of Kota. It was a rich habitat for flora and fauna, especially the tiger.

It is called *Darrah* for short, the full name being *Mukundarrah*, after Rao Mukund Singh of Kota. *Darrah* in Persian means *pass* and this strategic pass is the only place between the rivers Chambal and the Kali Sind, a distance of nearly 130 km (80 miles), where an army can pass through. Many battles were fought near here between the Khinchi and the Hada Rajputs.

Beside the *mahals* are the ruins of the ancient **Bhim Chauri temples**. The name is derived from its link with the legendary Bhimsen of the Mahabharata, as it is believed he got married here to the *rakshasa* (demon) princess Hidimba. There is a stone inscription dating back to the 5th century AD which tells us that Dhruvaswamy, a general of the Imperial Guptas, died here fighting the Huns.

Processions celebrating weddings or announcing *melas* (fairs) often travel between villages.

Darrah was the finest *Shikargarh* in Kota where organized *shikar* (hunting) took place from the early 1700s until 1955. These forests and the cliffs with their tigers and other animals have been vividly painted by the master artists of the Kota Kalam. The forests and places still stand largely unchanged. These vast jungles used to shelter even wild buffalo and rhino, according to old records. This would be impossible nowadays, and it is difficult to believe that game was plentiful here just 40 years ago. There are good jungle roads and the visitor can drive in a jeep into the Darrah Valley to view the wildlife and also to sit in old *malas* or *odhis* (shikar towers) and watch the animals. There is a Forest Rest House at Darrah.

Jhalara-Patan: (about 80 km/50 miles south of Kota.) The Jhalawar State was created in 1838 and the old cantonment town of Chaoni Umedpura was named as its capital and renamed Jhalawar. The road to Jhalawar goes past Darrah through an extensive belt of limestone-bearing strata where the famous Kota stone is quarried in great quantity. The stone is widely known for its use as flooring and can be polished to a high shine. Jhalawar has a fairly good **Government Museum**. Six km (4 miles) away is the town of **Jhalara-Patan** (City of Temple Bells). Colonel

James Tod mentions counting 108 temples here. Enclosed within its old walls is the famous 10th century 30-metre (100-foot) high **Surya Temple**, also known as *Sat Sahelion Ka Mandir* (Seven Sisters Temple). The image of Surya here is perhaps the finest in India. Nearby is the beautiful group of 6th to 14th-century temples on the Chandrabhaga stream which rises from a spring. The **Chandramauleshwar Mahadeo Temple** (also called Shitleshwar Mahadeo) is a fine example of the temple builders' art. It dates from 689 AD according to an inscription found here and now lying in Jhalawar Government Museum. The other temples in this complex are equally outstanding.

On a low mound between the towns of Patan and Jhalawar is the small fortress of Naulakhi, thus called because it took *naulakh* (or 900,000) rupees to build it in the late 18th century.

Ten km (6 miles) from Jhalawar is the famous **Fort of Gagron**. It is perched on a low ridge at the confluence of the rivers Ahu and the Kali Sind whose waters surround it on three sides. On the fourth side there used to be a deep moat completing its defences. Gagron is one of the rare forts which are both a *vana* and a *jala durg* – both forest-protected and water-protected. It is surrounded by forests and has behind it the Mukundarrah range of hills.

Like all major forts, it has had its share of bloody battles and sieges. It was attacked by the Sultans of Delhi but it held out against them. It was conquered and sacked in 1423 by Sultan Hoshang Shah of Malwa. The Rajput women immolated themselves, rather than face dishonour and servitude. For the next century and a half there was an almost continuous struggle for its possession until, in 1561, the fort was annexed by Emperor Akbar and it remained under Mughal rule till 1715, when the fort was granted to and came under the rule of Maharao Bhim Singh I of Kota.

Outside the fort walls stands the **Dargah** (shrine) **of Sheikh Hamid-ud-din Mithe Shah**, which is a place of

Surya Mandir, Jhalara Patan.

pilgrimage for both Muslims and Hindus. It was named after a Sufi saint who lived here until his death in 1353.

Close by, on an island, is the *chatri* of Pipaji, the pious Khinchi poet king of Gagron, who ruled here from 1360 to 1385. His poems are enshrined in the Guru Granth Sahib of the Sikhs. Guru Nanak, the founder of the Sikh faith, once passed through here and paid his respects at Pipaji's shrine. Gagron, apart from its rich historical past, is a lovely spot, with the Kali Sind river, forest and fields, and precipitous cliffs.

Across the river lies the infamous 90-metre (300-foot) high **Gidh Kerai** (Cliff of the Vultures). It was here that state prisoners sentenced to death were executed by being hurled down on to the rocks below.

Kakuni-Bhimgarh: (145 km/90 miles southwest of Kota.) For those interested in ancient remains there is a fine group of temples and ruins at Kakuni, about 13 km (8 miles) from Sarthal (50 km/30 miles from Jhalawar). There is a huge full-length idol of Ganesh and an 8th-century Sehastralingam (phallic symbol).

Many figures and carved stones lie scattered around this place which show that in its time, it was an important urban centre. Across the Parvan river are the ruins of Bhimgarh Fort, built by Raja Bhim Deo in the same period.

Ramgarh: (35 km/60 miles north of Kota.) The road to Ramgarh goes via Anta and then along the Chambal Main Right Wing Canal. An interesting 10th-century site, Ramgarh lies about 6 km (4 miles) from the canal road near Mangrol. It is a curious, hollow, circular hill sprouting out of the plains. Only one entrance leads into the bowl, with a small, pretty lake situated in the middle. A **Shiva temple** stands near the lake, with many beautiful carved pillars and perhaps the finest of the erotic sculptures to be found in this region. The place is known as *Bhand Deora* by the local people. This temple was built by Raja Mallaya Varma of the Meda dynasty. On top of the hill, with some 750 steep steps leading up to it, is the small temple of Kishnai Mata. At the side of the hill,

Shiva temple, Ramgarh.

near the entrance, are the ruins of an old palace built in medieval times.

Bundi: The town lies 40 km (25 miles) northwest of Kota, has a population of 65,000 and takes its name from the *bindo* or *bando nal*, the narrow passage between the rugged hills. It is best visited as a day excursion from Kota. The road into the town from the opposite side of the valley affords a picturesque view of the whole site.

Under Rao Bar Singh, the work on the **Taragarh** (Star Fort) crowning the top of the 150-metre (500-foot) hill was completed in 1354. There are huge water reservoirs inside the fort hewn out of solid rock, strong battlements and bastions, the biggest one called **Bhim Burj**, on which the large cannon, **Garbh Ganjam**, is mounted.

The fort commands a marvellous view of the plains of Hadaoti towards the east, with the towers of Kota vaguely visible in the haze, the lovely azure waters of Jait Sagar below on one side, the town of Bundi on the other, and forests and hills all around.

Below Taragarh, hugging the hill, is the big pile of the early 16th-century **Bundi Palace**. It is one of the least Mughal-influenced examples of Rajput architecture. To reach it, a flagged ramp goes up from the town. It is an easy climb. One passes through the **Hazari Pol** where a guard of 1,000 troops used to be quartered and the **Naubat Khana** where ceremonial music was played, and enters the inner courtyard of the palace through the **Hathi Pol**, a tall portal surmounted by the stone elephants typical of Hadaoti. The small square inside is called the **Nauthana-ka-Chowk** where nine steeds of the king used to be stalled. Climbing the steep stairs one reaches the **Ratan Daulat**, the Diwan-i-Aam or public audience chamber, which was built by Rao Raja Ratan Singh, one of Bundi's greatest rulers. Here stands a simple white marble *takht* or throne on which the kings were anointed.

The living apartments of the ruler, **Chattra Mahal**, were built in 1660 by Rao Raja Chattar Sal. Inside, it has

Bundi town below the Paragarh Fort. The City Palace is to the left.

beautiful wall paintings of the famous Bundi Kalam. On the other side, across the open courtyard, is the many-pillared **Ratan Mahal** which has four small black stone elephants mounted as capitals on each pillar. Behind this are the **Zenana Mahals**, with the **Badal Mahal** which also has some good wall paintings and typical old Rajput courtyards with shady trees inside. On the other side is the **Chittra Shala** built by Rao Raja Umed Singh (1739–70). It is an open quadrangle with cloistered galleries running round it where some of the best of Bundi wall-paintings are to be seen. Depictions of the *Ras-lila* and other myths, gods and goddesses, processions, court life, and beautiful damsels adorn it. The dominant colour is blue-green. On one side of the interior is a small dark chamber with wall paintings in bright pigments. It can be seen only with the help of a torch. In the Chittra Shala is a small shrine dedicated to the memory of Rao Raja Umed Singh or Shriji Sahib, the saintly ruler of Bundi who abdicated to devote himself to religion and whose wooden sandals are worshipped here.

The rectangular **Naval Sagar**, built by Rao Raja Umed Singh, lies in the middle of the town. There is an island temple of Varuna in it which gets submerged when the lake is full.

North of Bundi lies **Jait Sagar** with **Sukh Niwas** (Palace of Bliss) built in 1773 by Rao Raja Bishen Singh. It is situated amidst a pretty garden on top of the *bund*. There are some lovely sculptures in the garden. Rudyard Kipling stayed here and found inspiration for some of the scenes in *Kim*. At the other end of the lake is the **Sar Bagh** with 66 royal cenotaphs, some beautifully adorned with statues and marble friezes. **Shika Burj**, a large shooting tower set in forest, stands not too far away. It was built by Rao Umed Singh who lived here after his abdication.

Adjacent to Shikar Burj are the **Hanuman-ki-Chatri** and the **temple of Kedareshwar Mahadeo** where Rao Kolhan was cured of leprosy. Perhaps one of the finest pieces of Rajput architecture is **Rani-ki-Baodi**, a step-well built in 1700 by Dowager Rani Nathawatiji, a Solanki princess, mother of Rao Raja Budh Singh. It lies in the town just off the main road as it starts to climb the by-pass. Wide steps lead down to the water under a graceful *torana* (archway) surmounted by a frieze of elephants. The *baodi* was built as a public amenity but unfortunately it is neglected today. Opposite the well is a small statue of Bundi's most illustrious poet-historian, Suryamal Mishran, who wrote the *Vansh Bhaskar*, a history of the Hadas in the old Dingal language. Another interesting monument is the splendid 64-pillared *chatri* built by Dhaibhai Devji in 1683. It lies not far from the main road as one enters Bundi from the direction of Kota.

The lovely **Phul Sagar Palace**, is situated 10 km (6 miles) to the west of Bundi. It was the residence of the last ruler, Maharao Raja Bahadur Singh. Located between two hills and forests below the bund of the lake, with the waters flowing through the palace, it is a typical Rajput building. Originally, it only had a small pavilion (which still stands) built in 1603 by Phul Lata, a concubine of Rao Raja Bhoj. The rectangular *kund* or pool was added later by Maharao Raja Ram Singh (1821–89). The palace itself was built in 1945 around this pool and pavilion but retaining the basic essence of the old architecture on the exterior while the interior has modern amenities. In decorating the palace, the considerable skills of the Italian prisoners of war, lodged at Deoli 50 km (30 miles) away, were used extensively.

Bijolian–Bambaoda–Menai–Mandalgarh: (50–80 km/30–50 miles west of Kota.) On the main highway to Chittaurgarh and Udaipur via Bundi lie three interesting places. The first is **Bijolian**, a great cultural centre of the Chauhan kingdom in the 10th century. It has yielded some key stone inscriptions listing the full genealogy of the Chauhan kings and the first historical mention of Delhi, dating back to 1170 AD. Later it came under Mewar and was a stronghold of a Parmar feudatory. It has some very ancient and beautiful temples, the Shiva and Ganesh temples in particular. There used to be as many as a hundred temples here but now many now lie in ruins.

Soon after leaving Bijolian, the road goes past **Menal**, which has another beautiful group of 12th-century temples and ruins of a palace situated at the edge of a deep gorge. Mehal, or *Mahanal* (the great gorge), was a place of considerable importance, evident from the numerous ruins. It was the retreat of Prithviraj II. Enter the temple of Shiva through a handsome gateway. A big Nandi (bull) of stone stands in front of it. The stones of the temples are extensively carved and decorated, showing Lord Shiva and his consort Parvati. There is a breathtaking view of the gorge from the courtyard of the temple.

A short distance along the top of the escarpment, towards the east, the road leads to the ancient temple of **Jognia Mata** and to the nearby ruined town of Bambaoda, the first place where the Hadas found shelter in the 12th century before establishing the town of Bundi as their capital.

About 30 km (20 miles) away from Menal towards the south, the road branching northeast from the main highway to Udaipur leads to the old fort of **Mandalgarh**. It was one of the very first of the 35 or so forts built by the king of Mewar, Rana Kumbha. It guards and protects the heartlands of Mewar. It was occupied by the Mughals in the 1560s and now lies in ruins. There is a good view from the top of the escarpment.

Sawai Madhopur-Ranthambore National Park: (90 km/55 miles north of Kota.) There is a good road to Sawai Madhopur from Kota via Keshorai Patan, Lakheri and Indargarh, where it crosses the Bundi range of the Aravalli Hills, and, soon after, reaches Sawai Madhopur.

Indargarh is a small town with a lovely fort climbing the hill behind it. The fort has some good wall paintings but permission to enter needs to be obtained in advance from the family that owns it. It was founded in 1605 by Indarsal, a cadet of the Royal House of Bundi and came under Kota State in 1763. Indargarh is also famous for its

Shiva temple, Bijolian.

temple of Bijasan Mata on top of a hill and Kuanwalji (Kamleshwar Mahadeo).

Sawai Madhopur is the usual entry point to the fort of Ranthambore and to the well known National Park of the same name. It is an important railway junction on the main Delhi–Bombay route and also links with Jaipur along a new broad-gauge line.

The great historic fort of Ranthambore, which rises about 250 metres (800 feet) from the floor of the forested valley, surrounded by a range of hills, is one of the most ancient and famous in Rajasthan. It is said to have been founded by Raja Jayant in the 5th century. Later, around the 8th century, it became the stronghold of the Yadav kings, from whom it was wrested by the Chauhans in the late 10th century. When Prithviraj III was defeated by Muhammad Ghori in 1192, his son Govinda came here from Ajmer and made it his base.

The fort is sited on a rugged hill running east to west. The hill's flat summit spreads over an area of nearly 142 hectares (350 acres). Massive ramparts, crenellations, mighty gates and bastions have been built all around the hill, rising straight from near-vertical cliffs and rocks. The **Badal Mahal** (Palace of the Clouds) really does disappear into the clouds. There are two recognised ways to ascend to the fort. The northern one is the one most used now, a steady, paved climb with wide shallow steps going past four fortified gates. The other, the eastern entry, is now locked and not in use. There are several large water reservoirs on top and an underground spring called Patal Ganga which flows throughout the year. The 84-columned *chatri* of King Hamir Deva stands in good shape at the spot where he held audience and entertained. The other palaces, now in ruins, are spread around the site. The most famous places today are the ancient temples of Ganesh and of Shiva. Thousands of people worship at the Ganesh temple during Ganesh Chaturthi, when a large *mela* is organized. There is a spectacular view from the top, with the entire valley,

Sagars or small reservoirs at Menal (left) and at Mandalgarh Fort (right).

the forests, the hills, the three lakes and pavilions dotting the landscape.

Ranthambore is one of the most impregnable forts of India and has never been taken in straight fighting. It is an important and strategic fort commanding the roads to Malwa and Gujarat from Delhi and is one of the keys to Rajasthan. Many sieges and battles have taken place here during the last 800 years and it has changed masters often. The greatest king to live here, immortalised in history for his chivalry, courage and valour was Hamir Deva Chauhan. He gave shelter to the fugitive neo-Muslim Mongol commanders of Sultan Allauddin Khalji of Delhi and refused to yield them to the sultan. Soon a large army from Delhi besieged the fort, but it was beaten back. The next time the indefatigable sultan came personally and, after a prolonged siege, was successful in getting the gates opened only by treachery. The fort fell in 1303. The Rajput women committed *johar* (self-immolation) and Hamir beheaded himself as a penance and as a sacrifice to Lord Shiva. The fort was sacked and a great many beautiful buildings were destroyed.

Later the Mughal Emperor Akbar attempted to conquer the fort by force but faced great difficulties in positioning his artillery on top of the adjoining hills. Though heavily bombarded, the fort was ultimately taken over by good diplomacy. Rao Surjan of Bundi, who was the Commander of Ranthambore, saw wisdom in negotiating a dignified peace rather than face inglorious defeat and certain death. He surrendered the keys to Akbar in 1569 and secured honourable terms in return. Thereafter the fort became a prized Mughal possession.

An interesting monument to be seen on the road to Jaipur from Sawai Madhopur is the giant monolith elephant. It stands in the countryside about 12 km (8 miles) out of Uniara near the fortress of Kakor. Some other places of interest are the great forts of **Shahabad**, **Shergarh** and **Manoharthana** in the Kota area and the ancient Buddhist caves near **Kyasra** in Jhalawar.

Old wooden Gangaur figures, Mandalgarh.

RANTHAMBORE NATIONAL PARK

Situated at the junction of the Aravalli and the Vindhya ranges, Ranthambore is one of India's conservation success stories. Since becoming one of the original 11 areas under Project Tiger in 1973, the park has recovered much of its previous natural glory, proving that, with careful management, a once-wooded area which has since been reduced to arid scrub can be successfully restored.

In 1973, the original sanctuary of 156 sq. km (60 sq. miles) was expanded to 411 sq. km (158 sq. miles) with a core area of 169 sq. km (65 sq. miles) and later became a national park. In 1984 an adjoining area of 104 sq. km (40 sq. miles) to the south became the Sawai Man Singh Sanctuary (named after the last ruling Maharaja of Jaipur).

The link between environment and history is evident in this park, and like Bandhavgarh National Park in Madhya Pradesh, the fort, the temples, the tanks and other ruins are a constant reminder of man's involvement in the area.

The fort commanded a large area and until the late 13th century was the centre of a Hindu kingdom. During the 18th century, the area was protected as a hunting area for and by the Maharajas of Jaipur and it is thanks to an extension of this protection that the park exists today.

The fort is the natural focal point of the park with a series of well established artificial lakes stretching to the north.

Most of the area is covered by typical dry, mixed deciduous forest. The undulating hills have a few bare rockfaces and barren ridges. The area supports a mixed variety of birds, mammals and insects. On the gentler hillsides and in the valleys, dhok *(Anogeissus pendula)* is the main tree. The few areas of lush vegetation are around the lakes and have pipul, mango, palas and banyan, creating a thick forest. The huge banyan near Jogi Mahal at the base of the fort is reputedly the second-largest known.

The major predator here is the **tiger** but their territories overlap with those of the leopard, which are occasionally seen in areas on the park periphery. **Jackal**, **hyena**, **caracal** and **jungle cat** are also found in the park. In recent years, the tiger population has become increasingly diurnal and there have been many sightings of tigers hunting **sambar** on the banks of the lakes. The greater visibility of this magnificent animal, due to careful management, has made the park well known as one of the easier parks in which to spot and photograph tigers.

Sambar and **chital** are common throughout the park and are found in large concentrations near the lakes along with small groups of **nilgai**. In the scrub and thorn, **chinkara** are often observed. Other animals seen include the **marsh crocodile** (basking on rocks or along the banks of the lakes), **wild boar**, **ratel**, **monitor lizard** and **sloth bear**.

The rich birdlife reflects the varied range of flora on which it feeds. During the winter months the lakes attract a variety of migrant water birds.

The park entrance is only 13 km (8 miles) from Sawai Madhopur station on the main Bombay–Delhi line. A new broad-gauge line connects Sawai Madhopur with Jaipur (162 km/100 miles). ∎

Jogi Mahal.

BHARATPUR, DEEG AND DHOLPUR

Bharatpur: This area occupies an important place in the cultural history of Rajasthan. It was closely associated with the ancient kingdom of *Matsyadesa*. During the 5th and 4th centuries BC, the region covered by Bharatpur, Dholpur and Karauli formed part of the Sursena Janpada with its capital at Mathura to the northeast. Many late Mauryan (2nd century BC) sculptures and remains of pottery have been found at Noh on the Agra road east of Bharatpur and can now be seen in the local museum.

Unlike most of Rajasthan, this area is populated by Jats, farmers, who, over much of northwestern India, form the backbone of the agricultural population. They were settled in this region long before either the Rajputs or the Marathas became the dominant powers. In many areas, Jat leaders made marriage alliances with the new overlords, but they continued to harass the Mughal armies and often revolted against the Rajput princes.

During the late 17th century, a Jat headman from the Sinsinwar family called Churaman formed a loose coalition of fellow Jats and began systematically to raid the surrounding countryside, but the Mughal governor in Agra retaliated and in turn destroyed many Jat villages. Under Badan Singh, the Jats regrouped and by 1752 controlled a large area west of the Jamuna river between Delhi and Agra. The Amber (Jaipur) rulers gave Badan Singh the title of Brij-Raj and in 1725 the building of the fort of Deeg with gardens and palaces was started. In 1732 Badan Singh's son and regent, Suraj Mal, began work on the Bharatpur Fort and building continued for the next 60 years.

The **Bharatpur Fort** was, perhaps, among the most formidable in India at that time and in 1805 Lord Lake unsuccessfully laid siege to it for four months and had to retreat after suffering the largest losses experienced by the British in India up until then. Maharaja Ranjit Singh took advantage of this and

Bharatpur was the first state in India to sign a treaty of "Permanent Equal Friendship" with the East India Company.

Throughout the 19th century Bharatpur remained at peace and this continued till Independence came to India. In 1948, four princely states, Alwar, Bharatpur, Dholpur and Karauli, formed the *Matsya Union* with the Maharaja of Dholpur as *Rajpramukh* and in May 1949 the Union joined the new state of Rajasthan.

The local language around Bharatpur is the *Braj Bhasha* dialect of Rajasthani while south, toward Karauli, the *Dang* dialect is more widespread.

Music, dance and drama: As with most of northern India, festivals are celebrated throughout the year and a few have particular local significance. The *Ramlila* performances are most impressive and, while principally performed during *Dussehra*, are also sometimes performed at other more local festivals.

Bharatpur is close to the Braj region of Lord Krishna's birth and childhood. The *Ras-lila* depicting the life of Krishna is performed by professions drawn from the Rai community. During the *Narsingh Chaturdashi* festival, the dancers and other performers wear masks depicting various gods, saints and demons. The *khyal* form of rural drama is popular throughout Rajasthan but the *nautankis* (village actors) of Bharatpur, using a well-build stage and coloured backcloths, have developed their own technique of playing *nagaras* (kettledrums) and a form of dancing including high, and often violent, jumps, earning the name *takhta-tod*. The stories depicted are usually centred on the lives of Rama and Krishna.

Bharatpur is well located and there is a good road from Jaipur to the west and the 150 km (115 miles) can be covered in about 3½ hours. To the east is Akbar's capital, Fatehpur Sikri (18 km/11 miles) and Agra (50 km/32 miles). To the north, Delhi is only 184 km (125 miles) away. Besides being at the hub of an excellent road network, Bharatpur is a junction of the main Delhi–Bombay railway (with connections to Sawai Madhopur and

Preceding pages: a woman in colourful dress. Left, the family tree of the Bharatpur rulers recorded on an iron pillar, Lohagarh Fort.

Kota to the south) and the line running east–west between Agra and Jaipur.

The Iron Fort: While most visitors to Bharatpur now visit the area for the nearby bird sanctuary, the **Lohagarh Fort** is still the focal point of the town. The fort takes its name (*lohagarh*: iron fort) from its supposedly impregnable defenses. Its ingenious design gave it an awesome reputation. Surrounded by two massive earthen ramparts, each encircled by a moat, the mud walls were so thick that all missiles were absorbed and the inner fort remained intact. The moats were 45 metres (150 feet) wide in part and up to 15 metres (50 feet) deep. Now all that remains is part of the inner mud wall (the original outer wall was levelled in 1826) and the moat surrounding the masonry walls. The outermost wall was originally 11 km (7 miles) in circumference and took eight years to complete. A cannon still points defensively to the northeast from a remnant of the mud and rubble wall.

The entrance to the fort from the north is over an ancient brick and stone bridge and through the **Assaldati Gate**. On either side of the gate are fading murals of elephants. This "Gate of Seven Metals", possibly belonged to the Sisodia Rajputs of Chittaurgarh but was removed to Delhi by Allauddin Khilji, and the south gate, more often known as the *Loha Darwaza* (Iron Gate), was brought from Delhi by Maharaja Jawahar Singh in 1764.

The old walled city within the fort forms an irregular oblong and the inner fort contains three palaces and many new buildings. Numerous local government offices now occupy parts of the fort.

The **palace** within the fort was, like many throughout Rajasthan, built by different generations. Most of the buildings adopted Rajput and Mughal styles but in simplified forms, reflecting the Jat lack of ostentation. Of the three palaces, the central building is the oldest, being built by Badan Singh. Part of it now houses the museum. The **Kamra Palace** to the west, some of which is now part of the museum, previously housed the Bharatpur State armoury and

Central portion of Bharatpur Fort.

treasury. To the east is the raja's palace or **Mahal Khas**, including the royal apartments built by Maharaj Balwant Singh (1826–53). The rooms are compact, with stone-latticed windows set in long, arched alcoves. Many walls are still covered with multi-coloured, painted designs. On the ground floor is a set of *hamams*, sunken baths for both hot and cold water. These rooms with painted walls and domed roofs are, along with the rest of the royal apartments, in strong contrast to much of this otherwise unadorned fort.

The State Museum: Primarily an archaeological collection, this museum was founded in 1944 by Maharaj Sawai Brijendra Singh. While overshadowed by the older and better known collections at Mathura and Agra, it is certainly worth visiting. It has some interesting sculptures, including a late Gupta Shiva-Parvati from the 8th century, a Jain *tirthankara* dated *circa* 1020 and a 10th-century Ganesh. One of the most interesting pieces is a 2nd-century red sandstone *Shivalinga*. From the nearby

village of Noh are terracotta toys from the 1st to 3rd-century Kushan period.

Two other places of interest within the fort are its bastions. The central tower known as the **Jawahar Burj** was built in 1765 to commemorate a successful assault on Delhi. The coronation ceremony of the maharajas of Bharatpur took place here and nearby is an Iron Pillar about 30 cm (12 inches) in diameter with the names of the rulers from the time of Lord Krishna to the present inscribed on it in Hindi. The other tower, known as **Fateh Burj**, was built to remind the fort's inhabitants of the successful defence of Bharatpur from the British attack in 1805.

The villages of **Noh**, a few kilometres to the east, and **Mallah** to the south, have both produced interesting archaeological finds, many of which are now in the museum. At Noh a 2-metre (7-foot) high *yaksha* sculpture of the Kushan (1st century AD) period was found, similar to the one in the Mathura museum. About 40 km (25 miles) southeast of Bharatpur, at **Rupbas** is a

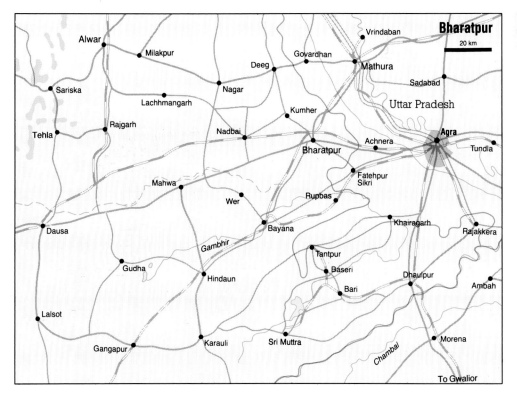

8-metre (27-foot) long sequence of rock-cut images showing "Baldeoji, his consort Reoti, Lakshmi-Narayan and the Pandava hero Yudhishthira with Vishnu". The now ruined, but still attractive palace and tank at Rupbas was used as a shooting lodge by Akbar on hunting visits from Fatehpur Sikri.

Deeg: The road north of Bharatpur goes via Kumher to Deeg (34 km/22 miles). Kumher was founded by Kumbi Jat of Sinsini and was at one time the second capital of Bharatpur State. Badan Singh in 1722 built the palaces and many of the fortifications which are now impressive ruins to the east of the road. The now small and dusty village was in 1754 the site of an important siege when Suraj Mal withstood a combined Mughal and Maratha army of over 80,000 men. During the siege, one of the opposing generals, Khandeo Rao Holkar, was shot and, with his typical generosity, Suraj Mal later built an impressive *chatri* (cenotaph) in his memory at the spot where he fell.

Deeg is now a small agricultural town with a busy, dusty market. It is also approachable from either Kosi or Mathura (36 km/23 miles) on the Delhi–Agra highway. Any visitor going by road from Delhi to Bharatpur is well advised to take the slower (and slightly rougher) road via Deeg. When approached from the south, the massive fortifications divert the road. The **fort** forms part of the town's fortifications and massive masonry walls tower up to 28 metres (85 feet) above a moat 17 metres (55 feet) wide. The fort has 12 bastions, the largest on the northwest corner, known as **Lakla Burj** and still mounted with cannon. The only gate is on the northern side and within the fort today still lie some locally cast guns and a partially ruined, simple *haveli*.

Deeg is justly known for its palaces and gardens begun by Badan Singh and laid out by Suraj Mal following the tradition brought to India by the early Mughals. The palace pavilions and gardens are laid out with an excellent sense of balance. The present area is probably only half of what was originally **Gopal Bhawan Deeg.**

planned. However, what was built is exciting and well preserved, with the buildings forming a large rectangle enclosing the gardens and two large tanks at the eastern and western ends.

The largest and most impressive building, **Gopal Bhawan**, was built around 1763 and overlooks the **Gopal Sagar** (tank) to the west. It is flanked by two smaller pavilions (Sawan and Bhadon – named after the two monsoon months) which purport, in their curved roofs and pillars, to simulate a large pleasure barge, and is fronted by two marble thrones with the gardens beyond. Seen from the garden, Gopal Bhawan seems only two storeys high while, actually, two lower levels also overlook the water. Many rooms in Gopal Bhawan still have their original furniture and since few tourists visit Deeg, it has been possible to maintain the palace very much as it was when the maharaja and his family occasionally stayed here up to the early 1970s. On the northern side of the garden is a large audience hall known as **Nand Bhawan**, while

opposite, to the south, is **Krishna Bhawan**. The focal point of the garden is the pillared summer pavilion (**Keshav Bhawan**) with its ingeniously designed waterworks overlooking Rup Sagar to the east. Five hundred fountains, many of which still play during local festivals, used to spout coloured water on special occasions against a backdrop of lavish firework displays.

At the southwestern corner is **Suraj Bhawan**, completed by Suraj Mal's son, Jawahar Singh (1764–68). Unlike most of the other buildings which use cream-coloured sandstone, Suraj Bhawan is built of white marble, decorated with a mosaic and inlay of semi-precious stones. Much of this marble, including the inlay, was probably looted from Delhi.

Many of the fountains and decorations were also brought to Deeg as booty after Suraj Mal's occupation of Delhi and Agra. A black marble "bed" used for laying out a dead ruler was brought from Delhi and is now in Gopal Bhawan.

One of the original buildings built by

The Bharatpur family chattris, Govardhan.

KEOLADEO GHANA NATIONAL PARK

I n the middle of the 18th century a small reservoir was created 5 km (3 miles) to the southeast of the Bharatpur fort. The building of the Ajan Bund and the subsequent flooding of this natural depression has created, during the subsequent 250 years, one of the world's most fascinating and spectacular bird reserves.

This created wilderness was encouraged and for many years was the shooting preserve of the Majarajas of Bharatpur until it was given to the Rajasthan Government to become a sanctuary in 1956. It is commonly referred to as the Bharatpur Bird Sanctuary.

Despite its becoming a national park in 1982, human pressures on it are still tremendous. A stone wall built in the late 1970s has helped control grazing by large numbers of domestic buffalo and cattle, but illegal collection of fodder continues. Of the total area of only 29 sq. km (11 sq. miles), or about one-third, is under some 1–1.5

metres (3–5 feet) of water following a satisfactory monsoon.

The range of flora in the park is impressive for such a small area. Dozens of grasses provide cover, nest material and food to a range of birds and mammals. Trees range from the thorny acacia or babul which dominates much of the park, to ber, khajur and khejri. Babul and kadam are nesting trees for many bird species. The lakes with their rich range of floating plants, algae, reeds, flowering plants and aquatic grasses provide food and cover to crustaceans, amphibians, insects and fish in large enough quantities that thousands of birds can depend on the area for raising their young and as a winter home.

From August until November, thousands of indigenous water birds breed and raise their young here. **Painted storks**, **spoonbills**, **cormorants**, three kinds of **egret**, **open-billed storks**, **purple herons**, **night herons** and **sarus cranes** are some of the main breeding species. From the onset of the monsoon, nest-building begins, and by October all eggs will have been laid and soon after, young birds of all sizes demand a constant supply of food.

In early October, the first migrants arrive from the high plateaus of Central Asia, Mongolia and Siberia. The **ducks**, **geese** and **waders** arrive first. Raptors, including the **steppe eagle**, **golden eagle**, **osprey** and **harrier** follow. A few years ago there were some 35 to 40 Siberian cranes to be seen, but sadly they seem to have disappeared, a warning of what might happen to other rare species.

The scrub forest and grassland of the park support a wide range of animals, including **nilgai**, **sambar**, **wild boar**, **feral cattle**, **civet**, **jacket** and the **rhesus macaque** amongst others. **Fishing cat**, **jungle cat**, **otter** and **mongoose** are among the smaller species seen.

A metalled road runs through the park from the north gate near the main Agra–Jaipur road. Vehicles are now allowed only as far as the tourist and forest lodges. A good network of raised paths along tree-lined *bunds* give good cover for bird-watching and the visitor can walk along them through much of the park. Visting the park at any time of the year is a rewarding experience. ■

Spoonbill in breeding plumage.

Badan Singh, **Purana Mahal**, at the southeastern corner, has a display of Rajput wall paintings, many influenced by the Mughal schools. This building is now used as a government office but it is worth visiting as an example of the simpler style of Jat building.

About 15 km (9 miles) east of Deeg, en route to Mathura, is the pilgrimage centre of **Govardhan**. The town is small and lies along a narrow range of hills which Lord Krishna is said to have held aloft on the tip of his finger for seven days and nights to protect the people of Braj from the flood poured down on them by Indra. The focal point of the town is the large stone tank called **Mahasi Ganga** which is surrounded by houses. The **Harideva Temple** nearby was built by Raja Bhagwan Das of Amber (Jaipur) during Akbar's reign. The temple is fairly large and worth visiting. On the opposite side of the tank are the *chatris* of two rajas of Bharatpur (Ranjit Singh and Balwant Singh) in which the painted ceilings of the pavilions depict incidents in the rajas' lives. The paintings of unsuccessful assaults by Lord Lake on Bharatpur Fort in Ranjit Singh's *chatri* are especially vivid.

On the road north of Govardhan to **Radha Kund** (3 km/2 miles) is the magnificent *chatri* erected in honour of Suraj Mal who was killed in 1763 at Shahdara to the east of Delhi. The paintings in the *chatri* are now in poor condition but, interestingly, show French officers in Suraj Mal's service. Beside the *chatri* is a tank, **Kusum Sarovar**, and an extensive garden lies behind the buildings.

South to Karauli: Southwest of Bharatpur, Suraj Mal also started to build a fort, palaces and gardens at **Wer** (48 km/30 miles), on lines similar to those of the Deeg complex. Situated between two ranges of the Aravalli hills, 41 km (26 miles) south of Bharatpur on the bank of the Gambir river, is the once famous but now dusty town of **Bayana**. Babur defeated the Sanga Rana of Chittaurgarh nearby on March 16, 1527. Of the numerous Mughal buildings in the town, most are now in a poor state, but there is still a fine gateway to a

garden which was laid out by Jahangir's mother when Akbar visited the town in 1601. The now ruined fort was described by Babur in his memoirs as one of the most famous in India.

A few kilometres east, in the Baretha hills, famous for their fine stone, is the man-made lake, **Kishan Sagar**, formed by damming the Kakund river. During the winter months, the lake is often the home of numerous species of migrating birds, in addition to the many resident species who breed here during the post-monsoon months. On the eastern ridge, a small, attractive palace built during the 1920s overlooks the lake.

Dholpur: Southeast of Bharatpur, on the National Highway between Agra (57 km/36 miles) and Gwalior (64 km/40 miles) to the south, is the capital of the former princely state of Dholpur. The state was created in 1805 when the British governor-general gave the last Jat Rana of Gohad (a state founded in 1505) three of the defeated Scindia's districts north of the Chambal river, and gave Gwalior and Gohal to the Scindia family. The ruling family belonged to the Bamrolian Jats who took this name from Bamroli, their adopted home during the 14th century.

Dholpur is today a quiet, agricultural town, famous for its locally quarried sandstone of which the palace and many of the older buildings are built. This sandstone is finely grained, dark reddish-purple in colour and easily worked. It hardens on weathering and is therefore often used for building. The same stone was later used in the building of New Delhi. To connect Delhi with the stone quarries at Barauli, a 10-km (6-mile) light railway was specially built by the Imperial Delhi Committee.

Because of the ford and ferry point a short distance south of the town and its proximity to the old Mughal capital at Agra, the area around Dholpur has been the scene of many crucial battles. In 1658, 5 km (3 miles) east of the town, at Ranka Chabutra, the last great Mughal Emperor, Aurangzeb, defeated his elder brother, Dara Shikoh, during a war of succession. The Chambal river has long been a natural boundary between the territories of the Rajput states and those of the Marathas to the south. For hundreds of kilometres, a labyrinth of ravines, extending up to 6 km (4 miles) from the river banks, has been the home and refuge for deposed princes and *dacoits* (bandits). During the 1970s, redevelopment of the agricultural potential of the area tried, with limited success, to bring greater security and prosperity to the area. On the north bank, a large, impressive, and now ruined fort, dominates the old ferry crossing.

Babur's lost garden: At the village of **Jhor**, 16 km (10 miles) from Dholpur, in 1978, Elizabeth Moynihan rediscovered the oldest Mughal garden in South Asia. In August 1527, on a large outcrop of sandstone above the dry bed of a lake, Babur started building a garden. The ridge stretches north, and 96 km (60 miles) away along it, Babur's grandson, Akbar, built his city of Fatehpur Sikri. The lake bed (formed by a dam built by Sikandra Lodi in about 1500) and part of the garden are now farmed by the villagers. Few of Babur's buildings and

little of his garden, which must have covered a large area, have survived. The surrounding walls have now gone, but part of the watercourse cut from a single outcrop of sandstone remains, although damaged. Originally there were three water channels, but only the one remaining can be traced: the water flowed from a small, octagonal pool on the edge of the upper terrace, down through a large hexagonal pool on the central terrace, onto a large central pool and the gardens below.

The lotus garden is the first example of Mughal design incorporating Indian skills with Central Asian concepts of garden architecture. A plain rectangular stucture now used as a stable was Babur's hot bath and remains almost as built in 1528. The sunken bath is of white stone. To the west are many abandoned Mughal wells and one pavilion which is now a Hindu shrine. Nearby is a large pre-Mughal tank with three sets of steps, each 30 metres (100 feet) long. Not far away is **Mach Kund**, a deep, spring-fed lake surrounded by over a hundred

Flags hoisted during the Kaila Devi Mela, Karauli.

temples. It is deserted for most of the year but is the site of an annual pilgrimage.

Wildlife and gardens: About 29 km (18 miles) southwest of Dholpur, over a dry, sparsely populated ridge of sandstone, is the small town of **Bari**. The headquarters of the *tehsil* (local administrative district) now occupies the fort built in 1286 by the Ghori king, Firoz Shah. Five km (3 miles) south is the **Talabe Shahi lake** where duck shoots previously took place and which now forms part of the **Van Vihar Wildlife Sanctuary** together with the adjoining **Ram Sagar Sanctuary**. The Ram Sagar lake forms part of an extensive irrigation system constructed by Maharaja Rana Ram Singh from 1901–11.

Beside the Talabe Shahi lake is a long and attractive series of buildings known as **Kanpur Mahal**. Built for Shah Jahan in about 1640, the palace was never occupied. Half of it is now a police post and the other half (fitted with some fascinating Victorian plumbing by a previous maharaja) is now a Public Works Department guest house.

These handsome red sandstone buildings along the west shore are reflected in the lake which, after a good monsoon, fills and attracts a wide range of waterbirds. A double row of octagonal sandstone *chatris* with deep eaves and arches line the *bund*. The pavilions of the gardens are to the north.

Some 61 km (38 miles) away lies **Karauli**, once the capital of a small principality belonging to the Jadon-Rajput family, which merged in 1948 with Bharatpur, Dholpur and Alwar to form the Matsya Union. The best time to visit is during the cattle market in February or the Kaila Devi Chaitra festival in April. The area has a fascinating history. Many villages were once the site of a hunting lodge, garden, or the scene of a battle. Owing to the proximity of the Mughal capitals, many of the region's cultural influences originate from the north and east rather than from the arid semi-desert of Rajasthan to the west.

Rajguru Temple, Machkund, near Dholpur, c. 1910.

INSIGHT GUIDES
TRAVEL TIPS

New Insight Maps

Maps in Insight Guides are tailored to complement the text. But when you're on the road you sometimes need the big picture that only a large-scale map can provide. This new range of durable Insight Fleximaps has been designed to meet just that need.

Detailed, clear cartography
makes the comprehensive route and city maps easy to follow, highlights all the major tourist sites and provides valuable motoring information plus a full index.

Informative and easy to use
with additional text and photographs covering a destination's top 10 essential sites, plus useful addresses, facts about the destination and handy tips on getting around.

Laminated finish
allows you to mark your route on the map using a non-permanent marker pen, and wipe it off. It makes the maps more durable and easier to fold than traditional maps.

The first titles
cover many popular destinations. They include Algarve, Amsterdam, Bangkok, California, Cyprus, Dominican Republic, Florence, Hong Kong, Ireland, London, Mallorca, Paris, Prague, Rome, San Francisco, Sydney, Thailand, Tuscany, USA Southwest, Venice, and Vienna.

🐾 INSIGHT GUIDES

The world's largest collection of visual travel guides

CONTENTS

Getting Acquainted

The Place

Area 342,239 sq. km (132,139 sq. miles).
Capital Jaipur.
Population 44 million at the last census in 1991, with 910 females to every 1,000 males. Currently around 50 million.
Languages Rajasthani, of which the major dialects are Marwari, Jaipuri, Malwi and Mewati. Hindi is also widely spoken and understood.
Peoples The majority of Rajasthanis are farmers or rural labourers. The Kshatriya Rajputs are the traditional ruling caste, while the Mewaris dominate trade. 12 percent of the population are Adivasi, including Bhil, Mina, Bhil-Mina, Bishnoi, Damariya, Gaduliya Lohar, Garasia and Sahariya peoples.
Literacy Total literacy is 38.5 percent. Female literacy is 20 percent.

Religions Hindu (89 percent); Muslim (7 percent); Jain (2 percent); Sikh (1.5 percent); Christian (0.1 percent).
Time Zones 5½ hours ahead of GMT.
Currency Decimal, with 100 paise to the rupee.
Weights & Measures The metric system is used for official purposes. Precious metals, especially gold, are often sold by the *tola* (11.5 grams/0.4 ounces). Gems are weighed in carats (0.2 grams/0.01 ounces).
   Financial outlays and population are usually expressed in *lakhs* (100 thousand) and *crores* (100 *lakhs* or 10 million).
Electricity The voltage system is 220V AC, 50 cycles. DC supplies also exist.
International Dialling Code 91.

The Land

The state is bisected by the Aravalli Hills running southwest–northeast. These are thought to to form one of the oldest ranges in the world. To the northwest is the Thar Desert with its rolling sand dunes. To the east and south of the Aravalli watershed the landscape consists of hilly tracts and plateaux, cut into by rivers such as the Banas, Chappan and Chambal.

Rajasthan is geologically diverse, ranging from the limestones of Jaisalmer, to the granites of Mewar, and the quartzites of the Aravallis. Mixed in with these rocks is a long-exploited mineral wealth, including lead, silver and zinc. Recently, drilling in the desert in Jaisalmer and Barmer districts has pointed to the existence of substantial deposits of oil – a potential danger to the delicate desert environment.
   As one of the driest regions of India, Rajasthan is prone to drought. This tendency is exacerbated by recent over-exploitation of groundwater reserves, and by traditional water conservation practices, such as the building of village tanks, falling into disuse. The summer of 2000 brought one of the worst droughts for years: crops failed, populations were displaced and many cattle died. When visiting the state try to use as little water as possible.

When to Go

The best time to visit Rajasthan is between October and March when the days are warm and the landscape is not too parched. However, from December to February at night it is cold (down to 2°C/36°F) and warm clothing is essential. From March–April

Average Monthly Temperatures & Rainfall

		Jan	Feb	Mar	Apr	May	June	July	Aug	Sep	Oct	Nov	Dec
Delhi	Max/Min °C	21/7	24/10	30/15	36/21	41/27	40/29	35/27	34/26	34/25	35/19	29/12	23/8
	Rainfall mm	25	22	17	7	8	65	211	173	150	31	1	5
Jaipur	Max/Min °C	22/8	25/11	31/15	37/21	41/26	39/27	34/26	32/24	33/23	33/18	29/12	24/9
	Rainfall mm	14	8	9	4	10	54	193	239	90	19	3	4
Jaisalmer	Max/Min °C	24/8	28/11	33/17	38/21	42/25	41/27	38/27	36/25	36/25	36/20	31/13	26/9
	Rainfall mm	2	1	3	1	5	7	89	86	14	1	5	2
Jodhpur	Max/Min °C	25/9	28/12	33/17	38/22	42/27	40/29	36/27	33/25	35/24	36/20	31/14	27/11
	Rainfall mm	7	5	2	2	6	31	122	145	47	7	3	1
Mumbai	Max/Min °C	31/16	32/17	33/20	33/24	33/26	32/26	30/25	29/24	30/24	32/23	33/20	32/18
	Rainfall mm	0	1	0	0	20	647	945	660	309	117	7	1
Udaipur	Max/Min °C	24/8	28/10	32/15	36/20	38/25	36/25	31/24	29/23	31/22	32/19	29/11	26/8
	Rainfall mm	9	4	3	3	5	87	197	207	120	16	6	3

onwards the weather becomes very hot, peaking in May–June when daytime temperatures can reach 50°C (122°F). The very high temperatures cause sand storms in the desert regions, that drive dust into every nook and cranny and block out the sun. The rains usually arrive in mid-July, cooling things down, and last until mid-September.

Etiquette

● Shoes must be removed before entering a temple, mosque or gurdwara (sikh temple).
● Avoid taking leather goods of any kind into temples.
● Photography is prohibited inside the inner sanctum of many places of worship. Obtain permission before using a camera. Visitors are usually welcome to look around at their leisure and can sometimes stay during religious rituals. For visits to places of worship, modest clothing is essential. In Sikh temples, your head should be covered. In mosques, women should cover their head and arms and wear long skirts. A small contribution to the donation box is customary.
● In private, visitors are received as honoured guests and your unfamiliarity with Indian ways will be accepted and understood. When eating with your fingers, remember to use only the right hand.
● Avoid pointing the soles of your feet towards anyone as this is considered a sign of disrespect. Don't point with your index finger: use either your extended hand or your chin.

The Government

India is a federal republic and the constitution devolves many powers from central government to individual elected state assemblies. Rajasthan's state government is unusual in India in having only one chamber, the Vidhan Sabha. The 200 Members of the Legislative Assembly (known as MLAs) are elected every five years and are headed by a Chief Minister who

appoints a cabinet. The state is also overseen by the State Governor, the representative of the Indian President who may, under special circumstances, assume control of the state.

Currently Rajasthan is ruled by the Indian National Congress which took over from the right-wing BJP (Bharatiya Janata Party) in 1998, after 10 years of BJP rule. The Chief Minister is Ashok Gehlot, who comes from Jodhpur, and the Congress now have 154 seats to the BJP's 30. The current State Governor is Anshuman Singh, an ex-High Court judge.

The Economy

Even with its substantial mineral wealth, Rajasthan remains one of the poorest and least industrialised states in India – a legacy of feudal rule, which lasted up to Independence in 1947. It also has one of the lowest population densities. Around 77 percent of the population are rural, with most people working in agriculture or as pastoralists. Tourism has become an important part of the state economy, although this recently took a knock through the severe drought of 2000, and the nuclear tests carried out at Pokaran in the Thar Desert in 1998.

Greetings

The namaste, the greeting with folded hands, is the Indian form of salutation and its use will be appreciated, though men, especially in the cities, will not hesitate to shake hands with you if you are a man. A handshake would even be appreciated as a gesture of special friendliness.

Most Indian women would be taken aback at the informality of interaction between the sexes common in the West and physical contact between men and women is to be avoided. Men should not shake hands with a woman (unless she first offers to).

Planning the Trip

What to Bring

Clothing
Travel light; during summer it is best to wear cotton. During winter, sweaters and jackets are required. Cotton shirts, blouses and skirts are inexpensive and easily available throughout the country. Remember to bring underwear (especially bras) and swimwear. Comfortable footwear, trainers for winter and sandals for summer, make walking on uneven surfaces easier.

For their own convenience, women should not wear sleeveless blouses, mini skirts and short, revealing dresses. Cover up – it's a good idea in the Indian sun anyway – locally available shalwar kamiz, a long tunic top worn over loose trousers, are ideal.

Film
Colour print film, developing and printing facilities are available in all big cities. Colour slide film can only be found in major cities and it may be safer to bring your own.

There are few places where prompt and reliable camera servicing can be done, so photographic equipment should be checked before the trip. Protect your camera and film from excessive exposure to heat, dust and humidity. Do not leave them in direct sun or in a locked car (which can get extremely hot) as heat affects film.

Carry film by hand in a plastic bag which can be given to airport security officers for inspection rather than being put through X-ray machines. There are restrictions on photography of military installations, bridges and dams, airports, border areas and Adivasi/restricted areas.

Other Essentials
If travelling away from the major cities or big hotels, take a sheet, sleeping bag, pillowcases, medical kit, padlock, sewing kit and earplugs among other items. Sun cream, sun block (vital in the mountains) and insect repellent are not readily available so they should be brought with you, along with cosmetics and tampons. A hat is a sensible item. A basin/bath plug is also useful in smaller hotels, which often do not have them.

Entry Regulations

Tourist visas for all nationalities are issued either for one month from the date of entry, with that entry having to be within a month of issue (this visa is not available by post), or for six months from the date of issue (not entry). It is safer and preferable to take a multiple-entry visa, in order to have the option of visiting a neighbouring country.

The best place to obtain a visa is from the embassy or high commission in your country of residence, rather than risk the complications and delays involved in applying for one in neighbouring countries.

Tourist visas can no longer be extended; you must leave the country and re-enter on a new one. It may be difficult to apply for a new visa from neighbouring countries.

Five-year visas are also issued to businessmen and students. Check with the embassy for current details.

If you stay for more than 180 days, before leaving the country you must have a tax clearance certificate. These can be obtained from the foreigner's section of the income tax department in every city. Tax clearance certificates are free, but take bank receipts to demonstrate that you have changed money legally.

In addition to visas, special permits are required for certain areas, while other areas are out of bounds to foreigners altogether (see

Restricted & Protected Areas below).

Restricted & Protected Areas

No access allowed to:
the western side (to the India-Pakistan Border) of National Highway 15 from Sri Ganganagar to Sanchore via Sri Ganganagar, Suratgarh, Lunkaransar, Bikaner, Gajner, Kolyat, Phalodi, Khera, Ram Deora, Pokaran, Lathi, Jaisalmer, Sangad, Fatehgarh, Sheo, Bhadewa, Kapoordi, Barmer, Hathitala, Sanwara, Lookhoo, Gandhwa and Dhamuna.
Exceptions:
peripheral areas of cities, towns, and villages on the National Highway; the cities of Suratgarh, Bikaner, Phalodi, Pokaran, Jaisalmer, Barmer and Sanchore; the villages or areas of Amarsagar, Ludarwa, Kuldara, Bada Bagh, Sam and Unda in Jaisalmer District.

Customs

Customs procedures have recently been simplified. Visitors fill in declaration forms on the plane, and then proceed to the relevant red or green channels. Tourists seldom have any trouble. Occasionally, customs officials ask to see one suitcase at random and make a quick check.

Prohibited articles
These include certain drugs, live plants, gold and silver bullion, and coins not in current use. Firearms require possession licences (valid for six months) issued by Indian embassies or consulates abroad or, on arrival in India, by a district magistrate. For further details, check with the issuing authority.

All checked luggage arriving at Delhi airport is X-rayed before reaching the baggage collection area in the arrival hall.

Duty-free imports
These include 200 cigarettes (or 50 cigars), 0.95 litres (1 pint) of alcohol, a camera with five rolls of

film and a reasonable amount of personal effects, including binoculars, laptop, sound recording instruments, etc.

Professional equipment and high-value articles must be declared or listed on arrival with a written undertaking to re-export them. Both the list and the articles must be produced on departure.

As this formality can be a lengthy process, allow extra time, both on arrival and at departure. For unaccompanied baggage or baggage misplaced by the airline, make sure you get a landing certificate from customs on arrival.

Exports
To avoid last-minute departure problems, remember that the export of antiques (over 100 years old), all animal products, and jewellery valued at over Rs2,000 (in the case of gold) and Rs10,000 (in the case of articles not made of gold) are banned. When in doubt about the age of semi-antiques, contact the office of the Archaeological Survey of India in Delhi, Mumbai, Calcutta, Chennai or Srinagar.

Currency declaration
At present, forms for amounts of cash in excess of US$10,000 must be completed at customs on arrival.

Health

No inoculations are legally required to enter India, but it is strongly advised that you get inoculations against typhoid (Typhim Vi gives protection for 3 years), hepatitis A (Havrix gives immunity for 1 year, up to 10 years if a 6-month booster is given), polio (a booster is needed every 5 years) and tetanus (booster injection every 10 years). Other diseases against which vaccinations might be considered, particularly for longer trips, include meningitis, rabies and Japanese B encephalitis.

Malaria prophylaxis is essential. The usual anti-malarial protection consists of a combination of daily proguanil (Paludrine) and weekly chloroquine (Avoclar, Nivaquin). These are now bought across the counter in the UK, but consult your doctor for the correct dosages. An alternative drug is mefloquine (Larium), taken weekly. However, its strong side effects mean it is rarely prescribed and then only for short periods. The best, and only certain, protection against malaria is not to get bitten. Sleep under a mosquito net whenever possible, cover up in the evenings and use an effective insect repellent such as DEET (diethyltoluamide). Burning mosquito coils during the evening, which are easily obtainable in India, is also effective.

Bring along a personal medical kit to take care of minor ailments. This should include anti-diarrhoea medication, a broad spectrum antibiotic, aspirin, clean needles and something for throat infections and allergies would be a good idea. Take your regular medications, tampons and panty-liners, contraceptives and condoms, as these may be difficult to find.

Also include plasters, antiseptic cream and water purification tablets. All cuts, however minor, should be cleaned and sterilised as immediately to prevent infection. Locally available oral rehydration powders (such as Vijay Electrolyte) containing salts and dextrose are an ideal additive to water, especially when travelling in the summer months or when suffering from diarrhoea. If oral rehydration salts are not available then one teaspoon each of salt and sugar in 500 ml of water is a useful substitute.

Prickly heat is a common complaint caused by excessive perspiration. Try to keep the skin dry by using talcum powder and wearing loose-fitting cotton clothes. Fungal infections are also common and can be treated by exposure to the sun and/or by the application of Caneston cream.

● **Traveller's diarrhoea** is usually caused by low-level food poisoning and can be avoided with a little care. When you arrive, rest on your first day and only eat simple food; well-cooked vegetarian dishes, a

Maps

Obtaining good maps of India can be difficult; the government forbids the sale of detailed maps in border areas, which includes the entire coastline, for security reasons, those which can be bought may not be exported.

Some good maps to bring along are: Bartholomew's 1:4,000,000 map of South Asia; Lascelles map of the same scale and Nelles Verlag maps. Tourist offices can supply larger scale city maps. State and city maps are also published by the TT company, 328 G.S.T. Road, Chromepet, Chennai, Tamil Nadu 600 044, or the Survey of India, Janpath Barracks A, New Delhi 110 001.

Other highly recommended maps are the Eicher series of detailed city maps, along with their guidebook to Delhi, available from local bookstores.

south Indian *thali* and peeled fruits are perhaps best. An upset stomach is often caused by eating too many rich Indian meat dishes (often cooked with vast amounts of oil and spices) and failing to rest and let your body acclimatise.

Drink plenty of fluids but never drink unboiled or unfiltered water. When in doubt, stick to soda, mineral water, or aerated drinks of standard brands. Avoid ice as this is often made with unboiled water. All food should be cooked and eaten hot. Don't eat salads and always peel fruit.

With all cases of diarrhoea, including dysentery and giardia described below, it is not a good idea to use imobilising drugs such as loperamide (Imodium) and atropine (Lomotil) as they prevent the body ridding itself of infection. These should only be used if you have to travel. The most important thing to do in cases of diarrhoea and/or vomiting is to rehydrate, preferably using oral rehydration salts.

● **Dysentery and giardia** are more serious forms of stomach infection and should be suspected and treated if the diarrhoea lasts for more than two days.

Dysentery is characterised by diarrhoea accompanied by the presence of mucus and blood in faeces. Other symptoms include severe stomach cramps and vomiting. Bacillic dysentery comes on quickly and is usually accompanied by fever. It may clear up by itself but its usual treatment is with 500mg of ciprofloxacin or tetracycline twice daily for 5 days. Amoebic dysentery has a slower onset and will not clear up on its own. If you suspect you have amoebic dysentery you should seek medical help as it can damage the gut. If this is not available then self-treat with 400mg of metronidazole (Flagyl) three times daily with food for 7 days. You must not drink alchohol when taking metronidazole.

Giardia is a similar infection caused by a parasite. Like amoebic dysentery it comes on slowly and its symptoms include very loose and foul-smelling diarrhoea, feeling bloated and nauseous, and stomach cramps. Giardia will not clear up on its own and will recur; its treatment is the same as for amoebic dysentery.

● **Heat exhaustion** is common, and indicated by shallow breathing, a rapid pulse, or pallor, and is often accompanied by leg cramps, headache or nausea.

The body temperature remains normal. Lying down in a cool place and sipping water mixed with rehydration salts or plain table salt will prevent loss of consciousness.

● **Heatstroke** is more serious, and more likely to occur when it is both hot and humid. Babies and elderly people are especially susceptible. The body temperature soars suddenly and the skin feels dry. The victim may feel confused, then pass out.

Take them quickly to a cool room, remove their clothes and

cover them with a wet sheet or towels soaked in cold water. Call for medical help and fan them constantly until their body temperature drops to 38°C (100°F).

HOSPITALS

Delhi
All India Institute of Medical Sciences, Ansari Nagar
Tel: 686 4851
Safdarjang General Hospital, Sri Aurobindo Marg
Tel: 616 5060

Jaipur
Santokba Durlabhji, Bhawani Singh Road
Tel: 566 251
SMS, Sawai Ram Marg
Tel: 560 291

Mumbai
Prince Ali Khan Hospital, Nesbit Road
Tel: 375 4343

Getting There

By Air
The majority of visitors now arrive in India by air. Mumbai and Delhi airports are the major entry points and are convenient for Rajasthan.

Discounts are often available during the off-peak season, so it is worth making enquiries. Many long-haul flights unfortunately arrive between midnight and 6am, apparently to suit the night landing regulations of European and East Asian cities but, in reality, often because of weight restrictions for a full plane taking off in the thin air of an Indian summer.

Once you have bought a ticket, check with the airline to confirm your booking then note down the ticket and flight numbers and computer reference code, and keep them separate from the ticket so, in case of loss or theft, you can obtain a replacement.

The major airports are constantly improving and all have left-luggage facilities. Porters and licensed taxis

are available. Delhi and Mumbai have duty-free shops in both the arrival and departure halls. Airport banks are open 24 hours for currency change.

By Rail
There is a train from Lahore in Pakistan to Amritsar in India which crosses the Wagah-Attari border. It stops for a couple of hours for customs and immigration at the border.

By Road
The border crossing from Pakistan to India is from Wagah to Attari. You used to have to travel to Wagah by public transport, cross the border on foot and take another bus or taxi to the nearest town, but there is now a direct bus from Lahore to Delhi. However, if the political situation worsens the service may be shelved, so check before you travel. The border with Nepal is only open for non-Indian or Nepalese nationals at Birganj/Raxhal, Bairwa and Kakarbitta/Naxalbari.

The old overland route through Turkey, Iran, Afghanistan and Pakistan is little-used by tourists now, but when peace returns to this fascinating area, it might again become popular with the more adventurous traveller. Some companies in the UK and Germany do, however, still operate a few departures. In London, Trailfinders (42–48 Earls Court Road, London W8 6EJ, tel: 020 7937 5400) can advise.

Special Facilities

Travelling with Children
Indians love children and are very tolerant and indulgent with them. The problem is that children can be more easily affected by the heat, unsafe drinking water and unfamiliar food seasoned with chillies and spices. In case of diarrhoea, rehydration salts are essential.

Keep the child away from stray animals, especially dogs and monkeys. To avoid the risk of

rabies, it may be safer to take an anti-rabies vaccine.

For infants, it is difficult to find nappies and places to change them. Consider bringing a supply of disposables, or changing to washables. A changing mat is essential, as is powdered milk of a brand that your child is familiar with.

For touring, walking and hiking, child-carrier backpacks or a folding pushchair or pram is worth its weight.

Disabled Travellers
Although disability is common in India, there are very few provisions for wheelchairs or special toilets. The roads are full of potholes and kerbs are often high and without ramps. If you have difficulty walking, it may be hard to negotiate street obstacles, beggars, or steep staircases.

On the other hand, Indians will always be willing to help you in and out of buses or cars, or up stairs. Taxis and rickshaws are cheap and the driver, with a little *bakshish*, will probably help.

You could employ a guide who will be prepared to help with obstacles. Another option is to go with a paid companion.

In the UK, the **Holiday Care Service**, 2 Old Bank Chambers, Station Road, Horley, Surrey RH6 9HW (tel: 01293 774535), could put you in touch with someone.

Some package holiday operators cater for travellers with disabilities, but first ensure that your needs have been understood before making a booking. Contact an organisation for the disabled for further information.

Gay & Lesbian Travellers

Homosexuality is still a taboo subject for many Indians. Sexual relations between men are punishable with long prison sentences and cruising in public could come under public disorder laws. There is no similar law against lesbians.

Public Holidays

There are many festivals in India, but only a few of these are full public holidays:

- **26 January:** Republic Day.
- **15 August:** Independence Day.
- **2 October:** Mahatma Gandhi's Birthday.
- **25 December:** Christmas Day.

See also **Festivals page 300**.

While general attitudes are discriminatory, things are changing slowly, and at least the issue of gay and lesbian rights is starting to be discussed, due in no small part to Deepa Mehta's 1998 film *Fire*, which depicted an affair between two married women. Attacks on cinemas by the religious right brought counter demonstations onto the streets of major cities.

However, gay and lesbian travellers should be discreet and avoid any public displays of affection (as should heterosexual couples). On the plus side, hotels will think nothing of two men or women sharing a room.

Embassies & Consulates

Delhi
Australian High Commission
Australian Compound, 1-50G
Shantipath, Chanakyapuri New
Delhi 110 021 (PO Box 5210)
Tel: 688 8223/687 2035/688 5637
Fax: 688 8223/687 2035/
British High Commission
Shantipath, Chanakyapuri, New
Delhi 110 021
Tel: 687 2161 (24 hrs)
Fax: 687 0065
Canadian High Commission
7–8 Shantipath, Chanakyapuri, New
Delhi 110 021 (P. O. Box 5207,
Chanakyapuri, New Delhi 110 021)
Tel: 687 6500
E-mail: delhi@delhi01.x400.gc.ca
Irish Embassy
13 Jor Bagh
Tel: 462 6714

New Zealand High Commission
50N Nyaya Marg, Chanyakapuri
Tel: 688 3170
US Embassy
Shantipath, Chanakyapuri
Tel: 419 8000
Fax: 419 0017

Mumbai
Australian Consulate-General
16th Floor, Maker Towers E, Cuffe
Parade, Colaba
Tel: 218 1071/218 1072
Fax: 218 8228/218 8189
Consulate of Canada
41–2 Maker Chamber VI, Jamnalal
Bajaj Marg, 220 Nariman Point
Tel: 287 6027–30/287 5479
E-mail: mmbai@dfait-maeci.gc.ca
**Office of the British Deputy High
Commissioner**
Maker Chambers IV, 2nd floor,
222 Jamnalal Bajaj Marg, Nariman
Point
Tel: 283 0517/283 2330
US Consulate General
Lincoln House, 78 Bhulabhai Desai
Road
Tel: 363 3611–8
Fax: 363 0350

Indian Embassies
Australia
High Commission of India, 3–5
Moonah Place, Yarralumla,
Canberra ACT-2600
Tel: (06) 273 3774/273 3999
Fax: (06) 273 3328/273 1308
Canada
High Commission of India, 10
Springfield Road, Ottawa, Ontario
KLM 1 C9
Tel: (613) 744 3751–3
Fax: (613) 744 0913

Great Britain
High Commission of India, India
House, Aldwych, London WC2B 4NA,
Tel: (0891) 880 800 (24-hours
recorded visa information);
(020) 7836 0990 (specific visa
enquiries);
(020) 7836-8484 (general)
US
Embassy of India, 2107
Massachusetts Avenue NW,
Washington DC 20008
Tel: (202) 939 7000
Fax: (202) 939 7027

Tourist Offices

Indian Tourist Offices Abroad
Australia
Level 2 Piccadilly, 210 Pitt Street,
Sydney, New South Wales 2000
Tel: (02) 9264 4855
Fax: (02) 9264 4860
Canada
60 Bloor Street West, Suite 1003,
Toronto, Ontario M4 N3 N6
Tel: (416) 962 3787–8
Fax: (416) 962 6279
France
13 Boulevard Haussmann, F-75009
Paris
Tel: (01) 45 23 30 45
Fax: (01) 45 23 33 45
Germany
Baseler Street, 48, D-60329
Frankfurt Am-Main 1
Tel: (069) 242 9490
Fax: (069) 242 9497
Great Britain
7 Cork Street, London W1X 2AB
Tel: (020) 8812 0929 (24-hour
tourist information);
(020) 7437 3677 (general)
Fax: (020) 7494 1048

Women Travelling Alone

Take the normal precautions such as avoiding local public transport, which can become crowded very quickly (crowds are a haven for gropers). "Eve-teasing" is the Indian euphemism for sexual harassment. Do not wear clothes that expose legs, arms and cleavage – *shalwar kamiz* are ideal, and a shawl is handy to use as a cover-all when required.

More serious sexual assaults on tourists are rare and tend to occur in the more popular tourist areas of Rajasthan, but in case something should happen, call for help from passers-by.

On the up-side, there are "ladies-only" queues at train and bus stations, and "ladies-only" waiting rooms at stations and compartments on trains.

Insurance

It is always advisable to obtain good travel insurance to cover the worst possible scenario. Take a copy of your policy and keep it separately as a safeguard.

Italy
Via Albricci 9, 21022 Milano
Tel: (02) 804 952/805 3506
Spain
Avenida Pio XII 30, 28016 Madrid
Tel: (91) 345 7339
US
1270 Avenue of America, Suite 1808, New York 10020
Tel: (212) 586 4901–3
Fax: (212) 582 3274

Alwar
Rajasthan Tourist Office
Railway Station
Tel: 331 868

Ajmer
Rajasthan Tourist Office
Savitri Girls' College Road
Tel: 52426

Bikaner
Rajasthan Tourist Office
Poonam Singh Circle
Tel: 527 445

Delhi
Government of India Tourist Office
88 Janpath
Tel: 332 0008
Fax: 332 0342
Domestic airport information counter
Tel: 329 5296
International airport information counter
Tel: 329 1171

Jaipur
Government of India Tourist Office
State Hotel Khasa Kothi
Tel/fax: 372 200
Rajasthan Tourist Office
Paryatan Bhavan, M.I. Road
Tel: 365 526
Fax: 376 362
Railway Station
Tel: 315 714

Jaisalmer
Rajasthan Tourist Office
Station Road, Gadi Sagar Pol
Tel: 52406

Jodhpur
Rajasthan Tourist Office
High Court Road
Tel: 44010

Mumbai
Government of India Tourist Office
123 Maharishi Karve Marg,
Opposite Churchgate
Tel: 203 2932/203 3144–5/203 6854
Fax: 201 4496

Udaipur
Rajasthan Tourist Office
Fath Memorial, Suraj Pol
Tel: 411 535
Railway Station
Tel: 412 984

Airline Offices

Delhi
Air India
Jeevan Bharti, 124 Janpath
Tel: 373 6446
Fax: 373 9796
E-mail: ddr@del2.vsnl.net.in
British Airways
DLF Plaza Tower, DLF Qatb Enclave, Phase 1, Gurgaon 122002, Haryana
Tel: 359 911
Fax: 359 926
Airport:
Tel: 565 2078
Gulf Air
G12 Connaught Place
Tel: 332 4293
Fax: 372 1756
Indian Airlines
Malhotra Building, F Block, Connaught Place (open 10am–5pm)
Tel: 371 9168/331 0517
Main Booking Office, Safdarjang Airport (open 24 hours)
Tel: 462 4332
Reservations: 462 0566/463 1337
Flight arr/dep: 301 4433
Jet Airways
Jetair House, 13 Community Centre, Yusuf Sarani
Tel: 652 3345/685 3700
Fax: 651 4996

Airport
Tel: 566 3404
Lufthansa
56, Janpath
Tel: 332 3310
Fax: 332 4524
Sahara India Airlines
7th Floor, Ambadeep Building, 14 Kasturba Gandhi Marg
Tel: 332 6851
Fax: 566 5362/566 2312

Jaipur
Air India
M.I. Road
Tel: 368 569
British Airways
Nijhawan Travel Service Pvt. Ltd., G2 Usha Plaza, M.I. Road
Tel: 370 374/361 065
Indian Airlines
Tel: 743 324
Fax: 743 407
Flight info: 743 500
Jet Airways
Tel: 360 763/370 594
Airport
Tel: 551 733
Sahara Indian Airlines
203 Shalimar Complex, Opposite Church, M.I. Road
Tel: 377 637/365 741/373 748
Fax: 367 808
Airport
Tel: 553 525

Mumbai
Air India
M.I. Road
Tel: 368 569
British Airways
Nijhawan Travel Service Pvt. Ltd., G2 Usha Plaza, M.I. Road
Tel: 370 374/361 065
Indian Airlines
Tel: 743 324
Fax: 743 407
Flight info: 743 500
Jet Airways
Tel: 360 763/370 594
Airport
Tel: 551 733
Sahara Indian Airlines
203 Shalimar Complex, Opposite Church, M.I. Road
Tel: 377 637/365 741/373 748
Fax: 367 808
Airport
Tel: 553 525

Cyber Cafés

Delhi
CyberHut
H35-3 Connaught Place
Open 9am–11pm, Rs100 per hour
The Internet Café @ Softcell
DishnetDSL
1st Floor, B45 Inner Circle, Above
Volga Restaurant, Connaught Place
Open 9am–11pm, Rs60 per hour
Steven's Cafe
1587 Main Bazaar, Paharganj
Open 10am–8pm, Rs180 per hour
X29
Hauz Khas
Open 10am–9pm, Rs60 per hour

Jaipur
Jaipur Communicator
G4–5, Jaipur Towers, M.I. Road
Open 8am–11pm, Rs60 per hour
Mewar Internet Café
Hotel Mewar, Sindhi Camp, Station
Road
Open 6am–11.30pm, Rs150 per
hour
Royal's Business Centre
Opposite A.I.R., M.I. Road
Open 8.30am–9.30pm, Rs60 per
hour
Tirupathi Communications
Sansar Chandra Road
Rs70 per hour

Mumbai
Access Infotech
3 East & West Building, Ground
Floor, South Side, Colaba Causeway
Open 10am–12am, Rs70 per hour
Interscape World
180 Himat Mansions, L.J. Road,
Shivaji Park
Open 9am–11pm, Rs80 per hour
24-hours Cybercafé
331 Dr Ambedkar Road, Pali Hill
Open 24 hours, Rs60 per hour

Pushkar
Internet Office
Varah Ghat
Rs2 per minute/Rs100 per hour

Udaipur
Mewar II Internet Café
Hotel Raj Palace, 103 Bhatiyani
Chotta
Open 8am–11.30pm, Rs900 per
hour

Practical Tips

Emergencies

Generally speaking, India is a safe place to travel, but a tourist is a natural target for thieves and pick-pockets, so take the usual precautions and keep money, credit cards, valuables and passport in a money belt or pouch well secured with a cord around your neck. A protective hand over this in a crowded place could save you a lot of heartache and hassle.

Do not leave belongings unattended, especially on a beach. Invest in good strong locks for all stages of travel. Chaining luggage to the berth on a train, or to your seat on a bus, is a precaution that travelling Indians often take. Watch your luggage carefully, especially during loading and unloading.

Credit card frauds do exist so make sure that shops and restaurants process your card in front of you.

Another sensible precaution is to keep a photocopy of your passport and visa, traveller's cheque numbers and receipts, ticket details, insurance policy number and telephone claims number, and some emergency money in a bag or case separate from your other cash and documents. If you are robbed, report the incident immediately to a police station.

Business Hours

Government offices
Officially 9.30am–6pm Monday to Friday, but most business is done between 10am and 5pm with a long lunch break.

Post Offices
Open from 10am–4.30pm Monday to Friday, and until 12 noon on Saturday. However, in most of the larger cities, the Central Post Office is open until 6.30pm on weekdays, 4.30pm on Saturday. On Sunday some open until noon. Major telegraph offices are open 24 hours.

Shops
Open from 10am–7pm. Some shops close for lunch. Although Sunday is an official holiday, different localities in major cities have staggered days off so that there are always some shopping areas open.

Restaurants
Usually open until 11pm. Some nightclubs and discoteques close very much later. Hotel coffee shops are often open around the clock.

Tipping

There is no harm expressing your appreciation with a small tip. Depending on services rendered and the type of establishment, this could range from Rs2–Rs10.

In restaurants, the tip is customarily 10–15 percent of the bill. Leading hotels add a 10 percent service surcharge and tipping in such places is optional.

Although tipping taxis and three-wheelers is not an established norm, it does not go amiss. Here again, 10 percent of the fare or leaving the change, if substantial, would be adequate. Porters at railway stations would expect around Rs2 a bag. At airports, a Rs5 tip in addition to the fee charged by the airport authority would be welcome.

If you have been a house guest, check with your host whether he has any objections to your tipping any of his domestic helpers (for instance, a chauffeur who may have driven you around) before doing so.

Banks

Open from 10am–2pm weekdays, 10am–noon Saturday for most foreign banks and nationalised Indian banks (of which the State Bank is the largest). Some banks operate evening branches, while others remain open on Sunday and close on another day of the week, and some open 9am–1pm. ANZ Grindlays has two branches open 24 hours; one in Connaught Place, New Delhi, the other at Breach Candy, Mumbai. All banks are closed on national holidays, on 30 June and 31 December. Most businesses close on public holidays.

Postal Services

The internal mail service is efficient in most areas. It is advisable to personally affix stamps to letters or postcards and hand them over to the post office counter for immediate franking rather than to post them in a letterbox.

Sending a registered parcel overseas is a complicated and time-consuming process. Most parcels should be stitched into cheap cotton cloth and then sealed (there are people outside major post offices offering this service). Two customs forms need to be completed. Once the parcel has been weighed and stamps affixed, make sure it is franked and a receipt of registration is issued. Important or valuable material should be registered.

Many shops offer to dispatch goods, but not all of them are reliable. It is usually only safe when handled by a government-run emporium.

Airfreighting purchases is possible but can be equally time-consuming. You will need to produce the bill and receipt, encashment certificate, your passport and onward airline ticket. There are many airfreight agents throughout India and most travel agents can provide assistance.

Telecommunications

India's telephone system is steadily improving and international calls can now be dialled direct to most parts of the world or booked through the operator. Calling from hotels can be extremely expensive, with surcharges up to 300 percent, so check rates first. Mobile telephones have also made an appearance in India and may be rented for the duration of your stay.

Privately run telephone services with international direct-dialling facilities are very widespread. Advertising themselves with the acronyms STD/ISD (standard trunk dialling/international subscriber dialling), they are quick and easy to use. Some stay open 24 hours a day. Both national and international calls are dialled direct. To call abroad, dial the international access code (00), the code for the country you want (44 for the UK, 1 for the US or Canada), the appropriate area code (without any initial zeros), and the number you want. Some booths have an electronic screen that keeps time and calculates cost during the call. Prices are similar to those at official telecommunications centres.

Home country direct services are now available from any telephone to the UK, US, Canada, Australia, New Zealand and a number of other countries. These allow you to make a reverse-charges or telephone credit card call to that country via the operator there. If you cannot find a telephone with home country direct buttons, you can use any phone toll-free by dialling 000, your country code and 17 (except Canada, which is 000-167).

Many privately run telephone services have fax machines and most large hotels have a fax.

E-mail and the internet are now very popular and widely available. All large cities, and many smaller towns, have internet cafés or similar places where you can surf the net or send e-mails. Charges are usually by the minute or hour, and average around 60 Rs per hour.

Money Matters

All encashments of traveller's cheques and exchange of foreign currency have to be recorded on a currency declaration form, or receipts kept as proof of legal conversion. The laws have eased, but some businesses and hotels may still insist. Visitors staying more than 180 days will have to produce proof of encashment of traveller's cheques or exchange of currency for income tax exemption and show they have been self-supporting.

Indian currency has 100 paise to the rupee. Coins are in denominations of 5, 10, 20, 25 and 50 paise. Also in use are 1, 2 and 5 rupee coins. Notes are in 1, 2, 5, 10, 20, 50, 100 and 500 rupee denominations. Indian rupees may not be brought in nor taken out of the country. Exchange rates fluctuate against other currencies.

Traveller's cheques should be well-known brands such as Thomas Cook, American Express and Visa. They can be inconvenient as not all banks will cash them.

Credit cards are increasingly accepted by hotels, restaurants, large shops, tourist emporia and airlines. Again, it is preferable to have a well-known card such as American Express, Access/ MasterCard or Visa. A number of banks will now issue rupees against a Visa card and Amex issues rupees or traveller's cheques to cardholders against a cheque at their offices. ATMs that will issue cash against a Visa card are now found in many cities.

Changing money on the black market is illegal and not worth the premium.

Media

Newspapers & Magazines

With a large number of English-language dailies and hundreds of newspapers in Indian languages, the press in India provides a wide and critical coverage of national and international events.

Among the better-known national English language dailies are the *Times of India*, *The Indian Express*, *The Hindu* and *The Hindustan Times* (all available on-line). There are also two Sunday papers, *The Sunday Observer* and *The Sunday Mail*. The main newspapers in Delhi are the *Asian Age* and *Pioneer*.

The top news magazines include *India Today*, *Outlook* and *Frontline* (also on-line). There are also excellent general-interest magazines such as *Sanctuary* (specialising in South Asian natural history) and *The India Magazine*. Travel magazines like *Travel Links* and city magazines such as *Delhi Diary* and *Hallo! Madras* give current information on internal travel and local cultural events.

International newspapers are on sale in Mumbai and Delhi within 24 hours and some international magazines are also available.

There are several glossy magazines in English, including *Society*, *Bombay* and *First City*, and women's magazines such as *Femina*. Indian editions of *Cosmopolitan* and *Elle* magazines are for sale.

Television & Radio Stations

Doordarshan is the government television company and broadcasts programmes in English, Hindi and regional languages. Local timings vary, but generally the news in English can be heard daily at 7.50am and 9.30pm.

Satellite television is available almost everywhere, including Star TV's five-channel network incorporating the BBC World Service and MTV. Other stations include VTV (local youth-orientated music channel) and Zee TV (Hindi). There are channels showing sport, American soaps and sitcoms and English-language movies. Up to 30 channels can be picked up, given the right equipment.

All India Radio (AIR) broadcasts on the short-wave, medium-wave and in Delhi, Mumbai and Chennai on FM (VHF). The frequencies vary, so check with your hotel.

Courier Services

Most of the major international courier networks have agency agreements with Indian companies. DHL, Skypak and IML all work under their own brand names while Federal Express operates as Blue Dart. These companies have offices in the major towns and operate both international and extensive domestic networks.

Note: The government's Speedpost service delivers quickly at a similar price.

On Arrival

Once through customs the visitor is often besieged by porters, taxi drivers and others. Choose one porter and stick to him. There is a system of paying porters a fixed amount per piece of baggage before leaving the terminal: a tip of Rs5, once the bags are aboard the taxi or bus, is sufficient. If a travel agent or a friend is meeting you, he or she may be waiting outside the building.

Some major hotels operate courtesy buses, and a public service known as EATS (Ex-Serviceman's Transport Service) operates an airport bus service in Delhi, Mumbai and Calcutta with stops at hotels and major points en route to the city centre.

On Departure

It is essential to reconfirm your reservations for all outward-bound flights 72 hours before departure, especially in the peak season, when most of the flights are overbooked.

Security procedures can be intensive and time-consuming, so allow at least two hours for check-in.

An airport/seaport tax is charged on departure and must be paid prior to check-in (check the cost with your airline at the time of booking). Do ensure that the name of your outward-bound carrier is endorsed on the tax receipt.

Poste Restante

Generally this works well, but make sure your name is clearly written. Most towns have only one main post office but there is often confusion between Delhi and New Delhi. New Delhi's main post office is near Connaught Circus while Delhi's main post office is between the Red Fort and Kashmir Gate in Old Delhi.

For visitors with entry permits, exit endorsements are necessary from the office where they were registered.

Should a stay exceed 180 days, an income tax exemption certificate must be obtained from the Foreign Section of the Income Tax Department in Delhi or Mumbai.

Repairs and Tailors

Traditionally, India's use of resources is very efficient, reflected in the way almost everything can be recycled and/or repaired. Since travelling around India can be hard on your shoes, baggage and clothes, this is very useful. Chappal-wallahs, shoe repairers, can be found everywhere, usually sitting by the side of the road with their tools in a wooden box. For an embarassingly small charge, they will be able to glue, nail or stitch almost any pair of shoes or sandals back into shape.

Indian tailors are very skillful and can run up a set of clothes quickly. Although they can do fair copies of Western fashions, they are, obviously, much better at stitching *sari* blouses or *shalwar kamiz*. The process of buying fabric is one of the great pleasures of visiting India, and if you want it made up, most shops will be able to recommend a good tailor.

Tailors will also be able to repair your existing clothes, even badly torn ones, and – just as useful – can stitch up rucksacks which are on the point of collapse.

Entrance Fees

The Archaeological Survey of India – which owns and looks after many of the sites in Rajasthan – has recently announced its intention of raising the entrance fee for foreign tourists to its sites (although there has been no indication of when this might happen). The proposals are to raise the fee from around Rs10 (this varies from place to place) to $US10, with further charges for photography and video cameras. The fee for Indian nationals is to go up from Rs5 to Rs10.

Hopefully, this large increase in revenue for the Archaeological Survey will result in better protection for valuable historical buildings. However, it will substantially add to the cost of a visit to Rajasthan for foreign travellers.

Departure Tax

Remember before you leave that there is a departure tax of Rs600 (Rs150 for neighbouring SAARC countries) for all international departures. This should be included in your ticket, but do check with your airline or ticket agent.

Getting Around

Travel by Air

Indian Airlines (not to be confused with the international carrier, Air India), has one of the world's largest domestic networks. The reservations system has been improved by the introduction of computers. For travel during the peak season (September–March), try and make reservations in advance as flights are usually heavily booked.

With time-consuming check-in and security procedures, you must be at the airport an hour before departure time. Coach services from some city terminals are available. In-flight service is adequate. Alcohol is only available on international flights.

Indian Airlines has a good safety record and its fares are often lower than those charged for comparable distances elsewhere. The baggage allowance per adult is 20kg and 30kg in business class.

Cancellation charges on tickets purchased locally are extremely high, but none are applicable for domestic sectors issued on international tickets.

The Discover India fare valid for 21 days of travel and the Tour India

Timetables

Airline timetables are published in *Divan* and *Excel* magazines and are shown on teletext. They are also available at travel agents and information counters at all major airports. A local travel magazine, *Travel Links*, also publishes air and rail timetables.

Scheme valid for 14 days and limited to six flight coupons, might be useful if you have limited time. These tickets must be purchased abroad, or paid for in India using foreign currency. For details, contact your travel agent or an Air India office abroad, or write to: Traffic Manager, Indian Airlines House, Parliament Street, New Delhi.

The privately operated airlines Jet Airways and Sahara Indian Airlines fly certain domestic routes.

Travel by Bus

Almost every part of the country is connected by an extensive and well-developed bus system with the railway stations being the natural hubs for both local and regional services. Some of the more rural routes are serviced by noisy dilapidated vehicles, but an increasing number of deluxe and air-conditioned expresses ply the trunk routes.

Many of the trunk routes are now operated by video coaches – if you have never been to an Indian cinema, a night bus journey is an introduction to the popular variety of Hindi or regional film.

There are many parts of the country where the bus service is the only means of public transport and at times may be more convenient (for instance, between Agra and Jaipur) than the train.

On many routes, even local ones, reservations can be made. Most baggage is carried on the bus roof, so all bags should be locked and checked on at intermediate stops. Most cities have a bus service, but it is usually preferable to use taxis or three-wheeled "auto-rickshaws".

Rickshaws

The most convenient way of getting around town is by rickshaw. These come in three types, a cycle rickshaw (a tricycle with a seat for two people on the back), an "auto" (a motorised three-wheeler) and, only in central Kolkata, rickshaws pulled by men on foot.

Taxis

When taking a taxi or bus into town from the airport, it is advisable to change money in the arrival hall. In Delhi, Mumbai and Bangalore, a system of prepayment for taxis into the city is operated by the traffic police. This saves considerable anguish when the occasional unscrupulous driver takes a long route or tries to overcharge. Elsewhere, enquire at the information desk for the going rate for a journey to your destination before getting into the taxi; and make sure the meter is "down" before you embark. It is alright to share a taxi even if the destination may not be the same (although in the same area). In some cities, taxis have fare charts which, when applied to the amount on the meter, give the correct fare. There is often a night surcharge of 10 percent between 11pm and 6am and a rate of Rs1 to Rs2 per piece of baggage.

Autos are, like taxis, supposed to use a meter. You should insist on this and get out if they refuse. Meter rates are subject to periodic changes, and extras for late-night journeys etc., which the driver should show you on a card. In popular tourist spots, during rush hour and bad weather, you may find it impossible to persuade the drivers to use the meter. A tactic that might work is to offer "meter plus five" (the cost plus Rs5). If not, you'll have to negotiate the fare. After a short while in the country you will get a feel for what is acceptable, given that as a relatively well-off foreign tourist you are expected, quite reasonably, to pay a little more.

Cycle rickshaws are more convenient in some places, like the very congested streets of Old Delhi. With these you should negotiate the fare before you set off.

Driving in India

The best advice to anyone who is thinking about driving in India is don't. Roads can be very congested and dangerous and there are many unwritten rules followed by other drivers. It is far better, and cheaper, to hire a car and driver.

However, if you do have to drive you will need your domestic licence, liability insurance, an international driver's permit and your vehicle's registration papers. Information regarding road conditions can be obtained from national and state automobile associations which periodically issue regional motoring maps, general information regarding roads and detailed route charts.

Contact: the **Automobile Association of Upper India** Lilaram Building, 14-F Connaught Circus, New Delhi 110001, tel: 331 4071, 331 2323–5; **Western India Automobile Association** Lalji Narainji Memorial Building, 76 Veer Nariman Road, Mumbai 400 020, tel: 291 085/291 192.

Car & Taxi Rental

Chauffeur-driven cars, costing about US$20 a day, can be arranged through tourist offices, hotels, local car rental firms, or branches of Hertz, Budget or Europcar.

The big international chains are best for self-drive car rental. They charge 30 percent less than for chauffeur-driven cars with about a Rs1,000 deposit against damage if paid in India, more if paid in country of residence. In some places motorbikes or mopeds are available for hire.

Taxis come both with and without air-conditioning. Charges vary, ranging from Rs325 for eight hours and 80 km (50 miles) to Rs450 for an air-conditioned car. For out-of-town travel, there is a per km charge, usually between Rs2.30–Rs3 per km in the plains (in the hills this rate is often Rs6 per km), with an overnight charge of Rs100. Package tours, sold by travel agencies and hotels, include assistance, guides and hotel accommodation, in addition to taxi charges.

The local yellow-top black taxis are metered, but with constant hikes in fuel prices, charges may often be higher than indicated on the meter. If so, this will be prominently stated in the taxi and the driver will have a card showing the excess over the meter reading that can be legitimately charged.

The fare for three-wheelers is about half that of taxis. Do not forget to ensure that the meter in the three-wheeler is flagged down to the minimum fare.

Travel by Rail

Rail travel is safe, comfortable and by far the best way to get around the country.

Indian Railways has a number of different classes, of varying degrees of comfort. In descending order of price, they are:
● First class AC, very comfortable with lockable cabins of four berths each.
● AC II tier, partitions arranged in groups of 6 berths with curtains that pull across to provide privacy.
● AC III tier, partitions with groups of 9 berths, the middle berths fold down for sleeping.
● AC chair car.
● First class, non-AC but with ceiling fans. Has lockable cabins of four berths each. There is one cabin of two berths halfway down each carriage.
● Sleeper class, partitions of 9 berths with ceiling fans.
● Second class, unreserved with no berths and hard seats.
Reservations are required for all classes other than second class. In the summer months it is best to go AC. When the weather is cooler then first class can be an excellent

Hitchhike Warning

It is unsafe to hitchhike in India, except in emergencies. Even then only a bus or truck is likely to stop and the ride would be slow and uncomfortable.

option as it is possible to see the passing countryside without having to stare through the darkened windows of AC.

All carriages have both Western and Indian-style toilets. If you are up to squatting on a moving train always use the Indian toilet as they are invariably cleaner and better maintained.

Advance reservation is strongly recommended. Many stations now have very efficient computerised booking counters from where you can book any ticket for any route. Reservations may be made up to 60 days in advance and cancellations (for which you will need to fill in the same form as for a reservation) can be made with varying degrees of penalty depending on the class and how close the cancellation is made to the time of departure. In the larger cities, the major stations have tourist sections with English-speaking staff to reduce the queues for foreigners and non-resident Indians buying tickets; payment is in pounds sterling or US dollars (traveller's cheques or cash). If reservations are not available then certain trains have a tourist quota that may be available. Other options are to take a waitlisted ticket or the more assured reservation against cancellation (RAC); the booking clerk should be able to advise you on how likely you are to get a reservation. It is also possible to make bookings from abroad through Indian Railways representatives. They will accept bookings up to six months ahead, with a minimum of one month for first class, three months for second.

Trains are slow compared to those in the West, so if you are in a hurry, stick to the expresses. Fares are generally low. The Indrail Pass, available to foreign nationals and Indians resident abroad and paid for in foreign currency, can cut down on time getting reservations and be good value if you plan on travelling nearly every day (it is not valid for the Palace on Wheels, Royal Orient and Fairy Queen). In the UK the

pass can be obtained through S.D. Enterprises, 103 Wembley Park Drive, Wembley, Middlesex HA9 8HG, tel: (020) 8903 3411; fax: (020) 8903 0392. They can also book single-journey tickets in advance for you. The Indrail pass can be bought in India at Railway Central Reservations Offices in Mumbai Central (tel: 292 122/ 222 126/292 042/291 952); Mumbai CST (tel: 415 0079); and New Delhi (tel: 344 877/345 080/345 181).

Tourist Guide Offices at railway reservation centres are helpful in planning itineraries and obtaining reservations. Tourist Guides are available at New Delhi, tel: 352 164, and Mumbai, Churchgate, tel: 298 016 4577. Railway timetables available at Indian Tourist Offices abroad also contain much useful information.

Each regional railway prints its full timetable in Hindi and English. There is also the monthly *Indian Bradshaw*, which lists all services across the country, or the concise but comprehensive *Trains At A Glance*, probably the most useful timetable for foreign tourists. These publications should be available from railway stations but they are updated and reprinted regularly so are periodically unavailable.

Remember to check which station your train departs from and do allow at least an hour to find your seat/berth. Lists of passengers with the compartment and seat/berth numbers allotted to them are displayed on platforms and on each carriage an hour before departure. The station superintendent and the conductor attached to the train are usually available for assistance.

Food can usually be ordered through the coach attendant and, on Shatabdi and Rajdhani trains, the fare covers food, drinks and snacks as well. Bedding consisting of two sheets, a pillow and a blanket is provided in first class AC, AC II tier and III tier, and is also available from the attendant for Rps20 in first class.

In theory, if they want bedding, first class passengers should contact the Station Manager before travelling, but extra bedding is often available. If travelling sleeper class then it is a good idea to take a sheet sleeping bag (any Indian tailor will run one up for you).

Retiring rooms (for short-term occupation only) are available at over 1,100 stations on a first-come first-served basis, but these are usually heavily booked. All first class waiting rooms have couches for passengers using their own bedding. At New Delhi station, a Rail Yatri Niwas has been built for transit passengers. Rooms for this can be booked in advance.

Reservation Forms

To buy your ticket you must first fill out a Reservation Requisition Form, which will be available from one of the windows in the booking office. The form is in Hindi on one side and English on the reverse. In addition to the obvious information such as where you wish to leave from and go to and when, to fill in the form you also need to know:

● The train number and name. You can get this from a timetable, or, if the train departs from the station you are booking from, it is usually displayed on a board in the booking office.

● The class you wish to travel and whether you require a berth (for overnight journeys, or any journey between 9pm and 6am), or only a seat.

● Whether you require a lower, middle or upper berth. An upper berth is a good idea as it can be used throughout the day, whereas the other two may only be used for sleeping 9pm–6am.

Foreign travellers should also fill in their passport numbers in the column that asks for your Concession Travel Authority Number, which is needed if the ticket is issued under the foreign tourist quota.

Most stations have cloakrooms where travellers can leave their luggage. Bags must be locked and you must have the reclaim ticket. Check opening times of the cloakroom for collection. Pre-paid taxi and/or auto-rickshaw services are available at some stations.

Useful Trains

The following list gives each train's starting and destination stations, the train's number and name, arrival and departure times, and the days it leaves on – always leave at least a couple of hours wait when planning connections.

From Abu Road
Abu Road–Ajmer–Jaipur: 9707 Aravali Express, dept. 11.15, arr. Ajmer 17.12, Jaipur 20.15, Daily
Abu Road–Ajmer–Jaipur–Delhi: 2915 Ashram Express, dept. 21.25, arr. Ajmer 02.10, Jaipur 04.35, Delhi 10.15, Daily
Abu Road–Ajmer–Jaipur–Delhi: 9105 Ahmadabad Delhi Mail, dept. 14.35, arr. Ajmer 20.20, Jaipur 23.25, Delhi 05.20, Daily
Abu Road–Jodhpur: 4846 Suryanagari Express, dept. 02.05, arr. 07.30, Daily
Abu Road–Jodhpur–Bikaner: 4708 Bandra Bikaner Express, dept. 04.45, arr. Jodhpur 10.35, Bikaner 15.40, Daily

From Ahmadabad
Ahmadabad–Jaipur–Delhi: 2915 Ashram Express, dept. 17.35, arr. Abu Road 21.05, Ajmer 02.10, Jaipur 04.35, Alwar 07.02, Delhi 10.15, Daily
Ahmadabad–Jaipur–Delhi: 9105 Ahmadabad Delhi Mail, dept. 09.55, arr. Abu Road 14.15, Ajmer 20.20, Jaipur 23.25, Alwar 02.22, Delhi 05.20, Daily
Ahamdabad–Jaipur–New Delhi: 2957 Swarnajayanti Rajdhani, dept. 17.10, arr. Abu Road 20.25, Ajmer 00.40, Jaipur 02.40, New Delhi 07.50, Mon, Wed, Fri
Ahmadabad–Jodhpur: 4846 Suryanagari Express, dept. 21.50, arr. Abu Road 01.45, Jodhpur 07.30, Daily

Ahmadabad–Udaipur–Delhi Sarai Rohilla: 9944 Ahmadabad Delhi Sarai Rohilla Express, dept. 22.40, arr. Udaipur City 07.35, Ajmer 19.10, Jaipur 23.30, Delhi Sarai Rohilla 07.05, Daily

From Ajmer
Ajmer–Abu Road: 2916 Ashram Express, dept. 23.25, arr. 04.05, Daily
Ajmer–Abu Road: 9106 Delhi Ahmadabad Mail, dept. 07.35, arr. 12.50, Daily
Ajmer–Abu Road: 9708 Aravali Express, dept. 11.05, arr. 16.30, Daily
Ajmer–Jaipur: 9652 Express, dept. 06.35, arr. 09.45, Daily
Ajmer–Jaipur–Delhi: 9105 Ahmadabad Delhi Mail, dept. 20.35, arr. Jaipur 23.25, Delhi 05.20, Daily
Ajmer–Jaipur–New Delhi: 2016 Shatabdi, dept. 15.30, arr. Jaipur 17.25, New Delhi 22.15, Mon–Sat
Ajmer–Jaipur–New Delhi: 2957 Swarnajayanti Rajdhani, dept. 00.45, arr. Jaipur 02.40, New Delhi 07.50, Mon, Wed, Fri
Ajmer–Jaipur–Delhi Sarai Rohilla: 9944 Ahmadabad Delhi Sarai Rohilla Express, dept. 19.45, arr. Jaipur 23.30, Delhi Sarai Rohilla 07.45, Daily
Ajmer–Udaipur City: 9615 Chetak Express, dept. 01.50, arr. 10.25, Daily
Ajmer–Udaipur City: 9943 Delhi Sarai Rohilla Ahmadabad Express, dept. 08.45, arr. 18.00, Daily

From Bikaner
Bikaner–Delhi Sarai Rohilla: 4790 Express, dept. 08.45, arr. 19.10, Daily
Bikaner–Delhi Sarai Rohilla: 4792 Mail, dept. 19.45, arr. 06.40, Daily
Bikaner–Jaipur–Ajmer: 4738 Express, dept. 20.30, arr. Jaipur 06.55, Ajmer 11.30, Daily
Bikaner–Jodhpur: 4805 Jammu Tawi Jodhpur Express, dept. 01.25, arr. 06.10, Daily
Bikaner–Jodhpur: 4887 Kalka Jodhpur Chandigarh Express, dept. 12.35, arr. 17.45 Daily
Bikaner–Jodhpur–Abu Road: 4707 Bikaner Bandra Express, dept.

09.35, arr. Jodhpur 15.00, Abu Road 20.20, Daily

From Delhi
Delhi–Jaipur–Abu Road: 2916 Ashram Express, dept. 15.05, arr. Alwar 17.55, Jaipur 20.35, Ajmer 23.15, Abu Road 04.05, Daily
Delhi–Jaipur–Abu Road: 9106 Delhi Ahmadabad Mail, dept. 22.50, arr. Alwar 01.30, Jaipur 04.20, Ajmer 07.20, Abu Road 12.50, Daily
Delhi–Jaipur–Jodhpur: 2461 Mandore Express, dept. 21.00, arr. Alwar 23.52, Jaipur 22.35, Jodhpur 06.40, Daily
Delhi–Jaipur–Jodhpur: 4859 Delhi Jodhpur Express, dept. 16.55, arr. Alwar 19.50, Jaipur 22.35, Jodhpur 06.40
Delhi Sarai Rohilla–Bikaner: 4709 Link Express, dept. 23.05, arr. 10.25, Daily
Delhi Sarai Rohilla–Bikaner: 4789 Express, dept. 08.35, arr. 19.15, Daily
Delhi Sarai Rohilla–Bikaner: 4791 Mail, dept. 21.25, arr. 08.10, Daily
Delhi Sarai Rohilla–Jaipur–Udaipur: 9615 Chetak Express, dept. 14.10, arr. Jaipur 21.50, Ajmer 01.40, Udaipur City 10.25, Daily
Delhi Sarai Rohilla–Jaipur–Udaipur: 9943 Ahmadabad Express, dept. 21.00, arr. Jaipur 04.30, Ajmer 08.30, Udaipur City 18.00, Daily
New Delhi–Jaipur–Abu Road: 2958 Swarnajayanti Rajdhani, dept. 14.40, arr. Jaipur 19.35, Ajmer 21.42, Abu Road 01.40, Tue, Thur, Sat
New Delhi–Jaipur–Ajmer: 2015 Shatabdi, dept. 06.15, arr. Jaipur 10.30, Ajmer 12.45, Mon–Sat

From Jaipur
Jaipur–Ajmer: 2015 Shatabdi, dept. 10.40, arr. 12.45, Mon–Sat
Jaipur–Ajmer: 2413A Link Express, dept. 11.30, arr. 13.50, Daily
Jaipur–Ajmer: 9651 Express, dept. 17.30, arr. 20.45, Daily
Jaipur–Alwar: 4854/4864 Marudhar Express, dept. 15.20, arr. 17.55, Mon, Thur and Sat/Tue, Wed, Fri and Sun
Jaipur–Alwar: 9771 Amritsar Express, dept. 19.10, arr. 22.25, Tue, Sat

Jaipur–Bikaner: 2468 Intercity Express, dept. 15.20, arr. 22.15, Daily
Jaipur–Bikaner: 4737 Ajmer Bikaner Express, dept. 21.00, arr. 07.00, Daily
Jaipur–Delhi: 2414 Express, dept. 16.30, arr. 21.50, Daily
Jaipur–New Delhi: 2016 Shatabdi, dept. 17.55, arr. 22.15, Mon–Sat
Jaipur–Jodhpur: 2461 Mandore Express, dept. 02.45, arr. 07.55, Daily
Jaipur–Jodhpur: 2465 Intercity Express, dept. 17.30, arr. 22.45, Daily
Jaipur–Jodhpur: 4859 Express, dept. 23.30, arr. 06.40, Daily
Jaipur–Udaipur: 9615 Chetak Express, dept. 22.10, arr. 10.25, Daily
Jaipur–Udaipur: 9943 Delhi Sarai Rohila Ahmadabad Express, dept. 04.50, arr. 18.00

From Jaisalmer
Jaisalmer–Jodhpur: 4809 Express, dept. 22.30, arr. 05.35, Daily

From Jodhpur
Jodhpur–Abu Road: 4707 Bikaner Bandra Express, dept. 15.20, arr. 20.20, Daily
Jodhpur–Abu Road: 4845 Suryanagari Express, dept. 18.15, arr. 23.20, Daily
Jodhpur–Bikaner: 4708 Bandra Bikaner Express, dept. 11.00, arr. 15.40, Daily
Jodhpur–Bikaner: 4888 Jodhpur Kalka Chandigarh Express, dept. 10.30, arr. 15.40, Daily
Jodhpur–Jaipur: 2308 Jodhpur Howrah Express, dept. 17.15, arr. 23.00, Thurs–Tue
Jodhpur–Jaipur: 2466 Intercity Express, dept. 05.45, arr. 10.35, Daily
Jodhpur–Jaipur: 4864/4865 Marudhar Express, dept. 09.00, arr. 15.05, Tue, Wed, Fri, Sun/Mon, Thur, Sat
Jodhpur–Jaipur–Delhi: 2462 Mandore Express, dept. 19.30, arr. Jaipur 00.35, Delhi 06.15, Daily
Jodhpur–Jaipur–Delhi: 4860 Express, dept. 23.15, arr. Jaipur 05.30, Delhi 11.25, Daily

Jodhpur–Jaisalmer: 4810 Express, dept. 22.55, arr. 05.30, Daily

From Mumbai
Bandra Terminus–Ahmadabad: 9215 Saurashtra Express, dept. 07.55, arr. 19.30, Daily
Bandra Terminus–Ahmadabad–Jodhpur–Bikaner, dept. 15.00, arr. Ahmadabad 00.10, Abu Road 04.45, Jodhpur 10.35, Bikaner 15.40, Daily
Bandra Terminus–Ahmadabad–Jaipur: 9707 Aravali Express, dept. 20.50, arr. Ahmadabad 05.55, Abu Road 10.55, Ajmer 17.12, Jaipur 20.15, Daily
Mumbai Central–Ahmadabad: 2009 Shatabdi, dept. 06.25, arr. 13.20, Sat–Thur
Mumbai Central–Ahmadabad: 9011 Gujarat Express, dept. 05.45, arr. 15.15, Daily
Mumbai Central–Ahmadabad: 2901 Gujarat Mail, dept. 21.50, arr. 06.40, Daily

From Udaipur
Udaipur–Jaipur–Delhi Sarai Rohila: 9616 Chetak Express, dept. 18.10, arr. Ajmer 02.15, Jaipur 05.45, Delhi Sarai Rohila 13.35, Daily
Udaipur–Jaipur–Delhi Sarai Rohila: 9944 Ahmadabad Delhi Sarai Rohila Express, dept. 08.00, arr. Ajmer 19.10, Jaipur 23.30, Delhi Sarai Rohila 07.05, Daily

Railway Tours

Indian Railways run three "Royal Trains" through Rajasthan and Gujarat, using luxury carriages – modelled on those of the maharajas – with on-board catering. Book well in advance for these popular tours.

The Royal Orient Using the famous picturesque carriages of the Palace on Wheels, this is a luxury, refurbished, air-conditioned, metre-gauge train. Accommodation is mainly in coupés, with each carriage having a mini-bar, kitchenette and Western toilets. It departs from Delhi Cantonment Station on Wednesdays at 2.30pm and travels through Chittaurgarh, Udaipur, Junagadh, Veraval, Sasan Gir, Delwada, Palitana, Sarkhej, Ahmedabad and Jaipur over the next six days, arriving back in Delhi at 6am the following Wednesday. The train runs between September and April; a two-berth cabin costs from $150 to $200 per day. Bookings can be made through travel agents abroad.

In India contact:
Tourism Corporation of Gujarat Limited
Nigam Bhavan, Sector 16, Gandhinagar, 382 016
Tel: 22029/22645/22528
Fax: 02712/22029
12-4 First Floor, East Patel Nagar, New Delhi 110 008
Tel: 572 0379

The Palace on Wheels Many of the tracks in Rajasthan have now been converted to broad gauge and the original Royal Train, the Palace on Wheels, has new rolling stock. The 14 carriages leave Delhi every Wednesday between September and April, and stop at Jaipur, Bharatpur, Chittaurgarh, Udaipur, Sawai Modhopur, Jaisalmer, Jodhpur and Agra, returning to Delhi on the 8th day. A double cabin costs between $295 and $350. Contact a travel agent abroad.

In India contact:
Senior Manager, Palace on Wheels, Rajasthan Tourist Reception Centre, Bikaner House, Pandara Road, New Delhi 110 011
Tel: 381 884
Fax: 382 823
Rajasthan Tourism Development Corporation
Hotel Swagatam Campus, Jaipur 302 006
E-mail: jaipur@palaceonwheels.net

The Fairy Queen Named after the engine which pulls the train (the oldest working broad-gauge steam engine in the world), this tour leaves one Saturday every month between November and February. It runs to Alwar, from where passengers are taken to the tiger reserve at Sariska. The next day they return to Alwar to see the fort and museum and return to Delhi in the evening. The cost is $235 per person. Contact travel agents for booking details.

Where to Stay and Eat

Ajmer (0145)

££££
Mansingh Palace
Vaishali Nagar, Ajmer 305 001
Tel: 425 855/425 857/425
702/425 956
Fax: 425 858
E-mail: mansinghajmer@ mailcity.com
Top hotel in town, with comfortable
rooms, bar and decent restaurant.
££
Hotel Regency
Delhi Gate, Ajmer 305 001
Tel: 620 296/622 439
Fax: 621 750/420 747
Central and pleasant hotel with
some AC rooms. Good vegetarian
restaurant.

Heritage Hotels

Some of India's most atmospheric
and romantic hotels are in
Rajasthan, many of them in
converted palaces, forts or *havelis*
(merchants' houses).

When the civil list of the Indian
aristocracy was abolished by Indira
Gandhi in the 1970s, some of the
ex-rulers of the princely states,
particularly in Rajasthan, turned to
tourism to fund the upkeep of their
properties by turning them into
luxury hotels. These proved
popular, and profitable, and soon
many owners of run-down old
buildings were busy renovating
them and taking in guests.

The facilities can be luxurious –
and expensive – with marble
swimming pools, beautifully
decorated suites and well-
maintained grounds. Food is
usually available to guests, most
commonly an Indian buffet of
about seven different dishes.

Alwar (0144)

££
Hotel Alwar
26 Manu Marg, Alwar 301 001
Tel: 335 754
Fax: 332 250
E-mail: ukrustagi@hotmail.com
Good rooms with attached bath.
Restaurant and pleasant garden.

Bambora

££££
Karni Fort
Reservations
Palace Road, Jodhpur 342 006
Tel: (0291) 512101/512102
Fax: (0291) 512105
E-mail: karani@jp1.dot.net.in
A beautifully restored hill-top palace
50 km (30 miles) south of Udaipur.
Great views from all rooms, lovely
pool and restaurant.

Bharatpur (05644)

££££
Bharatpur Forest Lodge
Keoladeo Ghana National Park
Tel: 22722
Fax: 22864
Situated inside the park, this hotel
offers luxury rooms with balconies,
an excellent buffet restaurant and a
bar. Book in advance.
Laxmi Vilas Palace
Kakaji ki Kothi
Tel: 23523
Fax: 25259
This former palace on the outskirts
of the city dates from 1899. It has
some luxury suites and comfortable
rooms. The food is recommended
and the service is excellent.
£££
Chandra Mahal Haveli
Peharsar
Tel: (05643) 3238
The turn-off for this lovely 1850s
haveli, set in the middle of a small
village, is 22 km (14 miles) out of
town down the Jaipur–Agra road.
There are suites overlooking the
garden, and a good restaurant.
££
Forest Rest House
Tel: 22777
Situated in the forest, popular

Hotel Price Categories

The rates below are for a double
room (AC where available) in high
season, including taxes.
£££££   Rs4,000 and above
££££   Rs2,000–4,000
£££   Rs1,000–2,000
££   Rs400–1,000
£   Up to Rs400

rooms with bath, restaurant and
gardens. Book in advance.
Tented Camp
For reservations contact:
Asian Adventurers
Tel/fax: (011) 852 5014
North West Safaris
Tel: (079) 656 0962
Fax: (02712) 23729
Situated near the park entrance, the
grounds have de luxe twin-bed tents
with attached baths and good food.
£
Spoonbill
Fatehpur Sikri Road
Tel: 23571
Decent rooms and dormitory beds
with very good food and friendly
service.

Bijaipur

£££
Castle Bijaipur
40 km south of Chittaurgarh
Tel: (01472) 40099
Fax: (01472) 41042
Very quiet and pleasant Heritage
Hotel. Horse riding and jeep safaris
arranged. Book through **Pratap
Palace Hotel** in Chittaurgarh.

Bikaner (0151)

£££££
Lallgarh Palace Hotel
Lallgarh Palace, Bikaner 334 001
Tel: 540 201/540 254
Fax: 522 253
E-mail: gm.bikaner@welcomemail.
wiprobt.ems.vsnl.net.in
A number of the 38 rooms still have
the original furnishings and carpets
made in a local prison. Part of the
palace houses a museum, another
part is a private residence. Golf
course and squash court.

Hotel Price Categories

The rates below are for a double room (AC where available) in high season, including taxes.

£££££	Rs4,000 and above
££££	Rs2,000–4,000
£££	Rs1,000–2,000
££	Rs400–1,000
£	Up to Rs400

££££
Bhanwar Niwas
Rampuria Street, Old City
Tel: 521 043
Fax: 521 880
Beautifully decorated *haveli* with 14 atmospheric rooms. Excellent food.
Karni Bhawan Palace
Gandhi Colony, Bikaner 343 001
Tel: 524 701–5
Fax: 522 408
Previously the residence of the *maharaja* of Bikaner. Great period rooms in a late-art deco house.
£££
Maan Bilas
Lallgarh Palace Complex, Bikaner 343 001
Tel: 524 711–2
Fax: 522 408
Comfortable rooms in converted buildings in the grounds of the Lallgarh Palace.
££
Dholamaru Tourist
Major Puran Singh Circle
Tel: 528 621
A range of decent rooms from dormitory to mid-budget. Good, inexpensive food.

Bundi (0747)

£££
Ishwari Niwas
1 Civil Lines
Tel: 32414
Fax: 32486
Quiet rooms around an attractive courtyard. Helpful staff and meals available.
££
Haveli Braj Bhushanjee
Opposite the Ayurvedic Hospital
Tel: 32322
Fax: 32142
Characterful rooms with attached

bath in old *haveli*. Good views from terrace and vegetarian food cooked for guests.

Chittaurgarh (01472)

££
Hotel Padmini
Chanderiya Road
Tel: 41718
Fax: 40072
A good, quiet option a little way out of town. Clean rooms and decent restaurant.
£
Pratap Palace Hotel
Sri Gurukal Road
Tel: 40099
Fax: 41042
Popular budget hotel. Clean rooms with attached bath and good restaurant.

Delhi (011)

WHERE TO STAY

£££££
Ashok Hotel
50-B Chanakyapuri, New Delhi 110 021
Tel: 611 0101
Fax: 687 3216/687 6060
E-mail: ashoknd@ndb.vsnl.net.in
Huge, mock-Mughal luxury hotel, flagship of the Ashok group. Amenities include 6 restaurants, pool and beauty parlour.
Claridges
12 Aurangzeb Road, New Delhi 110 011
Tel: 301 0211
Fax: 301 0625
E-mail: claridge@del2.vsnl.net.in
Elegant, old-fashioned hotel with great restaurants, good pool and beauty parlour.
Hotel Diplomat
9 Sardar Patel Marg, Diplomatic Enclave, New Delhi 110 021
Tel: 301 0204
Fax: 301 8605
E-mail: diplomat@nda.vsnl.net in
Quiet and popular hotel with pleasant garden. Advance booking advisable.
Hyatt Regency
Bhikaji Cama Place, Ring Road, New Delhi 110 066
Tel: 679 1234

Fax: 679 1024
E-mail: hyatt@del2.vsnl.net.in
Luxury hotel in South Delhi. Pleasant environment, excellent restaurants, very good pastry shop, airy bar with live jazz, good pool. Disco is free for women every Wednesday.
Hotel Imperial
Janpath, New Delhi 110 001
Tel: 334 1234/334 5678
Fax: 334 2255/334 8149
E-mail: gminp@giasdl.01.vsnl.net.in
Colonial-style hotel, centrally located, with a popular open-air restaurant, large bar, nice pool and shopping arcade.
Le Meridien
Windsor Place, Janpath, New Delhi 110 001
Tel: 371 0101
Fax: 371 4545
E-mail: info@lemeridien-newdelhi.com
Five-star, ultra-modern hotel south of India Gate. Restaurants, bars, swimming pool and disco.
Welcomgroup Maurya Sheraton Hotel and Towers
Diplomatic Enclave, Sardar Patel Marg, New Delhi 110 021
Tel: 611 2233
Fax: 611 3333
Luxury hotel, great restaurants and the best lap-swimming pool. Small disco (Ghungroo), popular with young Delhiites.
Oberoi
Dr Zakir Hussain Marg, New Delhi 110 003
Tel: 436 3030
Fax: 436 0484/430 4084
E-mail: oberoi2@giasde101.vsnl.net.in
Centrally located, elegant, exclusive and very expensive. Restaurants and good bakery, bars, bookshop (the Ritka Book House), pool, beauty parlour and health club.
The Oberoi Maidens
7 Sham Nath Marg, Delhi 110 054
Tel: 397 5464/291 4841/252 5464
Fax: 398 0771
E-mail: bsparmar@tomdel.com
Colonial-style hotel in Old Delhi. Large rooms, attentive service, pleasant gardens, swimming pool and restaurant. Recommended.

Taj Mahal
1 Man Singh Road, New Delhi
110 011
Tel: 302 6162
Fax: 302 6070
E-mail: tajmahal@giasdel01.vsnl.
net.in
The flagship of the Taj Group.
Luxurious and comfortable with
good restaurants, coffee shop, pool
and beauty parlour.
Taj Palace
Sardar Patel Marg, Diplomatic
Enclave, New Delhi 110 021
Tel: 611 0202
Fax: 611 0808
E-mail: bctpd@tajgroup.sprintrpg.
ems.vsnl.net.in
Another luxury Taj Group hotel.
Large and comfortable, all five-star
facilities, disco (My Kind of Place).
Convenient for the airport.
££££
Jukaso Inn Downtown
L-1, Connaught Place, New Delhi
110 001
Tel: 332 4451–3
Fax: 332 4448
Good value, central hotel close to

Nirula's. Modern and clean AC
rooms.
Hotel Marina
G-59 Connaught Place, New Delhi
110 001
Tel: 332 4658
Fax: 332 8609
E-mail: marina@nde.vsnl.net.in
Well-established, renovated hotel
with comfortable rooms, restaurant
and good travel service.
Nirula's Hotel
L-Block, Connaught Place, New
Delhi 110 001
Tel: 332 2419
Fax: 335 3957
E-mail: delhihotel@nirula.com
Well-established little hotel with AC
single and double rooms. Two
restaurants and a very popular ice-
cream parlour. Book in advance.
£££
Hotel Broadway
4–15A Asaf Ali Road, Delhi 110
002
Tel: 327 3821
Fax: 326 9966
E-mail: owhpl@nda.vsnl.net.in
A lovely hotel close to Old Delhi.

Clean rooms, good service and an
excellent restaurant.
Hotel Fifty Five
H-55 Connaught Place, New Delhi
110 001
Tel: 332 1244/332 1278
Fax: 332 0769
E-mail: hotelfiftyfive@hotmail.com
Centrally located with AC rooms,
attached baths and 24-hour room
service.
YWCA International Guest House
10 Sansad Marg
Tel: 336 1561
Fax: 334 1763
Clean AC rooms with attached bath.
Convenient location and reasonable
restaurant.
££
Metropolis
1634 Main Bazaar, Paharganj
Tel: 753 5766
Fax: 752 5600
The best hotel in Paharganj. Clean
and comfortable rooms, hot water
and a good restaurant.
Naari
B1–7 Vishal Bhawan, 95 Nehru
Place, New Delhi 19

Delhi's Hotel Restaurants

Some of the best food in India can
be found in Delhi, and many of the
top restaurants are found in its
five-star hotels. All of them are
expensive (count on at least
Rs1,200 for two people) and
reservations are recommended.

Ashok
Tokyo Elegant Japanese restaurant
with an emphasis on seafood.

Hyatt Regency
La Piazza Excellent Italian food,
including pizzas cooked in a wood-
fired oven.

The Oberoi
Baan Thai One of the best Thai
restaurants in Delhi.
La Rochelle Expensive and formal
French restaurant.

Le Meridien
Golden Phoenix Great Cantonese
and Schezwan food.

Le Belvedere Continental and
Indian dishes.
Pakwan Top tandoori restaurant.
Pierre Very fine French cuisine.

Maurya Sheraton
Bukhara Beautifully prepared food
from NWFP.
Dum Phukt Delicious Avadhi
dishes prepared by lengthy
steaming in a sealed pot.

Taj Mahal
Captain's Cabin Great seafood.
Haveli North Indian dishes
accompanied by live music.
House of Ming Exceptional Chinese
food, possibly the best in Delhi.
Longchamp Widely considered to
be the best French restaurant in
Delhi.

Taj Palace
Orient Express Excellent
Continental food served in a
recreated railway carriage.

Tea House of the August Moon
Superb Chinese restaurant, with
lotus pond, pagoda and goldfish.

Park Hotel
La Meninas Delhi's first Spanish
restaurant serving great *tapas*.

Oberoi Maidens
The Curzon Room Food from the
British Raj in period surroundings.

Claridges
Corbett's Garden *tandoori*
restaurant with a jungle theme.
Dhaba A recreation of a Punjabi
wayside *dhaba*, complete with
lorry.
Jade Garden Good Chinese food in
an evocative setting.

The Imperial
Garden Party Open-air restaurant,
good for a breakfast splurge.
Spice Route High-quality Thai
dishes, very popular.

Tel: 646 5711/618 7401
Fax: 647 2549/623 4621
A women-only guesthouse in South
Delhi. Comfortable rooms, pleasant
garden and meals. Tours arranged.
Safe and hassle-free for women
travelling on their own.
Recommended.
£
Hotel New City Palace
725 Jama Masjid, Delhi 110 006
Tel: 327 9548/325 520
Fax: 328 9923
Just behind the mosque in Old Delhi,
in the same building as the post
office. Clean, light, air-cooled rooms
with attached bath. Rooms at front
have great view. Recommended.
Major's Den
2314 Lakshmi Narain Street,
Paharganj, New Delhi 110 055
Tel: 262 9599/355 6665/351
4163/353 9010
A cheap, well-run hotel with clean,
air-cooled rooms and attached bath.
Youth Hostel
5 Naya Marg, Chanakyapuri
Tel: 611 9841
Inconvenient location but modern
and very good value. YHA members
only (membership fee Rs250).

WHERE TO EAT

Basil & Thyme
Santushi Shopping Complex,
Chanakyapuri
Tel: 467 4933
A place to be seen, with good and
reasonably priced Western food.
Open 10.30am–5.30pm.
Café 100
20-B Connaught Place, New Delhi
110 001
Tel: 335 0051
Burgers, pizzas and ice creams to
eat in or take away. Very popular.
Open 10.30am–11.30pm.
Karim's
Gali Kababiyan, Matia Mahal, near
Jama Masjid, Delhi 110 006
Tel: 326 9880/326 4981
The best Muslim food in the city.
Mouthwatering non-vegetarian
tandoori dishes and excellent
breads. There is a more expensive,
and less good, branch in
Nizamuddin, South Delhi.

**Nirula's Pot Pourri and Chinese
Room**
L-Block, Connaught Place, New
Delhi 110 001
Tel: 332 2419
The popular Pot Pourri (open
7.30am–11pm) has tasty
Continental and Indian food,
including a salad bar, and is a good
place for breakfast. The more
expensive Chinese Room upstairs
(open 12.30pm–4pm, 7–11pm)
serves standard Chinese dishes.
Park Balluchi Restaurant
Inside Deer Park, Hauz Khas
Village, New Delhi 110 016
Tel: 685 9369/696 9829
Award-winning restaurant serving
Mughlai and Afghan dishes. In a
lovely setting on the edge of the
park. Open 12pm–3pm, 7–11pm.
Pizza Express
D-10, Inner Circle, Connaught Place,
New Delhi 110 001; 2–3, Block C,
Ansal Plaza, Khel Gaon Marg
Tel: 373 9306/373 6391
Branches of the British chain, with
the same menu. Great pizza, wine
and desserts; a welcome relief from
Indian food. Open 11am–11pm.
Rodeo
12-A Connaught Place, New Delhi
110 001
Tel: 371 3780–1
Good Tex-Mex food and cocktails
served by waiters in cowboy outfits.
A pleasant place for a drink, which
must be with food after 7pm. Open
noon–11pm.
The Buck Stops Here
CG-01 Ansal Plaza, Khel Gaon
Marg, New Delhi 110 017
Tel: 625 7696–7
Inventive new café and restaurant
serving Mediterranean-inspired
food. Displays of designer cutlery
and crockery, paintings and the
furniture are all for sale. Soon to
acquire an *espresso* machine. Open
11am–11pm.
**The Village Bistro Restaurant
Complex**
12 Hauz Khas Village, Near Deer
Park, New Delhi 110 016
Tel: 685 2227/685 3857/656
3905/656 3970/652 2227
A group of six restaurants serving
Indian (**Village Mohalla**, **Khas Bagh**,
Top of the Village, open

12.30–3.30pm, 7.30–11.30pm),
Chinese (**The Village Kowloon**, open
12.30–3.30pm, 7.30–11.30pm), and
Continental food (**Le Cafe**, a coffee
shop open open 11am–midnight).
The **Village Durbar** (open
12.30–3.30pm, 7.30–11.30pm) is
multi-cuisine. The rooftop Top of the
Village looks out over the ruined
madarsa and tomb of Firoz Shah
Tughlaq, and stages a daily
traditional dance show, 7–7.45pm.
Zen
B-25 Connaught Place, New Delhi
110 001
Tel: 335 7444/335 7455
A Chinese restaurant, which also
serves good Japanese dishes, very
popular with Delhi's middle class. A
great place for people watching.
Open 10.30am–11pm.

Delwara (02953)

£££££
Devi Garh
P.O. Box 144, Udaipur 313 001
Tel: 89211–20
Fax: 89357
E-mail: reservations@
deviresorts.com
A beautifully restored palace hotel,
26 km (16 miles) outside Udaipur.
Wonderful modernist suites, one of
which has its own black-marble
swimming pool. Peaceful and
luxurious.

Deogarh (02951)

££££
Deogarh Mahal
Tel: 52555
Fax: 52777
E-mail: deogarh@jp1.net.in
A lovely old fort with tastefully
refurbished rooms. Excellent
service and good meals. Activities
and safaris arranged.

Dungarpur (02964)

££££
Udai Bilas Palace Hotel
Udai Bilas Palace, Dungarpur
314 001
Tel: 30808
Fax: 31008
E-mail: udaibilas@planetindia.net

Fascinating mid-19th century palace in lovely lakeside location. Art deco rooms and bathrooms, and eccentric decor. Recommended.

Eklingji

££££
Heritage Resorts
Lake Baghela, Nagda, Eklingji
Tel: (0294) 440382
A modern resort, 22 km from Udaipur, built of local stone and set in beautiful grounds. Meals are cooked from organic fruit and vegetables grown in the gardens. Recommended.

Gajner (01534)

££££
Gajner Palace Hotel
Gajner, Bikaner District 334 301
Tel: 55063–5
A comfortable lakeside palace hotel with access to a wildlife sanctuary. Good for bird watching.

Ghanerao (02934)

£££
Ghanerao Royal Castle
Tel: 84035
An atmospheric hotel 5 km (3 miles) from the Kumbhalgarh sanctuary. More basic than some Heritage Hotels but has friendly management and the rates are reasonable.

Jaipur (0141)

WHERE TO STAY

£££££
Rajvilas
Goner Road, Jaipur 302 016
Tel: 640 101
Fax: 640 202
E-mail: reservations@rajvilas.com
This is as good as it gets: an ultra-luxurious and ultra-expensive 13-hectare (32-acre) complex, 12km (7.5 miles) outside the city. Elegant rooms and suites in beautiful gardens with every conceivable amenity. Excellent food and an adventurous menu.

Rambagh Palace Hotel
Bhawani Singh Road, Jaipur
302 005
Tel: 381 919
Fax: 381 098
E-mail: rambagh@jp1.dot.net.in
The ultimate art deco palace for film-star fantasies. Posh interiors, health club, squash court and indoor pool. Folklore programmes nightly on fountained lawns.

Jai Mahal Palace Hotel
Jacob Road, Civil Lines, Jaipur
302 006
Tel: 371 616
Fax: 365 237
A top-class Taj-group hotel. Lovely gardens and an excellent restaurant.

Welcomgroup Rajputana Palace Sheraton
Palace Road, Jaipur 302 006
Tel: 360 011
Fax: 367 848
E-mail: rajputana@welcomgroup.com
Modern and luxurious five-star hotel. All amenities, including good pool and restaurants.

Raj Mahal Palace Hotel
Sardar Patel Marg, C Scheme, Jaipur 302 001
Tel: 381 757381 676/381 625
Fax: 381 887
Old British Residency converted into a tasteful lodging.

££££
Bissau Palace
Chandpole Gate, Jaipur 302 016
Tel: 304 371/304 391
Fax: 304 628
E-mail: sanjai@jpl.dot.net.in
Grand building with Rajput warrior decor. Gardens, pool and tennis court. Some rooms lack AC, but with lofty ceilings stay cool.

Narain Niwas Palace
Kanota Bagh, Narain Singh Road, Jaipur 302 004
Tel: 561 291/563 448
Fax: 561 045
Roomy and regal, with 19th-century royal relics of the Kanota ruler's family. Vegetarian restaurant and pool. Rooms completed in September 2000 now overlook the very attractive garden.

Samode Haveli
Gangapole, Jaipur 302 002
Tel: 632 370/632 407/631 068
Fax: 631 397

Hotel Price Categories

The rates below are for a double room (AC where available) in high season, including taxes.

£££££	Rs4,000 and above
££££	Rs2,000–4,000
£££	Rs1,000–2,000
££	Rs400–1,000
£	Up to Rs400

E-mail: reservations@samode.com
An excellent place to stay. This 150-year-old converted *haveli* has 20 spacious rooms and two wonderfully decorated suites (no. 115, covered in wall-paintings, and no. 116 with mirror-work overlooking the garden). Recommended.

£££
LMB
Johari Bazaar, Jaipur 302 003
Tel: 565 844/565 856–7
Fax: 562 176
E-mail: info@lmbsweets.com
Vegetarian hotel in walled city.

Madhuban Guest House
D237 Behari Marg, Banipark, Jaipur
302 016
Tel: 200 033/205 427
Fax: 202 344
20 rooms, some AC (standard rooms better, de luxe rooms a little dark), in very friendly, family-run hotel which was renovated in 2000. Quiet and secluded with nice garden.

Nana ki Haveli
Moti Dungra Road, Fatehtibba, Jaipur 302 004
Tel/fax: 605 481
An intimate, central hotel in a family home. Comfortable and close to the Central Museum. Excellent cooking. Recommended.

££
Diggi Palace
Diggi House, Shivaji Marg, Hospital Road
Tel: 373 091
Fax: 370 359
Good deal for budget travellers. Beautiful old palace with lawns and good terrace restaurant.

Hotel Arya Niwas
Behind Amber Tower, Sansar Chandra Road, Jaipur 302 001
Tel: 372 456/371 773/368 524/371 776

Hotel Price Categories

The rates below are for a double room (AC where available) in high season, including taxes.

£££££	Rs4,000 and above
££££	Rs2,000–4,000
£££	Rs1,000–2,000
££	Rs400–1,000
£	Up to Rs400

Fax: 361 871
E-mail: aryahotl@jp1.dot.net.in
The best budget hotel in Jaipur. Very clean and comfortable, AC and non-AC rooms. Also bizarre, but cheap and spotless, self-service restaurant, which will appeal to those who like being institutionalised. Pleasant terrace overlooking the front lawn. Recommended.

£
Jaipur Inn
17 Shiv Marg, Bani Park
Tel: 316 821
Clean rooms and dormitory. Food and camping facilities. Popular so book ahead.

WHERE TO EAT

NB: food poisoning scams have been reported in restaurants in the Walled City. The restaurants below are all safe.

Chanakya Restaurant
M.I. Road, Jaipur 302 001
Tel: 376 161/378 461
Very well-presented food in posh surroundings. Has a reputation for the best traditional Rajasthani food in Jaipur. However, this may be a shock to the unwary – lots of *ghi* is used in the cooking, which may not sit well on a weak stomach. Open 12–11pm.
Lassiwala
M.I. Road
Series of streetside stalls serving snacks and renowned clay cups of *lassi* to long queues of customers. Early morning–late evening.
Neel Mahal and **Polo Bar**
Rambagh Palace Hotel, Bhawani Singh Road
Tel: 381 919
The restaurant and bar of the famous

five-star hotel. You can wallow in luxury here even if you can't afford a room. The bar is great and even has a marble fountain. Ask to take your drinks out on to the terrace, which looks out over the beautiful gardens.
Niros
M.I. Road, Jaipur 302 001
Tel: 371 746/374 493/371 874
Cool, AC restaurant, very clean and central. Tasty food and prompt service from an extensive menu of Indian, Chinese and Continental dishes. A little more expensive than other places in town.
LMB
Johari Bazaar
Tel: 565 844/565 846–7
Below the hotel with the same initials. Jaipur's most famous sweet shop. The restaurant serves traditional high-caste Rajasthani vegetarian food (cooked in lots of *ghi* with no onions or garlic).
Mediterraneo
9 Khandela House, behind Amber Tower, S.C. Road
Rooftop Italian restaurant just along from the Arya Niwas hotel. Great fresh pasta, and pizzas cooked in a wood-fired oven.

Jaisalmer (02992)

WHERE TO STAY

££££
Gorbandh Palace
1 Tourist Complex, Sam Road, Jaisalmer 345 001
Tel: 51511–3
Fax: 52749
Luxury hotel on the outskirts of town. Traditionally decorated rooms and good pool.
£££
Jawahar Niwas Palace
Amar Sagar Road
Tel: 52208
Beautiful, old palace converted into an hotel, with spacious rooms, open-air coffee shop, restaurant and billiards room.
Hotel Dholamaru
P.O. Box 49, Jeth Bai Road, Jaisalmer 345 001
Tel: 52863/53122–3/53125
Fax: 52761/53124
Comfortable and pleasant.

££
RTDC Moomal Tourist Bungalow
Amar Sagar Road
Tel: 52392
Range of clean rooms, some of which are in round huts, with bath. Bar, decent restaurant and dance performances on Sundays.
Suraj
By the Jain Temples
Tel: 53023
In old converted *haveli*, large rooms with attached bath, and vegetarian restaurant.

WHERE TO EAT

Trio
Gandhi Chowk
Good food and live folk music.
Natraj
Opposite Salim Singh ki Haveli
Good restaurant.

Jaisamund Lake

££££
Jaisamund Island Resort
51 km south of Udaipur
Tel: (02906) 2222
Comfortable, well-appointed rooms. Beautiful setting, gardens and pool.

Jodhpur (0291)

WHERE TO STAY

£££££
Welcomheritage Umaid Bhawan Palace
Umaid Bhawan Palace, Jodhpur 342 006
Tel: 510 101
Fax: 510 100
E-mail: ubp@ndf.vsnl.net.in
Magnificent, expensive hotel, previously the largest private residence in the world, with spacious rooms, large gardens, restaurants, bars and an underground pool.
££££
Ajit Bhawan Palace
Opposite Circuit House, Jodhpur 343 006
Tel: 510 410/510 610/511 410
Fax: 510 674
E-mail: abhawan@del3.vsnl.net.in
Well-maintained palace converted

into an hotel with "ethnic hut" rooms. Good traditional meals.
£££
Hotel Adarsh Niwas
Station Road, Jodhpur 342 001
Tel: 624 066/615 871/627 338
Fax: 627 314
Centrally located, comfortable with good restaurant.
Hotel Karni Bhawan
Defence Lab. Road, Ratanada, Jodhpur 342 006
Tel: 639 380/432 220
Fax: 433 495
E-mail: marwar@del3.vsnl.net.in
1940s Sandstone bungalow with attractive rooms. Lovely pool and "dhani" huts for dining in the gardens.
££
Shanti Bhawan Lodge
Station Road, Jodhpur 342 001
Tel: 637 001/621 689/627 373/639 074
Fax: 639 211
Central hotel with a wide range of rooms.

WHERE TO EAT

Kalinga
near Shanti Bhawan Hotel
Good inexpensive food.

Kanota

£££
Royal Castle Kanota
15 km east of Jaipur
A converted-palace and Heritage Hotel set in lovely orchard and gardens. Ornately decorated and comfortable interiors. Large collection of rare books. Book through **Narain Niwas Palace Hotel** in Jaipur.

Karauli (07464)

££££
Bhanwar Vilas Palace
Tel: 20024
Reservations
Tel: (0141) 211 532
Converted palace hotel south of Bharatpur, off the NH11. Comfortable rooms, pool and restaurant.

Khimsar (01585)

£££££
Welcomgroup Khimsar Fort
Khimsar P.O., Nagaur District 341 025
Tel: 62345
Fax: 62228
Comfortable rooms in 16th-century fort. Pool set in pleasant gardens, restaurant and jeep safaris.

Kishangarh (01497)

££££
Roopangarh Fort
Ajmer District 305 814
Tel: 20217/20444
Heritage Hotel about 27 km from Ajmer, run by the local maharaja. Well decorated rooms, local cuisine and good views.

Kota (0744)

££££
Umed Bhavan Palace
Station Road
Tel: 325 262
Fax: 451 110
17 AC rooms in palace conversion.
£££
Brijraj Bhavan Palace Hotel
Civil Lines, Kota 324 001
Tel: 450 529
Fax: 450 057
A former palace by the river. Restaurant and room service. Recommended.
££
Chambal Tourist Bungalow
Nayapura
Tel: 327 695
An RTDC motel with OK rooms and restaurant.
Hotel Navrang
Civil Lines, Nayapura, Kota 324 001
Tel: 451 253/323 294
Fax: 450 044
Comfortable hotel with some AC rooms. Pleasant restaurant.

Kuchaman (01586)

£££££
The Kuchaman Fort
Nagaur District 341 508
Tel: 20882/20884
Fax: 20476

A stunningly decorated luxury hotel. Sensitive restoration has preserved the original interiors of the rooms. Excellent facilities. Recommended.

Kumbhalgarh (02954)

££££
Aodhi Hotel
Kelwara P.O., Rajasmand District
Tel: 42341–6
Fax: 42349
A lovely hotel set in the Aravalli hills. Very peaceful and close to the wildlife sanctuary. Fabulous pool and good restaurant.

Luni

££££
Fort Chanwa
Booking
Dalip Bhawan, No. 1 House, P.W.D. Road, Jodhpur- 342 001
Tel: (0291) 84216
Tel/Fax: (0291) 32460
23 individually-decorated rooms in 19th-century sandstone fort. Good pool and restaurant, and interesting excursions to surrounding area. Recommended.

Mount Abu (02974)

££££
Palace Hotel (Bikaner House)
Delwara Road, Mount Abu 307 501
Tel: 43121/38673
Fax: 38674
Quiet, well-run and respectfully converted hunting lodge. Large gardens with private lake. Advance booking advised.
£££
Cama Rajputana Club Resort
Adhar Devi Road, Mount Abu 307 501
Tel: 38205–6
Fax: 38412
E-mail: inquiry@camahotels.com
125-year-old converted club building. Comfortable rooms, restaurant and good sports facilities.
Connaught House
Rajendenra Marg, Sirohi District, Mount Abu 307 501
Tel: 38560/43439
Fax: 542 240
E-mail: marwar@del3.vsnl.net.in

Hotel Price Categories

The rates below are for a double room (AC where available) in high season, including taxes.

£££££ Rs4,000 and above
££££   Rs2,000–4,000
£££   Rs1,000–2,000
££   Rs400–1,000
£   Up to Rs400

British bungalow, the former summer residence of the Chief Minister of Marwar, with 14 period rooms and peaceful gardens. Book ahead.

Mumbai (022)

WHERE TO STAY

£££££
The Taj Mahal Hotel
Apollo Bunder, Mumbai 400 001
Tel: 202 3366
Fax: 287 2711
E-mail: business.centre@vsnl.com
India's most famous hotel, situated opposite the Gateway of India. Very grand and very expensive with beautiful rooms in both the old and new wings. Excellent restaurants (including the **Tanjore**, serving North and South Indian food), outdoor pool and beauty parlour.
The Oberoi Towers
Nariman Point, Mumbai 400 021
Tel: 202 4343
Fax: 204 3282
E-mail: reservation@oberoi-mumbai.com
Ultra-luxurious five-star hotel (India's most expensive) with great sea-view rooms. Several restaurants (including a Polynesian one) and bars, terrace garden pool on the 9th floor, large shopping arcade and disco.
The Oberoi
Nariman Point, Mumbai 400 021
Tel: 202 5757
Fax: 204 3282
E-mail: reservation@oberoi-mumbai.com
Next door to the Oberoi Towers. Very chic, with good restaurants, health club, pool and shops.
The Orchid
79C Nehru Road, Vile Parle East, Mumbai 400 099

Tel: 616 4040
Fax: 616 141
E-mail: ohmu@orchidhotel.com
Environmentally friendly five-star. Very comfortable with good restaurants (try the buffet at the **Boulevard**). Recommended.
The Leela Kempinski
Sahar, Andheri East, Mumbai 400 059
Tel: 836 3636/835 3535
Fax: 836 0606
E-mail: leela.bom@leela.sprintrpg.ems.vsnl.net.in
Ultra de luxe business-oriented hotel close to the international airport. Some great restaurants.
££££
Shelly's Hotel
30 P.J. Ramachandani Marg, Colaba Sea Face, Mumbai 400 039
Tel: 284 0229/284 0210/288 1436–7
Fax: 284 0385
Great-value hotel, lovely rooms with a period feel and good service.
£££
Hotel Diplomat
24–6 B.K. Boman Behram Marg, Apollo Bunder, Mumbai 400 001
Tel: 202 1661
Fax: 283 0000
E-mail: diplomat@bom3.vsnl.net.in
Well-run, friendly hotel with comfortable rooms. Centrally located and good value.
Hotel Whalley's
Jaiji Mansion, 41 Mereweather Road, Mumbai 400 001
Tel: 283 4206/282 1802
Fax: 287 1592
Popular hotel in characterful building. Rates include breakfast.
YWCA
18 Madam Cama Road
Tel: 202 0445
For both women and men. Doubles, family rooms and dormitories. Rates include membership, breakfast and buffet. Try to make a cash booking well in advance.
££
Bentley's Hotel
17 Oliver Road
Tel: 284 1474
Fax: 287 1846
E-mail: bentleyshotel@hotmail.com
Good-value, large and clean rooms. Price includes breakfast.

Lawrence
3rd Floor, 33 Rope Walk Lane
Tel: 284 3618
Opposite the Jehangir Art Gallery, it has a few great-value rooms, but reservations are essential.
£
Salvation Army Hostel Red Shield Hostel
30 Merriweather Road
Tel: 284 1824
Behind the Taj Mahal Hotel. Double rooms and dormitories (lockers available), canteen. A bit institutional but very good value.

WHERE TO EAT

Bade Mian
Behind Taj Mahal Hotel, Tulloch Road
Open-air pavement grill, famous for kebabs. Open 7.30pm–late.
China Garden
Om Chambers, 123 August Kranti Marg, Kemps Corner, Mumbai 400 036
Tel: 363 0841–2
Expensive but excellent Chinese, Korean, Thai and Japanese cuisine. Open 12.30–3pm, 7pm–12am.
Copper Chimney
18 K. Dubash Marg
Tel: 204 1661
Excellent but pricey *tandoori* and North Indian dishes. Reservations essential.
Golden Gate Restaurant
B-1 Amerchand Mansion, Madame Cama Road (near YWCA), Colaba, Mumbai 400 039
Tel: 202 6306/202 7989/282 8200
Pricey seafood, Chinese and Indian cuisine. Great salad bar lunch. Open 12–3.30pm, 6–11.30pm.
Khyber
145 M.G. Road, Kalaghoda Fort, Mumbai 400 001
Tel: 267 3227–9/267 3584
Very rich Mughlai and Punjabi cuisine. Expensive, reserve ahead. Open 12.30–4pm, 7.30pm–12am.
Leopold Café
Colaba Causeway
Tel: 202 0131
Legendary travellers' haunt. Good Western food and bar.

New Martin
near Strand Cinema, Sir P.J. Marg
Goan specialities and seafood.
Piccolo
11A Sir Homi Mody Street
Tel: 267 4537
Authentic Parsi food and good
desserts. (Also at **Landmark**, 35 S.
Patkar Road.) Open 9am–6pm.
Samovar
Jehangir Art Gallery, 161 B M.G.
Road
The gallery café, popular for snacks
and lunch. Open Mon–Sat
11am–7pm.

Narlai

£££
Rawla Narlai
Traditionally decorated rooms in a
characterful palace halfway
between Udaipur and Jodhpur, close
to Ranakpur. Horse riding and
camel safaris offered. Booking
through **Ajit Bhawan** in Jodhpur.

Pachewar (01437)

££££
Pachewar Fort
Pachewar, Via Malpura, Tonk
District 304 509
Tel: 28756
A well-preserved 300-year-old fort 90
km south of Jaipur, now converted
into a Heritage Hotel. Outdoor dining
on rooftop or in courtyard. Jeep,
horseback or camel safaris arranged.

Pushkar (0145)

££££
Pushkar Resorts
Motisar Road, Village Ganhera,
Pushkar
Tel: 72017/72944–5
Fax: 72946
E-mail: pushkar@pushkarresorts.com
Out-of-town luxury accommodation in
cottages. Good pool and restaurant.
£££
Hotel Pushkar Palace
Pushkar Palace, Pushkar 305 022
Tel: 72001/72401–3
Fax: 72226
The best place in town. Wide range
of rooms in a 400-year-old
maharaja's palace, some with lake

view, and good vegetarian
restaurant. Book ahead.
£
Payal Guest House
Main Bazaar
Tel: 72163
Pleasant, cheap hotel with rooms
around a courtyard.
VK Tourist Palace
By Pushkar Palace
Tel: 72174
Popular and cheap hotel with
excellent restaurant.

Raj Mahal

£££
Raj Mahal Palace Hotel and Resort
This secluded palace hotel is 67 km
north of Bundi in a beautiful
location on the banks of the Banas
river. Traditional, well decorated
rooms and good food. Boats are
available and there are good walks
in the surrounding hills. Make
reservations through **Narain Niwas
Palace** in Jaipur.

Ramgarh (014262)

£££££
Ramgarh Lodge
35 km north of Jaipur
Tel: 552217
Fax: 381098
Taj Group hotel in old hunting lodge
by Ramgarh Lake. Lovely, peaceful
location. Plenty of stuffed trophies
showing off the previous owners'
murderous past.

Ranakpur (02934)

££££
Maharani Bagh
Near Ranakpur Temple, Pali District
Tel: 3705/3751
Fax: (0291) 542540
Cottage accommodation in lovely
gardens. Good outdoor restaurant
in a mango orchard. Pool and jeep
safaris.

Ranthambore (07462)

£££££
Sawai Madhopur Lodge
Ranthambore Road, Sawai
Madhopur 322 001

Paying Guests

The State Tourist Board operates
a Paying Guest Scheme in Ajmer,
Bikaner, Bundi, Jaipur, Jaisalmer,
Jodhpur, Mount Abu, Pushkar
and Udaipur. Staying with local
families you will meet some
lovely people, and get an insight
into the lives of ordinary
Rajasthanis. Rates vary
depending on the quality of the
accommodation.
  For details, contact your
nearest Government of India
Tourist Office, or the Director of
Tourism, Government of
Rajasthan, Government Hostel,
M.I. Road, Jaipur, Rajasthan, tel:
91 141 370 180/371 142; fax:
376 362.

Tel: 20541
Fax: 20718
E-mail: sawai.madhopur@
tajhotels.com
Taj group palace hotel. Comfortable
accommodation with all the usual
luxuries. Well managed and close to
the park.
£££
Castle Jhoomar Baori
8 km from the station.
Tel: 20495
A hill-top hunting lodge. A little run-
down but the great views are some
compensation.
££
Ankur Resorts
Ranthambore Road, Sawai
Madhopur 322 001
Tel: 20792
Fax: 20697
A good option. Clean, comfortable
rooms, some individual cottages,
and good restaurant.

Rohet (02936)

££££
Rohet Garh
Village P.O., Rohet, Pali District
Tel: 68231
E-mail: rohetgar@datainfosy.net
Simply-decorated AC rooms in old
fort. Lovely gardens and wonderful
pool. Trips to nearby Bishnoi
villages.

Hotel Price Categories

The rates below are for a double room (AC where available) in high season, including taxes.

££££	Rs4,000 and above
££££	Rs2,000–4,000
£££	Rs1,000–2,000
££	Rs400–1,000
£	Up to Rs400

Samode

££££
Samode Bagh
3 km (2 miles) from Samode village Run by the owners of the palace (below), accomodation is in luxury "tents", with attached bath, set in beautiful gardens. Lovely pool. Book through **Samode Haveli** in Jaipur.
Samode Palace Hotel
The palace, which has 20 rooms, is the main attraction of this small village. It contains an excellent *Sheesh Mahal* (hall of mirrors). The rooms are luxurious and beautifully furnished, and it has a great pool. Bookings can be made through **Samode Haveli** in Jaipur. Recommended.

Sardar Samand

££££
Sardar Samand Palace
Sardar Samand, Pali District 306 103
Tel: (0291) 545991
Fax: (0291) 542240
A lakeside art deco lodge built in 1933 for Maharaja Umaid Singh, 60 km from Jodhpur. Lovely peaceful location, excellent pool and decent restaurant. The lake is a good place for bird watching. Recommended.

Sariska (01465)

££££
Hotel Sariska Palace
Alwar District 301 022
Tel: 24247
The most elegant option close to the park. A converted, French-designed 1892 palace with the usual Heritage Hotel facilities.

Shekhavati

££££
Hotel Castle Mandawa
Mandawa, Jhunjhunu District, 333 704
Tel: (01592) 23124/23432–3
Fax: (01592) 23171
58 rooms with period furniture in evocative 240-year-old fort.
Mukundgarh Fort
Mukundgarh
Booking (Jaipur):
Tel: (0141) 696 8937
Fax: (0141) 696 9831
48 rooms in converted 18th-century fort. Restaurant, bar and pool.
The Desert Resort
Mandawa, Jhunjhunu District 333 704
Tel: (01592) 23245
Fax: (01592) 23151
Upmarket, chic resort with well-designed rooms and great pool.
£££
Dundlod Fort Hotel
Dundlod, Jhunjhunu District 333 702
Tel: (01594) 52519/52180
Fax: (01594) 52519
E-mail: dundlod@datainfosys.net
Range of rooms, some renovated, in friendly hotel (previously "Castle" and "Kila"). Tours arranged.
Golden Castle Resort
Pachar
Tel: (01576) 64611
Atmospheric rooms with great decorations. Meals provided and tours arranged.
Jamuna Resort
Jhunjhunun
Tel: (01592) 32871
Fax: (01592) 32603
Small but pleasant lodge with well decorated rooms a little way out of town. Reasonable outdoor restaurant and swimming pool.
Narayan Niwas Castle
Mahansar
Tel: (01562) 64322
Booking (Delhi):
Tel: (011) 688 6909
Fax: (011) 688 6122
Slightly down-at-heel 18th-century fort with bags of charm. Friendly and laid-back.

Piramal Haveli
Bagar
Booking (Delhi):
Tel: (011) 461 6145
E-mail: sales@neemrana.com
Sympathetic conversion of 20th century *haveli*. Friendly staff and good food.
Roop Niwas Palace
Nawalgarh
Tel: (015954) 22008
Fax: (015954) 233 388
Large, comfortable palace with gardens, restaurant and pool. Friendly service.
££
Apani Dhani
Nawalgarh
Tel: (015954) 22239
An eco-farm growing organic food on the edge of town. Comfortable, traditional accomodation in environmentally friendly huts.
Shiv Shekhawati
Khemi Sati Road, Jhunjhunu
Tel: (01592) 32909
Fax: (01592) 32603
Very clean rooms, some AC, with attached bath. Good vegetarian restaurant.

Siliserh (0144)

£££
Lake Castle Hotel
Tel: 86322
Palace hotel in fabulous position overlooking the lake. Some AC rooms and restaurant.

Sitamata (02950)

££££
Fort Dhariawad
Tel: 20050
Comfortable rooms in converted fort and modern cottages. Jeep safaris to the sanctuary arranged.

Sodawas

££££
Hotel Karni Kot
Small, modern palace set admid wheat and mustard fields, halfway between Jodhpur and Ranakpur. Friendly hosts and good food. Horse riding facilities. Book through **Hotel Karni Bhawan** in Jodhpur.

Udaipur (0294)

WHERE TO STAY

£££££

Fateh Prakash Palace
City Palace, Udaipur 313 001
Tel: 528 016–9
Fax: 528 006
E-mail: shelley@udaipur.hrhindia.com
Part of the City Palace complex, with 17 exclusive rooms. Restaurant with wonderful views of the lake, serves excellent afternoon teas.

Lake Palace Hotel
P.O. Box 5, Udaipur 313 001
Tel: 527 961/527 973
Fax: 527 974
E-mail: resv@udaipur.hrhindia.com
Exquisite, romantic, luxurious hotel with all amenities, pool and lakeview restaurant.

Shiv Niwas Palace
City Palace, Udaipur 313 001
Tel: 528 016–9
Fax: 528 006
E-mail: 1phm.hrh@axcess.net.in
The magnificent guest apartments of the City Palace have been converted into an exclusive hotel.

The Trident Udaipur
Haridas ji ki Magri, Mulla Talai, Udaipur 313 001
Tel: 432 200
Fax: 432 211
E-mail: bhushan@tridentudo.com
Excellent facilities in comfortable and well-run hotel. Good restaurants.

££££

Hotel Hilltop Palace
5 Ambavgarh, Fatehsagar, Udaipur 313 001
Tel: 521 997–9
Fax: 525 106
Efficient, modern hotel. Great views from rooftop restaurant.

Shikarbadi Hotel
Goverdhan Vilas, Udaipur 313 001
Tel: 583 200–4
Fax: 584 841
Formerly the Maharaja's hunting lodge, 4 km (2.5 miles) from the railway station, this attractive hotel has a restaurant, swimming pool, gardens and deer park.

£££

Caravanserai
14 Lalghat
Tel: 411 103

Fax: 521 252
Old *haveli* with pleasant rooms and restaurant.

Kankarwa Haveli
26 Lalghat
Tel: 411 457
Fax: 521 403
Lovely converted *haveli* overlooking the lake. Friendly and good value. Recommended.

££

Jagat Niwas Palace Hotel
25 Lalghat
Tel: 420 133
Fax: 520 023
Popular converted *haveli* with great restaurant.

£

Lalghat Guest House
33 Lalghat
Tel: 525 301
Fax: 418 508
Well-known travellers' haunt. Wide range of rooms and dormitory beds.

Ratan Palace Guest House
21 Lalghat
Tel: 561 153
Friendly and clean budget accommodation.

WHERE TO EAT

Berry's Restaurant
Chetak Circle, Udaipur 313 001
Tel: 419 927
Good Indian dishes and reasonable western snacks. Very clean. Open 9am–11pm.

Natural
55 Rang Sagar
Tel: 527 879
Hotel restaurant serving Continental food; good for breakfast.

Shopping

What to Buy

The bazaars in most towns reflect the rich culture of Rajasthan with a range of bright, colorful fabrics, handicrafts and cloths. Using local materials, these craftsmen manage to meet the everyday needs of the local people, producing simple utensils of great beauty. The same facilities that built and decorated the splendid forts, palaces and memorials throughout the state today keep alive these traditions and skills.

The traditional tie-dyed textiles made by knotting the material and dipping it in color to form the delicate *bandhani* patterns are found throughout the state. The block prints of Sanganer, many with *khari* (over-printing with gold); the *ajrah* prints from Barmer; the *jajam* prints of Chittaurgarhr and the floral prints from Bagru are found not only where they are made, but also in the old city bazaars of Jaipur and other large towns. In many large towns, Rajasthan Government Emporia sell fabric throughout the state by the yard, as made-up clothes or as wall hangings at fixed prices.

Jaipur and Sanganer are famous for their "blue pottery". All are hand-moulded and well glazed.

Leather workers using camel and other hides provide a variety of local traditional footwear. Combinations of camel leather, cloth and velvet are now also used to make other items, including purses, cases, handbags, and even garments.

In Jaipur and a few small villages, carpets and *dhurries* are made for both the local and export markets. Orders can be placed for both traditional and contemporary designs in any colour combination and many manufacturers keep a range for ready sale.

Throughout Rajasthan, local jewelers make splendid jewellery for the princes, and the same tradition of finely cut precious and semi-precious stones set in gold with enamel inlay work has continued.

In many village bazaars or *melas* (fairs), traditional silver jewelry belts, chains, bangles etc. can still be found, they are sold by weight.

The **Johari Bazaar** of Jaipur (and bazaars in other towns) also stock a range of bangles, beads and rings. Ear studs made of ivory, bone, lac and glass are also available.

Among the many other items available in the state are *pichwais* or cloth paintings. The best selection of both traditional and modern design is probably available in Jaipur. Engraved brassware, enamel work using cobalt and sulphate of copper mined in the hills near Khetri, and inlay work are made throughout the state.

Warning: the export of ivory in any form and items made from wild animal products is banned.

Shopping in Jaipur

Traditional tie-dyed textiles in *bandhani* patterns, block prints from Sanganer (many with *khari* over-printing in gold), *ajrah* prints, *jajam* prints, and the floral prints from Bagru can all be found in the bazaars of the old city. The **Rajasthali Government Emporium** (just of M.I. Road) is the **only** government-run shop. It sells fabric by the yard, or made up into garments and wall hangings, gemstones and other jewellery. Another good place for fabrics and clothing is the **Gramya** khadi handicraft emporium (Panch Batti, M.I. Road, tel: 373 821). Jaipur is also the home of **Anokhi** (2 Tilak Marg, C Scheme, tel: 381 247). They sell elegant *shalwar* (in colours that will appeal to Western tastes), T-shirts, skirts, bed linen, throws etc., all in good-quality fabrics that are reasonably priced and ethically sourced.

Jaipur is famous as a centre for semi-precious gemstones. If you do want to buy these, check what you are buying very carefully. Rajasthali, above, is recommended, as is **The Gem Palace** on M.I. Road (tel: 374 175/363 061). This long-established jewellers has beautiful, and expensive, work. If you are buying gems from elsewhere, ask to take them to the government's **Gem Testing Laboratory** (Chamber 1, 3rd Floor, M.I. Road). The tests take about two hours and the charge is Rs200 per stone.

Jaipur and Sanganer are famous for their "blue pottery". These hand-painted vessels are decorated with floral motifs and geometric patterns in combinations of blue, white and occasionally other colours.

Leather workers produce a range of traditional footwear, including *jhutis* with their turned-up toes. In Jaipur the cobblers also make *mojadis*, soft slippers embroidered with bright colours.

Jewellery can be found in the **Johari Bazaar**. Although it is well-known for its silver, the gold-work is finer. Make sure you bargain hard. Jaipur has the best selection of *pichwais* or cloth paintings. Try the **Friends of the Museum Master Craftsmen and Artists** display room inside the main courtyard of the City Palace, where you can watch the artists at work. Engraved brassware, and exquisite enamel work and inlay is also available; the best enamel work is done by **Kudrat Singh** (1565 Rasta Jarion, Chaura Rasta, tel: 561 135/572 284).

The HTDC bank on Ashok Marg has one of the only ATMS that will issue cash against a Visa card (available 9.30am–3.30pm).

Festivals

In addition to the many Hindu, Muslim, Christian and Sikh festivals celebrated throughout North India, Rajasthan has many local festivals which combine with traditional fairs.

Festivals A to Z

Desert Festival: At **Jaisalmer**. A festival started by Rajasthan Tourism in 1979 to promote local arts. It also includes acrobatics, turban tying displays and some of the best camel races with the desert units of the Border Security Force.

Baneshwar Festival: At **Baneshwar** (Dungarpur District). Situated at the confluence of the Mali and Som rivers about 60 km (37 miles) southeast of Dungarpur, this festival offers one of the few opportunities to see a large gathering of Bhil peoples.

Bikaner Festival: At **Bikaner**. The **Kolagat** *mela* and cattle fair is an important annual festival for the desert people, held on the banks of the holy lake, about 45 km (28 miles) from Bikaner.

Brij Festival: At **Bharatpur**. For a few days prior to Holi, this traditional festival includes performances of the *Raslila*, enacting the love story of Krishna and Radha.

Elephant Festival: At **Jaipur**, during Holi. A lively festival with lots of activities including elephant parades, polo and races.

Gangaur Festival: At **Jaipur**. A traditional spring festival that is celebrated throughout Rajasthan. Mainly celebrated by women who commemorate the love between Shiva and Parvati.

Hadoti Festival: At **Kota**. Local music, dance and culture from Bundi, Jalawar and Kota.

Kajli Tij: At **Bundi.** Celebrates Tij on the third day of the month of *Bhadra* and continues for eight days till **Janamastami**, which celebrates Lord Krishna's birthday.

Marwar Festival: At **Jodhpur.** Music and local dance performed on the night of the full moon.

Mewar Festival: At **Udaipur.** Also celebrated at Gangaur and dedicated to Parvati. The women of Udaipur gather to dress the images of Ishar and Gangaur (Shiva and Parvati) that are then carried in procession through the city to Gangaur Ghat at Lake Pichola, and then in boats along the shore.

Nagaur Fair: at **Nagaur.** This is a traditional cattle fair where villagers also trade in camels, horses and bullocks.

Pushkar Festival: At **Pushkar,** 7 miles (11 km) from **Ajmer.** At the full moon during the month of Kartik, thousands of pilgrims flock to the small town of Pushkar for a ritual bath in the lake. The nearby cattle, horse and camel fair takes place during the preceding four days.

Summer Festival: At **Mount Abu.** A 3-day festival of Rajasthani and Gujarati music and dance, held in June every year.

Tij Festival: At **Jaipur.** A traditional festival welcoming the monsoon with excitement and colour. Particularly important for women who apply henna patterns to their hands and feet, and buy new bangles and clothes.

Wildlife

A selection of wildlife sanctuaries follows, but avid naturalists should consult the *Insight Guide: Indian Wildlife* for a definitive listing of national parks, reserves, forests and sanctuaries.

Wildlife & Bird Parks

Darrah Sanctuary
Established in 1955, previously the Kota hunting reserve. The sanctuary covers 266 sq. km (102 sq. miles) of dry deciduous forest (mostly *Anogeissus penduai*). The animals include wolf, sloth bear, chinkara and leopard. Despite disturbance from local villages, it is still worth visiting.
Best time to visit: February–May
Contact: Range Officer, Darrah Wildlife Sanctuary, via Kamalpura, Kota District

Desert National Park
This large park of 3,172 sq. km (1,220 sq. miles) is 32 km (20 miles) from Jaisalmer. Much of the area is covered with patchy scrub and occasional trees and flowers. Fauna seen include blackbuck, chinkar, desert fox and cat, and birds of prey such as the tawny eagle, short-toed eagle and spotted eagle. There are approximately 350 great Indian bustard. The park also contains fossilized trees.
Best time to visit:
September–March (Summer temperature exceeds 50˚C/122˚F)
Contact: Deputy Director, Desert National Park, Jaisalmer

Kumbalgarh
This large sanctuary in the Aravalli hills is perhaps the only area in India where the highly endangered

wolf is breeding successfully. Other animals include leopard, sloth bear, chinkara, chousingha, ratel and flying squirrel.
Best time: September–November
Contact: Wildlife Warden, Kumbalgarh Sanctuary, Udaipur District, Rajasthan

Mount Abu Sanctuary
A small sanctuary in forested hills to the northeast of Mount Abu. Animals include leopard, chinkara and, in the lower areas, sloth bear, sambar and wild boar. Among the interesting birds is the grey jungle fowl.
Best time to visit: March–June
Contact: Wildlife Warden, Mount Abu

National Chambal Sanctuary
This runs along the Chambal river from Rana Pratap Sagar to the southwest of Kota to its confluence with the Jamuna. It was set up to protect the garial crocodilian. Southeast of Sawai Madhopur, the Chambal joins the Parbati river which forms the border with Madhya Pradesh. The Madhya Pradesh bank is also a sanctuary containing blackbuck, caracal, chinkara and wolf.
Best time to visit: October–March
Contact: Warden, National Chambal Sanctuary, Kota

Ranthambore
An impressive range of animal species including sambar, chital, nilgai, chinkara, monkey, wild boar, sloth bear, hyena, jackal, leopard and tiger. Excellent birdlife including crested serpent eagle.
Best time: October–April
Contact: The Field Director, Ranthambore National Park, Sawai Madhopur, Rajasthan

Sariska National Park, Tiger Reserve and Sanctuary
Originally the shooting area of the Alwar ruling family, Sariska became a sanctuary in 1958. Most of Sariska is hilly with a wide valley from the gate to Thana Gazi. It has a good network of roads. Animals seen include leopard, wild dog (first

sighted in 1986), nilgai, chital, chousingha, chinkara, ratel and tiger.
Best time to visit: November–June. Very dry summers make June good for game-viewing, although it is hot.
Contact: The Field Director, Sariska Tiger Reserve, Alwar district

Sitamata Sanctuary

In the southern forests of Rajasthan with 423 sq. km (163 sq. miles) of dry deciduous forest and bamboo. The flying squirrel is more often seen here than in other sanctuaries. Other species include leopard, caracal, chousingha, pangolin, sambar, wild boar and chinkara.
Best time to visit: April–July
Contact: Wildlife Warden, Sitamata Wildlife Sanctuary, Dhariawad, Udaipur District

Birdlife

Keoladeo Ghana (Rajasthan)

One of the world's greatest heronries is situated here. Famous for waterbirds, including crane and migratory fowl. Mammals include sambar, blackbuck, chital, nilgai, fishing cat, jungle cat, otter and mongoose.
Best time: breeding, August–October; migrants, October–February
Contact: Chief Wildlife Warden, Keoladeo National Park, Bharatpur, Rajasthan

Language

The language of the majority of speakers in the state is Rajasthani. Hindi is very closely related and is the next most widely spoken and/or understood language. In addition here are local dialects and languages, particularly those spoken by Adivasi peoples.

Indian languages are phonetically regular, based on syllables rather than an alphabet. Important differences are made between long and short vowels, and reteroflex, palatal and labial consonants – listen hard to get a feel for the vocabulary below. There are various systems of transliteration and you may see many of the words below spelt different ways in English. Where a consonant is followed by "h" this is an aspirated sound, "c" is usually pronounced "ch" (followed by "h", "chh").

Traveller's Hindi

Basics

Hello/goodbye *Namaste*
Yes *Ji ha*
No *Ji nehi*
Perhaps *Shayad*
Thank you *Dhanyavad/shukriya*
How are you? *Ap kaise hai?/Ap thik hai?*
I am well *Me thik hu/thik hai*
What is your name? *Apka nam kya hai?*
My name is (John/Jane) *Mera nam (John/Jane) hai*
Where do you come from? *Ap kahan se aye?*
From (England) *(England) se*
How much (money)? *Kitna paise hai?*
That is expensive *Bahut mahenga hai*
Cheap *Sasta*
I like (tea) *Mujhe (chai) pasand hai*

Is it possible? *Kya ye sambhav hai?*
I don't understand *Mujhe samajh nehi*
I don't know *Mujhe malum nehi*
Money *Paisa*
Newspaper *Akhbar*
Sheet *Chadar*
Blanket *Kambal*
Bed *Kot/palang*
Room *Kamra*
Please clean my room *Mera kamra saf kijie*
Clothes *Kapre*
Cloth *Kapra*
Market *Bajar*

Numbers

1	*ek*
2	*do*
3	*tin*
4	*char*
5	*panch*
6	*che*
7	*sat*
8	*arth*
9	*nau*
10	*das*
20	*bis*
30	*tis*
40	*chalis*
50	*pachas*
60	*sath*
70	*setur*
80	*assi*
90	*nabbe*
100	*sau*
1,000	*hazar*
100,000	*lakh*
10,000,000	*kror*

Pronouns

I am *Mai hun*
You are *Ap hain*
He/she/it is *Voh hai*
They are *Ve hain*

Verbs

To drink *Pina*
To eat *Khanna*
To do/make *Karna*
To buy *Kharidna*
To sleep *Sona*
To see *Dekhna*
To hear/listen to *Sunna*
To wash (clothes) *Dona*
To wash (yourself) *Nahana*
To get *Milna*

Prepositions, adverbs and adjectives

Now *Ab*
Right now *Abhi*
Quickly *Jaldi*
Slowly *Dirhe se*
A bit *Bahut*
A little *Tora*
Here *Yaha/idhar*
There *Vaha/udhar*
Open *Khola*
Closed *Bund*
Finished *Khatm hai*
Big/older *Bara*
Small/younger *Chota*
Beautiful *Sundar*
Old *Purana*
New *Naya*

Questions

What is? *Kya hai?*
Where is? *Kahan hai?*
Why? *Kyun?*
Who is? *Kaun hai?*
When is? *Kab hai?*
How? *Kaisa?*

Most sentences can be turned into a question by putting *"kya"* on the front and raising the pitch at the end, e.g. *"Dhobi hai"*, "There is a washerman", *"Kya dhobi hai?"*, "Is there a washerman?"

Days of the week

Monday *Somvar*
Tuesday *Mangalvar*
Wednesday *Budhvar*
Thursday *Guruvar*
Friday *Shukravar*
Saturday *Shanivar*
Sunday *Itvar*
Today *Aj*
Yesterday/tomorrow *kal*
Week *Hafta*

Months

January *Janvari*
February *Farvari*
March *March*
April *Aprail*
May *Mai*
June *Jun*
July *Julai*
August *Agast*
September *Sitambar*
October *Aktubar*
Novmber *Navambar*
December *Disambar*

Month *Mahina*
Year *Sal*

Relatives

Mother *Mata-ji*
Father *Pita-ji*
Sister *Behen*
Brother *Bhai*
Husband *Pati*
Wife *Patni*
Maternal grandmother *Nani*
Maternal grandfather *Nana*
Paternal grandmother *Dadi*
Paternal grandfather *Dada*
Elder sister (term of respect) *Didi*
Daughter *Beti*
Son *Beta*
Girl *Larki*
Boy *Larka*
Are you married? *Kya ap shadishuda hai?*
Are you alone (male/female)? *Kya ap akela/akeli?*
How many children have you got? *Apke kitne bache hai?*
How many brothers and sisters have you got? *Apke kitne bhai behen hai?*

Health

Doctor *Daktar*
Hospital *Aspatal*
Dentist *Dentist*
Pain *Dard*
I am ill *Main bimar hun*
I have been vomiting *Ulti ho rahi thi*
I have a temperature *Mujhe bukhar hai*
I have a headache *Mere sir men dard hai*
I have a stomach ache *Mere pat men dard hai*
I have diarrhoea *Mujhe dast ar raha hai*
The English word "motions" is a common expression for diarrhoea.

Travel

Where is (Delhi)? *(Dilli) kahan hai?*
Bus station *Bus adda*
Railway station *Tren stashan/railgari*
Airport *Hawai adda*
Car *Gari*
How far is it? *Kitna dur hai?*
In front of/opposite (the Taj Mahal) *(Taj Mahal) ke samne*
Near *Ke nazdik/ke pas*
Far *Dur*

Ticket *Tikat*
Stop *Rukh jaiye*
Let's go *Chele jao*
I have to go *Mujhe jana hai*
Come *Ayie*
Go *Jayie*

Food

I want (a thali) *Mujhe (thali) chahiye*
Without chilli *Mirch ke bina*
Little chilli *Kam mirch*
Hot *Garam*
Cold *Tanda*
Ripe/cooked *Pukka*
Unripe/raw *Kucha*
Basics
Mirch **Chilli**
Namak **Salt**
Ghi **Clarified butter**
Dahi **Yoghurt**
Raita **Yoghurt with cucumber**
Chaval **Rice**
Panir **Cheese**
Pani **Water**
Dudh **Milk**
Lassi **Yoghurt drink**
Nimbu pani **Lime water**
Tandur **Oven**
Pilao **Rice cooked with *ghi* and spices**
Biryani **Rice cooked with vegetables or meat**
Mithai **Sweets**
Breads (*Roti*)
Puri **Deep-fried and puffed-up wheat bread**
Chapati **Flat, unleavened bread**
Nan **Leavened flat bread**
Tanduri roti **Similar to *nan***
Paratha **Chapati cooked with *ghi***
Vegetables (*Sabzi*)
Palak **Spinach**
Allu **Potato**
Gobi **Cauliflower**
Bindi **Okra**
Pyaz **Onion**
Sarsun **Mustard greens**
Mattar **Peas**
Tamata **Tomato**
Baingain/brinjal **Aubergine**
Dal **Dried pulses**
Meat
Ghost **Lamb**
Murg **Chicken**
Machli **Fish**
Fruit
Kela **Banana**
Santra **Orange**
Aum **Mango**

Further Reading

History

Annals and Antiquities of Rajasthan, by James Tod (Low Price Publications, 1990). A reprint of the 1829–32 classic account of Rajasthani history and customs.

Freedom at Midnight, by Larry Collins and Dominique Lapierre (Tarang, 1975). Gripping popular history of the birth of the Indian nation.

A History of India, Volume I, by Romilar Thapar (Pelican, 1980). Highly acclaimed history. Volume 1 traces the history of South Asia from ancient times through to the Delhi sultanate; Volume II, by Perceval Spear, continues from the Mughals to the assassination of M.K. Gandhi.

India: a History, by John Keay (HarperCollins, 2000), A new one-volume history by a well-respected writer.

The Last Maharaja: a Biography of Sawai Man Singh II, Maharaja of Jaipur, by Quentin Crewe (Michael Joseph, 1985). The life of one of the best-known rulers of this princely state.

Liberty or Death: India's Journey to Independence and Division, by Patrick French (HarperCollins, 1997). Readable and well researched account of the freedom struggle and Partition.

A Princess Remembers, by Gayatri Devi (Weidenfeld & Nicholson, 1976). Autobiography of the Maharani of Jaipur who played a prominent part in the politics of the new state of Rajasthan.

This Fissured Land, by Madhav Gadgil and Ramachandra Guha (Oxford University Press, 1993). Searching and thought-provoking ecological history of South Asia.

The Wonder that Was India, by A.L. Basham (Rupa, 1967). Learned historical classic in idiosyncratic, rapturous prose.

Society, Culture & Religion

Gods, Demons and Others, by R.K. Narayan (Heineman, 1986). Retellings of some of India's most popular religious myths by one of the country's greatest writers. Also worth looking out for are his retellings of **The Ramayana** (Penguin, 1977), based on the Tamil Kamban version, and **The Mahabharata** (Heineman, 1986).

The Idea of India, by Sunil Khilnani (Hamish Hamilton, 1997). Intellectual *tour de force* examines concepts about an ancient civilisation and its status as a relatively new nation.

Intimate Relations: Exploring Indian Sexuality, Sudhir Kakar (University of Chicago Press, 1990). This study throws light on many aspects of Indian marital and family relations.

An Introduction to Hinduism, by Gavin Flood (Cambridge University Press, 1996). Perhaps the best general introduction to the complexities of this diverse religion. Recommended.

May You Be the Mother of a Hundred Sons, by Elisabeth Bumiller (Penguin, 1990). Women's issues tackled head-on, everything from dowries to infanticide, with dozens of poignant interviews.

The Other Side of Silence: Voices from the Partition of India, by Urvashi Butalia (Penguin, 1998). Tales of families torn apart for 50 years, compellingly told by India's leading literary feminist.

The Painted Walls of Shekhavati, by Francis Wacziarg and Aman Nath (Helm, 1982). A meticulously researched book which renewed interest in these Marwari mansions. Mughal and Rajput Painting, by Milo Cleveland Beach (Cambridge University Press, 1992). A scholarly investigation of the links between the two styles.

Plain Tales from the Raj, ed Charles Allen (Rupa, 1992). First-hand accounts from ex-colonialists.

Rajput Painting, Ananda Coomaraswamy (Hacker Art Books, 1975). Reprint of the 1916 book by a respected writer.

Fiction

Clear Light of Day, by Anita Desai (Penguin, 1982). The difficulties of post-Partition India seen through the eyes of a Hindu family living in Old Delhi.

Delhi, A Novel, by Kushwant Singh (Viking, 1989). A bawdy saga that takes us through 600 years of temptresses and traitors to unravel the Indian capital's mystique. Narrated in turns by a eunuch, an irreverent wag, potentates and poets. Superb. (It took this popular author 20 years to write.)

The Gift of a Cow, by Premchand (Allen & Unwin, 1968). The great Hindi novelist's tragic classic about the hardships endured by a North Indian peasant.

In Custody, by Anita Desai (Heineman, 1984). The last days of an Urdu poet, made into a beautiful Merchant-Ivory film.

Inside the Haveli, by Rama Mehta (The Women's Press, 1994). Novel about the claustrophobic domestic lives of Rajasthani women.

Kim, by Rudyard Kipling (Penguin Books, 2000, ed. by Edward Said). The wonderful adventures of a boy who wanders across North India in search of the Great Game.

Midnight's Children, by Salman Rushdie (Jonathan Cape, 1981). Rushdie burst onto the literary scene with this dazzling novel of post-Independence India.

A Passage to India, by E.M. Forster (Penguin, 2000). The classic novel of the misunderstandings that arose out of the East-West encounter. After a mysterious incident in a cave Dr Aziz is accused of assaulting a naive young Englishwoman, Adela Quested. The trial exposes the racism inherent in British colonialism.

The Raj Quartet, by Paul Scott (University of Chicago Press, 1998). Four novels – **The Jewel in the Crown, The Day of the Scorpion, The Towers of Silence** and **A Division of Spoils** – set during the last days of the British Raj and charting its decline and fall.

Red Earth and Pouring Rain, by Vikram Chandra (Viking, 1996).

Acclaimed debut novel, quick-paced and audacious.

A River Sutra, by Gita Mehta (Viking, 1993). Gently wrought stories which linger in the imagination.

A Suitable Boy, by Vikram Seth (Phoenix Press, 1994). A huge and multi-faceted novel set during the run up to Independent India's first elections, which centres around a mother's search for a suitable husband for her daughter. Highly recommended.

Train to Pakistan, by Kushwant Singh (various editions, 1954). Gripping story of the excesses of partition, penned when scars of the divided nations were still fresh.

Untouchable, by Mulk Raj Anand (Penguin, 1986). Grinding tale of poverty and discrimination.

Women Writing in India: 600BC to the Present, ed. Susie Tharu and K. Lalitha (Feminist Press, 1991). Wonderful and eclectic anthology bringing to light the neglected history of Indian women. Volume 1 includes writings from 600BC to the early 20th century, volume 2 concentrates on the 20th century alone.

Yaarana: Gay Writing from India, ed. Hoshang Merchant, and, **Facing the Mirror: Lesbian Writing from India**, ed. Ashwini Sukthankar (both Penguin, 1999). Anthologies of short stories, extracts from novels and poetry from gay and lesbian Indian writers.

Travel

Autobiography of a Princess, also being the Adventures of an American Film Director in the Land of the Maharajas, by James Ivory (John Murray, 1975). Illustrated book about the film, with a screenplay by Ruth Prawer Jhabvala.

Butter Chicken in Ludhiana: Travels in Small Town India, by Pankaj Mishra (Penguin, 1995). An urban Indian novelist casts a jaundiced eye over modern Indian life.

City of Djinns, by William Dalrymple (HarperCollins, 1993). Respected

travel-writer's account of a year spent in Delhi, full of historical references.

Desert Places, by Robyn Davidson (Viking, 1996). A woman's story of living and travelling with the desert nomads of Rajasthan.

Exploring Indian Railways, by Bill Aitken (Oxford University Press, 1996). Highly informed and occasionally idiosyncratic tour of the Indian railway system written by a clear enthusiast.

The Great Hedge of India, by Roy Moxham (Constable, 2000). One man's quest to find the hedge which marked the old British customs line. Very entertaining and packed full of historical detail. Recommended.

Old Delhi: Ten Easy Walks, by Gayner Barton and Lorraine Malone (South Asia Books, 1997). Very useful guide to the confusing maze of streets in Old Delhi.

Sorcerer's Apprentice, by Tahir Shah (Penguin, 1998). Travelogue of the author's attempts to learn the secrets of illusion and fraud of India's street magicians.

Food, Language & Images

Curries and Bugles, by Jennifer Brennan (Penguin, 1992). Legends and tales mixed up with the favourite recipes of Raj-era memsahibs and sahibs.

Hanklyn-Janklin, or a Stranger's Rumble Tumble Guide to some Words, Customs and Quiddities Indian and Indo-British, by Nigel B. Hankin (Banyan Books, New Delhi, 1992). Lives up to its title and is a delightful reference work.

Hobson-Jobson (Routledge and Kegan Paul, 1968), the 1886 glossary on which Hankin modelled his modern etymology. The pair complement one another.

Indian Style, by Suzanne Slesin, Stafford Cliff (Thames and Hudson, 1990). Colour prints of exterior and interior design, in exacting detail, capture the texture of India.

Mansions at Dusk: the Havelis of Old Delhi, by Pavan K. Varma (Spantech, 1992). Atmospheric

photographs by Sondeep Shankar illustrate this homage to the now decaying mansions of Muslim Delhi.

Other Insight Guides

The 190-title **Insight Guides** series has full coverage of India:

Insight Guide: Delhi, Agra and Jaipur is the perfect companion for travellers taking the classic tour of India's Golden Triangle.

Insight Guide: India takes you around this huge and fascinating country state by state, from the shores of Kerala to the mountains of the Garhwal.

Insight Guide: Indian Wildlife is an indispensable guide for nature lovers, combining expert text and astonishing photography.

Insight Guide: South India is a guide to the southern states of Andhra Pradesh, Karnataka, Tamil Nadu and Kerala.

Compact Guide: Goa is a great pocket companion to this very popular state, taking in beaches, history and the fabulous site at Hampi in Karnataka.

ART & PHOTO CREDITS

David Allardice 216
Ping Amranand 12/13, 119R, 178
Vivek Anand 59L&R, 61L&R, 66, 72, 169
David Beatty/APA front flap bottom, 185
Bodo Bondzio 48, 84, 109, 110, 126L
Bodo Bondzio/APA 214/215
Vivian Bose 206/207, 208
Marcus Brooke 38
A. Cassio 49
A. Cassio/APA 190, 221R
K. Debnicki 116
Gen. R. K. Gaur spine top, 70, 86, 182R, 192, 205
Hans Höfer back cover centre, 18/19, 20/21, 87, 96/97, 113, 114, 127, 162/163, 164, 167, 176/177, 188/189, 194, 197, 199, 203
Luca Invernizzi back cover right, 40, 107, 161
Caroline Jones 47, 63, 108
Thomas Kelly 111, 121

Wilhelm Klein 14/15, 16/17, 25, 52/53, 62, 117, 182L, 209, 219, 223, 226, 230, 232, 254
Jean Kuglar 233
Link Picture Library 44/45, 210
Lyle Lawson 2, 6/7, 56, 57
Lyle Lawson/APA 225, 260/261
D. Messent 124
D. Messent/APA 224
Francesco Milaneso 184, 193
Pramod Mistry 115, 175
Aman Nath 22, 28/29, 80, 82, 125, 129, 138, 147, 150, 152/153, 155, 156, 158, 172, 224
Kim Naylor 104, 118, 119L, 122, 160, 168, 198, 211, 212/213, 220, 221L, 222, 228
Avinash Pasricha 46, 65, 74, 245, 251
Aditya Patankar front flap top, back flap top, spine centre, back cover bottom, 1, 30, 32L&R, 35, 36, 37, 41, 42, 43, 50, 54/55, 64, 67, 68/69, 73L&R, 76, 77, 100/101,

112, 120, 130/131, 132, 135, 137, 139, 140, 149, 154, 170, 171, 173, 200, 201, 204 229, 231, 235, 238, 240, 241, 242/243, 248, 249, 252, 253, 256, 257L&R, 258, 262, 264, 266, 267, 270, 271, 272
Günter Pfannmuller 142/143, 181
Kailash Sankhala 159, 187
Shalini Saran back flap bottom, 18/19, 58L&R, 60L&R, 78/79, 98/99, 144, 148, 151
Geeti Sen 88/89, 90, 92L&R, 93, 94, 95
Toby Sinclair back cover top, 26/27, 126R, 128, 141, 202, 227, 236/237, 259, 268
Tony Stone 11
Joanna Van Gruisen 195

Map Production Berndtson & Berndtson, Dave Priestley
© 2000 Apa Publications GmbH & Co. Verlag KG (Singapore branch)

INSIGHT GUIDE
Rajasthan

Cartographic Editor **Zoë Goodwin**
Design Consultants
Carlotta Junger
Picture Research **Hilary Genin**

Index

66 I was first drawn to the Insight Guides by the excellent "Nepal" volume. I can think of no book which so effectively captures the essence of a country. Out of these pages leaped the Nepal I know – the captivating charm of a people and their culture. I've since discovered and enjoyed the entire Insight Guide series. Each volume deals with a country in the same sensitive depth, which is nowhere more evident than in the superb photography. 99

Sir Edmund Hillary

INSIGHT GUIDES

The world's largest collection of visual travel guides

Insight Guides – the Classic Series
that puts you in the picture

Alaska	China	Hong Kong	Montreal	Seattle
Alsace	Cologne	Hungary	Morocco	Sicily
Amazon Wildlife	Continental Europe		Moscow	Singapore
American Southwest	Corsica	Iceland	Munich	South Africa
Amsterdam	Costa Rica	India		South America
Argentina	Crete	India's Western	Namibia	South Tyrol
Asia, East	Cuba	Himalaya	Native America	Southeast Asia
Asia, South	Cyprus	India, South	Nepal	Wildlife
Asia, Southeast	Czech & Slovak	Indian Wildlife	Netherlands	Spain
Athens	Republics	Indonesia	New England	Spain, Northern
Atlanta		Ireland	New Orleans	Spain, Southern
Australia	Delhi, Jaipur & Agra	Israel	New York City	Sri Lanka
Austria	Denmark	Istanbul	New York State	Sweden
	Dominican Republic	Italy	New Zealand	Switzerland
Bahamas	Dresden	Italy, Northern	Nile	Sydney
Bali	Dublin	Italy, Southern	Normandy	Syria & Lebanon
Baltic States	Düsseldorf		Norway	
Bangkok		Jamaica		Taiwan
Barbados	East African Wildlife	Japan	Old South	Tenerife
Barcelona	Eastern Europe	Java	Oman & The UAE	Texas
Bay of Naples	Ecuador	Jerusalem	Oxford	Thailand
Beijing	Edinburgh	Jordan		Tokyo
Belgium	Egypt		Pacific Northwest	Trinidad & Tobago
Belize	England	Kathmandu	Pakistan	Tunisia
Berlin		Kenya	Paris	Turkey
Bermuda	Finland	Korea	Peru	Turkish Coast
Boston	Florence		Philadelphia	Tuscany
Brazil	Florida	Laos & Cambodia	Philippines	
Brittany	France	Lisbon	Poland	Umbria
Brussels	France, Southwest	Loire Valley	Portugal	USA: On The Road
Budapest	Frankfurt	London	Prague	USA: Western States
Buenos Aires	French Riviera	Los Angeles	Provence	US National Parks: East
Burgundy			Puerto Rico	US National Parks: West
Burma (Myanmar)	Gambia & Senegal	Madeira		
	Germany	Madrid	Rajasthan	Vancouver
Cairo	Glasgow	Malaysia	Rhine	Venezuela
Calcutta	Gran Canaria	Mallorca & Ibiza	Rio de Janeiro	Venice
California	Great Barrier Reef	Malta	Rockies	Vienna
California, Northern	Great Britain	Marine Life of the	Rome	Vietnam
California, Southern	Greece	South China Sea	Russia	
Canada	Greek Islands	Mauritius, Réunion		Wales
Caribbean	Guatemala, Belize &	& Seychelles	St Petersburg	Washington DC
Catalonia	Yucatán	Melbourne	San Francisco	Waterways of Europe
Channel Islands		Mexico City	Sardinia	Wild West
Chicago	Hamburg	Mexico	Scandinavia	
Chile	Hawaii	Miami	Scotland	Yemen

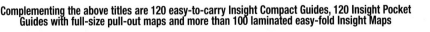

Complementing the above titles are 120 easy-to-carry Insight Compact Guides, 120 Insight Pocket
Guides with full-size pull-out maps and more than 100 laminated easy-fold Insight Maps